COURSE 28: HUSBAND, WIFE, PUMPKIN

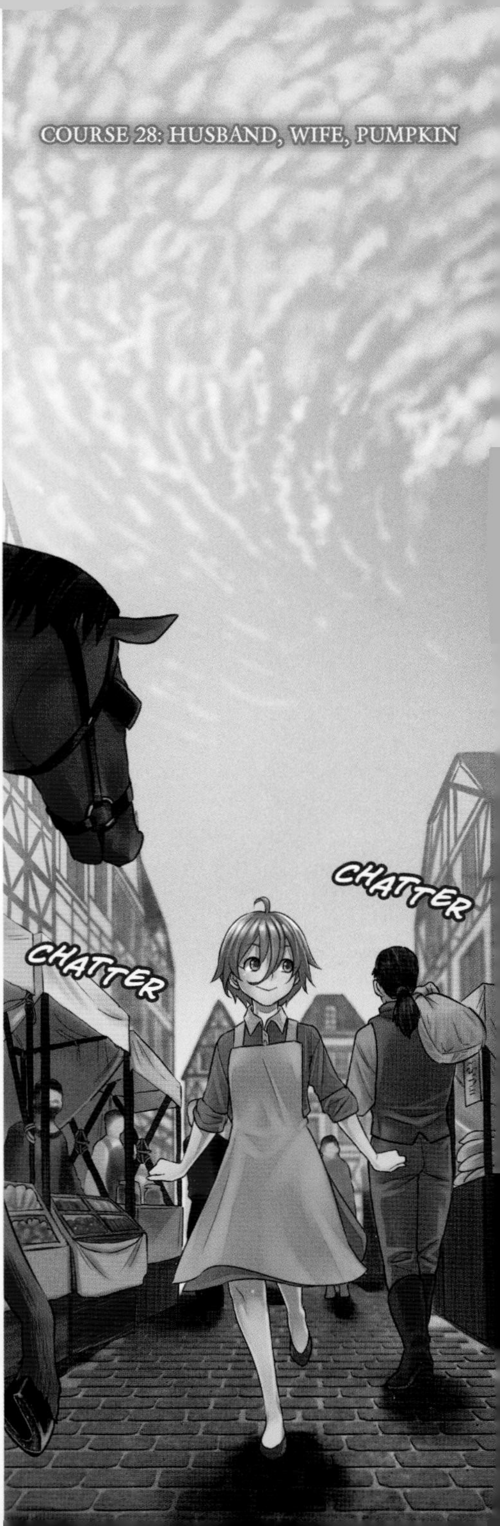
CHATTER
CHATTER

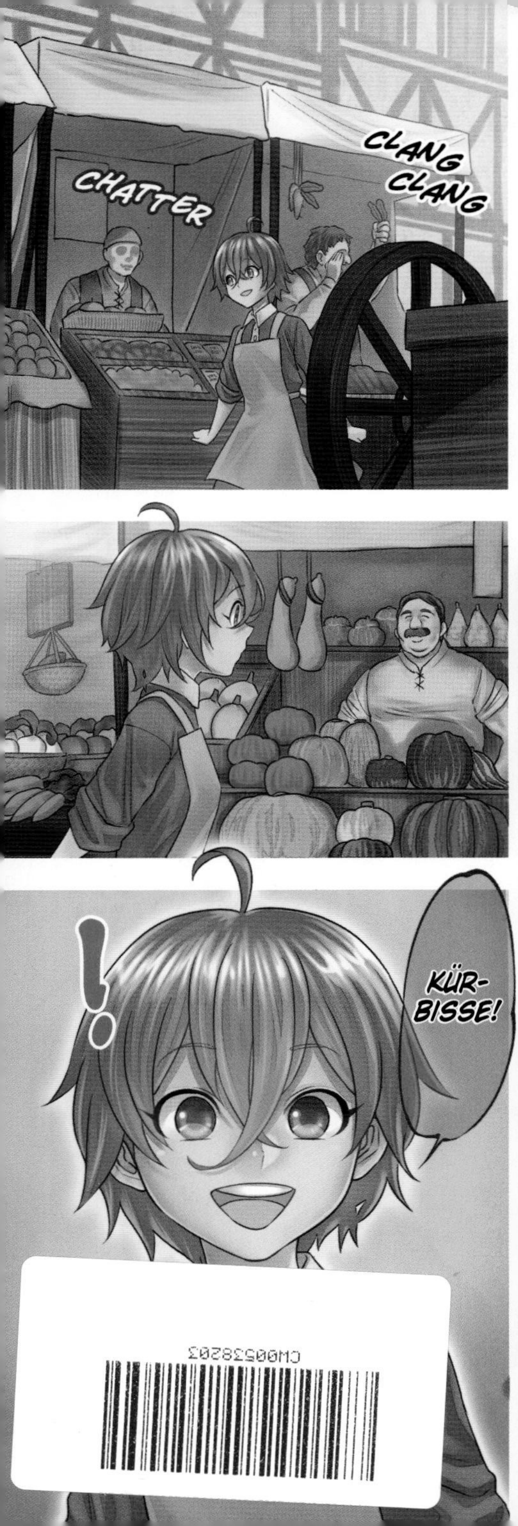
CLANG CLANG
CHATTER
KÜR-BISSE!
!

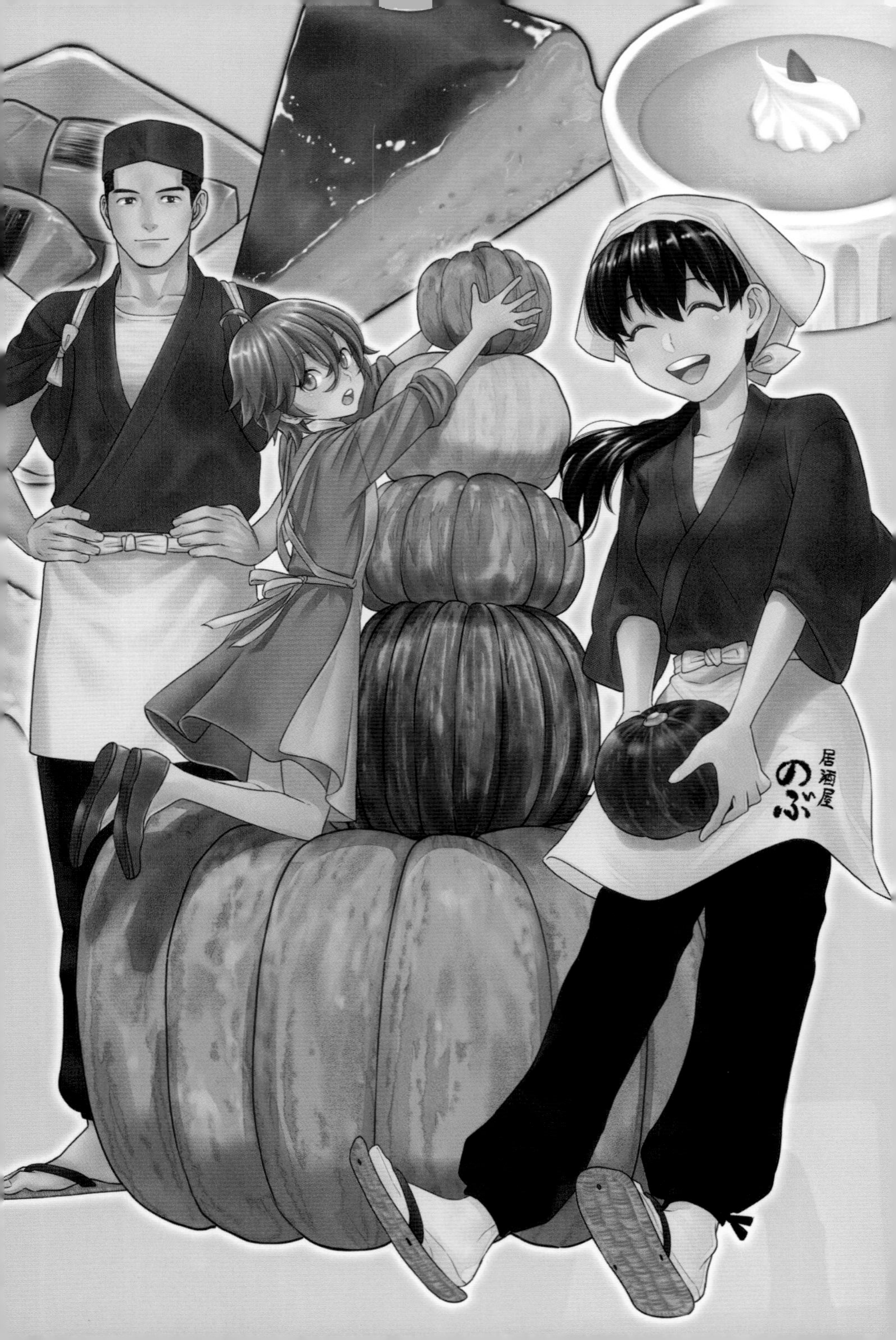
居酒屋
のぶ

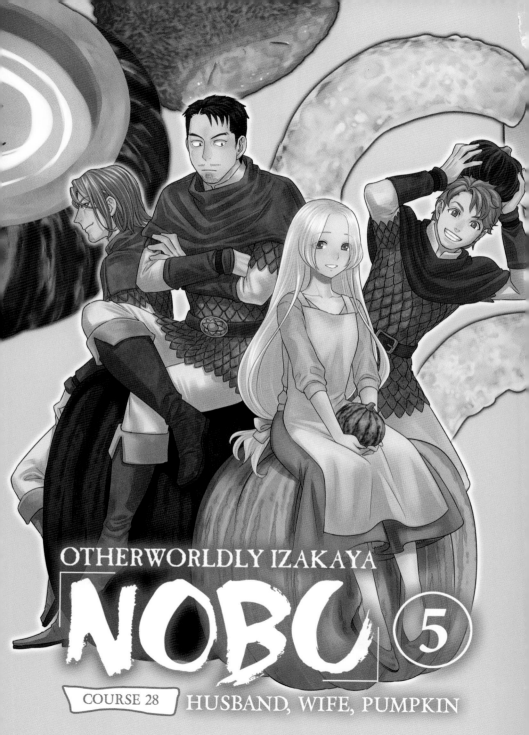

OTHERWORLDLY IZAKAYA

「NOBU」 ⑤

COURSE 28　HUSBAND, WIFE, PUMPKIN

MENU

OTHERWORLDLY IZAKAYA

NOBU ⑤

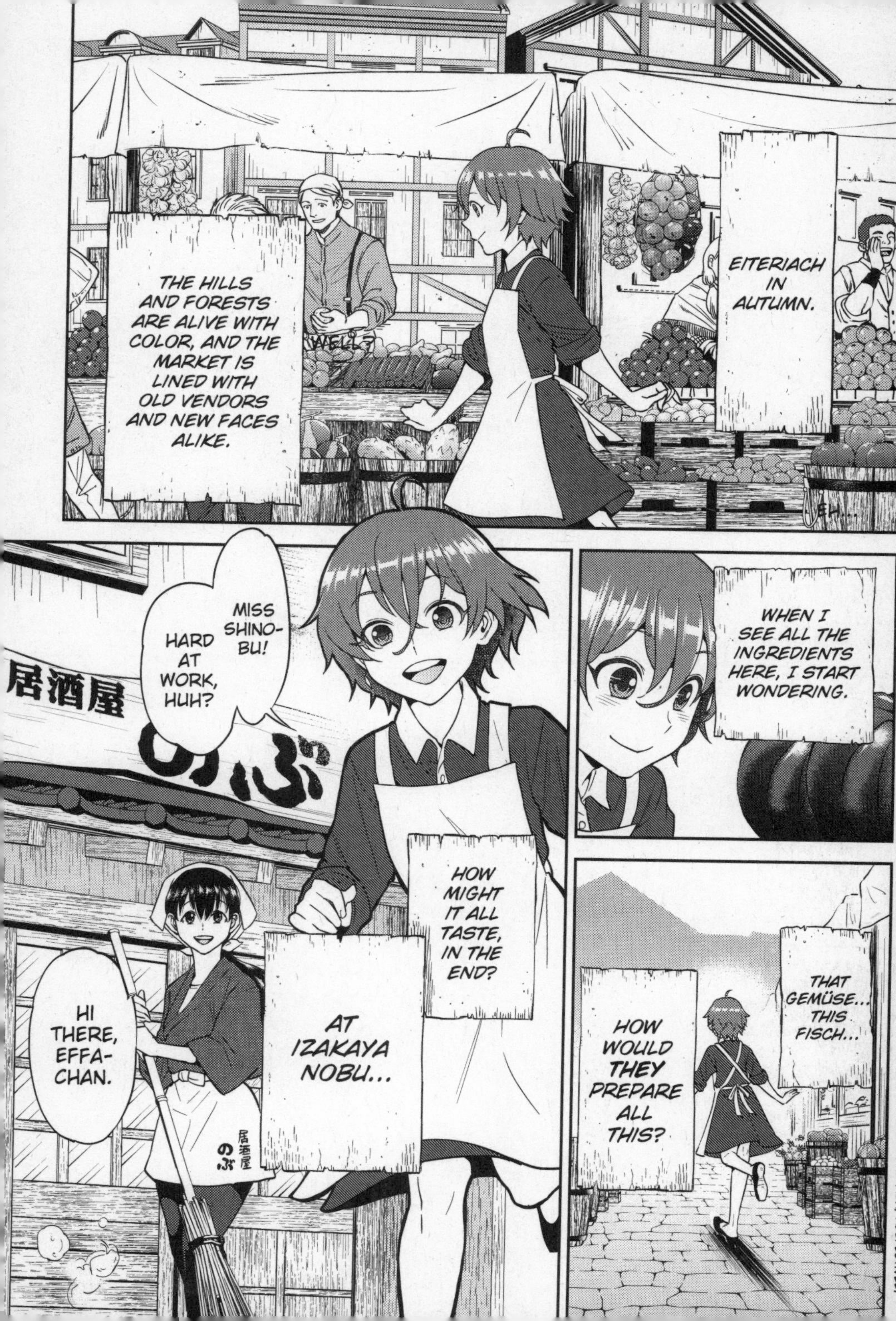
EITERIACH IN AUTUMN.
THE HILLS AND FORESTS ARE ALIVE WITH COLOR, AND THE MARKET IS LINED WITH OLD VENDORS AND NEW FACES ALIKE.
WELL?
EH...
WHEN I SEE ALL THE INGREDIENTS HERE, I START WONDERING.
THAT GEMÜSE... THIS FISCH...
HOW WOULD THEY PREPARE ALL THIS?
HOW MIGHT IT ALL TASTE, IN THE END?
AT IZAKAYA NOBU...
MISS SHINOBU!
HARD AT WORK, HUH?
居酒屋
のぶ
HI THERE, EFFA-CHAN.
居酒屋
のぶ

*GEMÜSE AND FISCH ARE GERMAN FOR VEGETABLE AND FISH, RESPECTIVELY

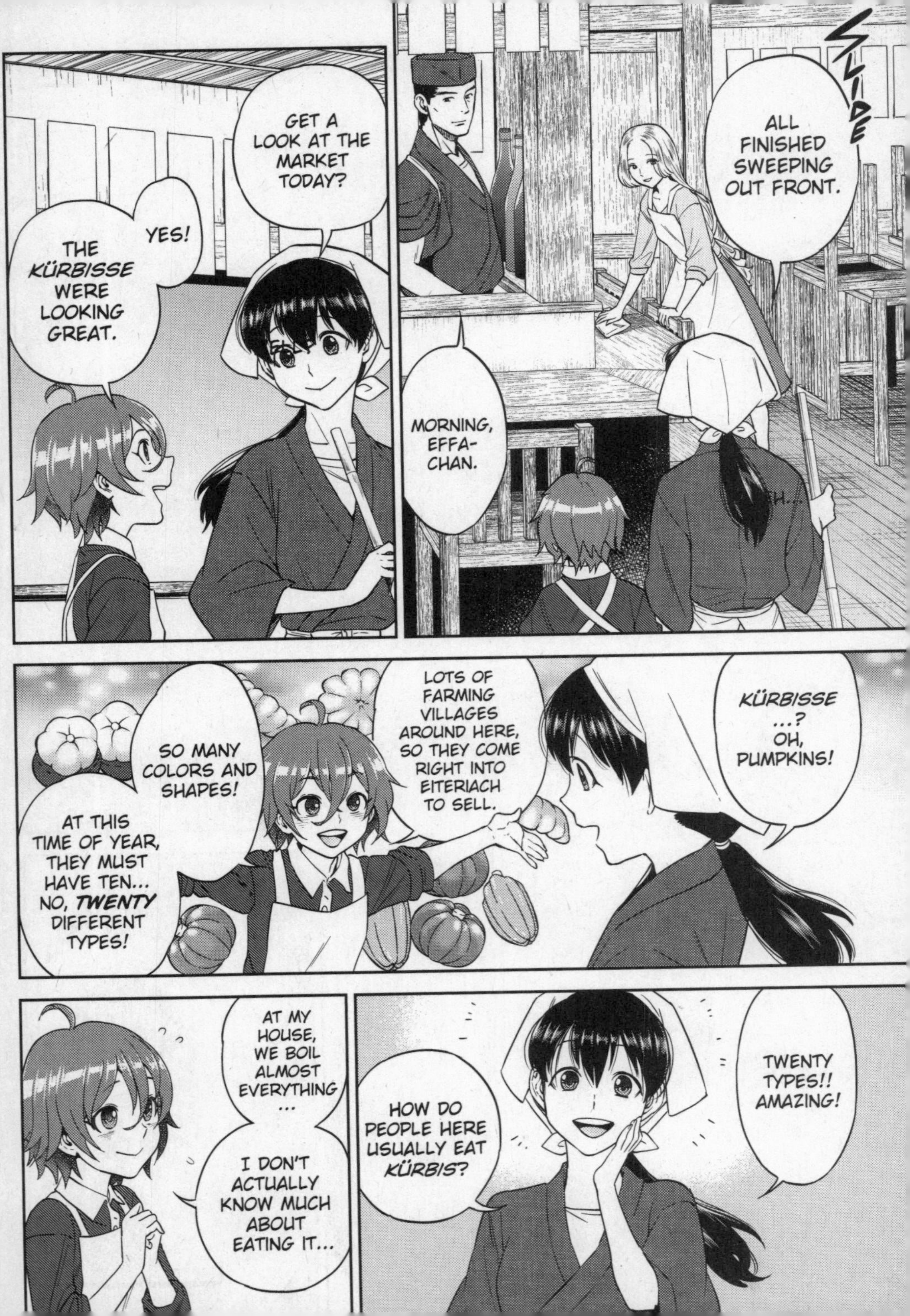
SLIDE
ALL FINISHED SWEEPING OUT FRONT.
MORNING, EFFA-CHAN.
GET A LOOK AT THE MARKET TODAY?
YES!
THE *KÜRBISSE* WERE LOOKING GREAT.
KÜRBISSE ...? OH, PUMPKINS!
LOTS OF FARMING VILLAGES AROUND HERE, SO THEY COME RIGHT INTO EITERIACH TO SELL.
SO MANY COLORS AND SHAPES!
AT THIS TIME OF YEAR, THEY MUST HAVE TEN... NO, ***TWENTY*** DIFFERENT TYPES!
TWENTY TYPES!! AMAZING!
HOW DO PEOPLE HERE USUALLY EAT *KÜRBIS*?
AT MY HOUSE, WE BOIL ALMOST EVERYTHING ...
I DON'T ACTUALLY KNOW MUCH ABOUT EATING IT...

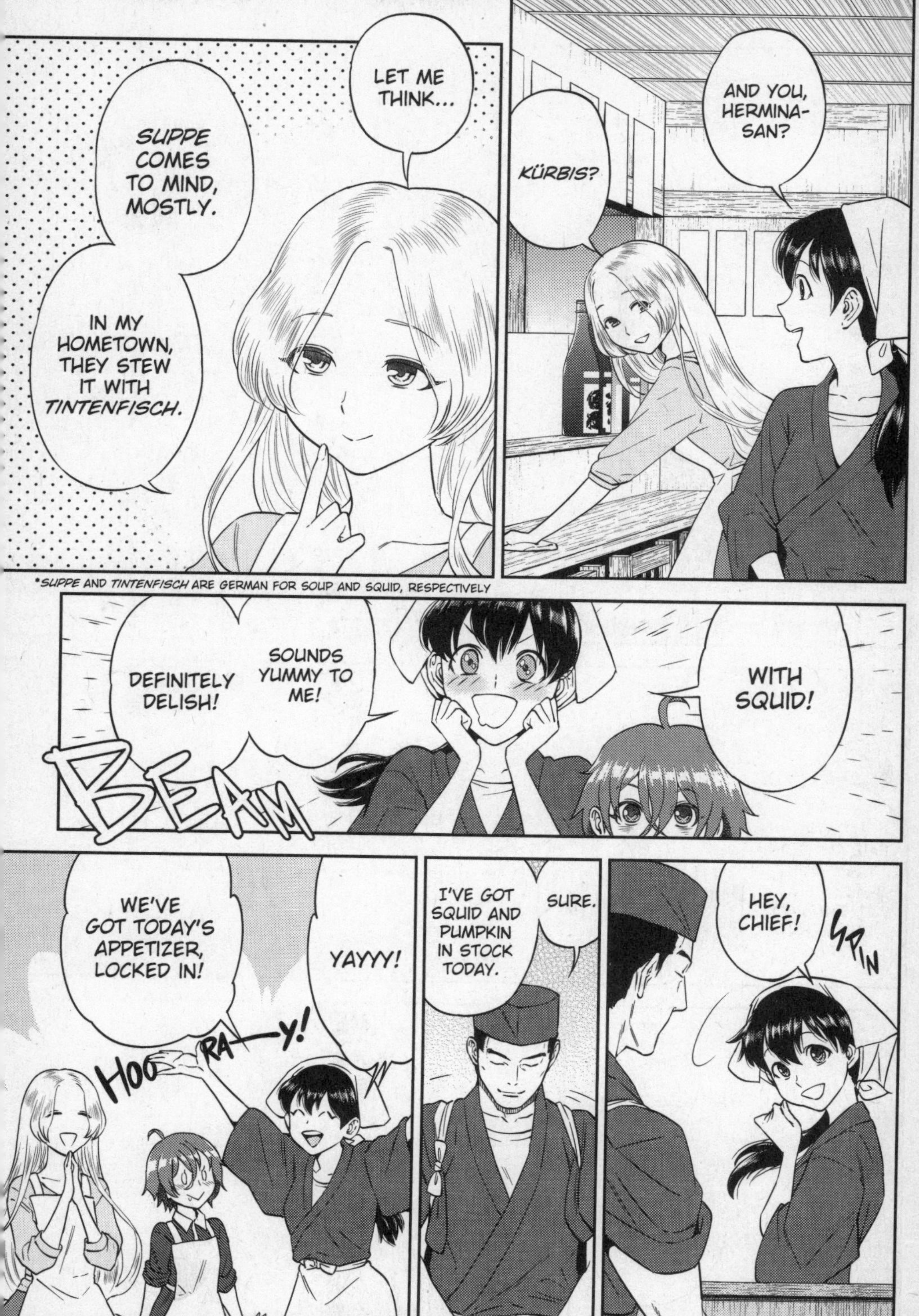
AND YOU, HERMINA-SAN?
KÜRBIS?
LET ME THINK...
SUPPE COMES TO MIND, MOSTLY.
IN MY HOMETOWN, THEY STEW IT WITH *TINTENFISCH*.
WITH SQUID!
SOUNDS YUMMY TO ME!
DEFINITELY DELISH!
BEAM
HEY, CHIEF!
SPIN
SURE.
I'VE GOT SQUID AND PUMPKIN IN STOCK TODAY.
YAYYY!
WE'VE GOT TODAY'S APPETIZER, LOCKED IN!
HOORA—Y!

**SUPPE* AND *TINTENFISCH* ARE GERMAN FOR SOUP AND SQUID, RESPECTIVELY

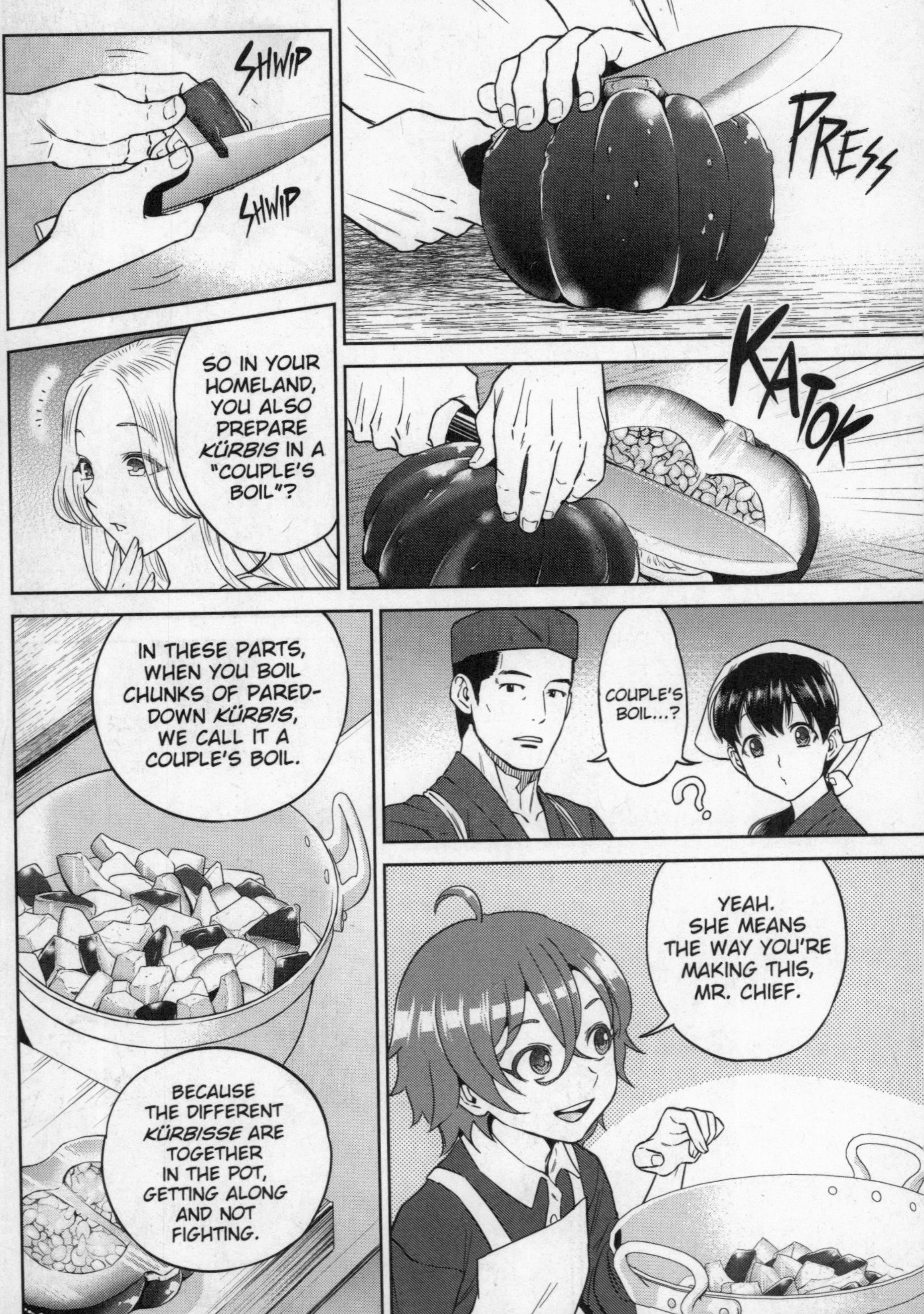
PRESS
SHWIP
SHWIP
KATOK
SO IN YOUR HOMELAND, YOU ALSO PREPARE *KÜRBIS* IN A "COUPLE'S BOIL"?
COUPLE'S BOIL...?
?
YEAH. SHE MEANS THE WAY YOU'RE MAKING THIS, MR. CHIEF.
IN THESE PARTS, WHEN YOU BOIL CHUNKS OF PARED-DOWN *KÜRBIS*, WE CALL IT A COUPLE'S BOIL.
BECAUSE THE DIFFERENT *KÜRBISSE* ARE TOGETHER IN THE POT, GETTING ALONG AND NOT FIGHTING.

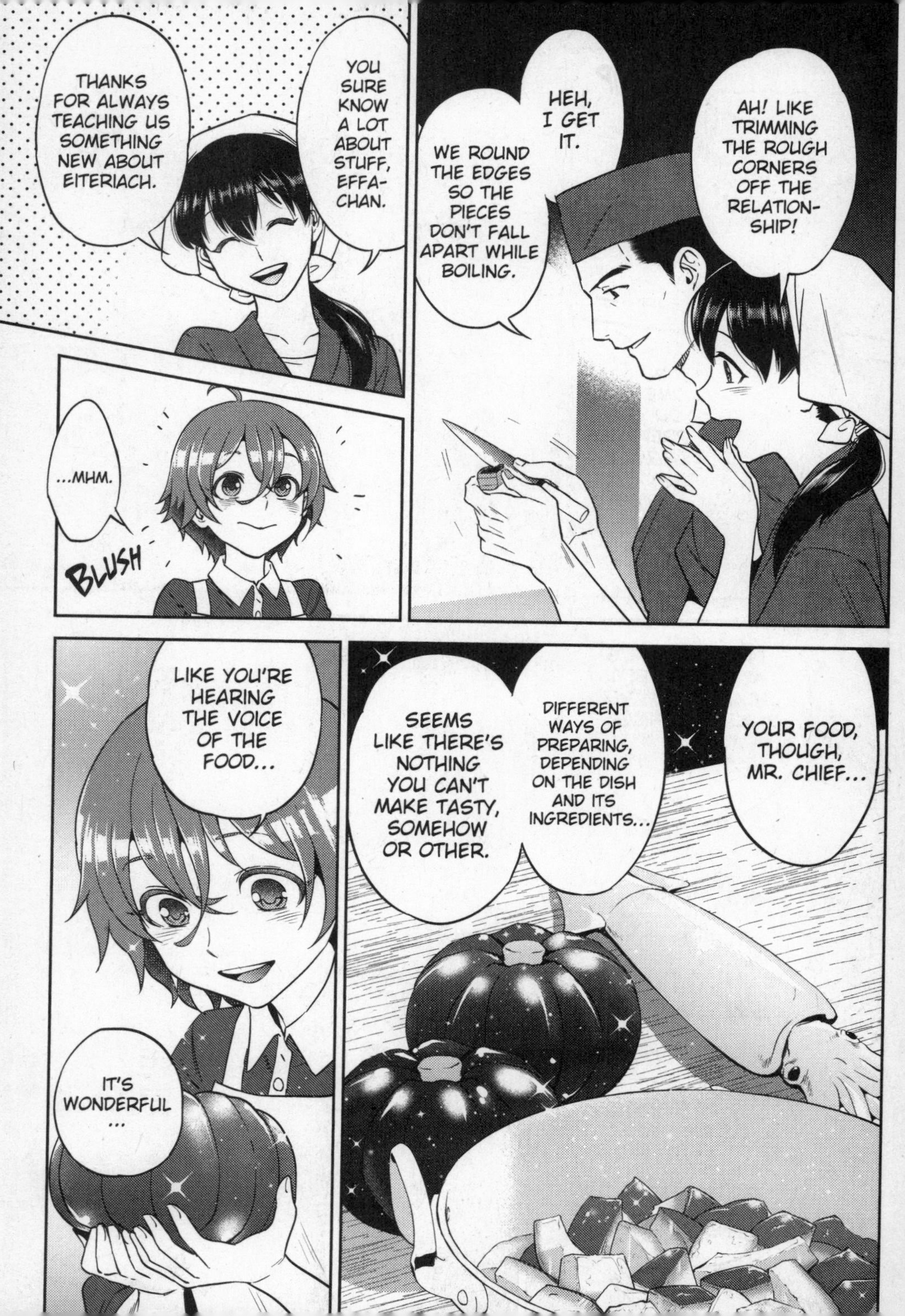
AH! LIKE TRIMMING THE ROUGH CORNERS OFF THE RELATION-SHIP!
HEH, I GET IT.
WE ROUND THE EDGES SO THE PIECES DON'T FALL APART WHILE BOILING.
YOU SURE KNOW A LOT ABOUT STUFF, EFFA-CHAN.
THANKS FOR ALWAYS TEACHING US SOMETHING NEW ABOUT EITERIACH.
...MHM.
BLUSH
YOUR FOOD, THOUGH, MR. CHIEF...
DIFFERENT WAYS OF PREPARING, DEPENDING ON THE DISH AND ITS INGREDIENTS...
SEEMS LIKE THERE'S NOTHING YOU CAN'T MAKE TASTY, SOMEHOW OR OTHER.
LIKE YOU'RE HEARING THE VOICE OF THE FOOD...
IT'S WONDERFUL ...

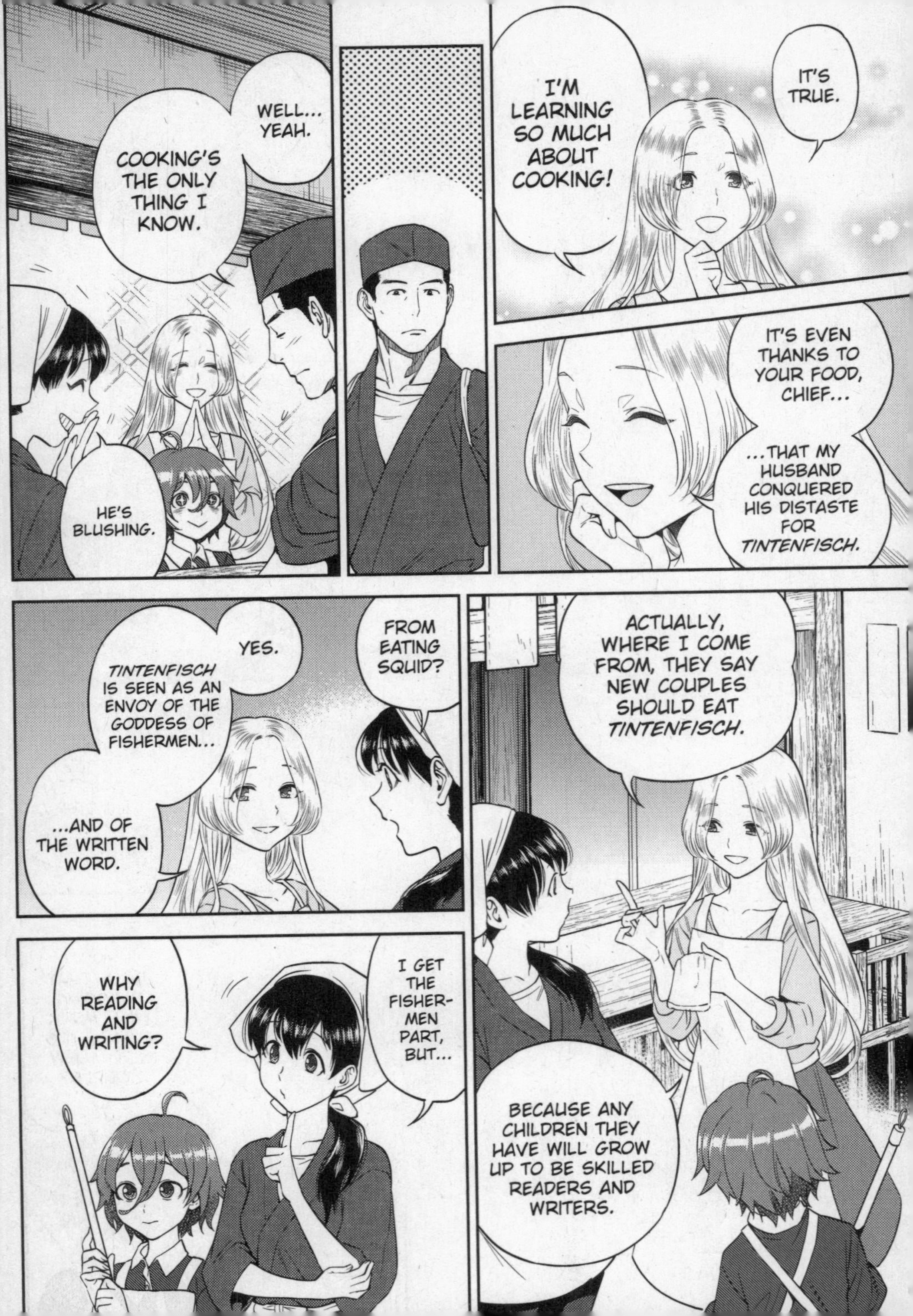
IT'S TRUE.
I'M LEARNING SO MUCH ABOUT COOKING!
IT'S EVEN THANKS TO YOUR FOOD, CHIEF...
...THAT MY HUSBAND CONQUERED HIS DISTASTE FOR *TINTENFISCH*.
WELL... YEAH.
COOKING'S THE ONLY THING I KNOW.
HE'S BLUSHING.
ACTUALLY, WHERE I COME FROM, THEY SAY NEW COUPLES SHOULD EAT *TINTENFISCH*.
BECAUSE ANY CHILDREN THEY HAVE WILL GROW UP TO BE SKILLED READERS AND WRITERS.
FROM EATING SQUID?
YES.
TINTENFISCH IS SEEN AS AN ENVOY OF THE GODDESS OF FISHERMEN...
...AND OF THE WRITTEN WORD.
I GET THE FISHER-MEN PART, BUT...
WHY READING AND WRITING?

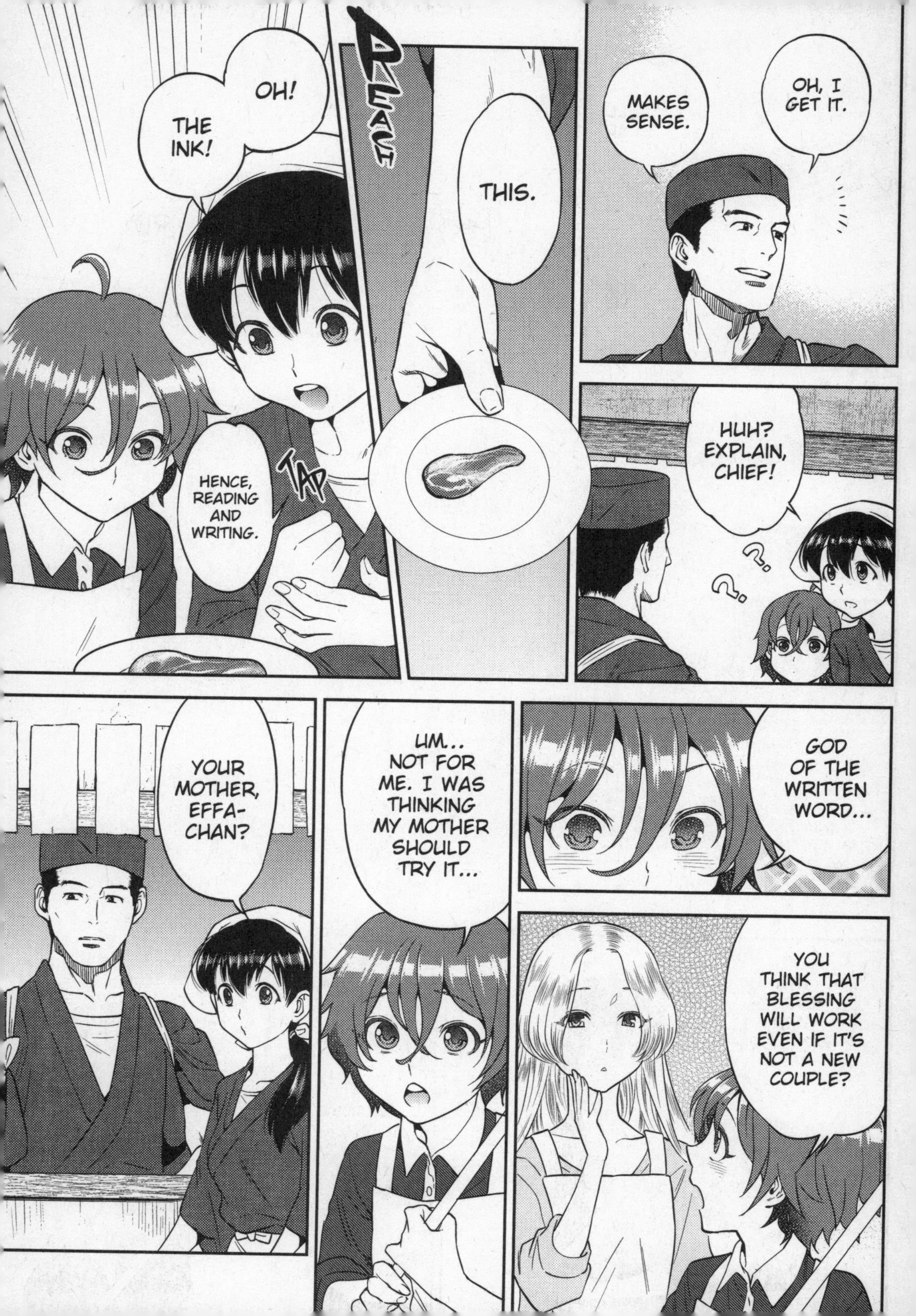
OH, I GET IT.
MAKES SENSE.
HUH? EXPLAIN, CHIEF!
REACH
THIS.
OH!
THE INK!
TAP
HENCE, READING AND WRITING.
GOD OF THE WRITTEN WORD...
YOU THINK THAT BLESSING WILL WORK EVEN IF IT'S NOT A NEW COUPLE?
UM... NOT FOR ME. I WAS THINKING MY MOTHER SHOULD TRY IT...
YOUR MOTHER, EFFA-CHAN?

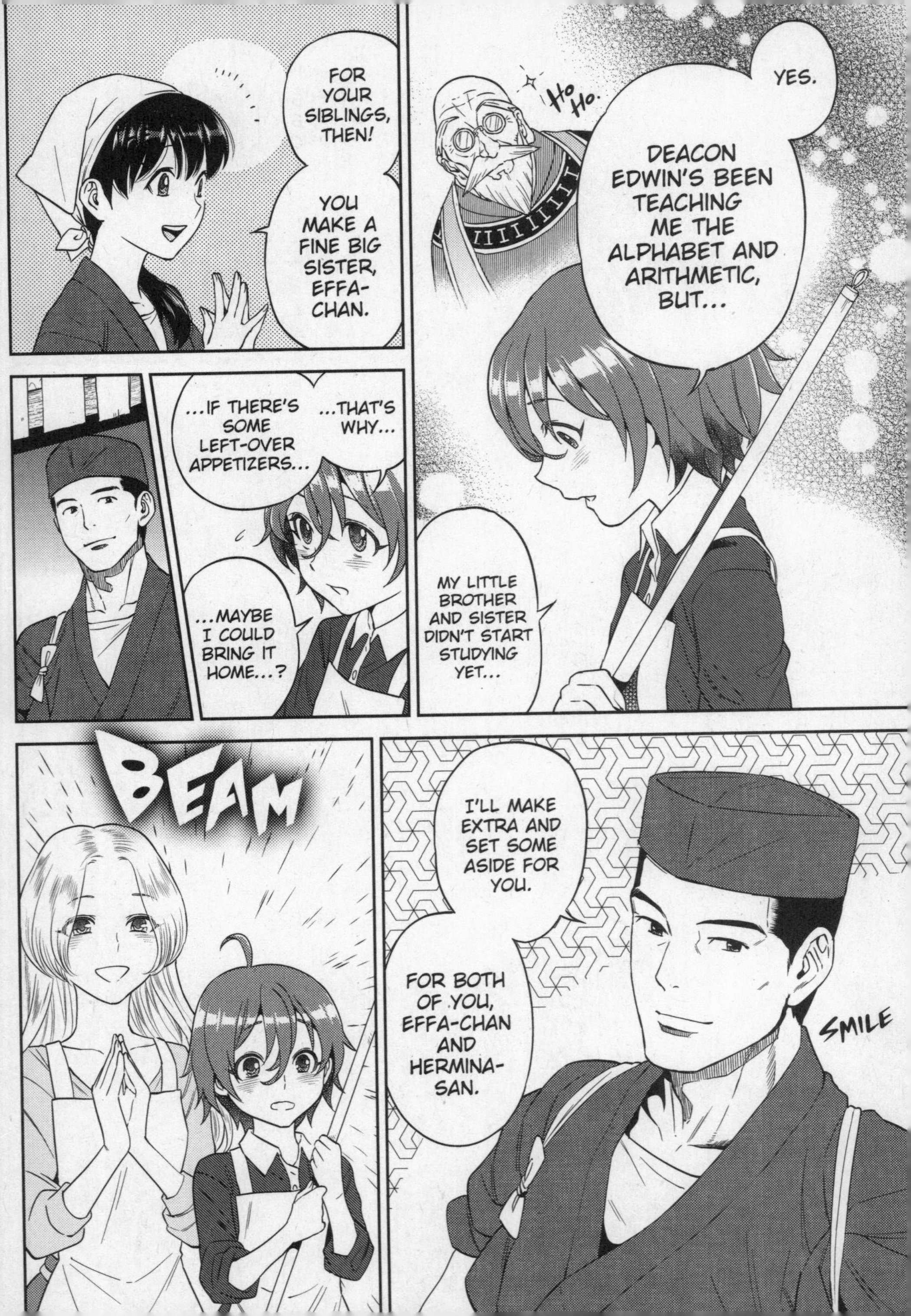
YES.
Ho Ho.
DEACON EDWIN'S BEEN TEACHING ME THE ALPHABET AND ARITHMETIC, BUT...
MY LITTLE BROTHER AND SISTER DIDN'T START STUDYING YET...
FOR YOUR SIBLINGS, THEN!
YOU MAKE A FINE BIG SISTER, EFFA-CHAN.
...THAT'S WHY...
...IF THERE'S SOME LEFT-OVER APPETIZERS...
...MAYBE I COULD BRING IT HOME...?
I'LL MAKE EXTRA AND SET SOME ASIDE FOR YOU.
FOR BOTH OF YOU, EFFA-CHAN AND HERMINA-SAN.
SMILE
BEAM

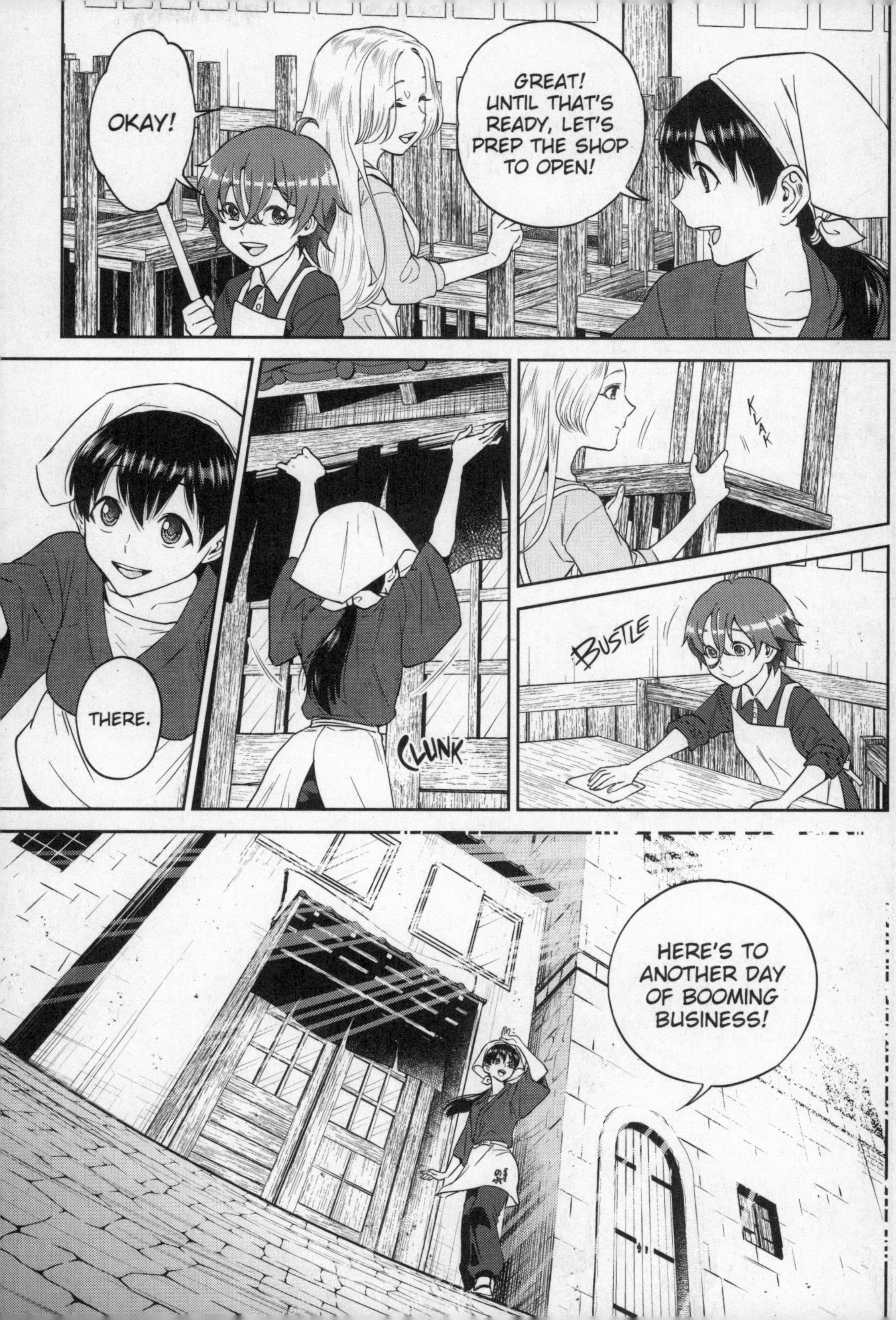
GREAT! UNTIL THAT'S READY, LET'S PREP THE SHOP TO OPEN!
OKAY!
KLAK
BUSTLE
CLUNK
THERE.
HERE'S TO ANOTHER DAY OF BOOMING BUSINESS!

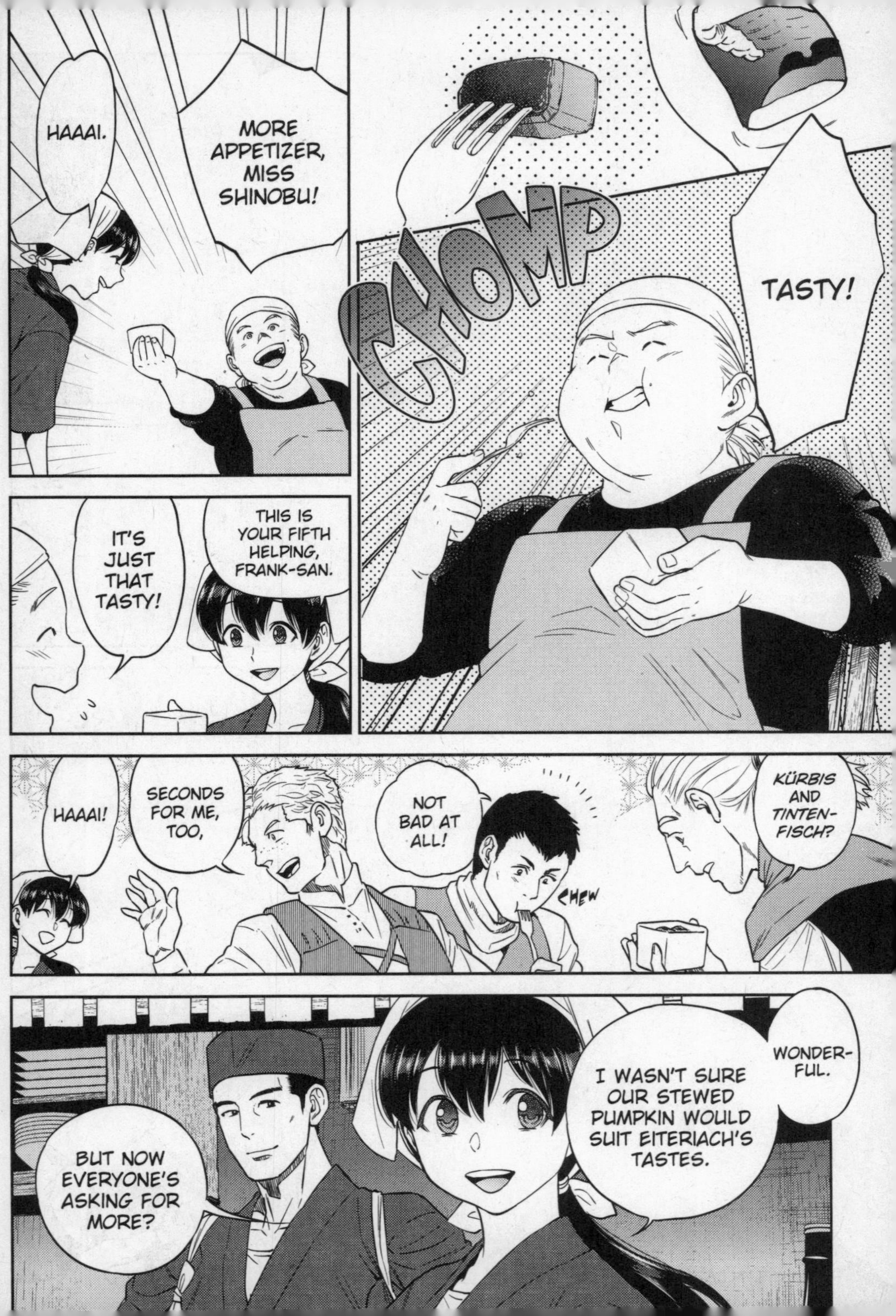
CHOMP
TASTY!
MORE APPETIZER, MISS SHINOBU!
HAAAI.
THIS IS YOUR FIFTH HELPING, FRANK-SAN.
IT'S JUST THAT TASTY!
KÜRBIS AND TINTEN-FISCH?
NOT BAD AT ALL!
CHEW
SECONDS FOR ME, TOO,
HAAAI!
WONDER-FUL.
I WASN'T SURE OUR STEWED PUMPKIN WOULD SUIT EITERIACH'S TASTES.
BUT NOW EVERYONE'S ASKING FOR MORE?

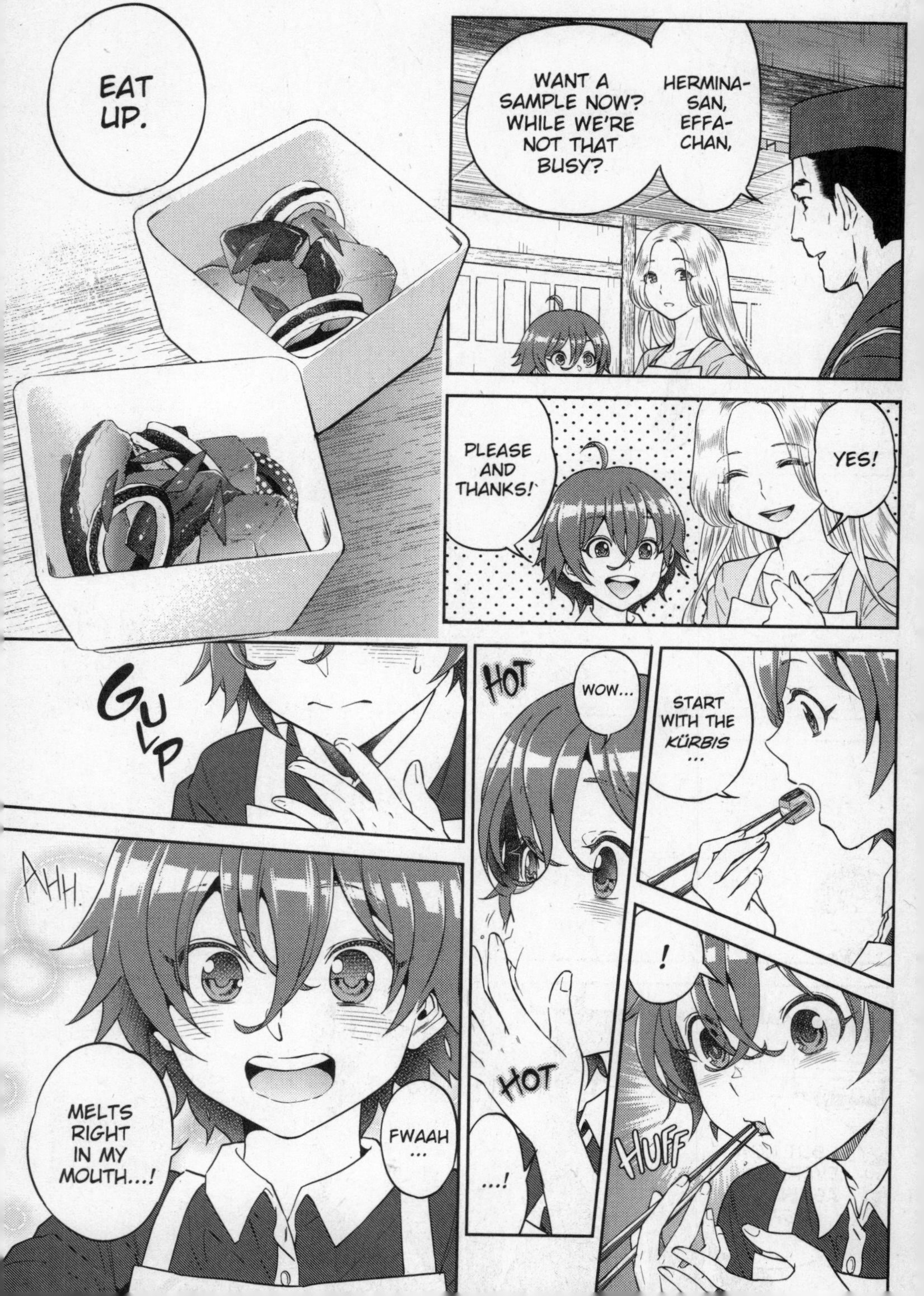
HERMINA-SAN, EFFA-CHAN,
WANT A SAMPLE NOW? WHILE WE'RE NOT THAT BUSY?
YES!
PLEASE AND THANKS!
EAT UP.
START WITH THE *KÜRBIS* ...
!
HUFF
HOT
WOW...
HOT
...!
GULP
AHH.
FWAAH ...
MELTS RIGHT IN MY MOUTH...!

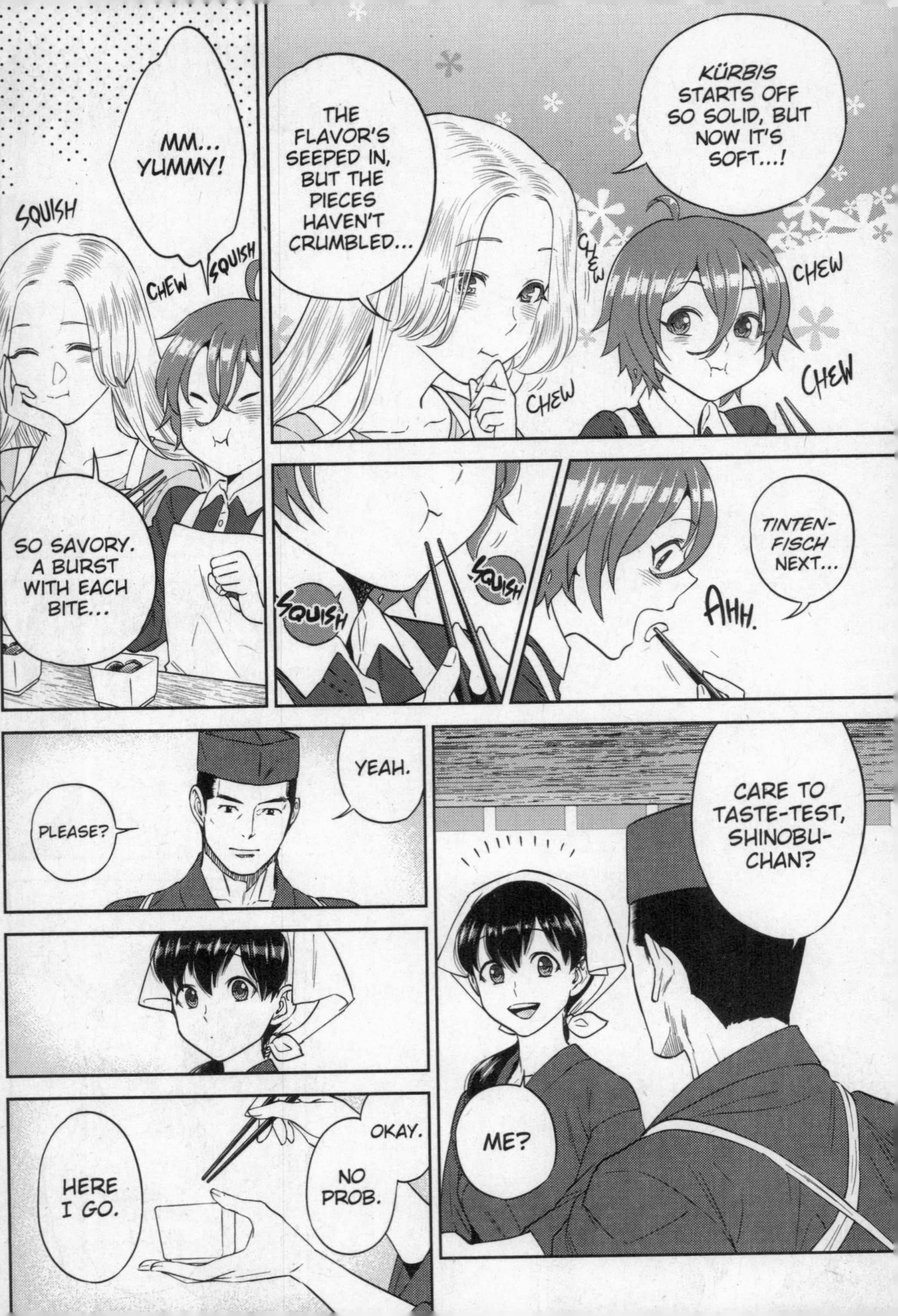
KÜRBIS STARTS OFF SO SOLID, BUT NOW IT'S SOFT...!
THE FLAVOR'S SEEPED IN, BUT THE PIECES HAVEN'T CRUMBLED...
CHEW
CHEW
CHEW
CHEW
TINTEN-FISCH NEXT...
AHH.
SQUISH
SQUISH
MM... YUMMY!
SQUISH
SQUISH
CHEW
SO SAVORY. A BURST WITH EACH BITE...
CARE TO TASTE-TEST, SHINOBU-CHAN?
ME?
YEAH.
PLEASE?
OKAY.
NO PROB.
HERE I GO.

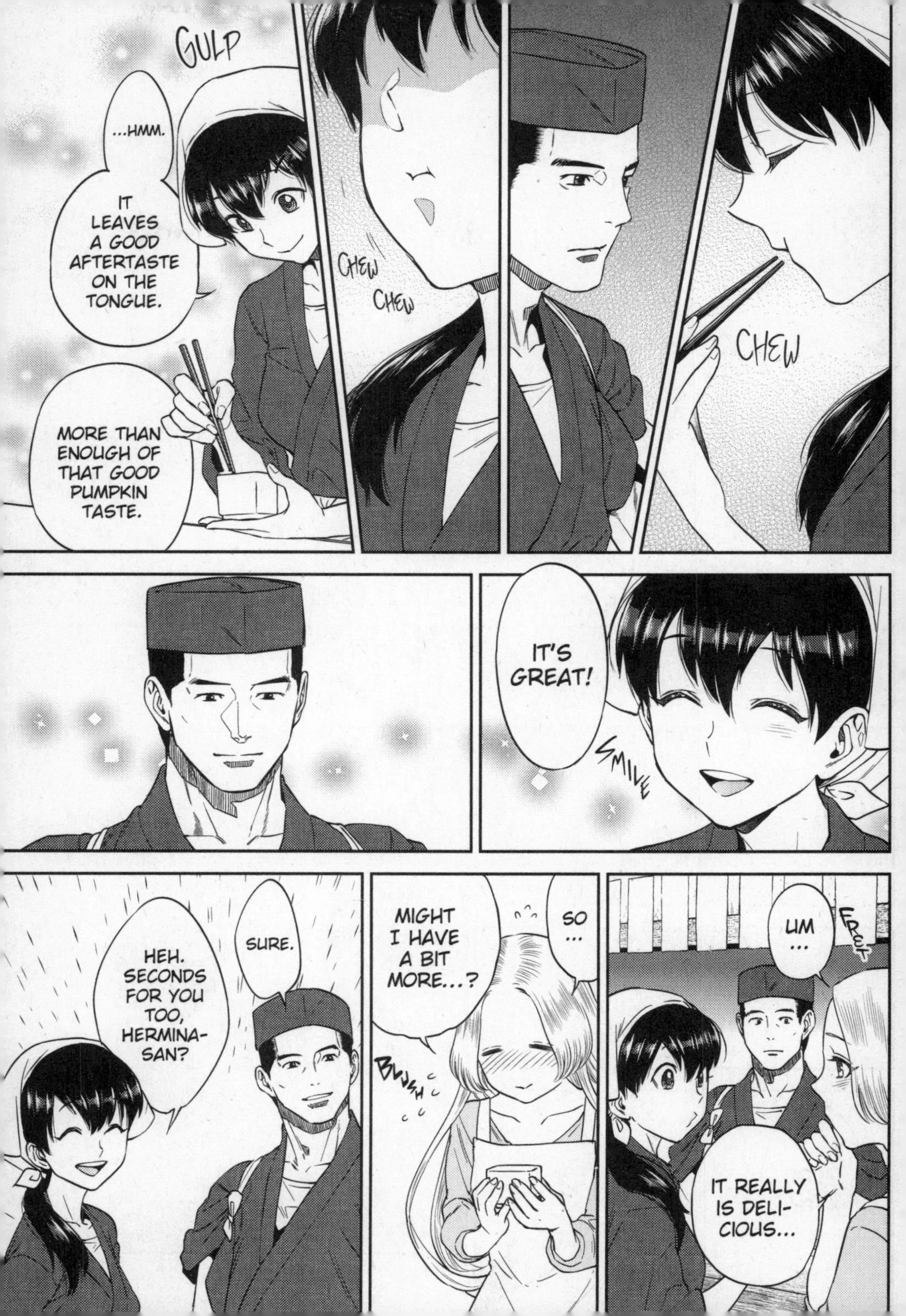
CHEW
CHEW
CHEW
GULP
...HMM.
IT LEAVES A GOOD AFTERTASTE ON THE TONGUE.
MORE THAN ENOUGH OF THAT GOOD PUMPKIN TASTE.
IT'S GREAT!
SMILE
UM ...
FRET
IT REALLY IS DELICIOUS...
SO ...
MIGHT I HAVE A BIT MORE...?
BLUSH
SURE.
HEH. SECONDS FOR YOU TOO, HERMINA-SAN?

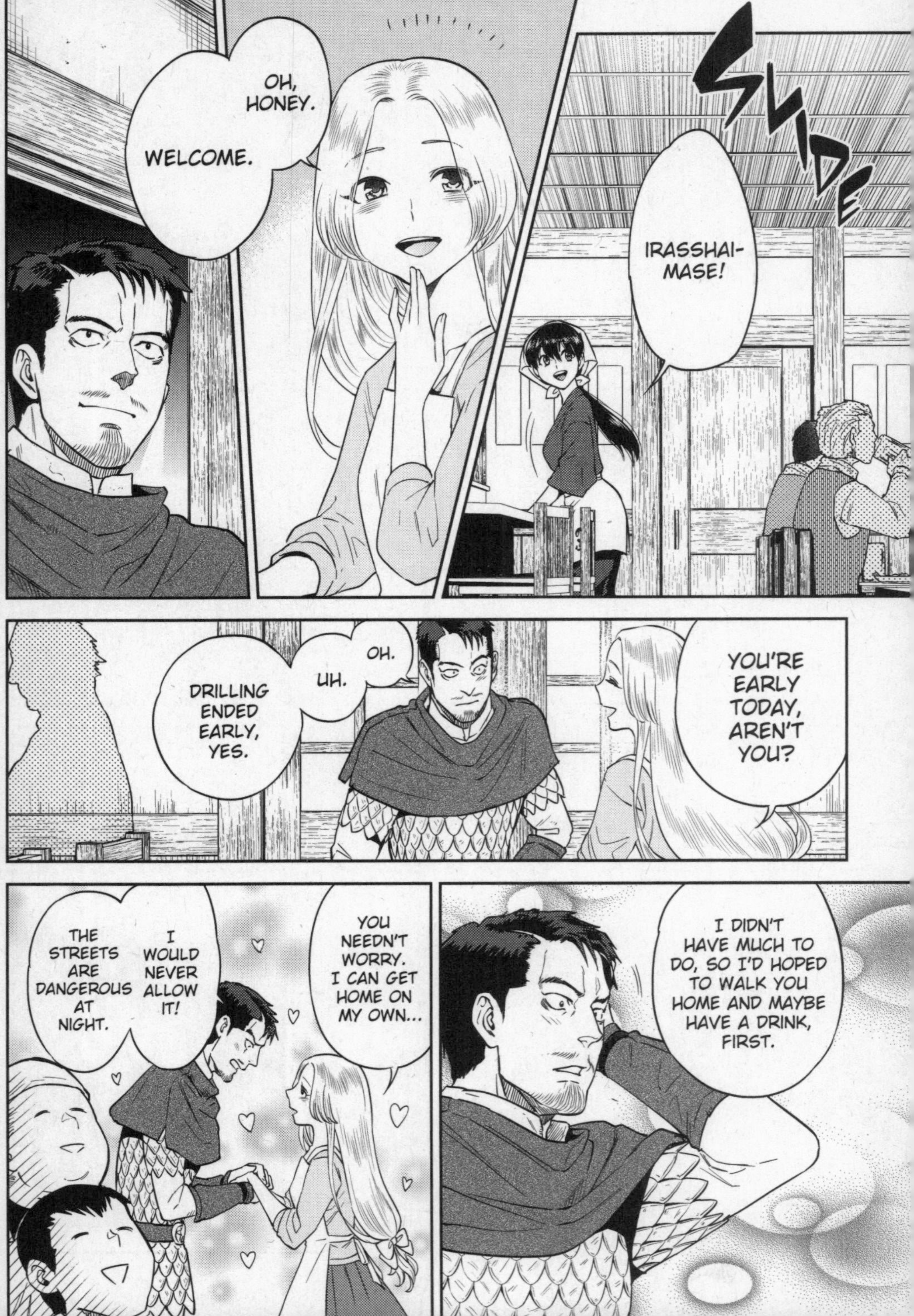
SLIDE
IRASSHAI-MASE!
OH, HONEY.
WELCOME.
YOU'RE EARLY TODAY, AREN'T YOU?
OH.
UH.
DRILLING ENDED EARLY, YES.
I DIDN'T HAVE MUCH TO DO, SO I'D HOPED TO WALK YOU HOME AND MAYBE HAVE A DRINK, FIRST.
YOU NEEDN'T WORRY. I CAN GET HOME ON MY OWN...
I WOULD NEVER ALLOW IT!
THE STREETS ARE DANGEROUS AT NIGHT.

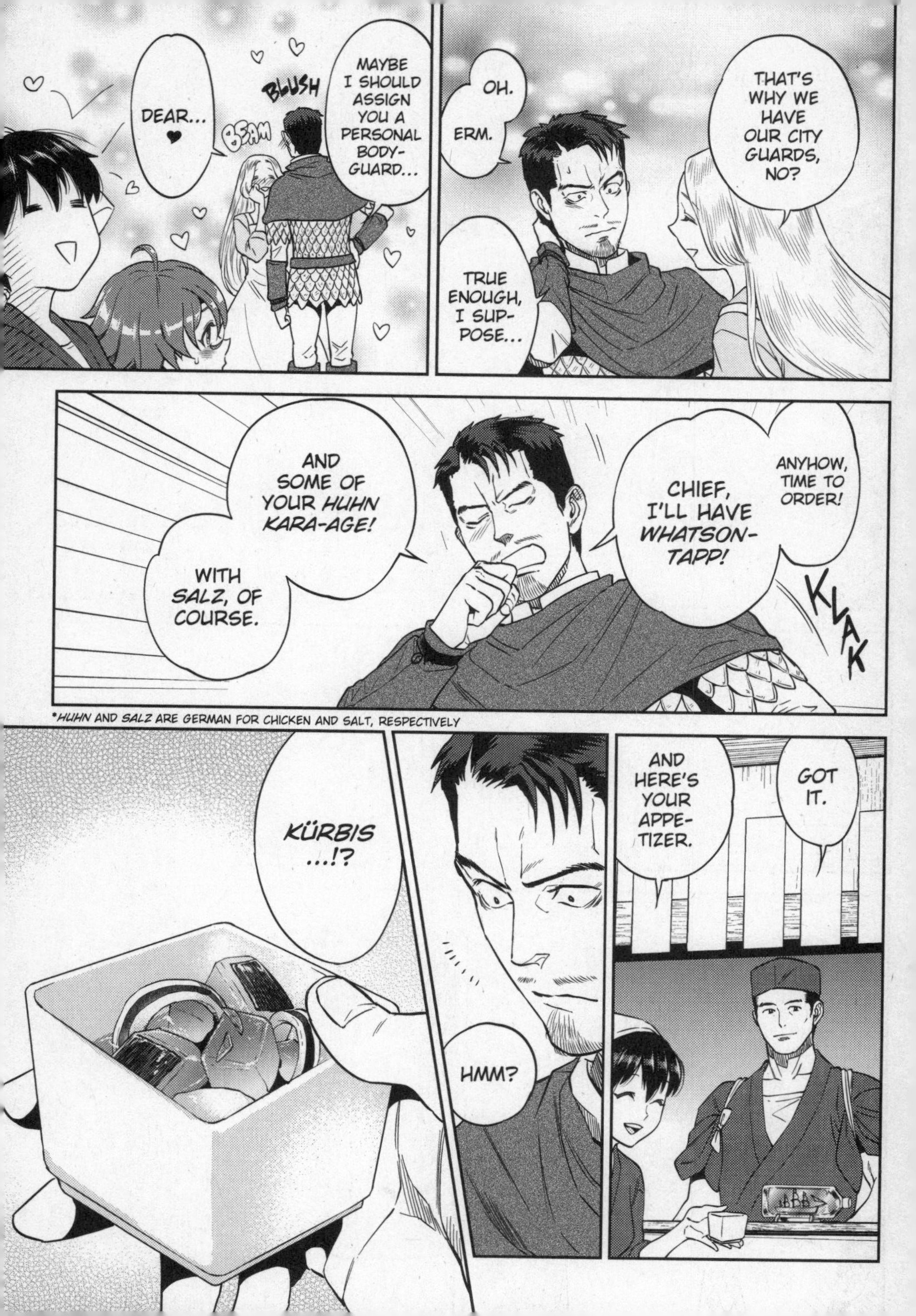
THAT'S WHY WE HAVE OUR CITY GUARDS, NO?
OH.
ERM.
TRUE ENOUGH, I SUP-POSE...
MAYBE I SHOULD ASSIGN YOU A PERSONAL BODY-GUARD...
BLUSH
BEAM
DEAR... ♥
KVAK
ANYHOW, TIME TO ORDER!
CHIEF, I'LL HAVE *WHATSON-TAPP!*
AND SOME OF YOUR *HUHN KARA-AGE!*
WITH *SALZ*, OF COURSE.
GOT IT.
AND HERE'S YOUR APPE-TIZER.
HMM?
KÜRBIS ...!?

**HUHN* AND *SALZ* ARE GERMAN FOR CHICKEN AND SALT, RESPECTIVELY

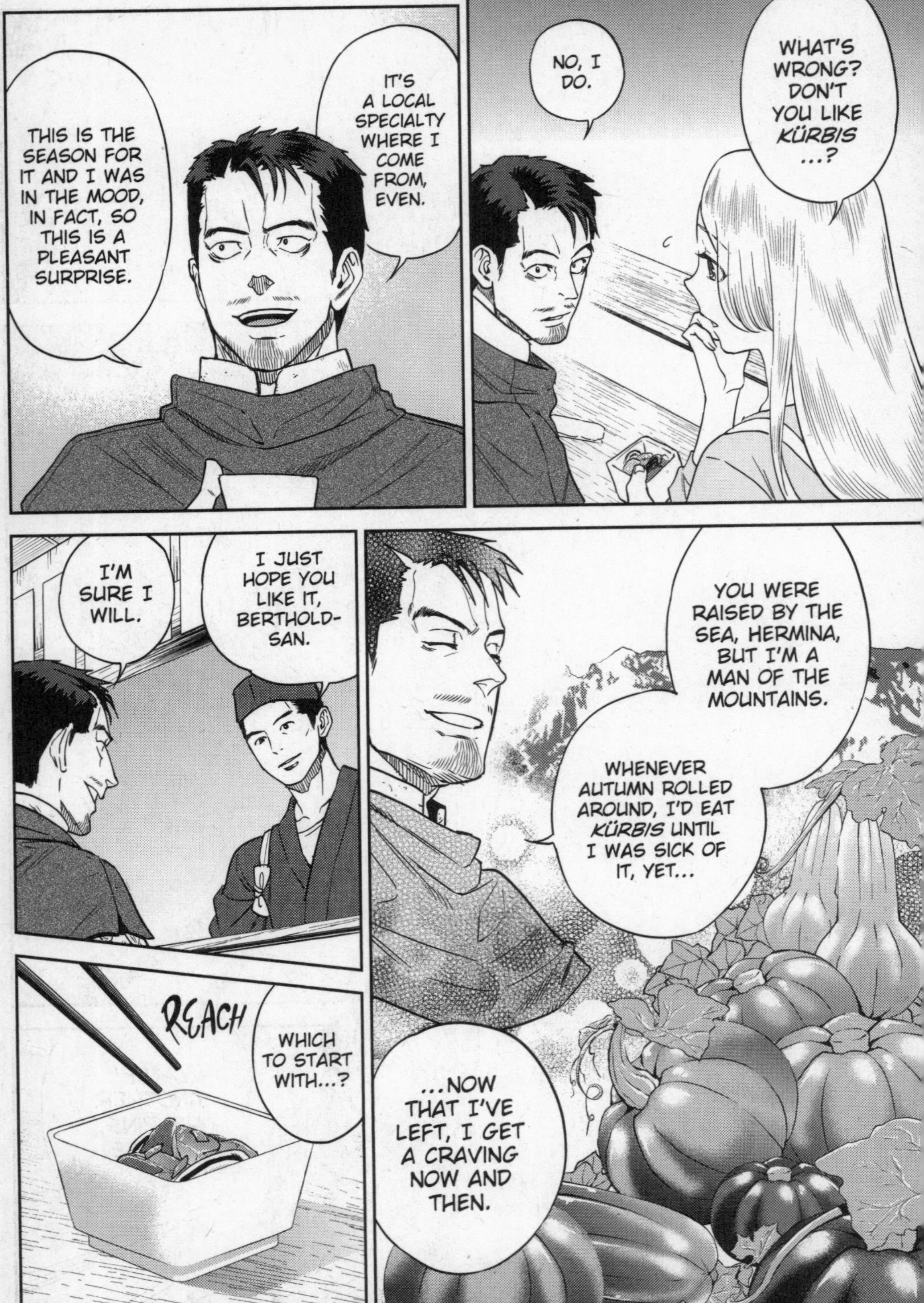
WHAT'S WRONG? DON'T YOU LIKE *KÜRBIS* ...?
NO, I DO.
IT'S A LOCAL SPECIALTY WHERE I COME FROM, EVEN.
THIS IS THE SEASON FOR IT AND I WAS IN THE MOOD, IN FACT, SO THIS IS A PLEASANT SURPRISE.
YOU WERE RAISED BY THE SEA, HERMINA, BUT I'M A MAN OF THE MOUNTAINS.
WHENEVER AUTUMN ROLLED AROUND, I'D EAT *KÜRBIS* UNTIL I WAS SICK OF IT, YET...
...NOW THAT I'VE LEFT, I GET A CRAVING NOW AND THEN.
I JUST HOPE YOU LIKE IT, BERTHOLD-SAN.
I'M SURE I WILL.
REACH
WHICH TO START WITH...?

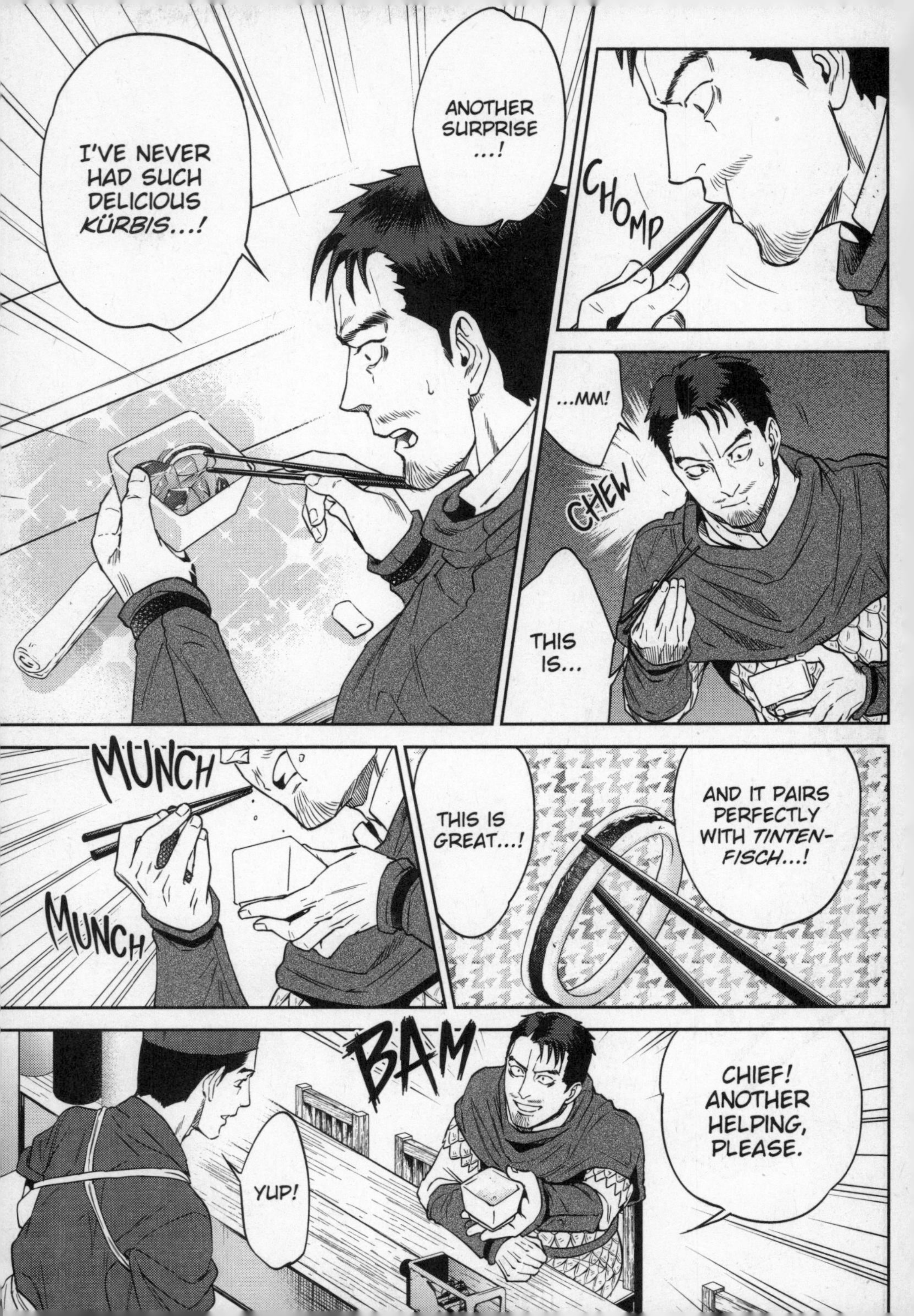
CHOMP
...MM!
CHEW
THIS IS...
ANOTHER SURPRISE ...!
I'VE NEVER HAD SUCH DELICIOUS *KÜRBIS*...!
AND IT PAIRS PERFECTLY WITH *TINTEN-FISCH*...!
THIS IS GREAT...!
MUNCH
MUNCH
CHIEF! ANOTHER HELPING, PLEASE.
BAM
YUP!

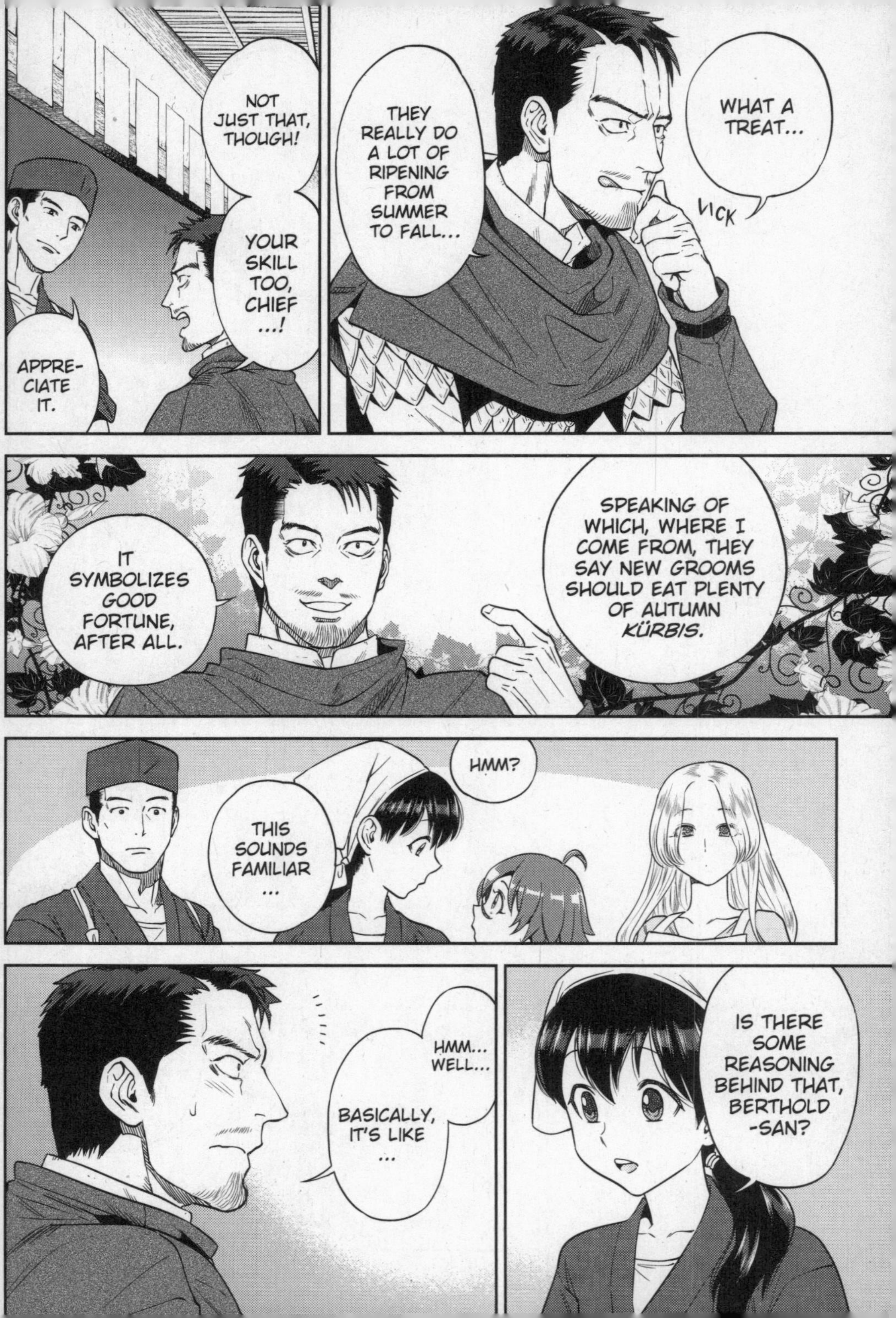
WHAT A TREAT...
LICK
THEY REALLY DO A LOT OF RIPENING FROM SUMMER TO FALL...
NOT JUST THAT, THOUGH!
YOUR SKILL TOO, CHIEF ...!
APPRE-CIATE IT.
SPEAKING OF WHICH, WHERE I COME FROM, THEY SAY NEW GROOMS SHOULD EAT PLENTY OF AUTUMN *KÜRBIS.*
IT SYMBOLIZES GOOD FORTUNE, AFTER ALL.
HMM?
THIS SOUNDS FAMILIAR ...
IS THERE SOME REASONING BEHIND THAT, BERTHOLD -SAN?
HMM... WELL...
BASICALLY, IT'S LIKE ...

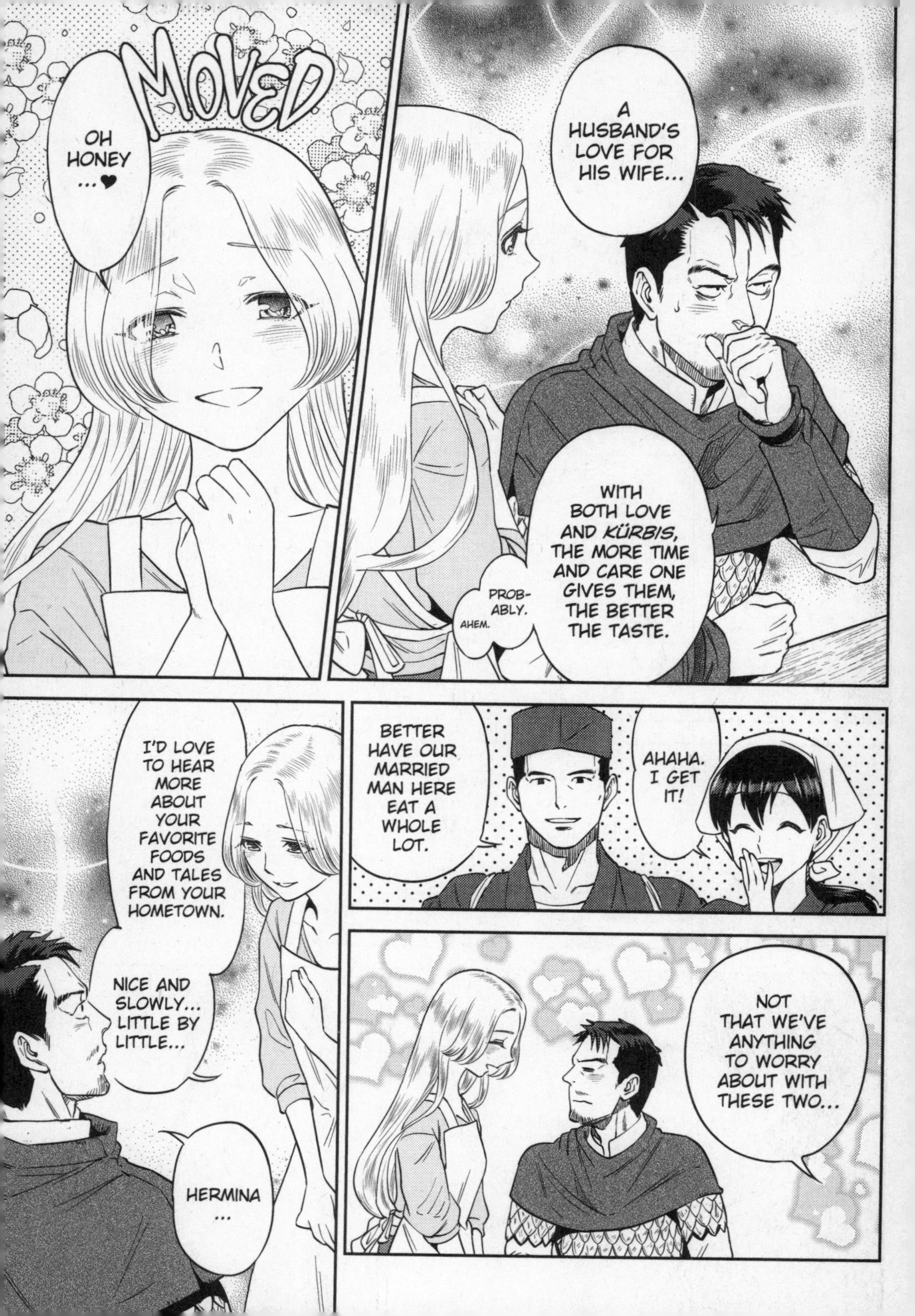
A HUSBAND'S LOVE FOR HIS WIFE...
WITH BOTH LOVE AND *KÜRBIS*, THE MORE TIME AND CARE ONE GIVES THEM, THE BETTER THE TASTE.
PROB-ABLY.
AHEM.
MOVED
OH HONEY ...♥
AHAHA. I GET IT!
BETTER HAVE OUR MARRIED MAN HERE EAT A WHOLE LOT.
NOT THAT WE'VE ANYTHING TO WORRY ABOUT WITH THESE TWO...
I'D LOVE TO HEAR MORE ABOUT YOUR FAVORITE FOODS AND TALES FROM YOUR HOMETOWN.
NICE AND SLOWLY... LITTLE BY LITTLE...
HERMINA ...

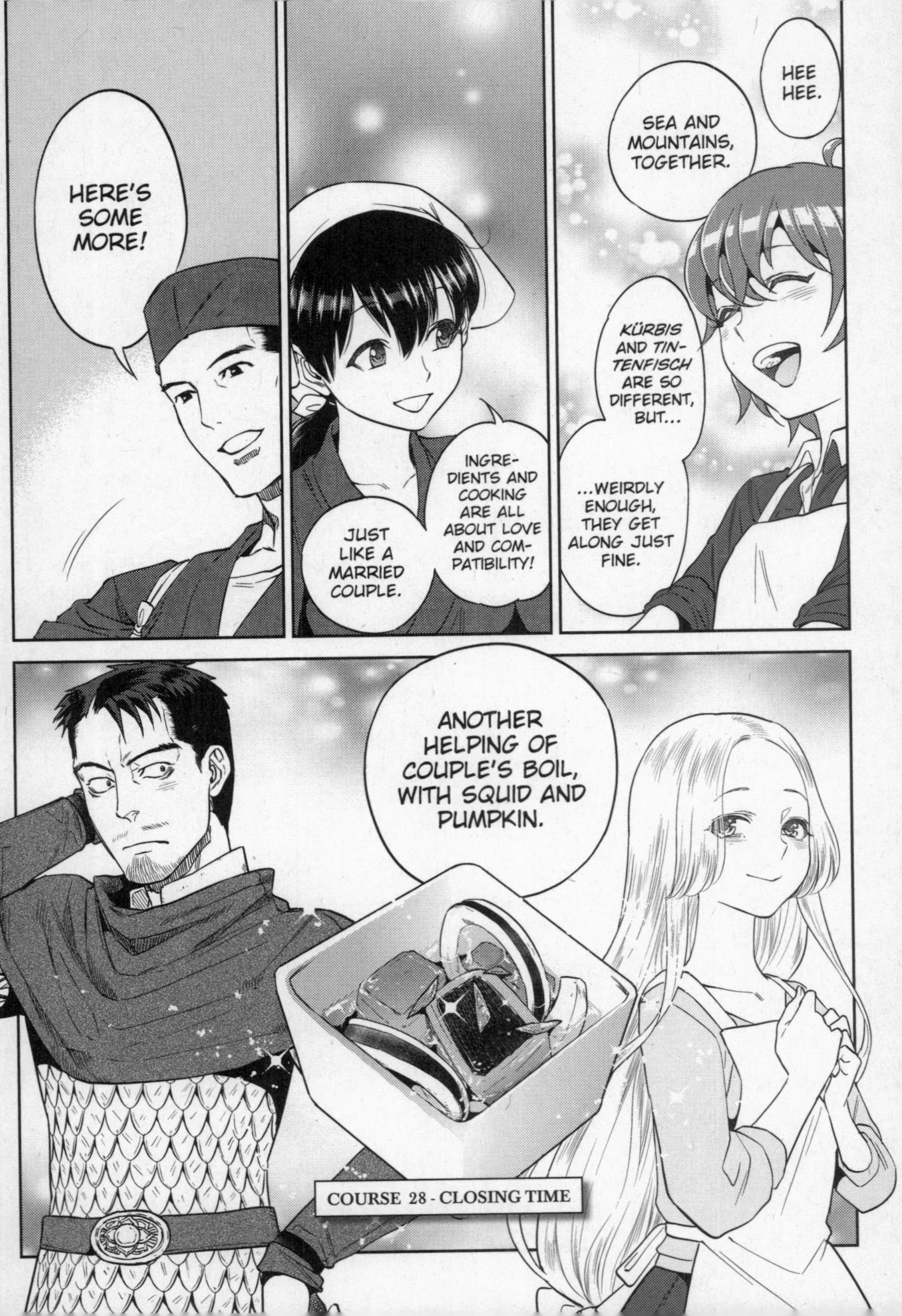
HEE HEE.
SEA AND MOUNTAINS, TOGETHER.
KÜRBIS AND *TINTENFISCH* ARE SO DIFFERENT, BUT...
...WEIRDLY ENOUGH, THEY GET ALONG JUST FINE.
INGREDIENTS AND COOKING ARE ALL ABOUT LOVE AND COMPATIBILITY!
JUST LIKE A MARRIED COUPLE.
HERE'S SOME MORE!
ANOTHER HELPING OF COUPLE'S BOIL, WITH SQUID AND PUMPKIN.
COURSE 28 - CLOSING TIME

Squid and Pumpkin Couple's Boil

OTHERWORLDLY IZAKAYA NOBU

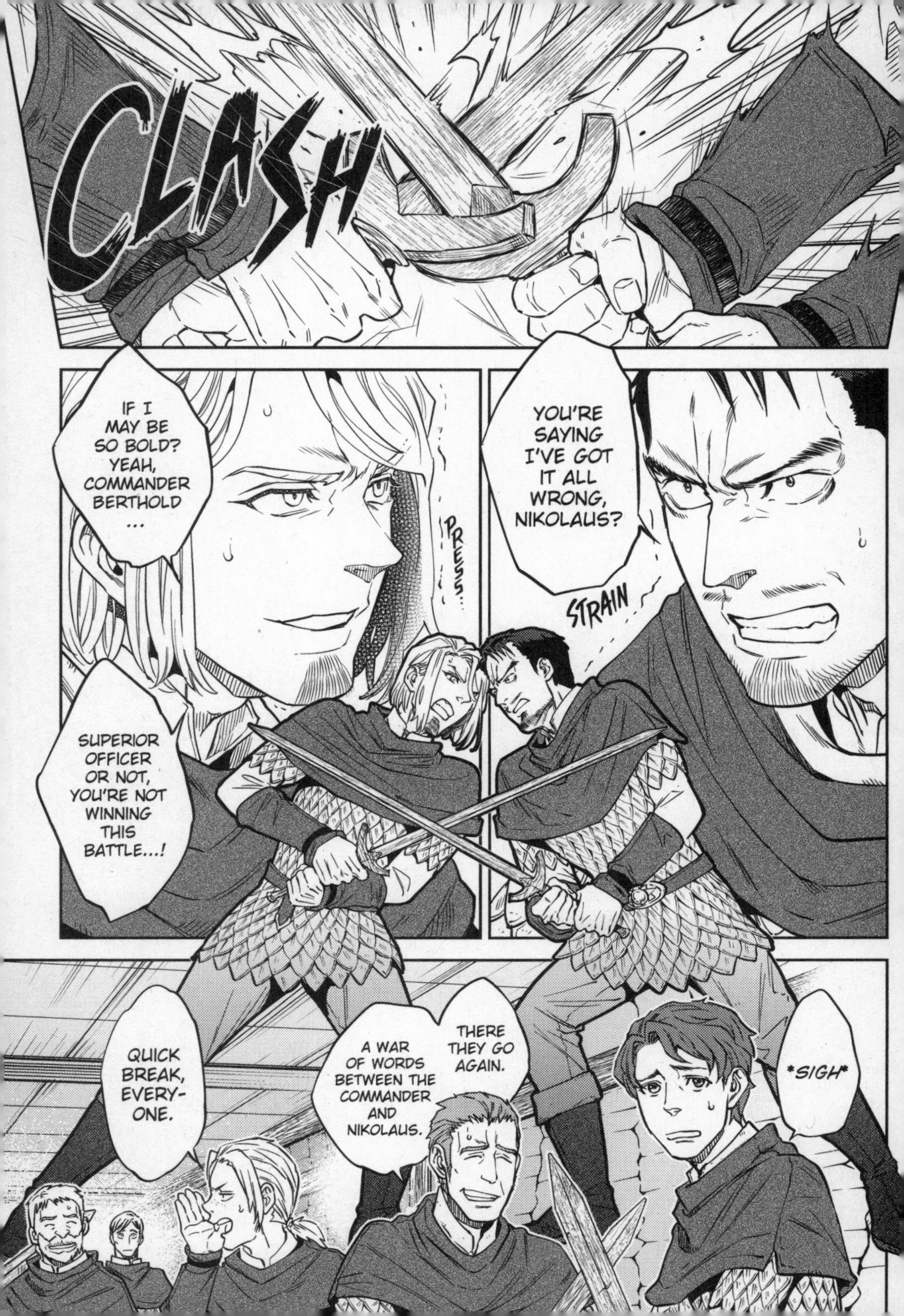
CLASH
YOU'RE SAYING I'VE GOT IT ALL WRONG, NIKOLAUS?
STRAIN
IF I MAY BE SO BOLD? YEAH, COMMANDER BERTHOLD ...
PRESS...
SUPERIOR OFFICER OR NOT, YOU'RE NOT WINNING THIS BATTLE...!
SIGH
THERE THEY GO AGAIN.
A WAR OF WORDS BETWEEN THE COMMANDER AND NIKOLAUS.
QUICK BREAK, EVERY-ONE.

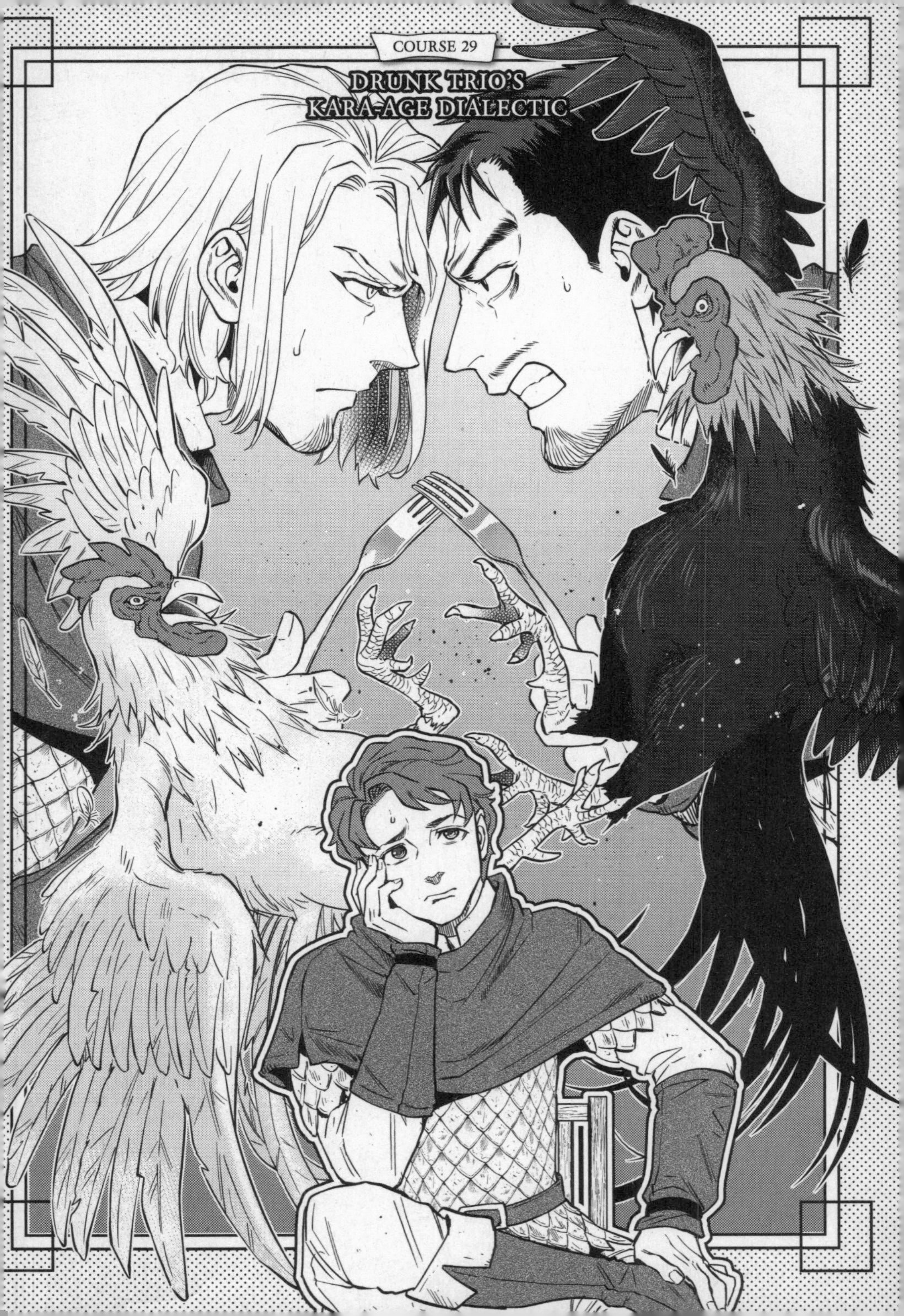
COURSE 29
DRUNK TRIO'S
KARA-AGE DIALECTIC

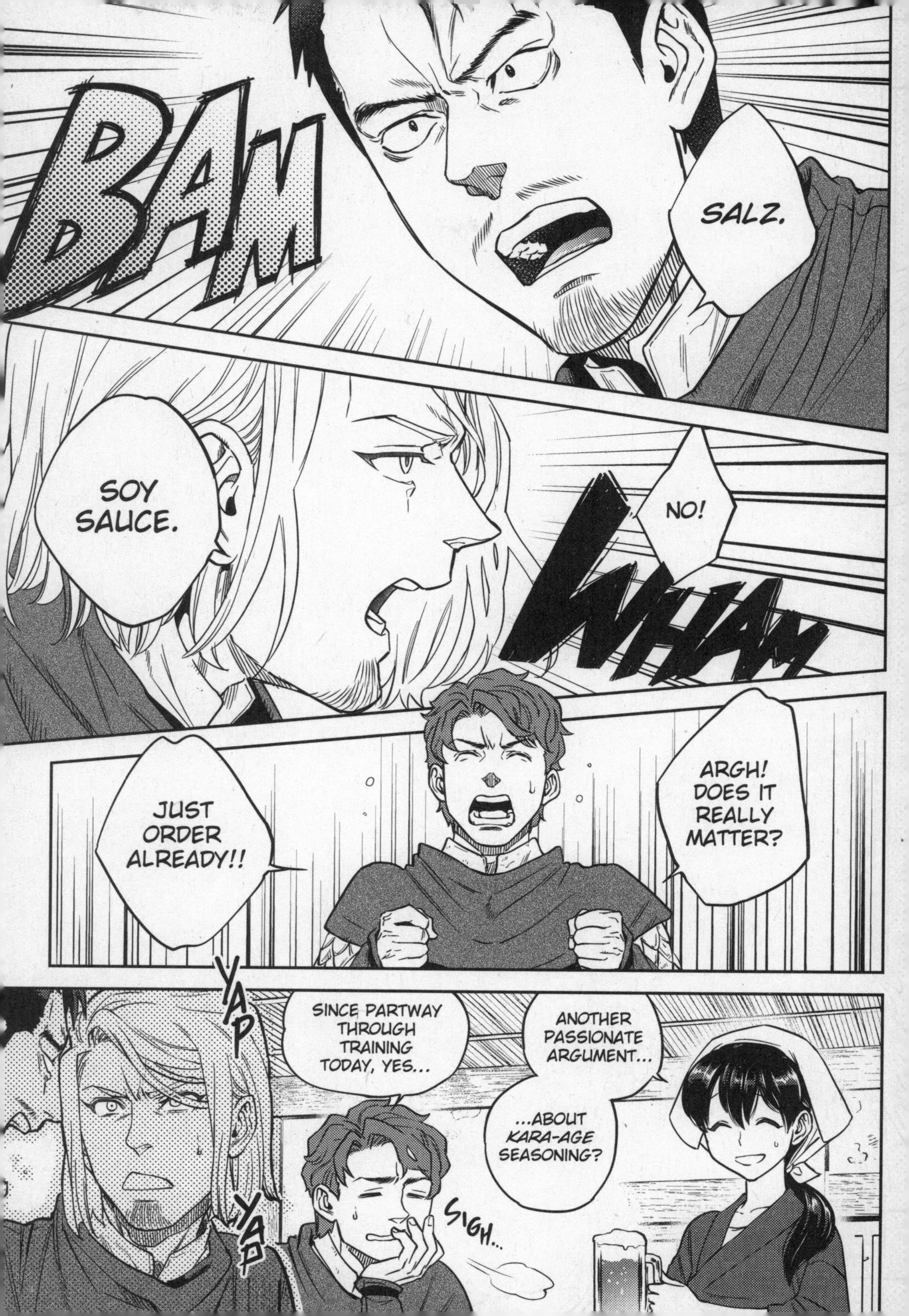
SALZ.
BAM
NO!
WHAM
SOY SAUCE.
ARGH! DOES IT REALLY MATTER?
JUST ORDER ALREADY!!
ANOTHER PASSIONATE ARGUMENT...
...ABOUT KARA-AGE SEASONING?
SINCE PARTWAY THROUGH TRAINING TODAY, YES...
YAP
YAP
YAP
SIGH...

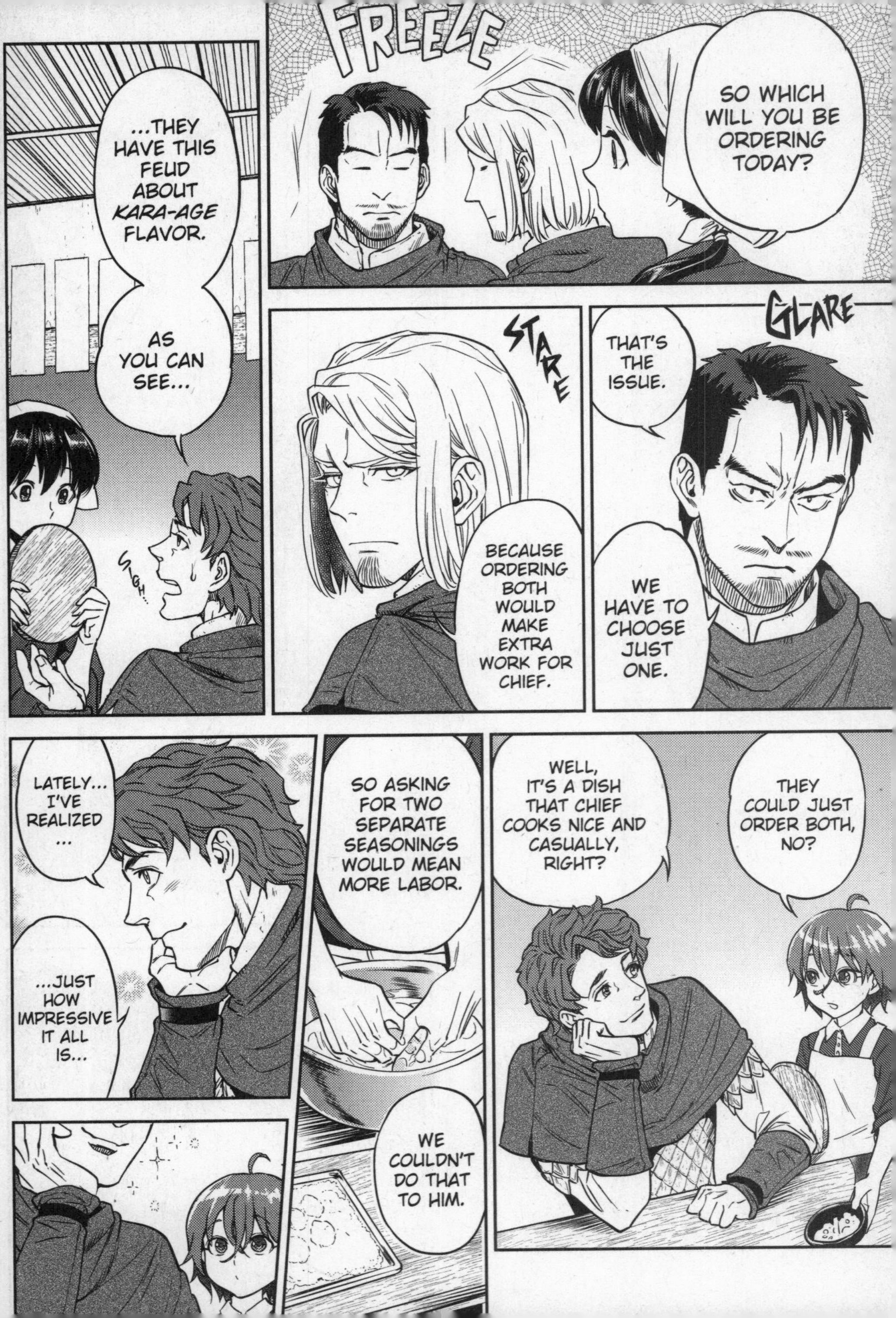
FREEZE
SO WHICH WILL YOU BE ORDERING TODAY?
GLARE
THAT'S THE ISSUE.
WE HAVE TO CHOOSE JUST ONE.
STARE
BECAUSE ORDERING BOTH WOULD MAKE EXTRA WORK FOR CHIEF.
...THEY HAVE THIS FEUD ABOUT KARA-AGE FLAVOR.
AS YOU CAN SEE...
SIGH...
THEY COULD JUST ORDER BOTH, NO?
WELL, IT'S A DISH THAT CHIEF COOKS NICE AND CASUALLY, RIGHT?
SO ASKING FOR TWO SEPARATE SEASONINGS WOULD MEAN MORE LABOR.
WE COULDN'T DO THAT TO HIM.
LATELY... I'VE REALIZED ...
...JUST HOW IMPRESSIVE IT ALL IS...

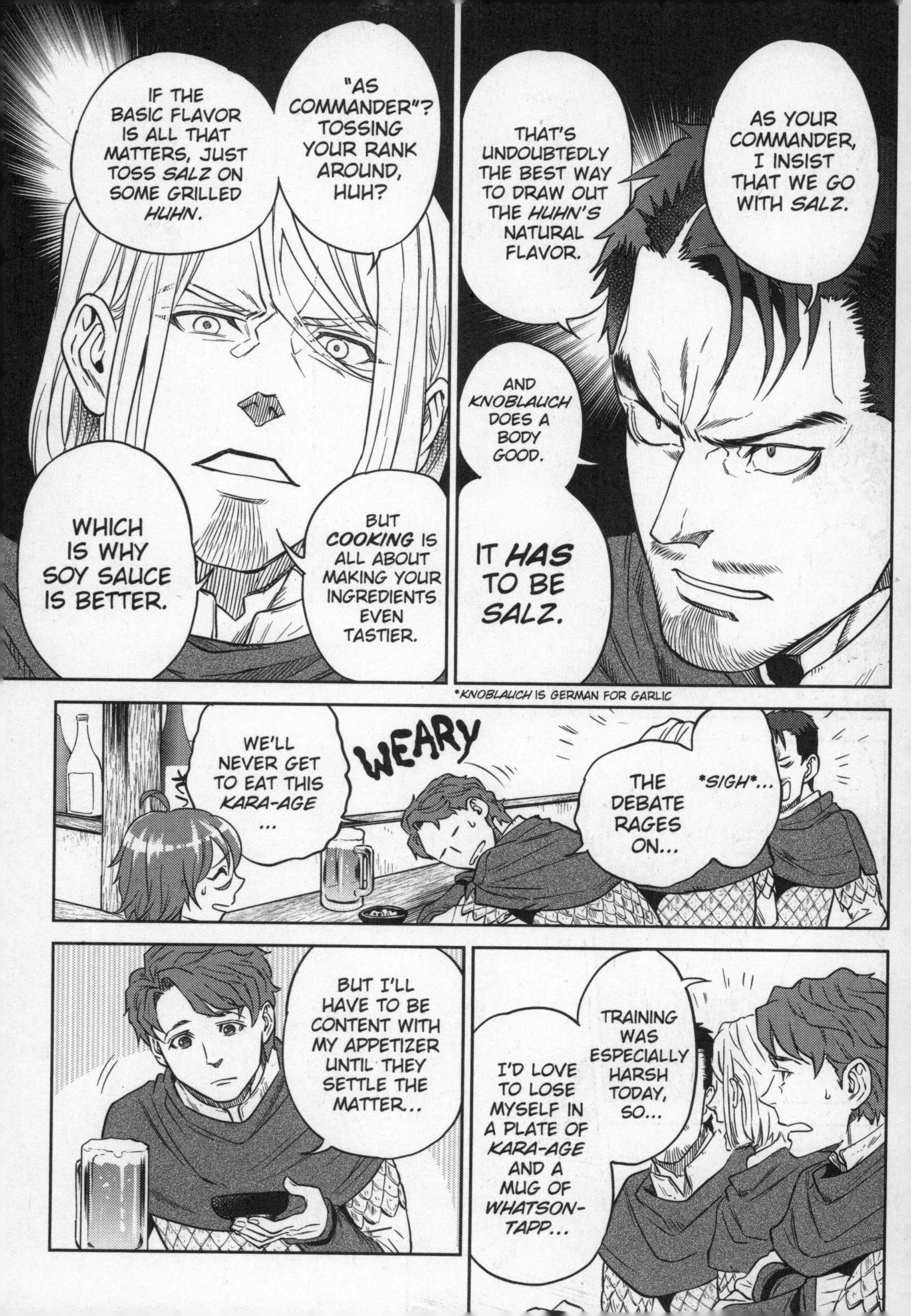
AS YOUR COMMANDER, I INSIST THAT WE GO WITH *SALZ*.
THAT'S UNDOUBTEDLY THE BEST WAY TO DRAW OUT THE *HUHN'S* NATURAL FLAVOR.
AND *KNOBLAUCH* DOES A BODY GOOD.
IT **HAS** TO BE *SALZ*.
"AS COMMANDER"? TOSSING YOUR RANK AROUND, HUH?
IF THE BASIC FLAVOR IS ALL THAT MATTERS, JUST TOSS *SALZ* ON SOME GRILLED *HUHN*.
BUT **COOKING** IS ALL ABOUT MAKING YOUR INGREDIENTS EVEN TASTIER.
WHICH IS WHY SOY SAUCE IS BETTER.
**KNOBLAUCH* IS GERMAN FOR GARLIC
SIGH...
THE DEBATE RAGES ON...
WEARY
WE'LL NEVER GET TO EAT THIS *KARA-AGE* ...
TRAINING WAS ESPECIALLY HARSH TODAY, SO...
I'D LOVE TO LOSE MYSELF IN A PLATE OF *KARA-AGE* AND A MUG OF *WHATSON-TAPP*...
BUT I'LL HAVE TO BE CONTENT WITH MY APPETIZER UNTIL THEY SETTLE THE MATTER...

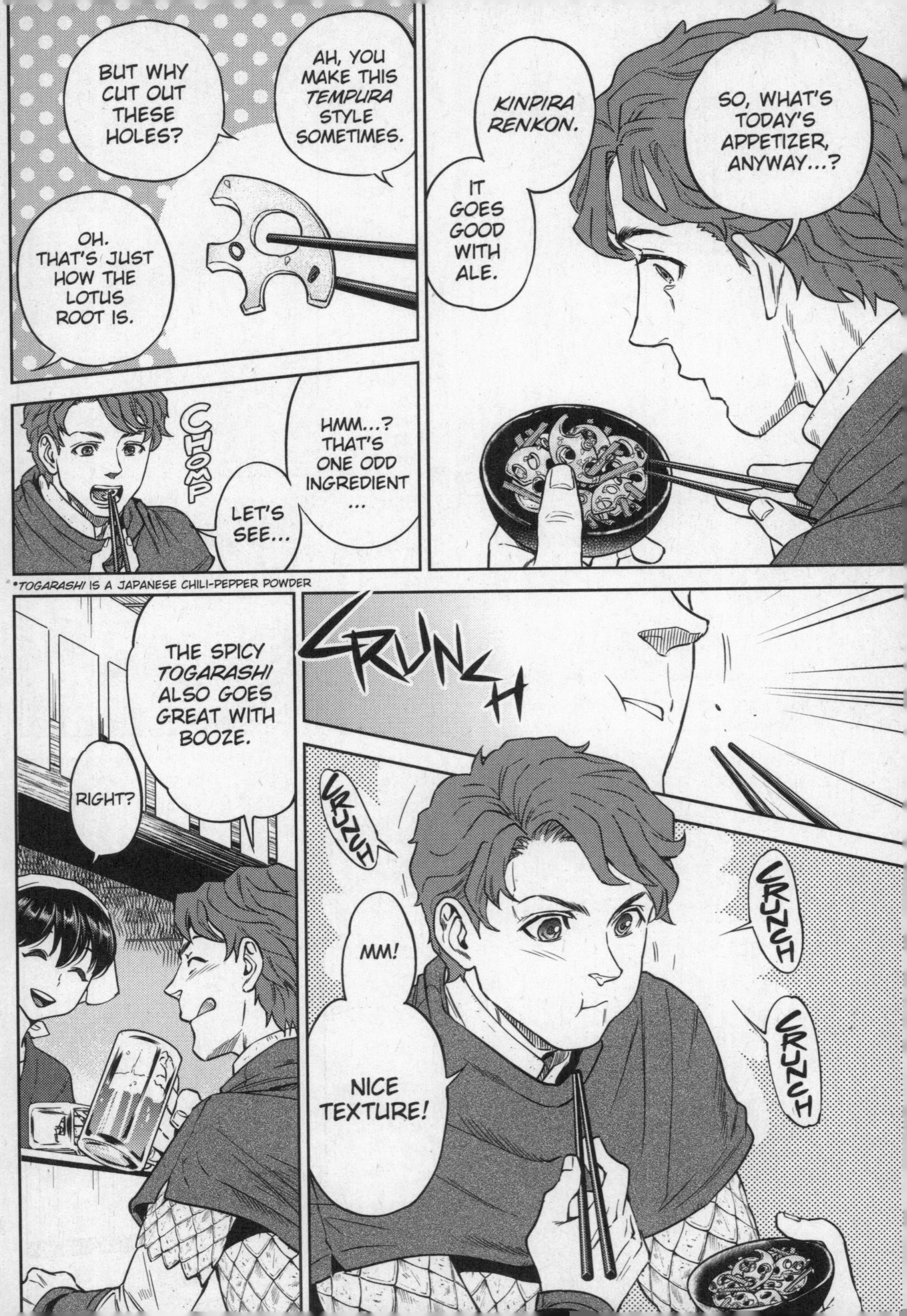
SO, WHAT'S TODAY'S APPETIZER, ANYWAY...?
KINPIRA RENKON.
IT GOES GOOD WITH ALE.
AH, YOU MAKE THIS TEMPURA STYLE SOMETIMES.
BUT WHY CUT OUT THESE HOLES?
OH. THAT'S JUST HOW THE LOTUS ROOT IS.
HMM...? THAT'S ONE ODD INGREDIENT ...
LET'S SEE...
CHOMP
CRUNCH
CRUNCH
CRUNCH
CRUNCH
MM!
NICE TEXTURE!
THE SPICY TOGARASHI ALSO GOES GREAT WITH BOOZE.
RIGHT?

*TOGARASHI IS A JAPANESE CHILI-PEPPER POWDER

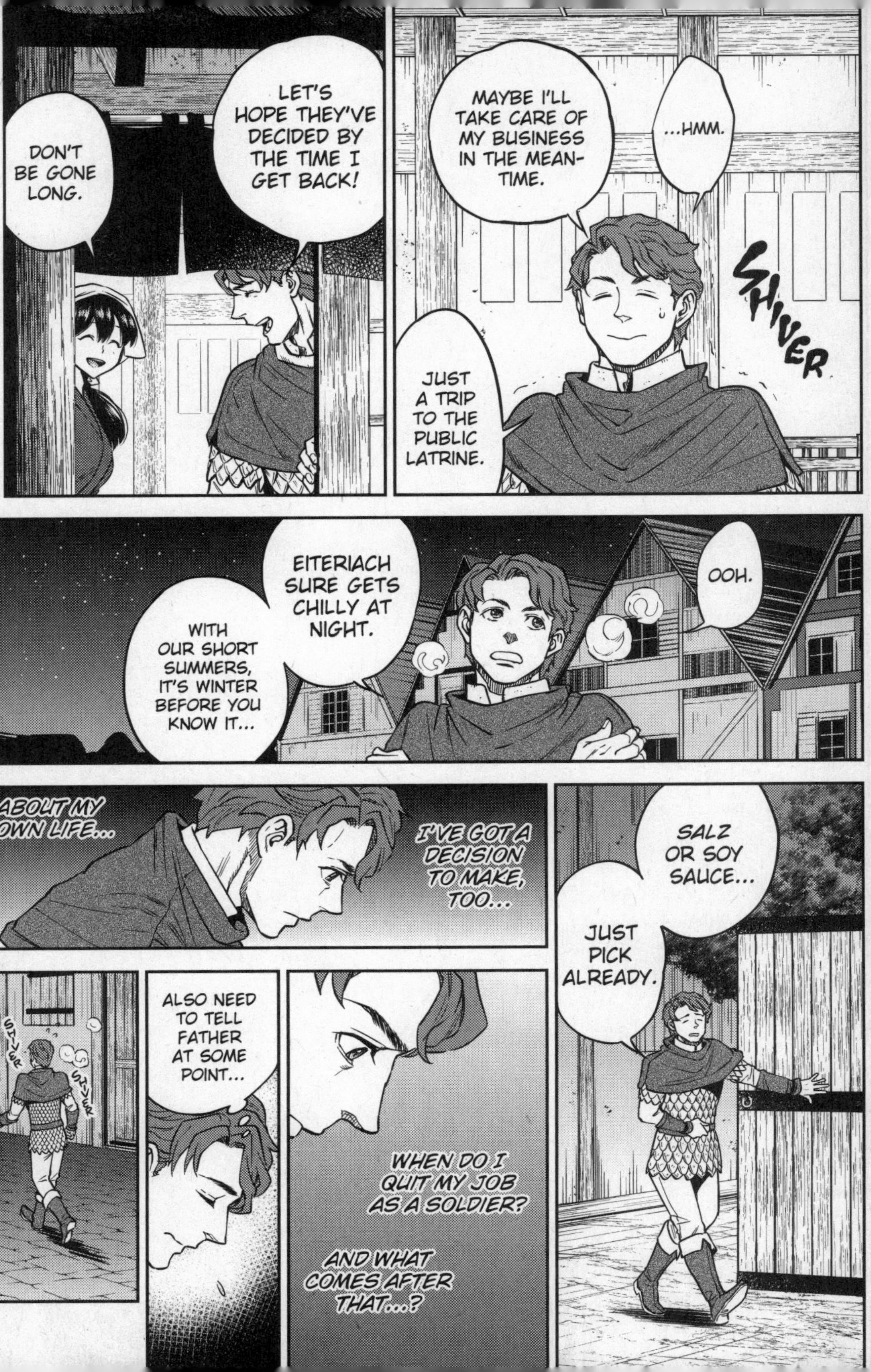
...HMM.
MAYBE I'LL TAKE CARE OF MY BUSINESS IN THE MEAN-TIME.
SHIVER
JUST A TRIP TO THE PUBLIC LATRINE.
LET'S HOPE THEY'VE DECIDED BY THE TIME I GET BACK!
DON'T BE GONE LONG.
OOH.
EITERIACH SURE GETS CHILLY AT NIGHT.
WITH OUR SHORT SUMMERS, IT'S WINTER BEFORE YOU KNOW IT...
SALZ OR SOY SAUCE...
JUST PICK ALREADY.
I'VE GOT A DECISION TO MAKE, TOO...
ABOUT MY OWN LIFE...
WHEN DO I QUIT MY JOB AS A SOLDIER?
AND WHAT COMES AFTER THAT...?
ALSO NEED TO TELL FATHER AT SOME POINT...
SHIVER
SHIVER

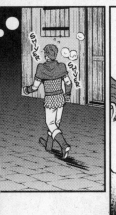

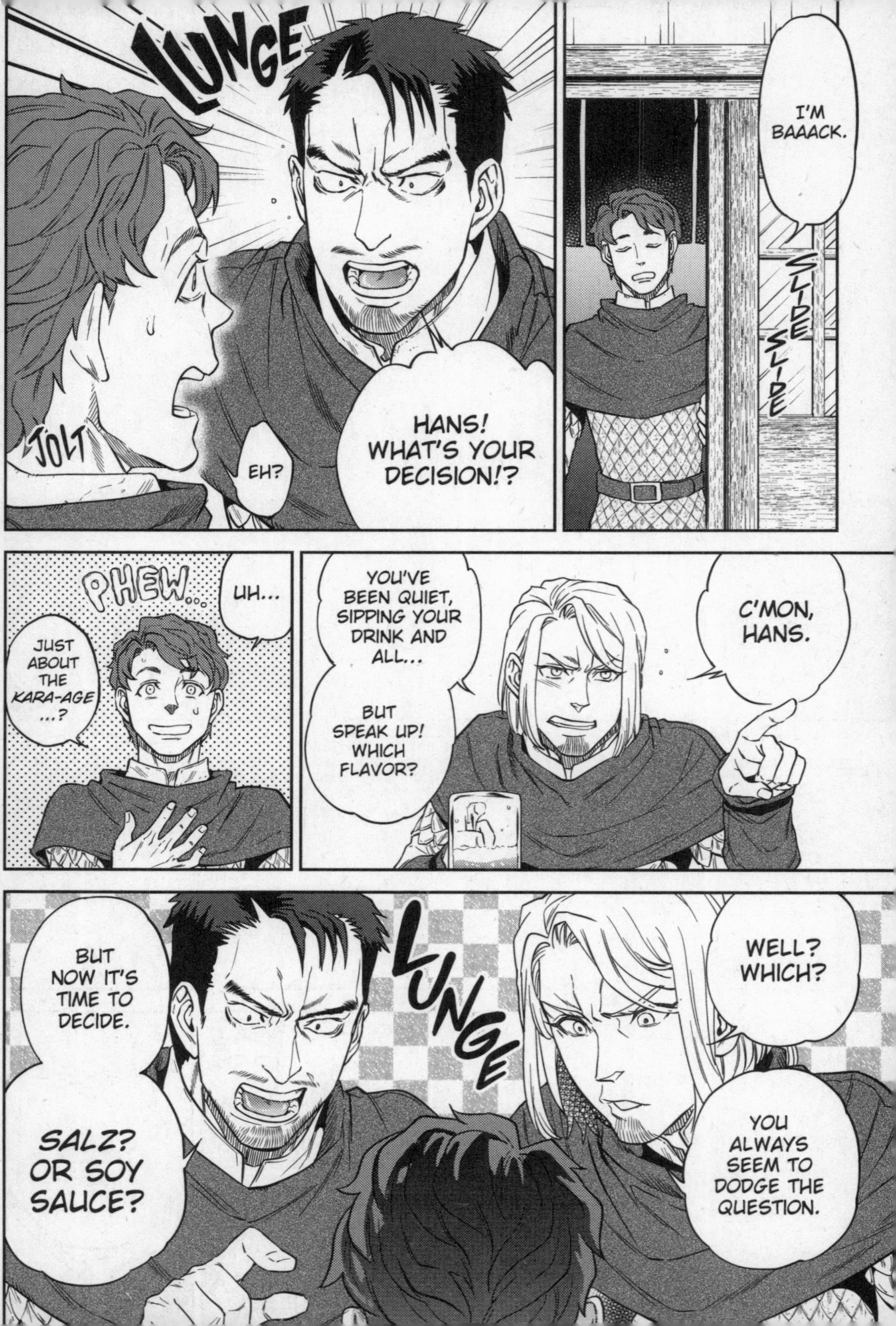
I'M BAAACK.
SLIDE
SLIDE
LUNGE
HANS! WHAT'S YOUR DECISION!?
EH?
JOLT
C'MON, HANS.
YOU'VE BEEN QUIET, SIPPING YOUR DRINK AND ALL...
BUT SPEAK UP! WHICH FLAVOR?
UH...
PHEW...
JUST ABOUT THE KARA-AGE ...?
WELL? WHICH?
BUT NOW IT'S TIME TO DECIDE.
LUNGE
YOU ALWAYS SEEM TO DODGE THE QUESTION.
SALZ? OR SOY SAUCE?

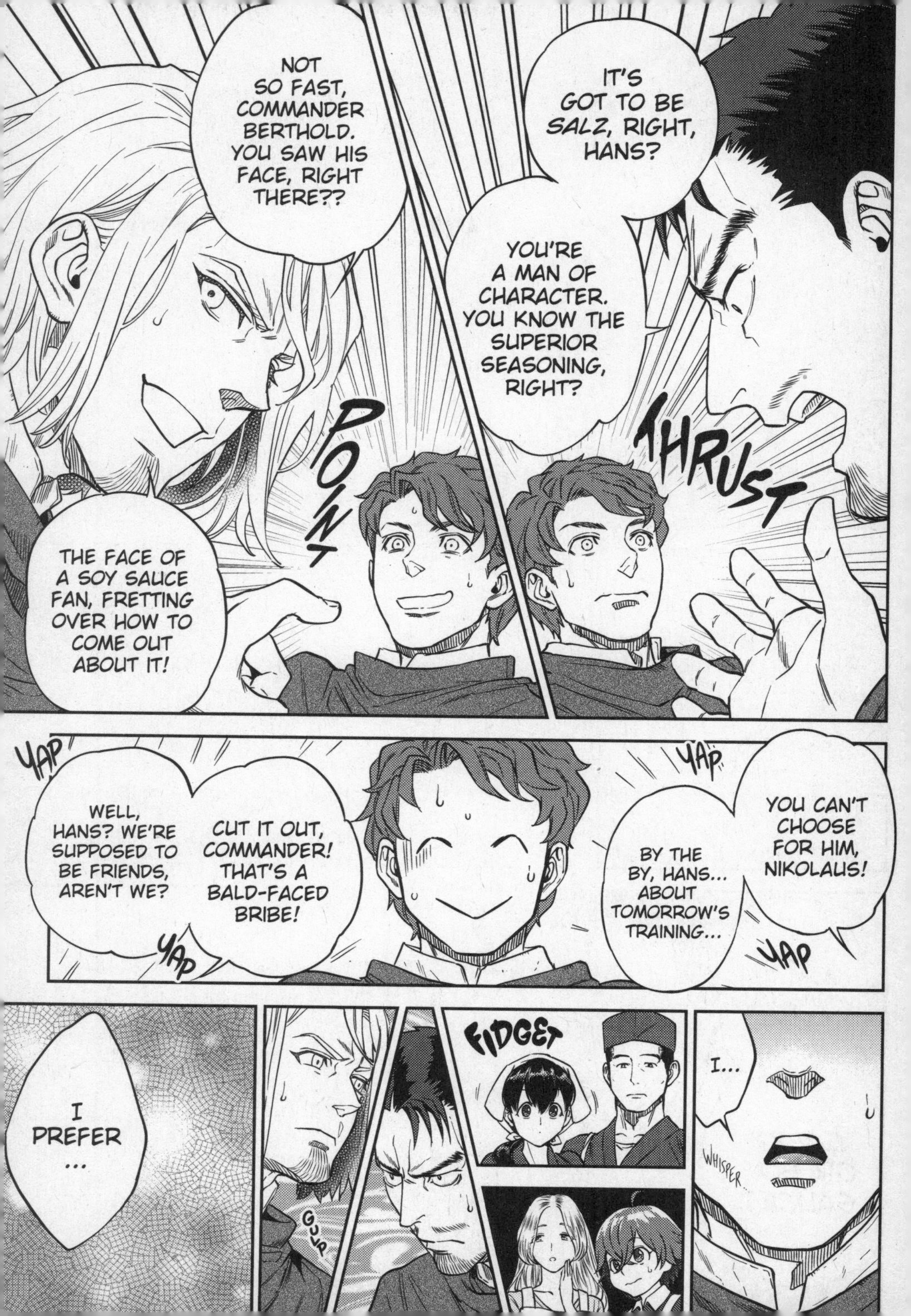
IT'S GOT TO BE SALZ, RIGHT, HANS?
YOU'RE A MAN OF CHARACTER. YOU KNOW THE SUPERIOR SEASONING, RIGHT?
THRUST
NOT SO FAST, COMMANDER BERTHOLD. YOU SAW HIS FACE, RIGHT THERE??
POINT
THE FACE OF A SOY SAUCE FAN, FRETTING OVER HOW TO COME OUT ABOUT IT!
YAP
YOU CAN'T CHOOSE FOR HIM, NIKOLAUS!
BY THE BY, HANS... ABOUT TOMORROW'S TRAINING...
YAP
CUT IT OUT, COMMANDER! THAT'S A BALD-FACED BRIBE!
WELL, HANS? WE'RE SUPPOSED TO BE FRIENDS, AREN'T WE?
YAP
YAP
I...
WHISPER...
FIDGET
GULP
I PREFER ...

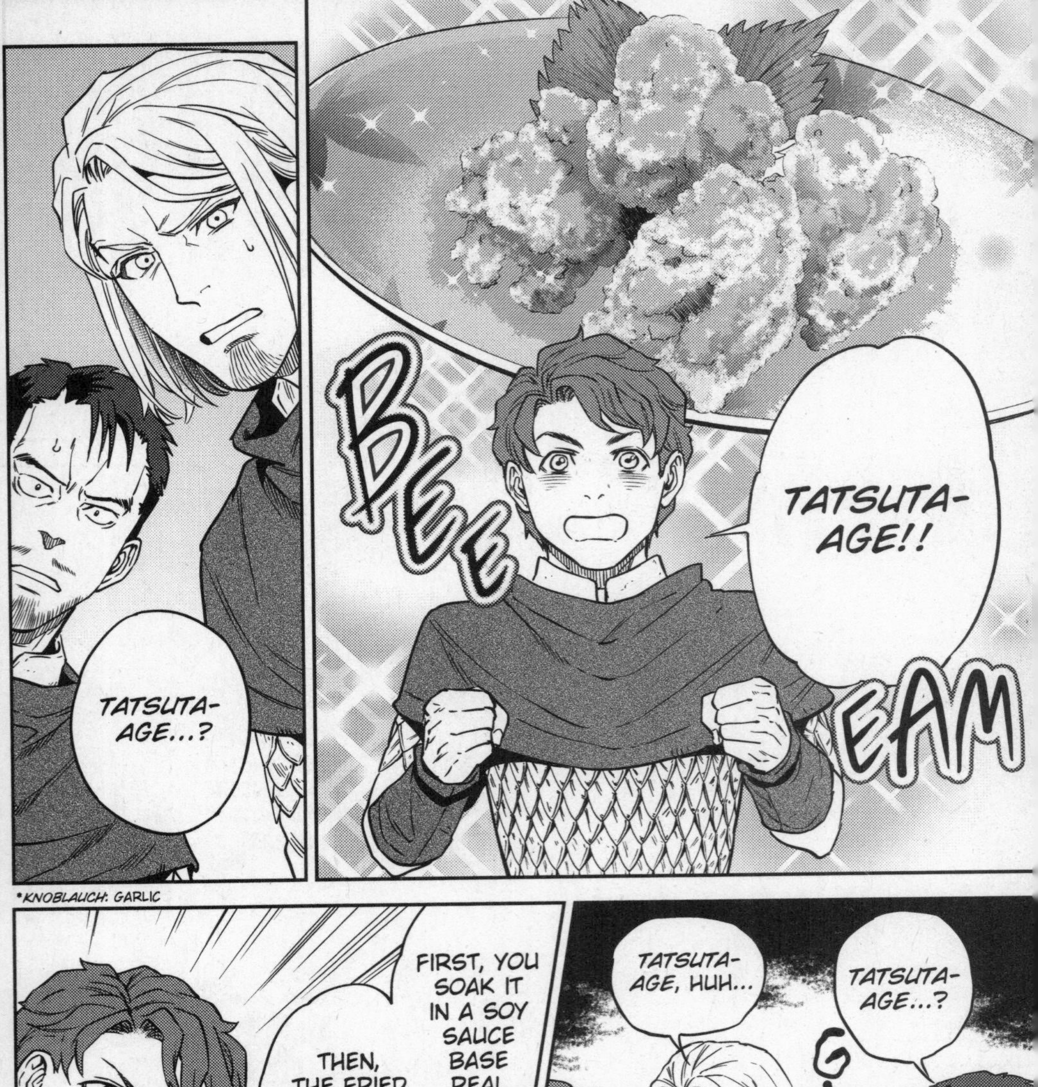
BEE
TATSUTA-AGE!!
EAM
TATSUTA-AGE...?

*KNOBLAUCH: GARLIC

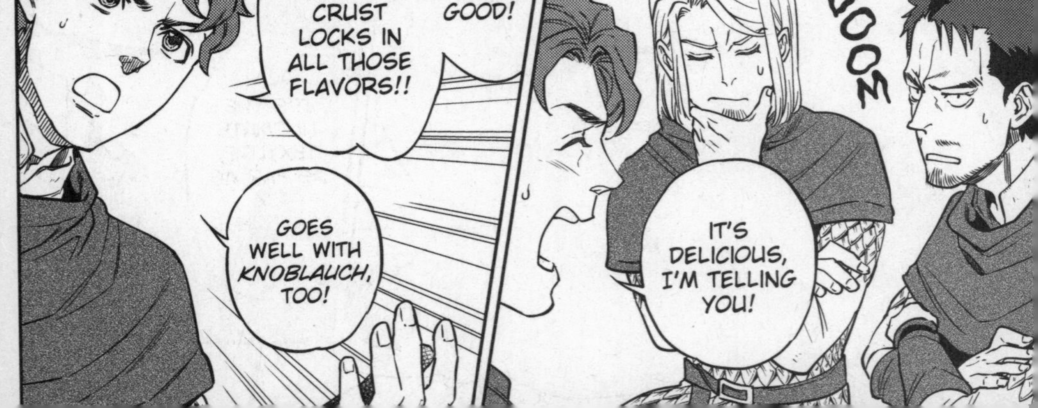
TATSUTA-AGE...?
TATSUTA-AGE, HUH...
GLOOM
IT'S DELICIOUS, I'M TELLING YOU!
FIRST, YOU SOAK IT IN A SOY SAUCE BASE REAL GOOD!
THEN, THE FRIED CRUST LOCKS IN ALL THOSE FLAVORS!!
GOES WELL WITH KNOBLAUCH, TOO!

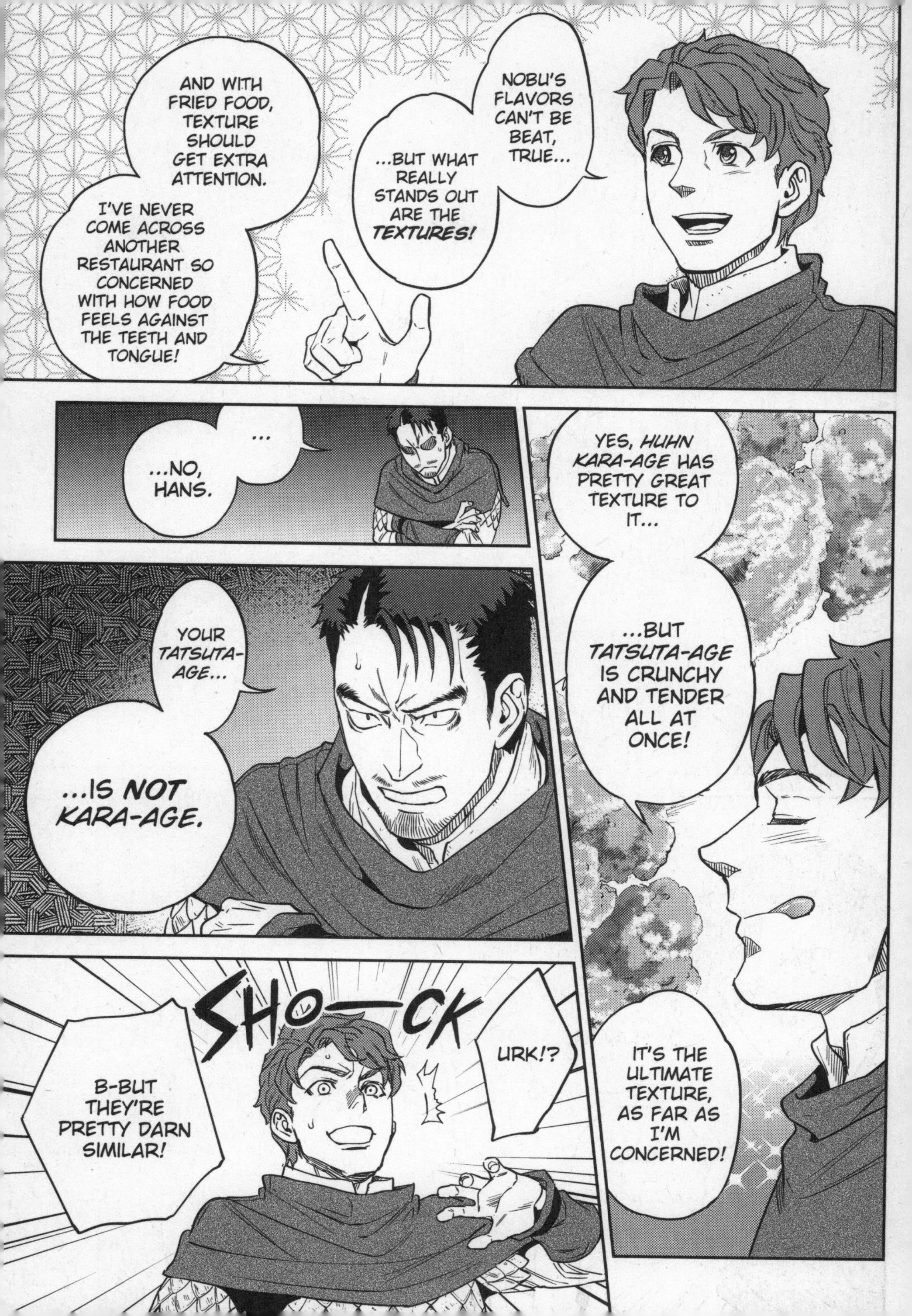
NOBU'S FLAVORS CAN'T BE BEAT, TRUE...
...BUT WHAT REALLY STANDS OUT ARE THE *TEXTURES!*
AND WITH FRIED FOOD, TEXTURE SHOULD GET EXTRA ATTENTION.
I'VE NEVER COME ACROSS ANOTHER RESTAURANT SO CONCERNED WITH HOW FOOD FEELS AGAINST THE TEETH AND TONGUE!
YES, *HUHN KARA-AGE* HAS PRETTY GREAT TEXTURE TO IT...
...BUT *TATSUTA-AGE* IS CRUNCHY AND TENDER ALL AT ONCE!
IT'S THE ULTIMATE TEXTURE, AS FAR AS I'M CONCERNED!
...
...NO, HANS.
YOUR *TATSUTA-AGE...*
...IS ***NOT KARA-AGE.***
SHO—CK
URK!?
B-BUT THEY'RE PRETTY DARN SIMILAR!

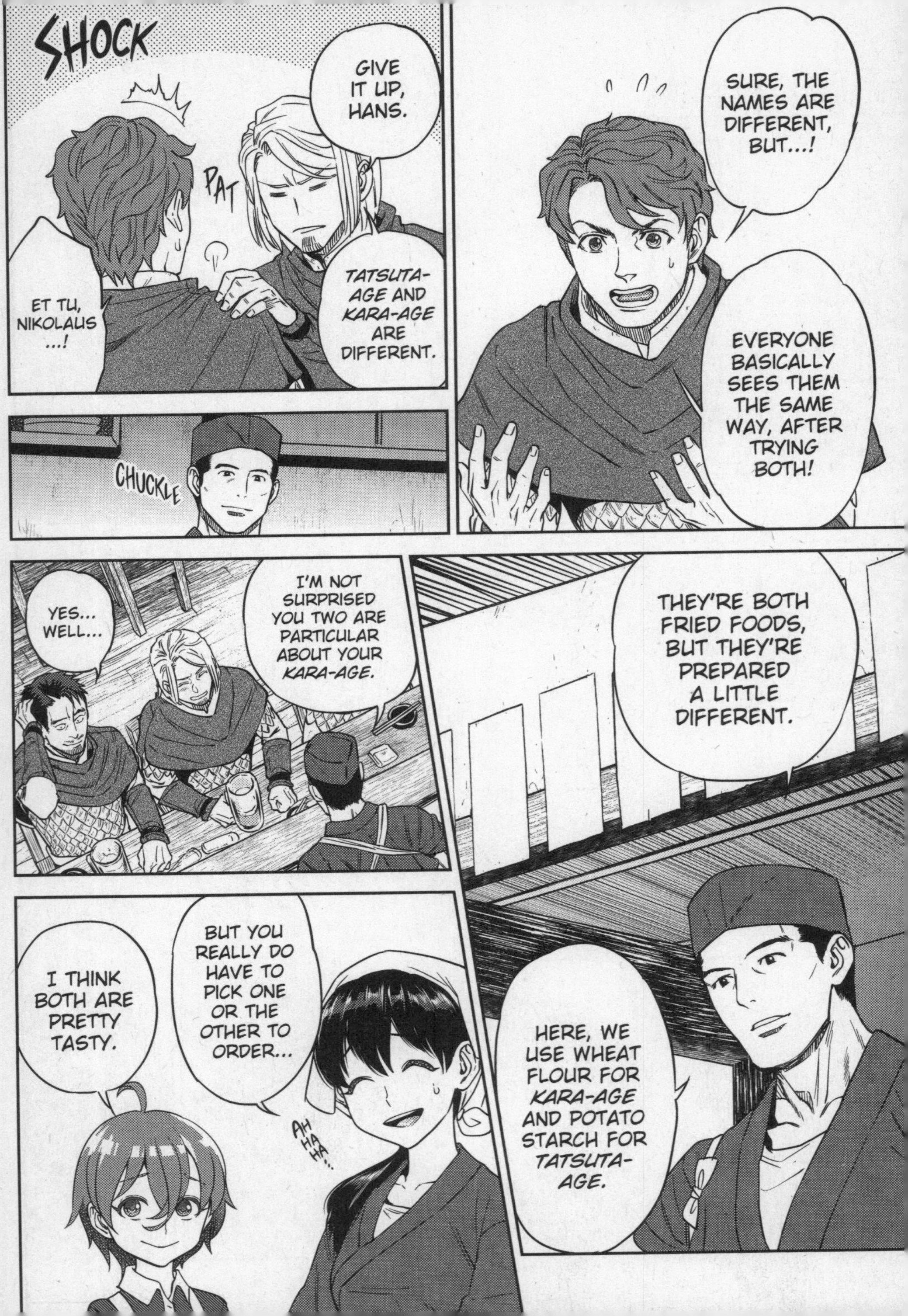
SURE, THE NAMES ARE DIFFERENT, BUT...!
EVERYONE BASICALLY SEES THEM THE SAME WAY, AFTER TRYING BOTH!
SHOCK
GIVE IT UP, HANS.
PAT
TATSUTA-AGE AND KARA-AGE ARE DIFFERENT.
ET TU, NIKOLAUS ...!
CHUCKLE
THEY'RE BOTH FRIED FOODS, BUT THEY'RE PREPARED A LITTLE DIFFERENT.
I'M NOT SURPRISED YOU TWO ARE PARTICULAR ABOUT YOUR KARA-AGE.
YES... WELL...
HERE, WE USE WHEAT FLOUR FOR KARA-AGE AND POTATO STARCH FOR TATSUTA-AGE.
BUT YOU REALLY DO HAVE TO PICK ONE OR THE OTHER TO ORDER...
AH HA HA...
I THINK BOTH ARE PRETTY TASTY.

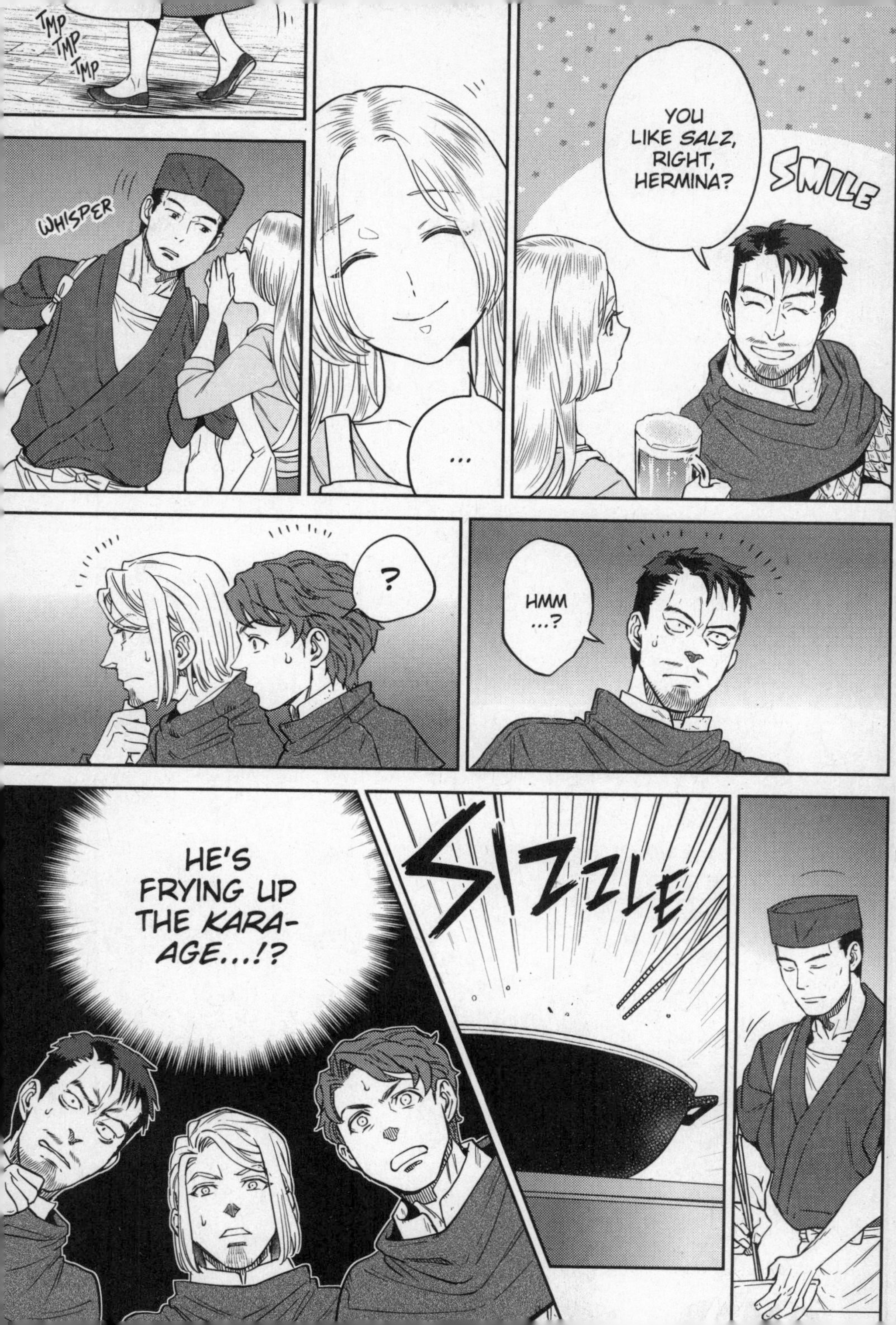
YOU LIKE SALZ, RIGHT, HERMINA?
SMILE
...
TMP TMP TMP
WHISPER
HMM ...?
?
SIZZLE
HE'S FRYING UP THE KARA-AGE...!?

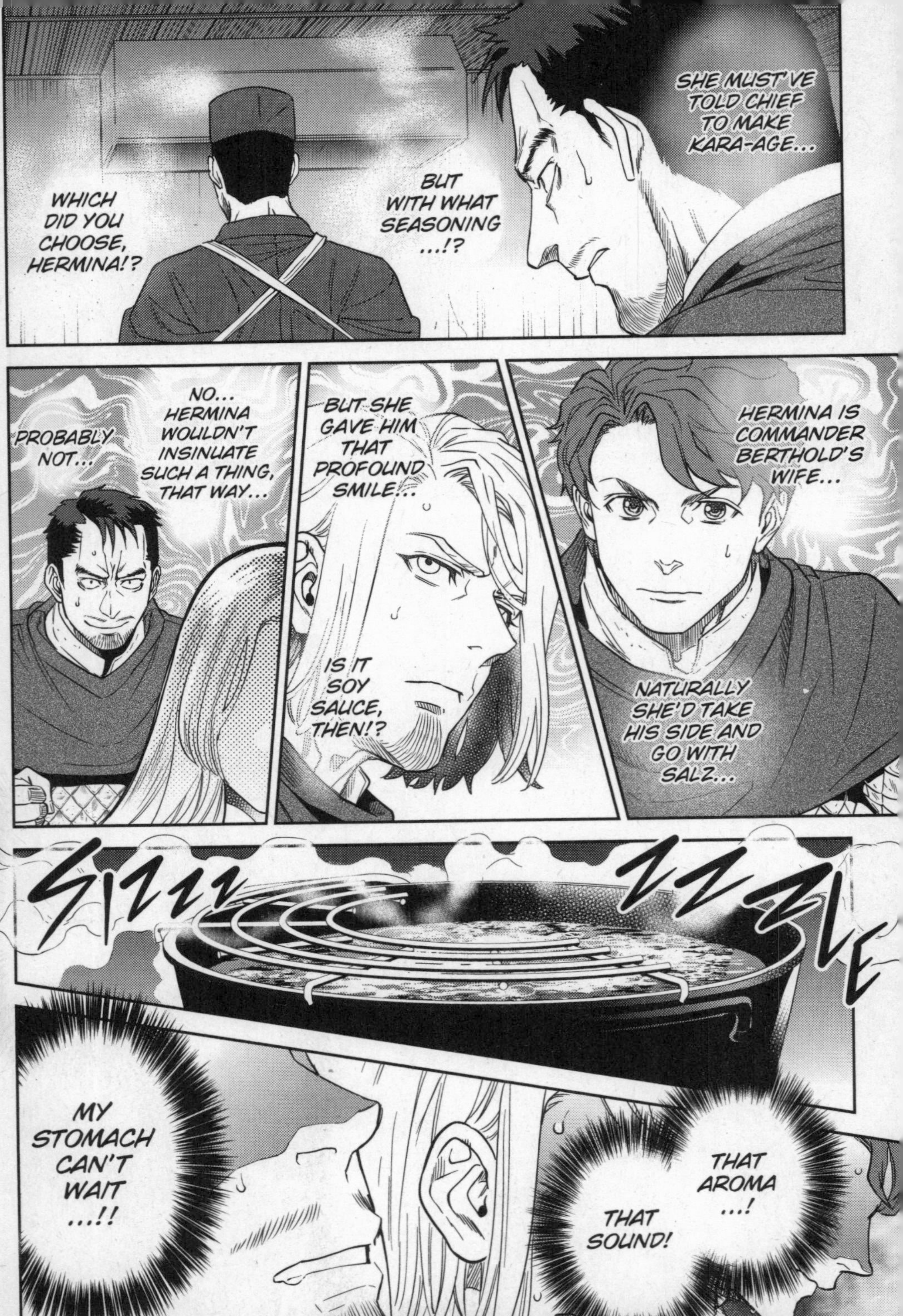
SHE MUST'VE TOLD CHIEF TO MAKE KARA-AGE...
BUT WITH WHAT SEASONING ...!?
WHICH DID YOU CHOOSE, HERMINA!?
HERMINA IS COMMANDER BERTHOLD'S WIFE...
NATURALLY SHE'D TAKE HIS SIDE AND GO WITH SALZ...
BUT SHE GAVE HIM THAT PROFOUND SMILE...
IS IT SOY SAUCE, THEN!?
NO... HERMINA WOULDN'T INSINUATE SUCH A THING, THAT WAY...
PROBABLY NOT...
SIZZZZ
ZZZZLE
THAT AROMA ...!
THAT SOUND!
MY STOMACH CAN'T WAIT ...!!

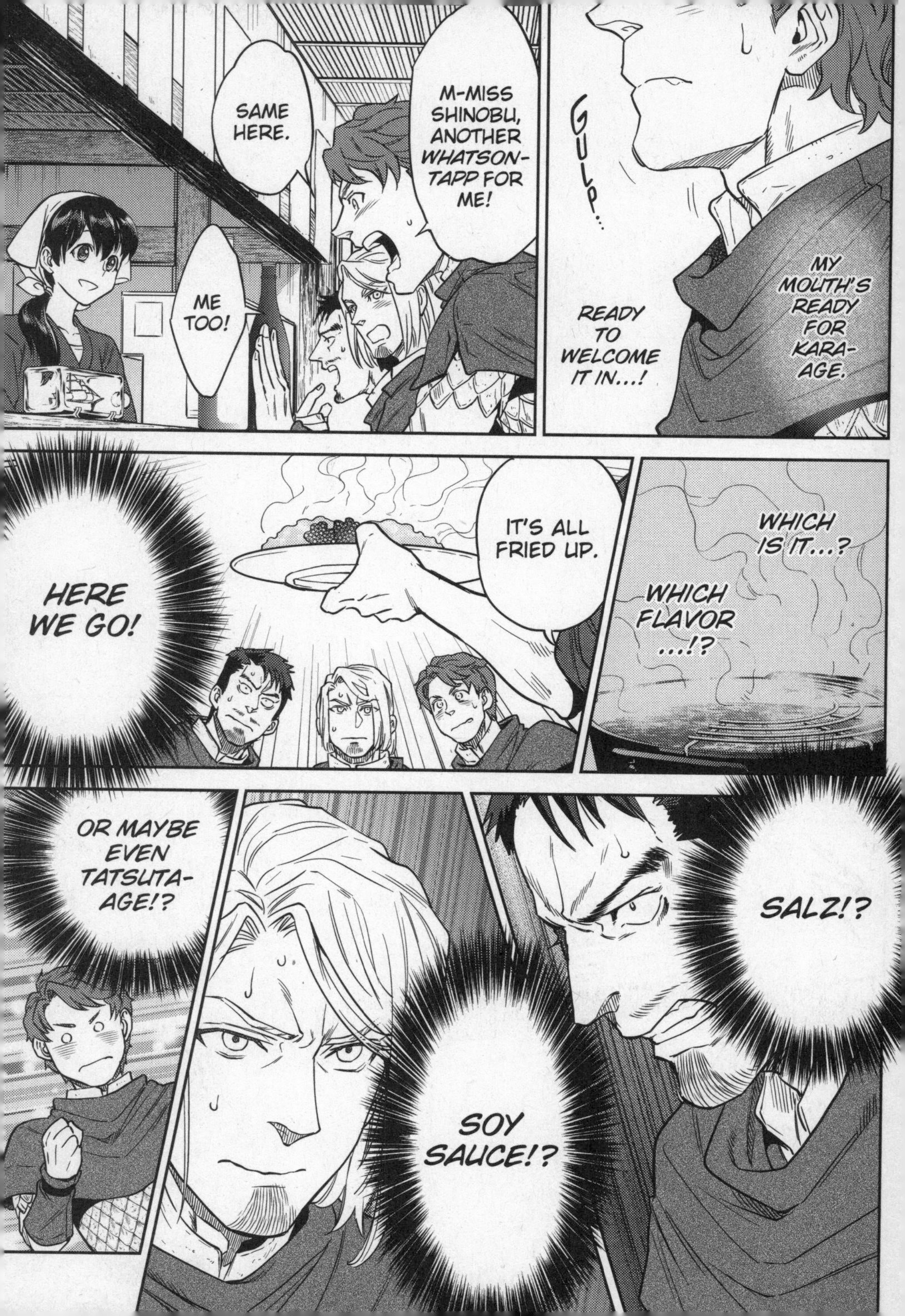
GULP...
MY MOUTH'S READY FOR KARA-AGE.
READY TO WELCOME IT IN...!
M-MISS SHINOBU, ANOTHER WHATSON-TAPP FOR ME!
SAME HERE.
ME TOO!
WHICH IS IT...?
WHICH FLAVOR ...!?
IT'S ALL FRIED UP.
HERE WE GO!
SALZ!?
SOY SAUCE!?
OR MAYBE EVEN TATSUTA-AGE!?

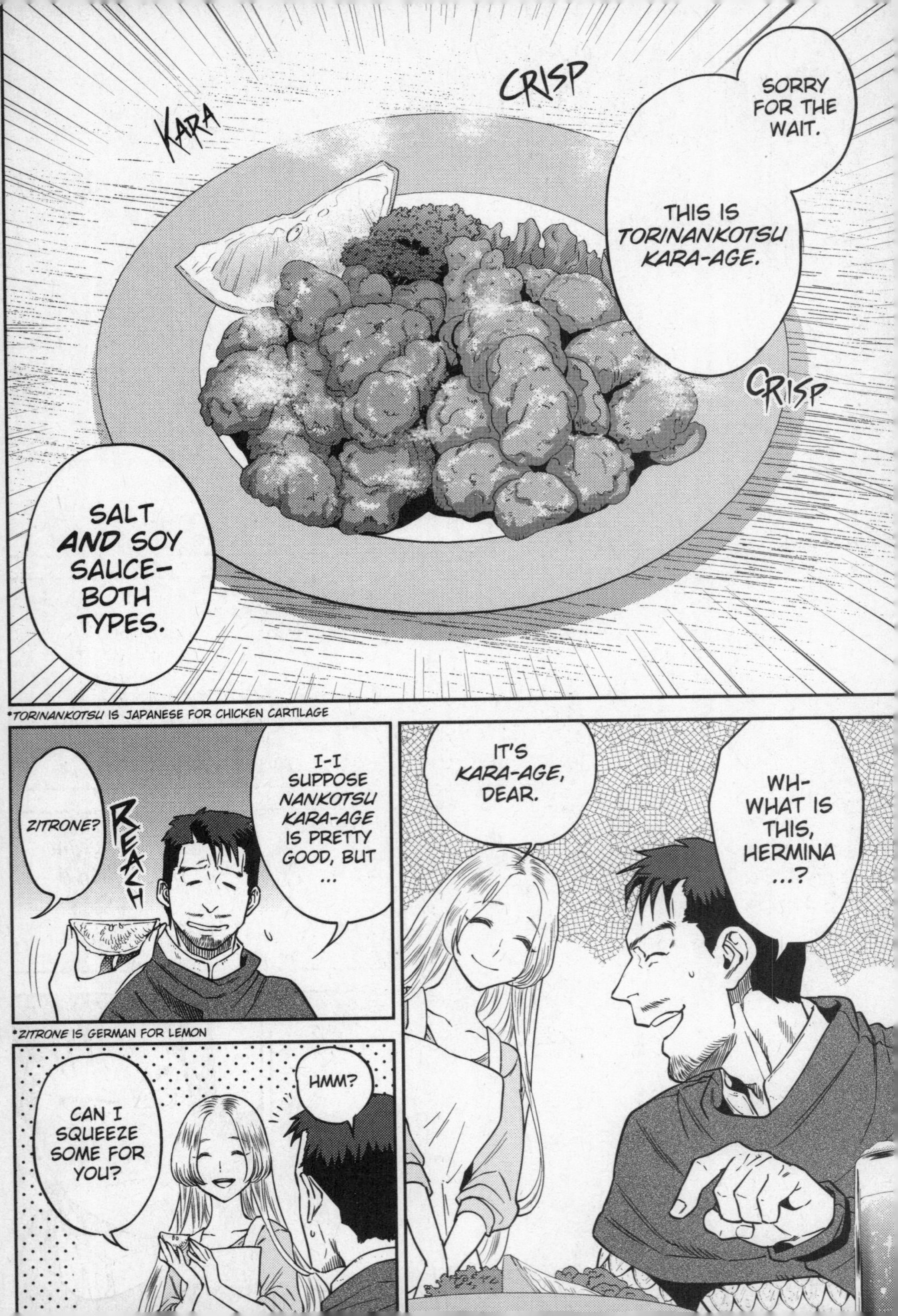
CRISP
SORRY FOR THE WAIT.
KARA
THIS IS *TORINANKOTSU KARA-AGE*.
CRISP
SALT ***AND*** SOY SAUCE-BOTH TYPES.
WH-WHAT IS THIS, HERMINA ...?
IT'S *KARA-AGE*, DEAR.
I-I SUPPOSE *NANKOTSU KARA-AGE* IS PRETTY GOOD, BUT ...
REACH
ZITRONE?
HMM?
CAN I SQUEEZE SOME FOR YOU?

**TORINANKOTSU* IS JAPANESE FOR CHICKEN CARTILAGE

**ZITRONE* IS GERMAN FOR LEMON

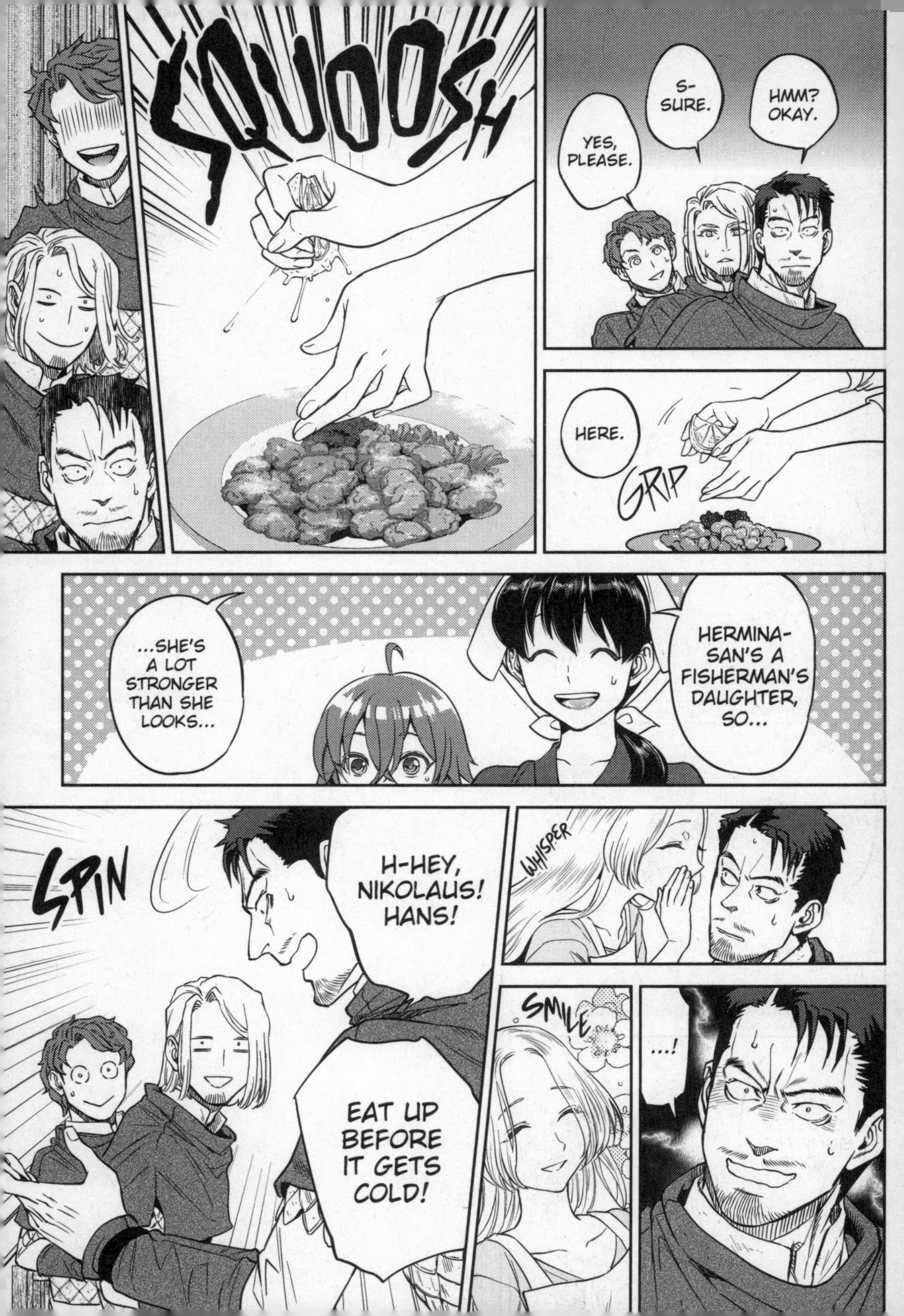
HMM? OKAY.
S-SURE.
YES, PLEASE.
HERE.
GRIP
SQUOOSH
HERMINA-SAN'S A FISHERMAN'S DAUGHTER, SO...
...SHE'S A LOT STRONGER THAN SHE LOOKS...
WHISPER
...!
SMILE
H-HEY, NIKOLAUS! HANS!
SPIN
EAT UP BEFORE IT GETS COLD!

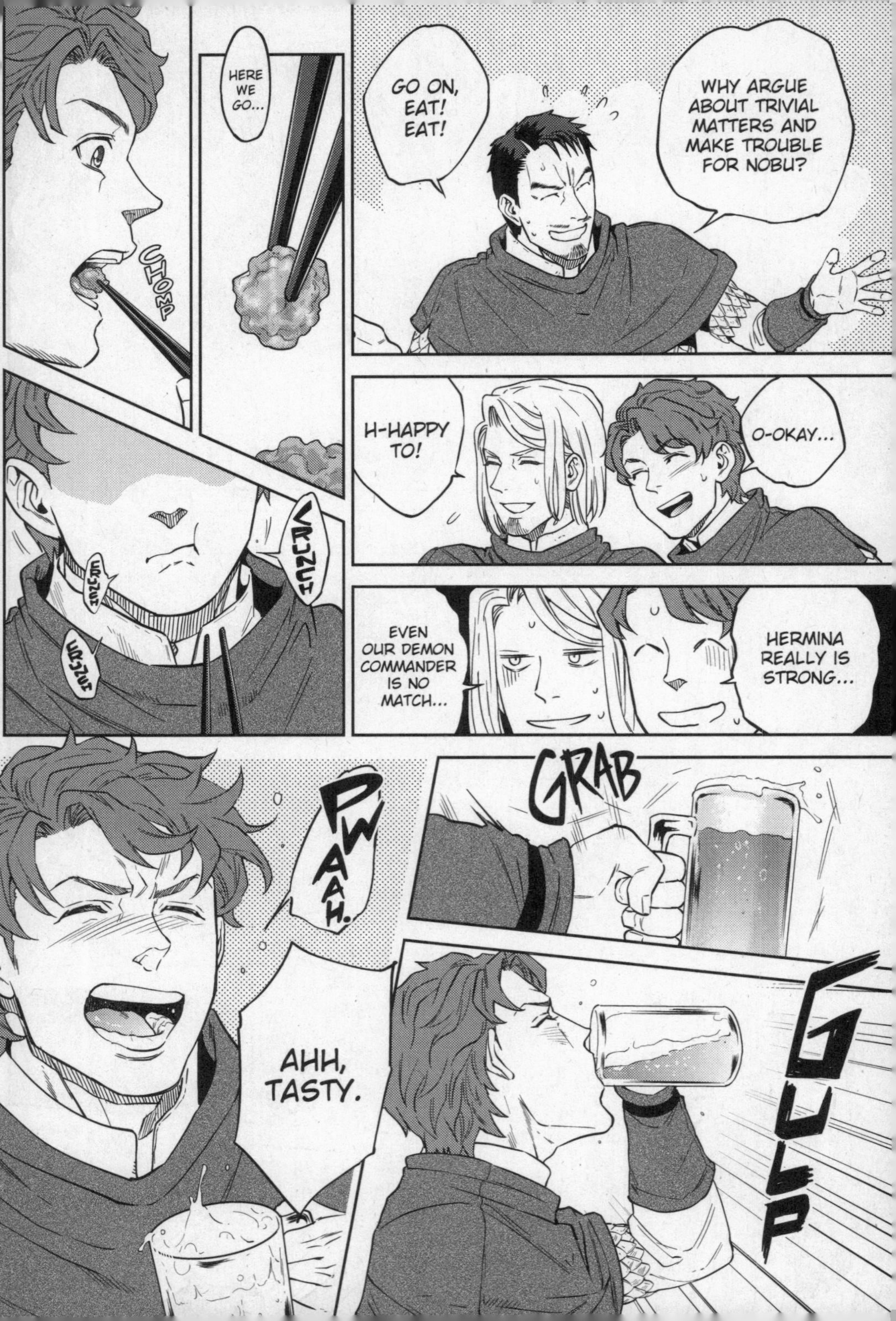
WHY ARGUE ABOUT TRIVIAL MATTERS AND MAKE TROUBLE FOR NOBU?
GO ON, EAT! EAT!
HERE WE GO...
CHOMP
O-OKAY...
H-HAPPY TO!
HERMINA REALLY IS STRONG...
EVEN OUR DEMON COMMANDER IS NO MATCH...
CRUNCH
CRUNCH
CRUNCH
GRAB
GULP
PWAAAH.
AHH, TASTY.

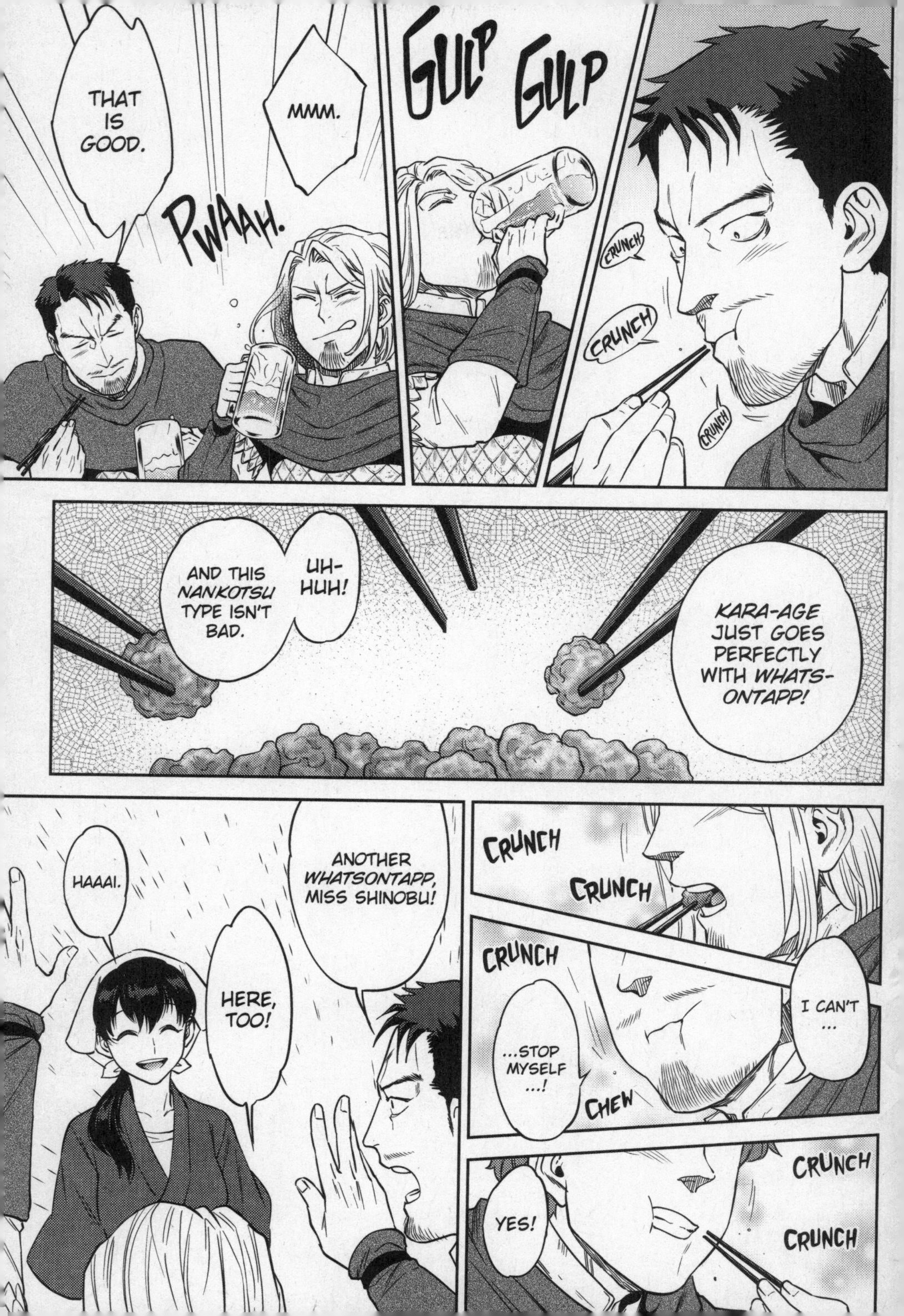
CRUNCH
CRUNCH
CRUNCH
GULP GULP
MMM.
THAT IS GOOD.
PWAAH.
KARA-AGE JUST GOES PERFECTLY WITH WHATSONTAPP!
UH-HUH!
AND THIS NANKOTSU TYPE ISN'T BAD.
CRUNCH
CRUNCH
I CAN'T ...
CRUNCH
...STOP MYSELF ...!
CHEW
CRUNCH
CRUNCH
YES!
ANOTHER WHATSONTAPP, MISS SHINOBU!
HERE, TOO!
HAAAI.

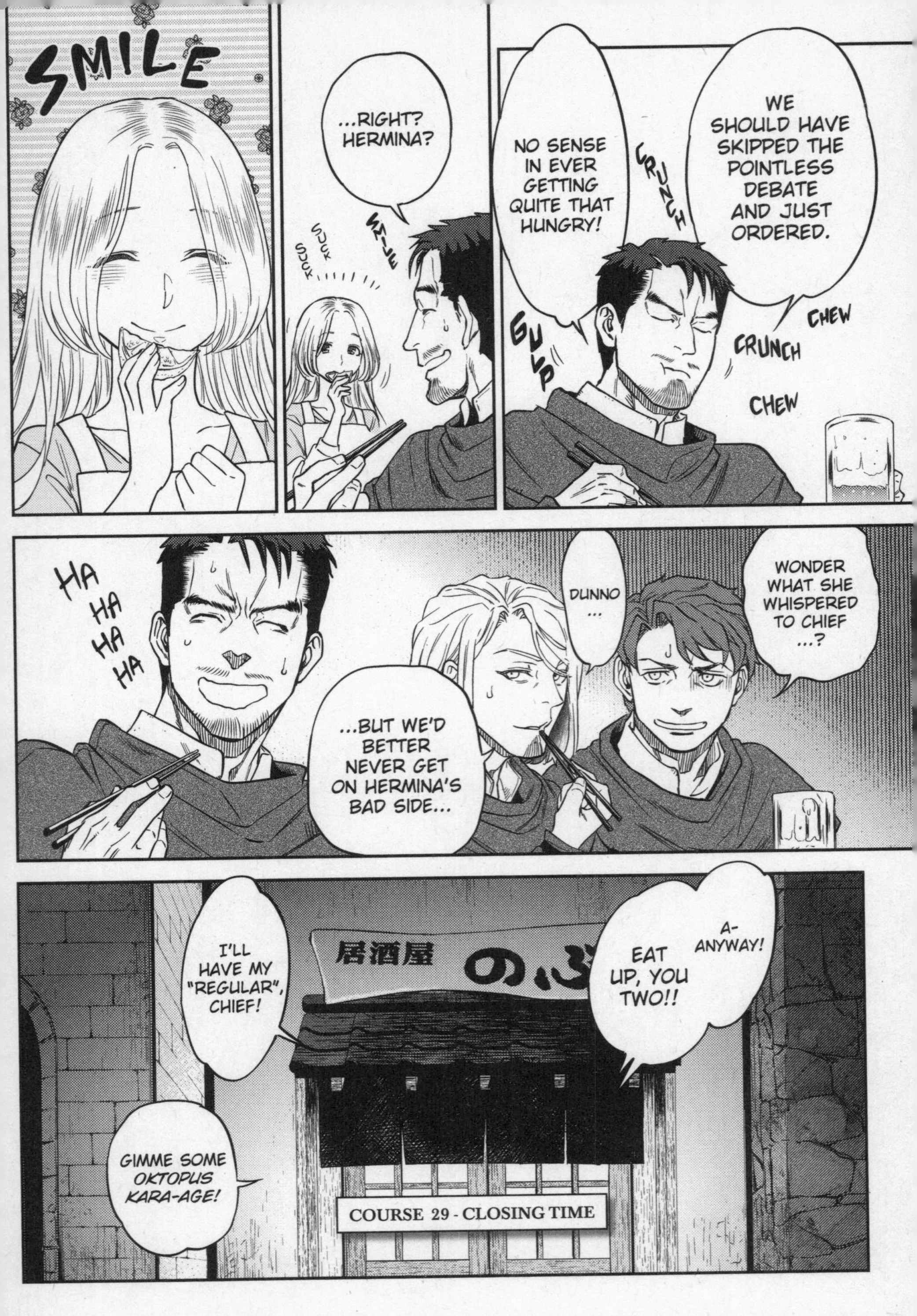
WE SHOULD HAVE SKIPPED THE POINTLESS DEBATE AND JUST ORDERED.
CRUNCH
NO SENSE IN EVER GETTING QUITE THAT HUNGRY!
GULP
CHEW
CRUNCH
CHEW
...RIGHT? HERMINA?
SUCK SUCK
SMILE
WONDER WHAT SHE WHISPERED TO CHIEF ...?
DUNNO ...
...BUT WE'D BETTER NEVER GET ON HERMINA'S BAD SIDE...
HA HA HA HA
A- ANYWAY!
EAT UP, YOU TWO!!
居酒屋 のぶ
I'LL HAVE MY "REGULAR", CHIEF!
GIMME SOME OKTOPUS KARA-AGE!
COURSE 29 - CLOSING TIME

Torinankotsu Kara-age

OTHERWORLDLY IZAKAYA

NOBU

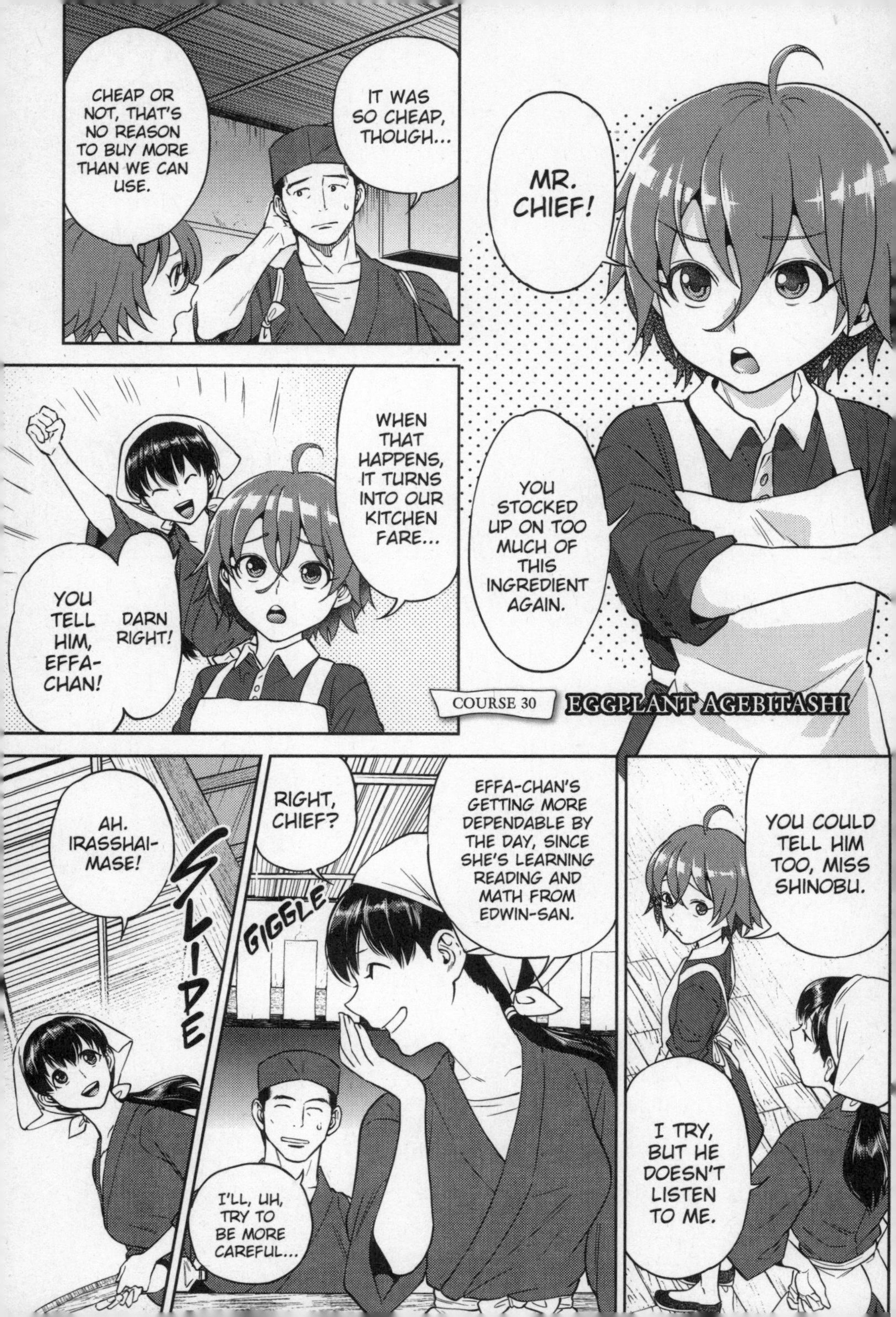
MR. CHIEF!
YOU STOCKED UP ON TOO MUCH OF THIS INGREDIENT AGAIN.
IT WAS SO CHEAP, THOUGH...
CHEAP OR NOT, THAT'S NO REASON TO BUY MORE THAN WE CAN USE.
WHEN THAT HAPPENS, IT TURNS INTO OUR KITCHEN FARE...
DARN RIGHT!
YOU TELL HIM, EFFA-CHAN!
COURSE 30
EGGPLANT AGEBITASHI
YOU COULD TELL HIM TOO, MISS SHINOBU.
I TRY, BUT HE DOESN'T LISTEN TO ME.
EFFA-CHAN'S GETTING MORE DEPENDABLE BY THE DAY, SINCE SHE'S LEARNING READING AND MATH FROM EDWIN-SAN.
RIGHT, CHIEF?
GIGGLE
I'LL, UH, TRY TO BE MORE CAREFUL...
SLIDE
AH. IRASSHAIMASE!

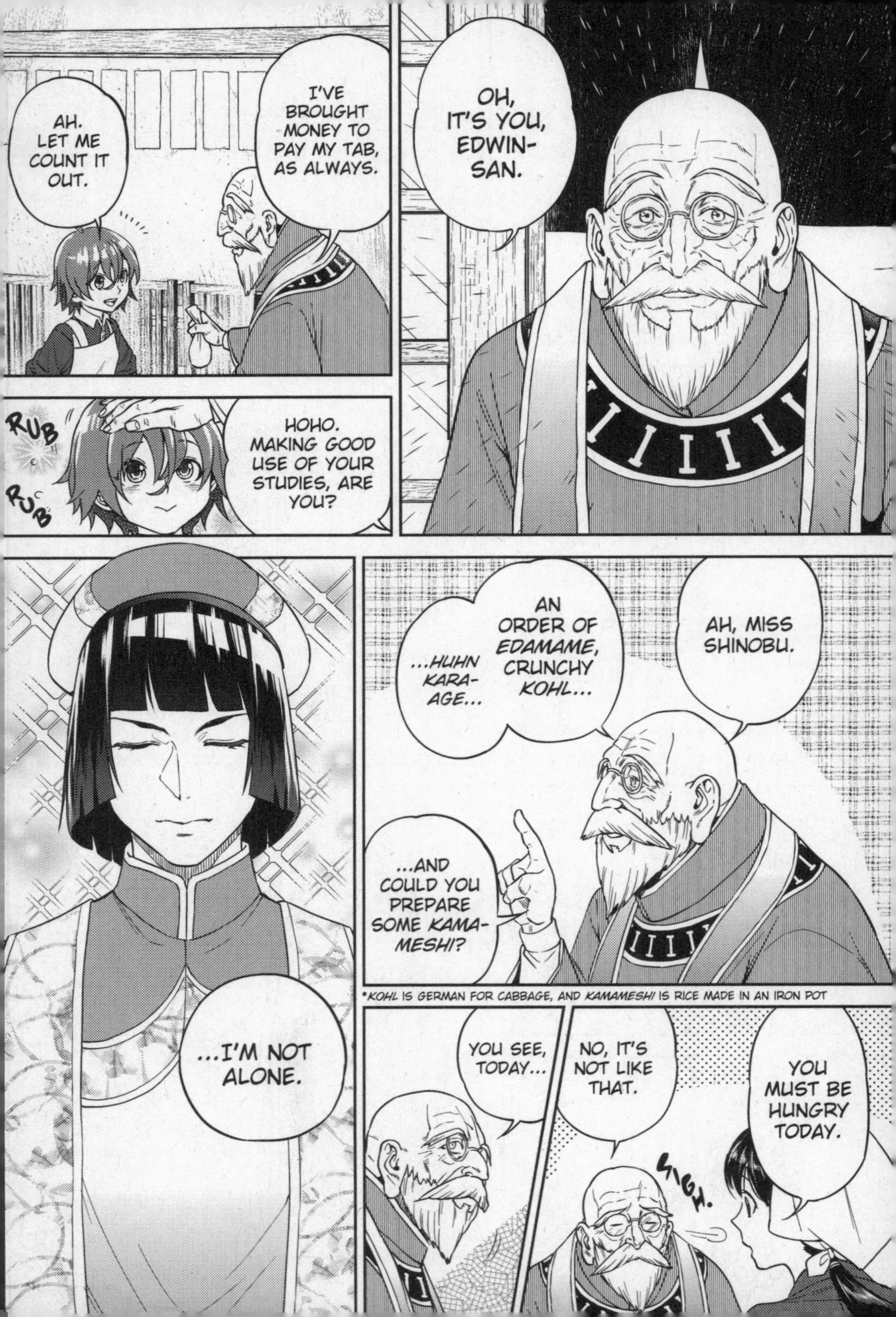
OH, IT'S YOU, EDWIN-SAN.
I'VE BROUGHT MONEY TO PAY MY TAB, AS ALWAYS.
AH. LET ME COUNT IT OUT.
HOHO. MAKING GOOD USE OF YOUR STUDIES, ARE YOU?
RUB
RUB
AH, MISS SHINOBU.
AN ORDER OF *EDAMAME*, CRUNCHY *KOHL*...
...*HUHN KARA-AGE*...
...AND COULD YOU PREPARE SOME *KAMA-MESHI*?
YOU MUST BE HUNGRY TODAY.
SIGH.
NO, IT'S NOT LIKE THAT.
YOU SEE, TODAY...
...I'M NOT ALONE.
**KOHL* IS GERMAN FOR CABBAGE, AND *KAMAMESHI* IS RICE MADE IN AN IRON POT

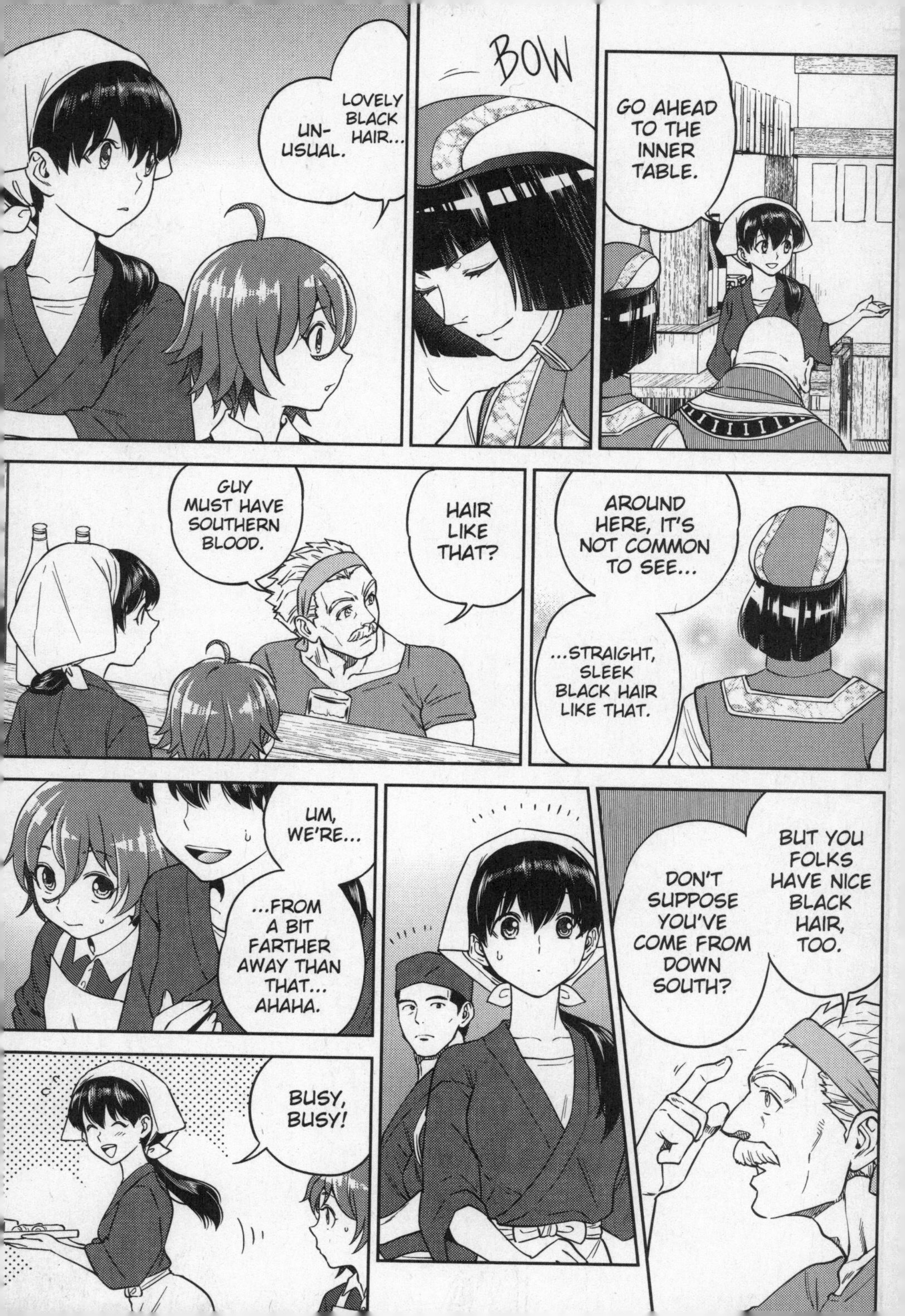

GO AHEAD TO THE INNER TABLE.
BOW
LOVELY BLACK HAIR...
UN-USUAL.
AROUND HERE, IT'S NOT COMMON TO SEE...
...STRAIGHT, SLEEK BLACK HAIR LIKE THAT.
HAIR LIKE THAT?
GUY MUST HAVE SOUTHERN BLOOD.
BUT YOU FOLKS HAVE NICE BLACK HAIR, TOO.
DON'T SUPPOSE YOU'VE COME FROM DOWN SOUTH?
UM, WE'RE...
...FROM A BIT FARTHER AWAY THAN THAT... AHAHA.
BUSY, BUSY!

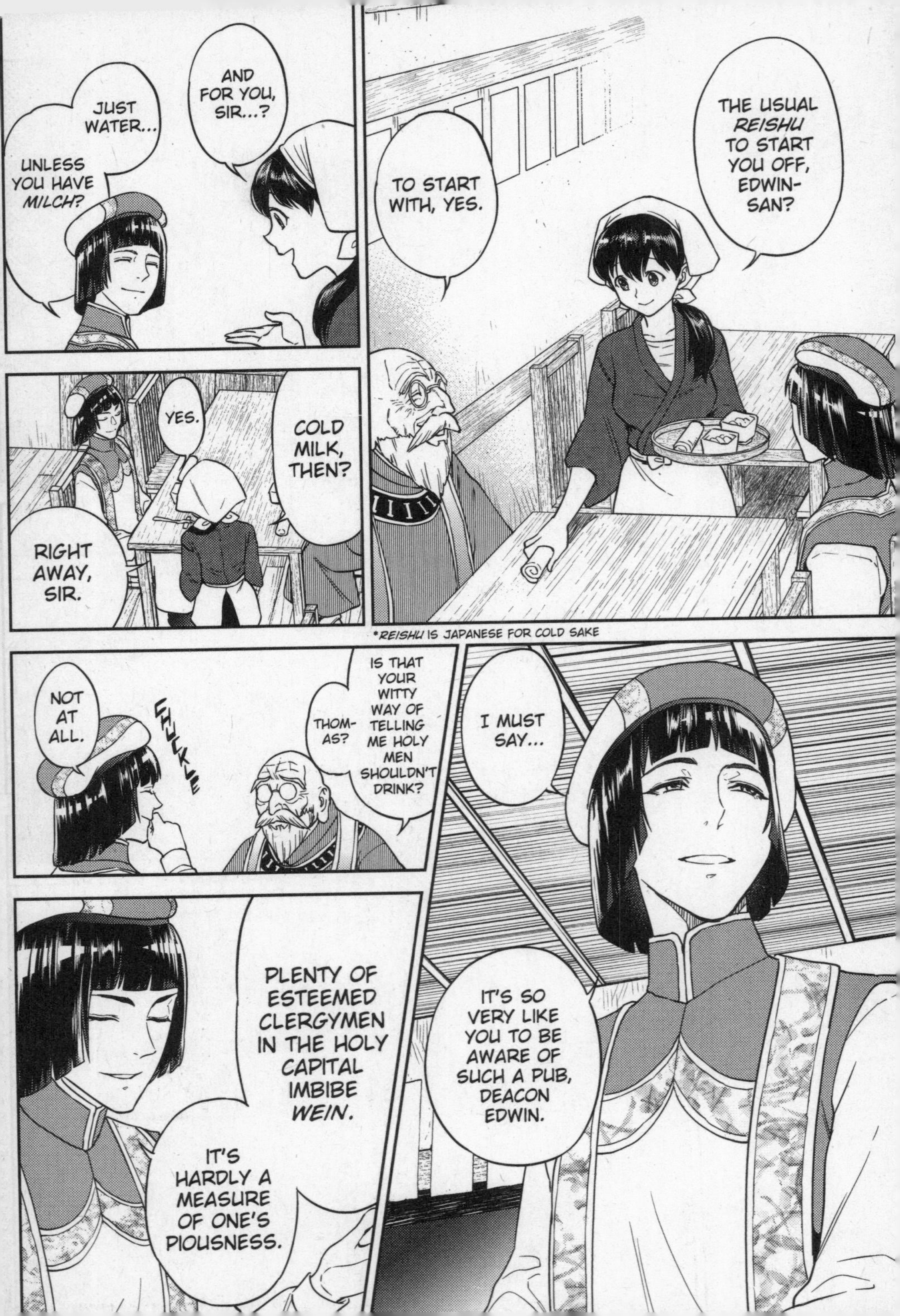
THE USUAL *REISHU* TO START YOU OFF, EDWIN-SAN?
TO START WITH, YES.
AND FOR YOU, SIR...?
JUST WATER...
UNLESS YOU HAVE *MILCH*?
COLD MILK, THEN?
YES.
RIGHT AWAY, SIR.
I MUST SAY...
IT'S SO VERY LIKE YOU TO BE AWARE OF SUCH A PUB, DEACON EDWIN.
IS THAT YOUR WITTY WAY OF TELLING ME HOLY MEN SHOULDN'T DRINK?
THOM-AS?
NOT AT ALL.
CHUCKLE
PLENTY OF ESTEEMED CLERGYMEN IN THE HOLY CAPITAL IMBIBE *WEIN*.
IT'S HARDLY A MEASURE OF ONE'S PIOUSNESS.

**REISHU* IS JAPANESE FOR COLD SAKE

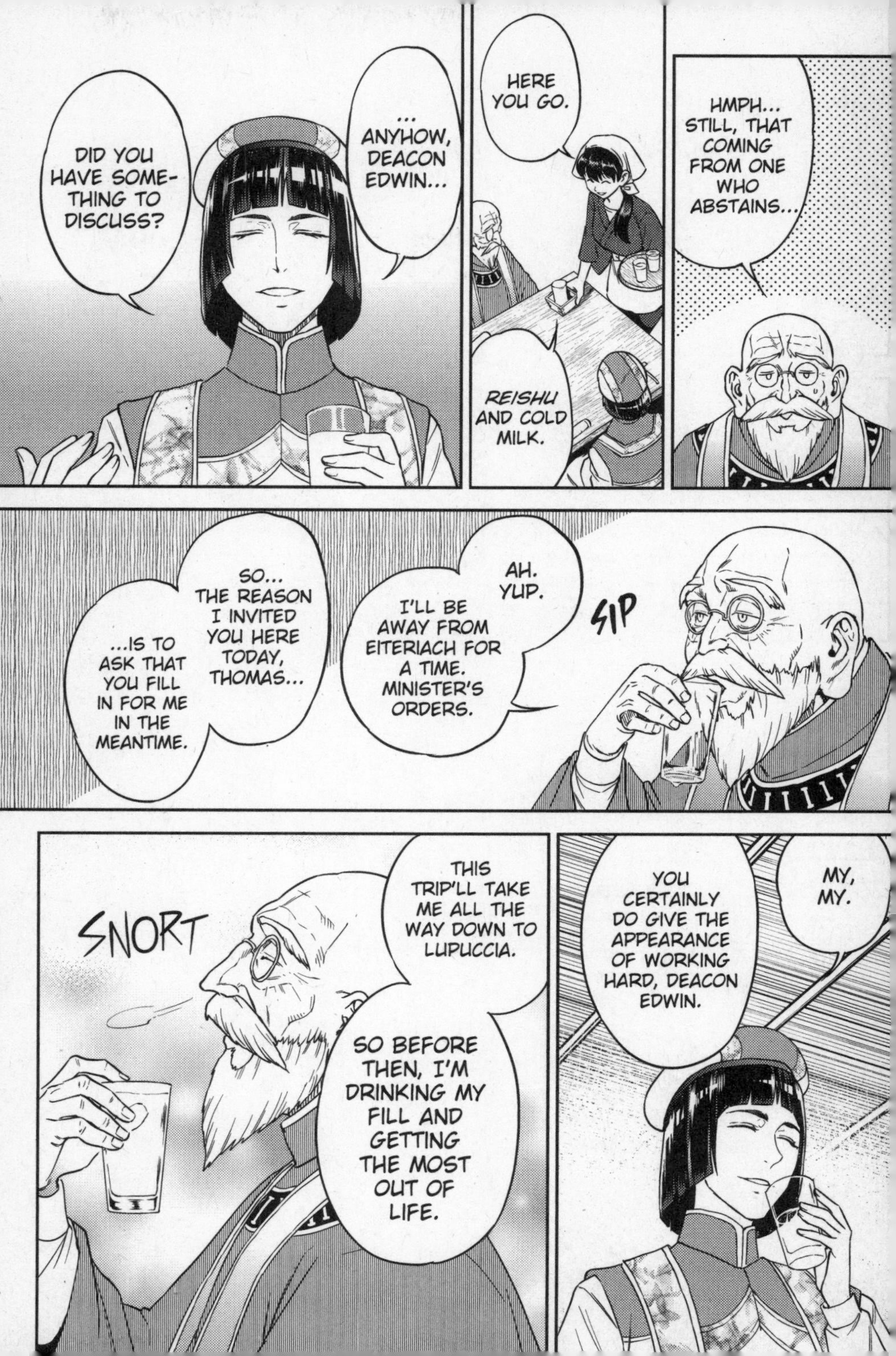
HMPH... STILL, THAT COMING FROM ONE WHO ABSTAINS...
HERE YOU GO.
REISHU AND COLD MILK.
... ANYHOW, DEACON EDWIN...
DID YOU HAVE SOME-THING TO DISCUSS?
SIP
AH. YUP.
I'LL BE AWAY FROM EITERIACH FOR A TIME. MINISTER'S ORDERS.
SO... THE REASON I INVITED YOU HERE TODAY, THOMAS...
...IS TO ASK THAT YOU FILL IN FOR ME IN THE MEANTIME.
MY, MY.
YOU CERTAINLY DO GIVE THE APPEARANCE OF WORKING HARD, DEACON EDWIN.
THIS TRIP'LL TAKE ME ALL THE WAY DOWN TO LUPUCCIA.
SO BEFORE THEN, I'M DRINKING MY FILL AND GETTING THE MOST OUT OF LIFE.
SNORT

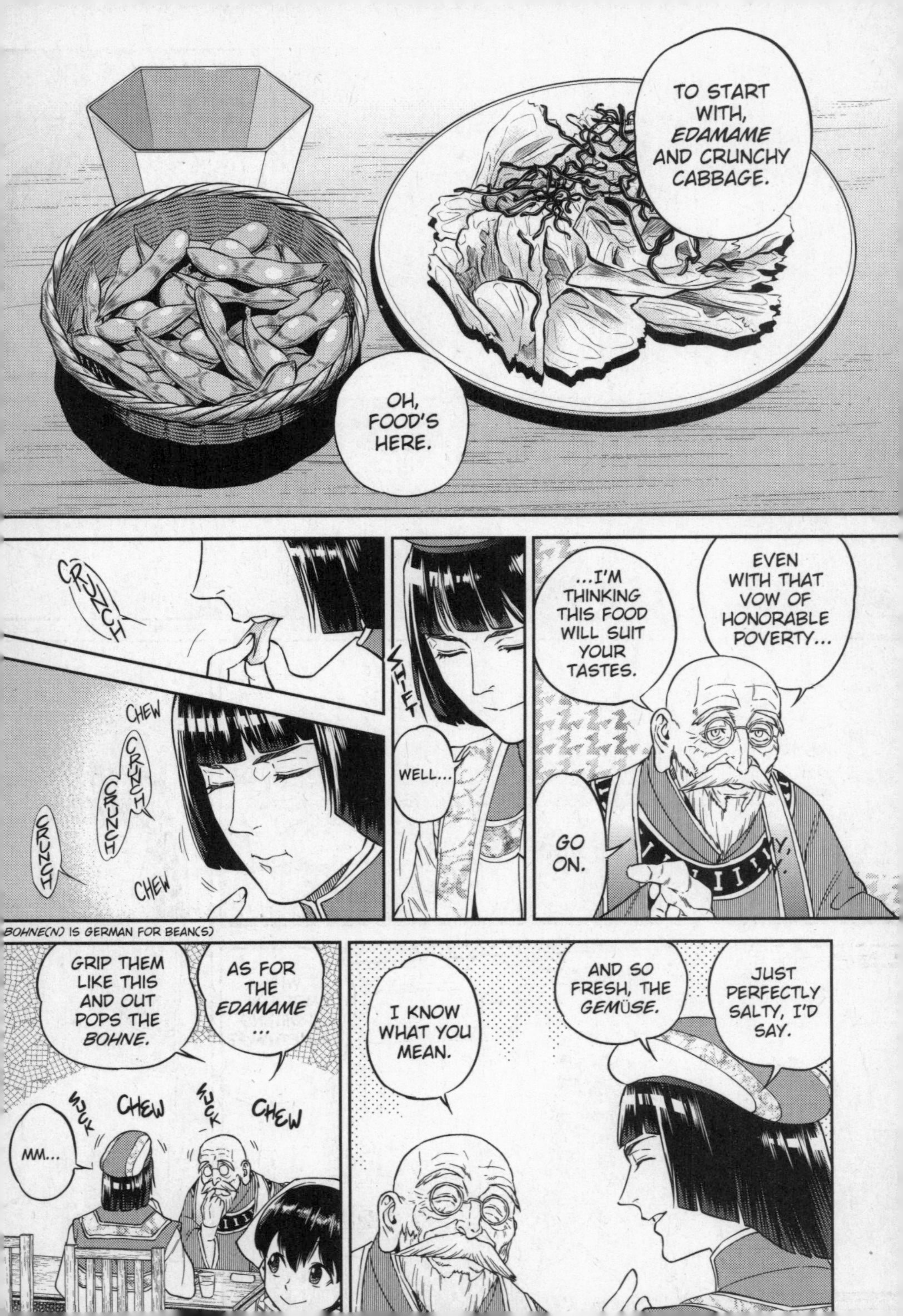
TO START WITH, *EDAMAME* AND CRUNCHY CABBAGE.
OH, FOOD'S HERE.
EVEN WITH THAT VOW OF HONORABLE POVERTY...
...I'M THINKING THIS FOOD WILL SUIT YOUR TASTES.
GO ON.
SHIFT
WELL...
CRUNCH
CHEW
CRUNCH
CRUNCH
CRUNCH
CHEW
JUST PERFECTLY SALTY, I'D SAY.
AND SO FRESH, THE *GEMÜSE*.
I KNOW WHAT YOU MEAN.
AS FOR THE *EDAMAME*...
GRIP THEM LIKE THIS AND OUT POPS THE *BOHNE*.
SHUCK
CHEW
SHUCK
CHEW
MM...

BOHNE(N) IS GERMAN FOR BEAN(S)

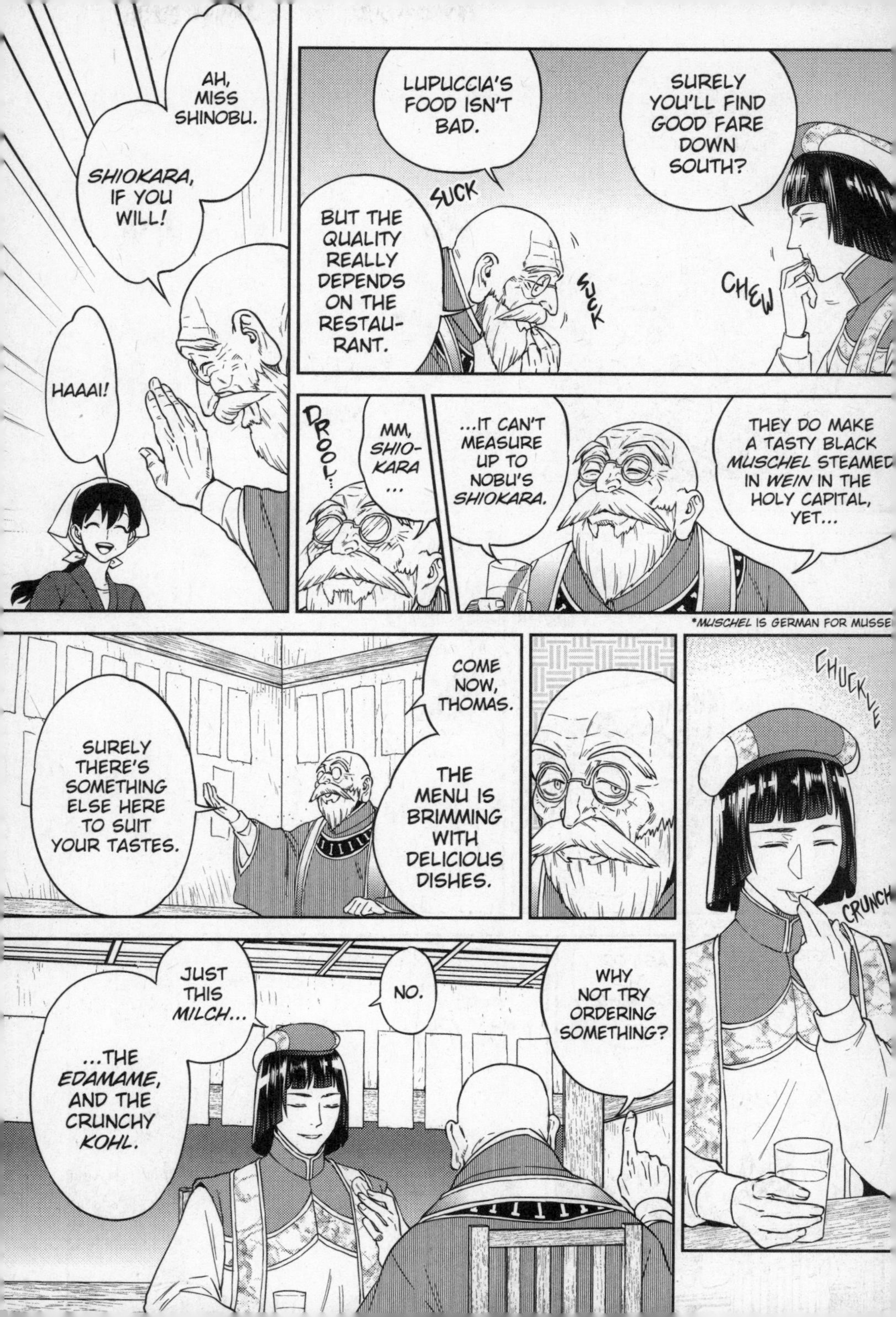
SURELY YOU'LL FIND GOOD FARE DOWN SOUTH?
CHEW
LUPUCCIA'S FOOD ISN'T BAD.
SUCK
BUT THE QUALITY REALLY DEPENDS ON THE RESTAU-RANT.
SUCK
THEY DO MAKE A TASTY BLACK *MUSCHEL* STEAMED IN *WEIN* IN THE HOLY CAPITAL, YET...
...IT CAN'T MEASURE UP TO NOBU'S *SHIOKARA.*
MM, SHIO-KARA...
DROOL...
AH, MISS SHINOBU.
SHIOKARA, IF YOU WILL!
HAAAI!
**MUSCHEL* IS GERMAN FOR MUSSE
CHUCKLE
CRUNCH
COME NOW, THOMAS.
THE MENU IS BRIMMING WITH DELICIOUS DISHES.
SURELY THERE'S SOMETHING ELSE HERE TO SUIT YOUR TASTES.
WHY NOT TRY ORDERING SOMETHING?
NO.
JUST THIS *MILCH*...
...THE *EDAMAME,* AND THE CRUNCHY *KOHL.*

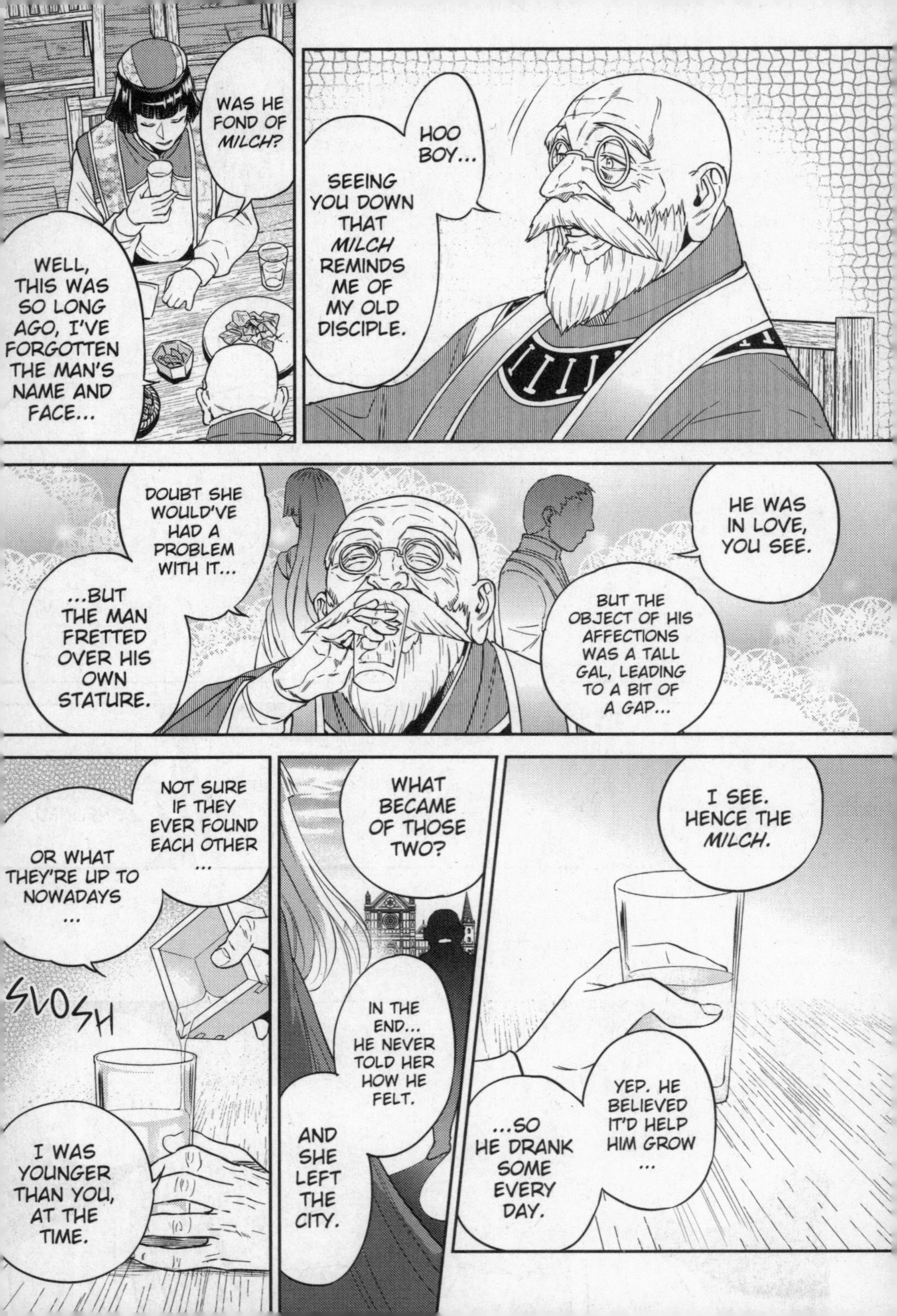
HOO BOY...
SEEING YOU DOWN THAT *MILCH* REMINDS ME OF MY OLD DISCIPLE.
WAS HE FOND OF *MILCH*?
WELL, THIS WAS SO LONG AGO, I'VE FORGOTTEN THE MAN'S NAME AND FACE...
HE WAS IN LOVE, YOU SEE.
BUT THE OBJECT OF HIS AFFECTIONS WAS A TALL GAL, LEADING TO A BIT OF A GAP...
DOUBT SHE WOULD'VE HAD A PROBLEM WITH IT...
...BUT THE MAN FRETTED OVER HIS OWN STATURE.
I SEE. HENCE THE *MILCH*.
YEP. HE BELIEVED IT'D HELP HIM GROW...
...SO HE DRANK SOME EVERY DAY.
WHAT BECAME OF THOSE TWO?
IN THE END... HE NEVER TOLD HER HOW HE FELT.
AND SHE LEFT THE CITY.
NOT SURE IF THEY EVER FOUND EACH OTHER...
OR WHAT THEY'RE UP TO NOWADAYS...
SLOSH
I WAS YOUNGER THAN YOU, AT THE TIME.

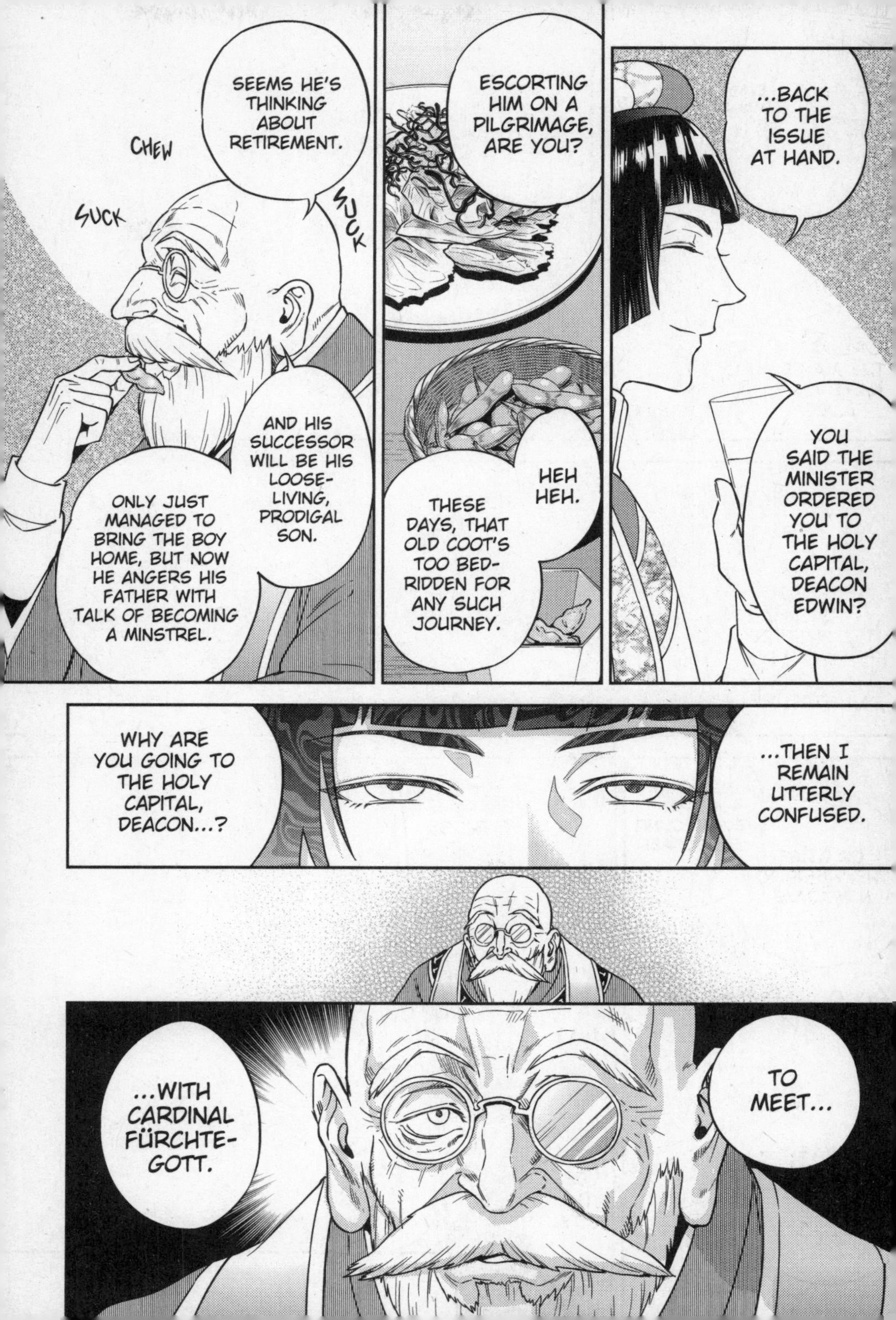
...BACK TO THE ISSUE AT HAND.
YOU SAID THE MINISTER ORDERED YOU TO THE HOLY CAPITAL, DEACON EDWIN?
ESCORTING HIM ON A PILGRIMAGE, ARE YOU?
HEH HEH.
THESE DAYS, THAT OLD COOT'S TOO BED-RIDDEN FOR ANY SUCH JOURNEY.
SUCK
SEEMS HE'S THINKING ABOUT RETIREMENT.
CHEW
SUCK
AND HIS SUCCESSOR WILL BE HIS LOOSE-LIVING, PRODIGAL SON.
ONLY JUST MANAGED TO BRING THE BOY HOME, BUT NOW HE ANGERS HIS FATHER WITH TALK OF BECOMING A MINSTREL.
...THEN I REMAIN UTTERLY CONFUSED.
WHY ARE YOU GOING TO THE HOLY CAPITAL, DEACON...?
TO MEET...
...WITH CARDINAL FÜRCHTE-GOTT.

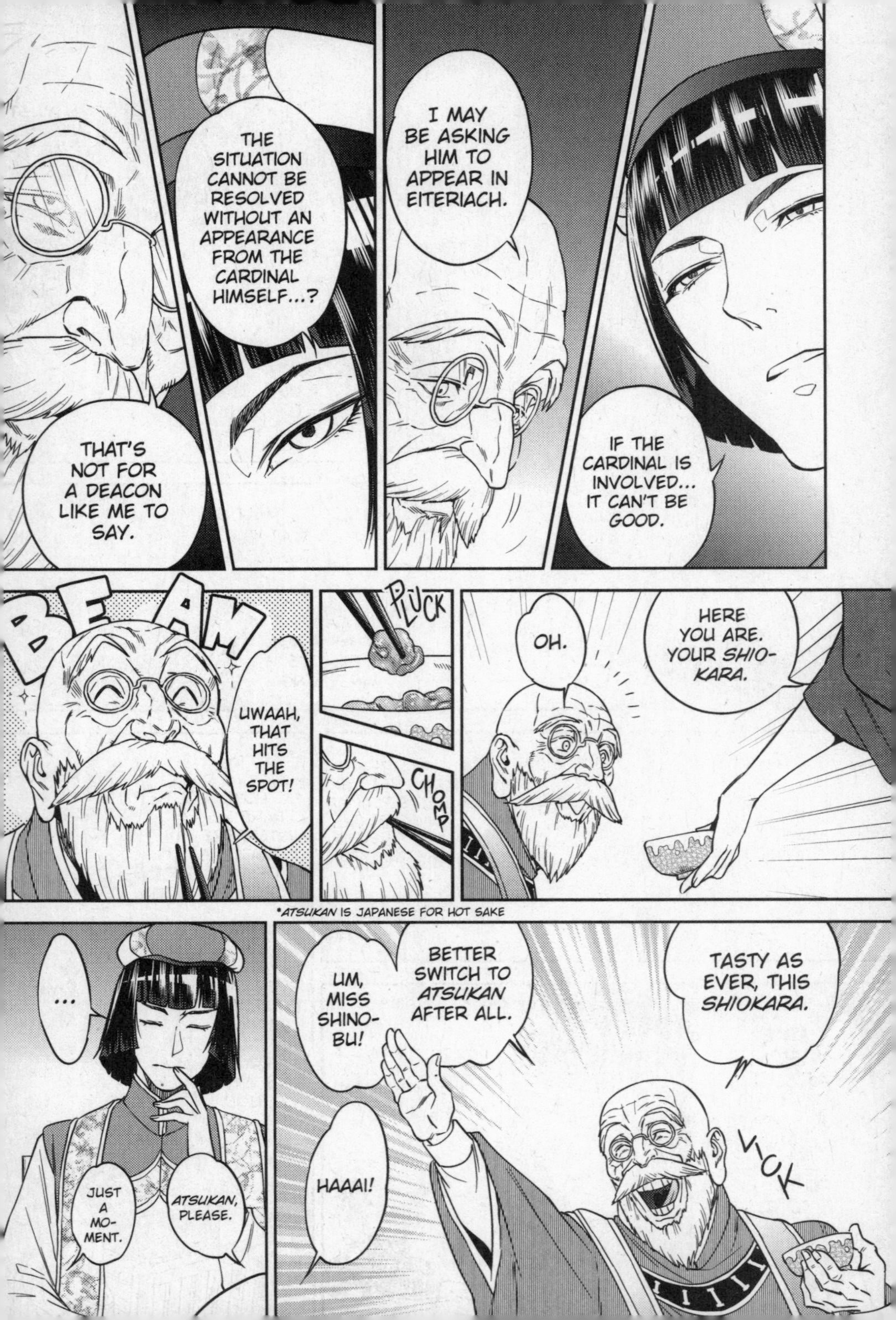
IF THE CARDINAL IS INVOLVED... IT CAN'T BE GOOD.
I MAY BE ASKING HIM TO APPEAR IN EITERIACH.
THE SITUATION CANNOT BE RESOLVED WITHOUT AN APPEARANCE FROM THE CARDINAL HIMSELF...?
THAT'S NOT FOR A DEACON LIKE ME TO SAY.
HERE YOU ARE. YOUR *SHIO-KARA.*
OH.
PLUCK
CHOMP
BEAM
UWAAH, THAT HITS THE SPOT!
TASTY AS EVER, THIS *SHIOKARA.*
VUCK
BETTER SWITCH TO *ATSUKAN* AFTER ALL.
UM, MISS SHINOBU!
HAAAI!
...
ATSUKAN, PLEASE.
JUST A MOMENT.

**ATSUKAN* IS JAPANESE FOR HOT SAKE

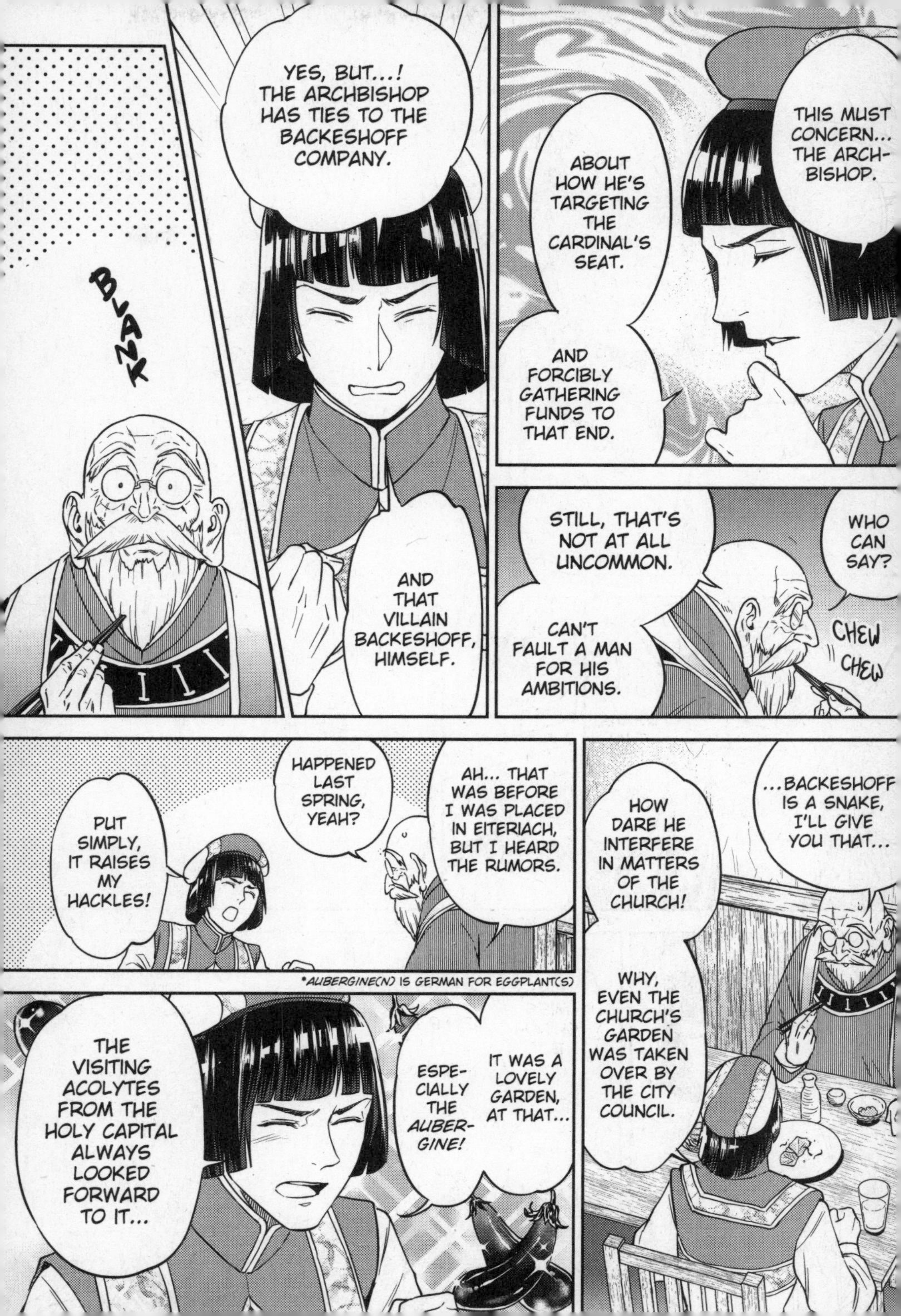
THIS MUST CONCERN... THE ARCH-BISHOP.
ABOUT HOW HE'S TARGETING THE CARDINAL'S SEAT.
AND FORCIBLY GATHERING FUNDS TO THAT END.
WHO CAN SAY?
STILL, THAT'S NOT AT ALL UNCOMMON.
CAN'T FAULT A MAN FOR HIS AMBITIONS.
CHEW CHEW
YES, BUT...! THE ARCHBISHOP HAS TIES TO THE BACKESHOFF COMPANY.
BLANK
AND THAT VILLAIN BACKESHOFF, HIMSELF.
...BACKESHOFF IS A SNAKE, I'LL GIVE YOU THAT...
HOW DARE HE INTERFERE IN MATTERS OF THE CHURCH!
WHY, EVEN THE CHURCH'S GARDEN WAS TAKEN OVER BY THE CITY COUNCIL.
AH... THAT WAS BEFORE I WAS PLACED IN EITERIACH, BUT I HEARD THE RUMORS.
HAPPENED LAST SPRING, YEAH?
PUT SIMPLY, IT RAISES MY HACKLES!
*AUBERGINE(N) IS GERMAN FOR EGGPLANT(S)
IT WAS A LOVELY GARDEN, AT THAT...
ESPE-CIALLY THE AUBER-GINE!
THE VISITING ACOLYTES FROM THE HOLY CAPITAL ALWAYS LOOKED FORWARD TO IT...

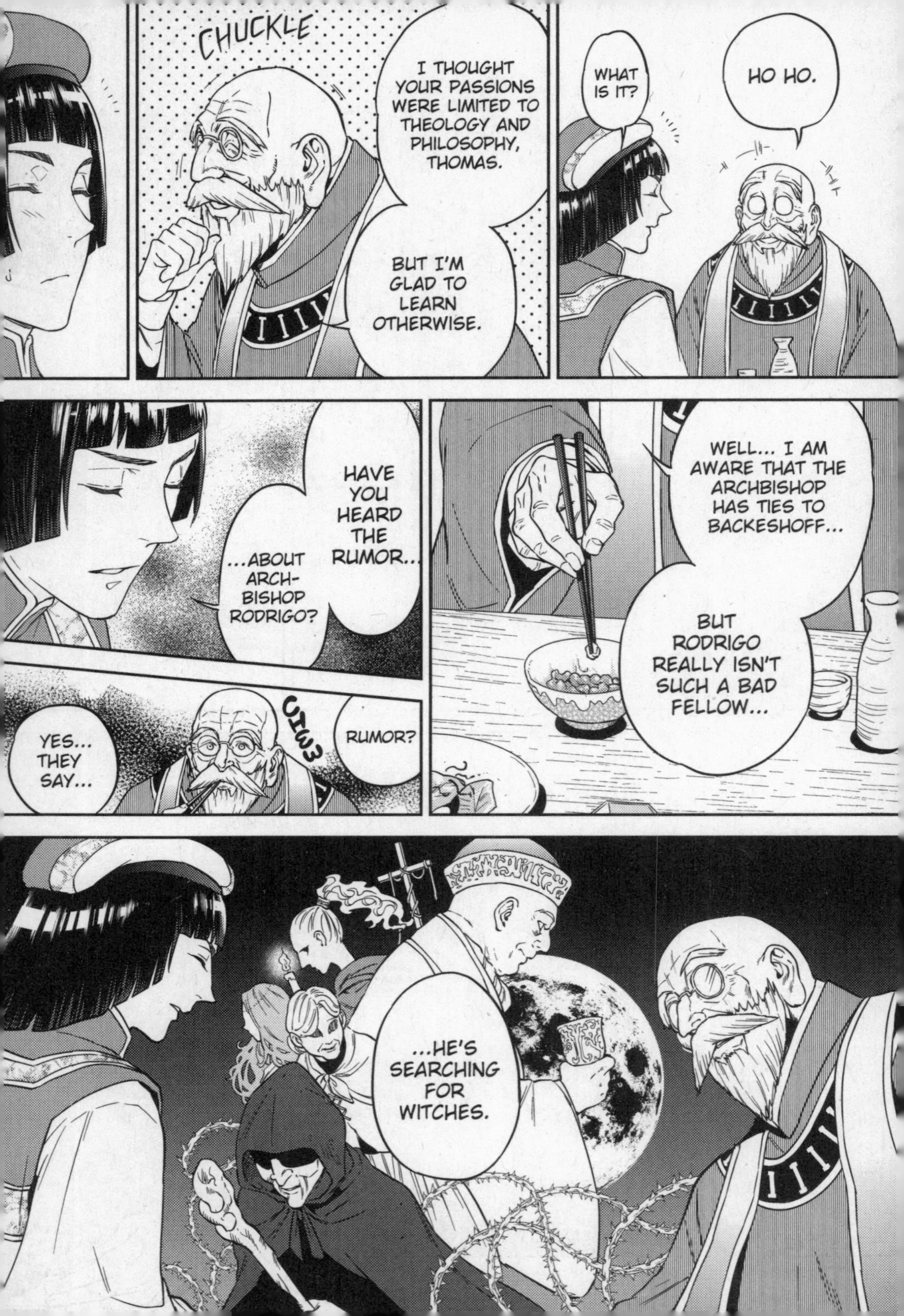
HO HO.
WHAT IS IT?
I THOUGHT YOUR PASSIONS WERE LIMITED TO THEOLOGY AND PHILOSOPHY, THOMAS.
CHUCKLE
BUT I'M GLAD TO LEARN OTHERWISE.
WELL... I AM AWARE THAT THE ARCHBISHOP HAS TIES TO BACKESHOFF...
BUT RODRIGO REALLY ISN'T SUCH A BAD FELLOW...
HAVE YOU HEARD THE RUMOR...
...ABOUT ARCH-BISHOP RODRIGO?
RUMOR?
YES... THEY SAY...
...HE'S SEARCHING FOR WITCHES.

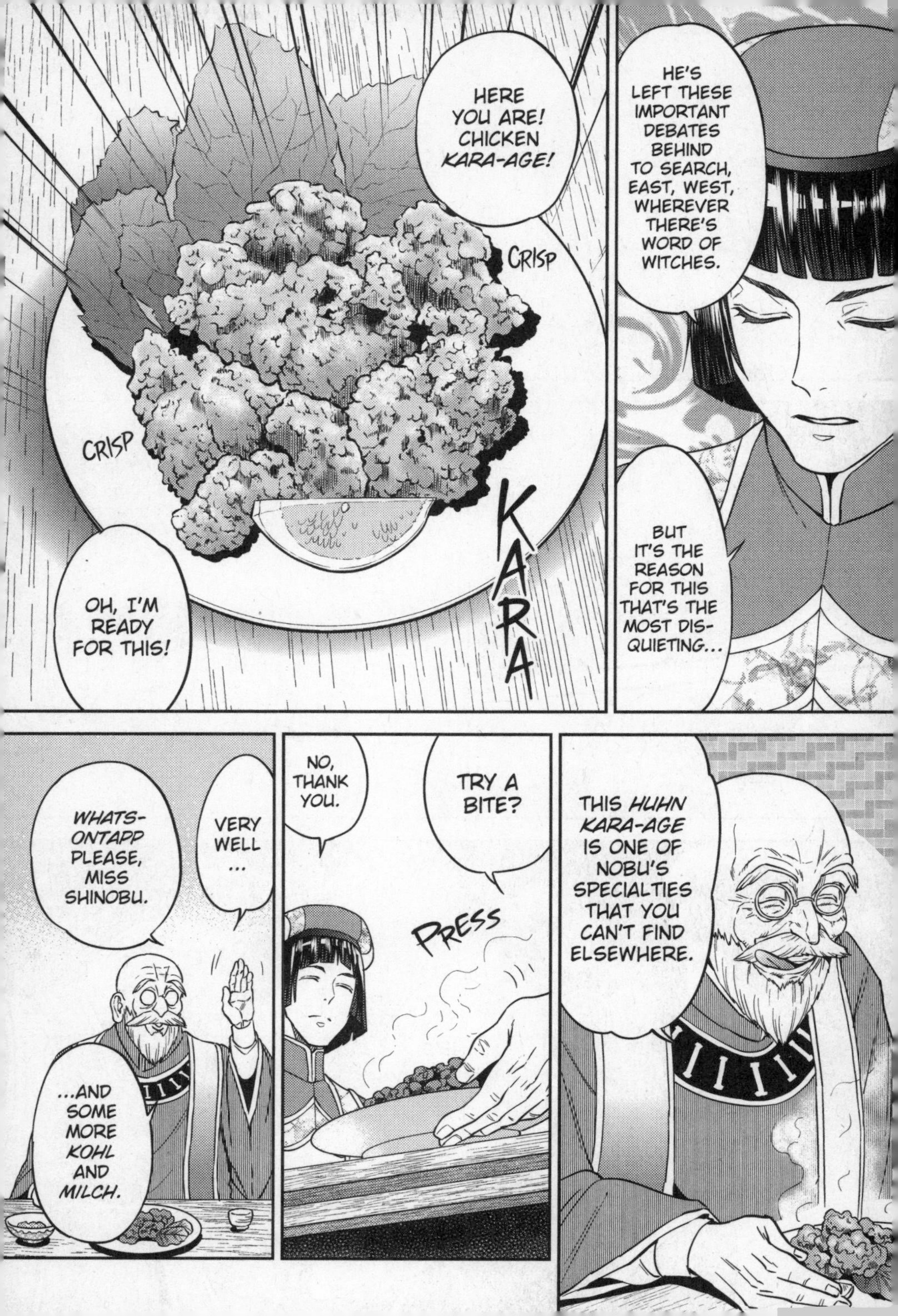
HE'S LEFT THESE IMPORTANT DEBATES BEHIND TO SEARCH, EAST, WEST, WHEREVER THERE'S WORD OF WITCHES.
BUT IT'S THE REASON FOR THIS THAT'S THE MOST DIS-QUIETING...
HERE YOU ARE! CHICKEN *KARA-AGE!*
CRISP
CRISP
KARA
OH, I'M READY FOR THIS!
THIS *HUHN KARA-AGE* IS ONE OF NOBU'S SPECIALTIES THAT YOU CAN'T FIND ELSEWHERE.
TRY A BITE?
NO, THANK YOU.
PRESS
VERY WELL ...
WHATS-ONTAPP PLEASE, MISS SHINOBU.
...AND SOME MORE *KOHL* AND *MILCH*.

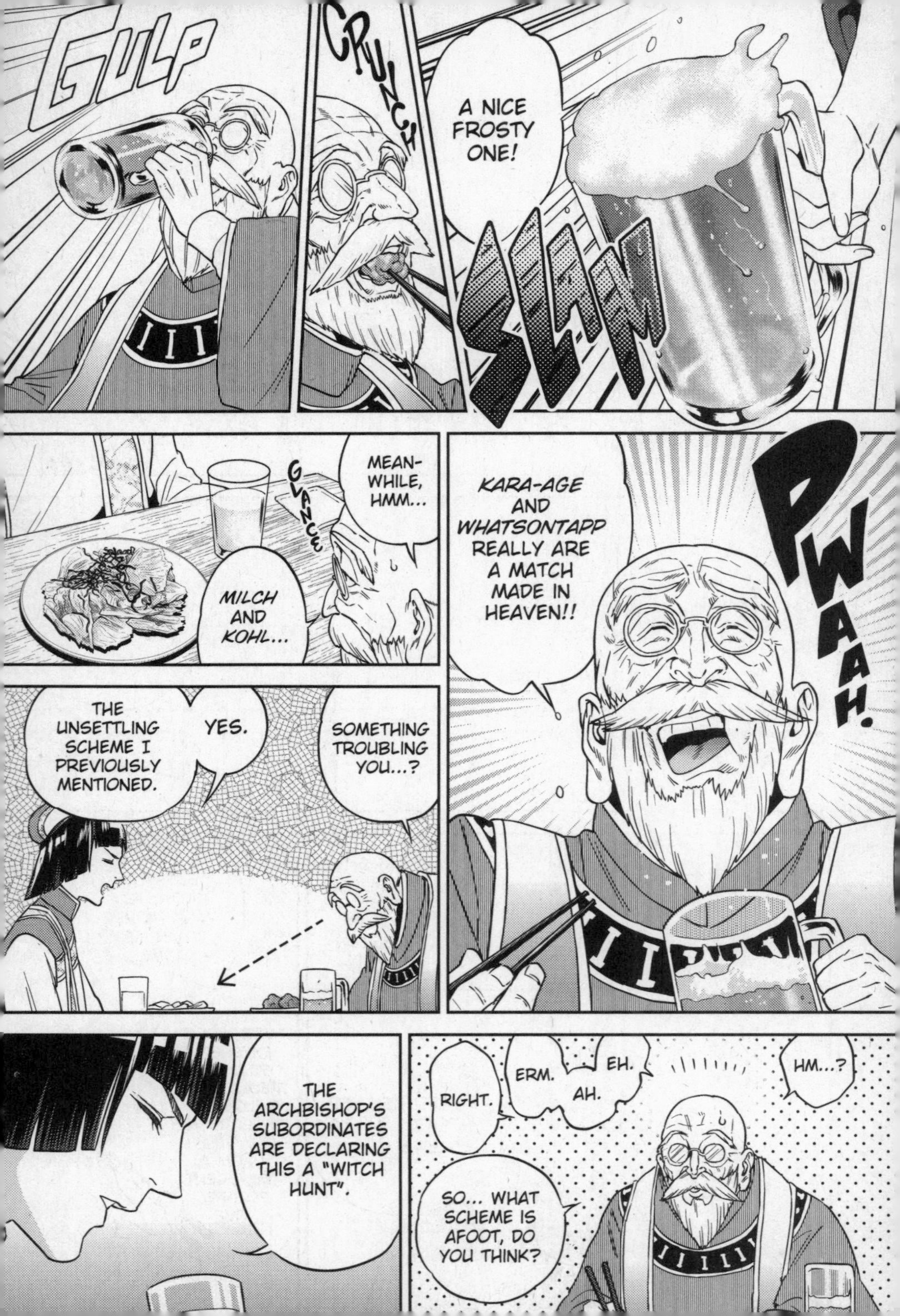
A NICE FROSTY ONE!
SLAM
CRUNCH
GULP
PWAH.
KARA-AGE AND WHATSONTAPP REALLY ARE A MATCH MADE IN HEAVEN!!
MEAN-WHILE, HMM...
GLANCE
MILCH AND KOHL...
SOMETHING TROUBLING YOU...?
YES.
THE UNSETTLING SCHEME I PREVIOUSLY MENTIONED.
HM...?
EH.
ERM.
AH.
RIGHT.
SO... WHAT SCHEME IS AFOOT, DO YOU THINK?
THE ARCHBISHOP'S SUBORDINATES ARE DECLARING THIS A "WITCH HUNT".

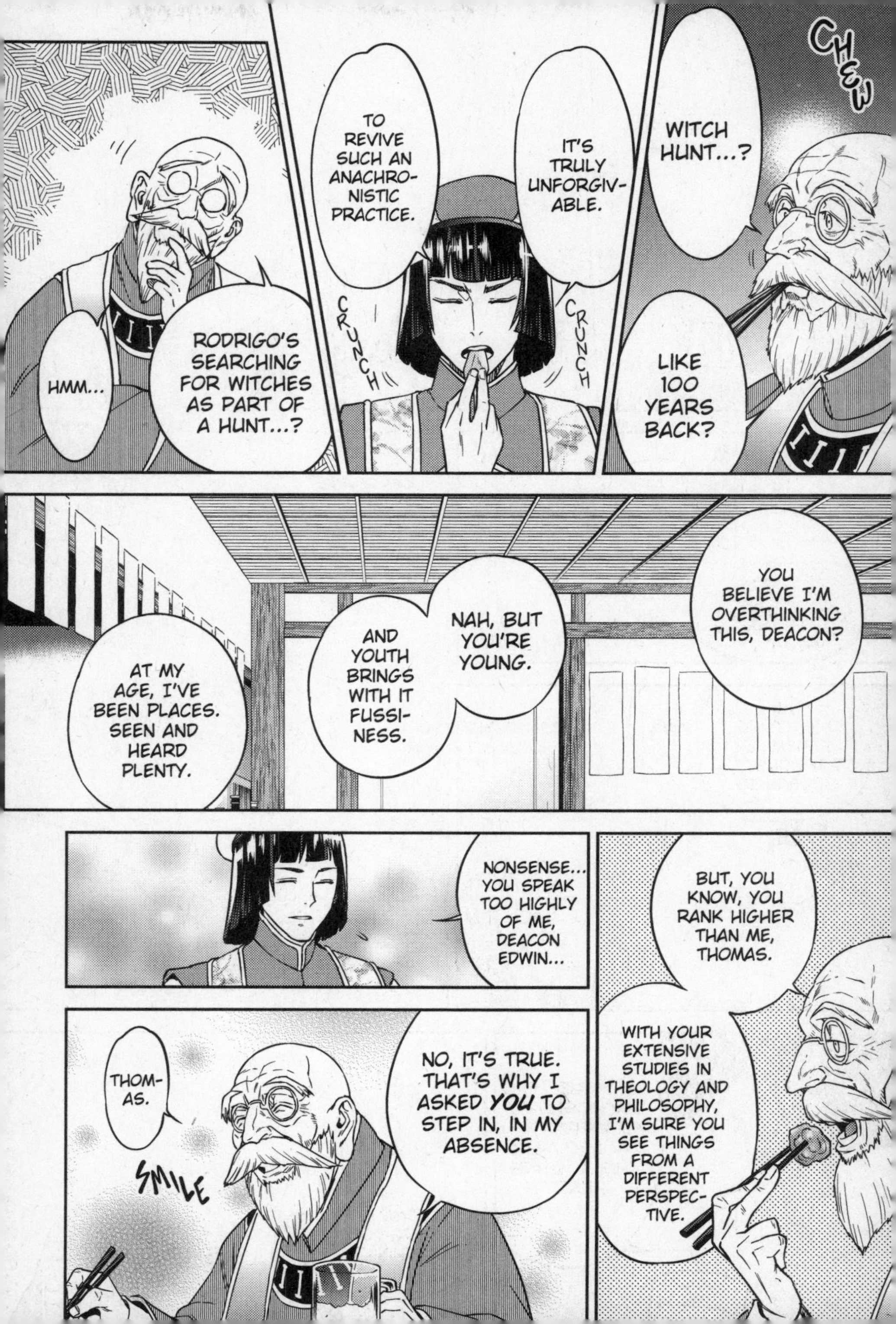
CHEW
WITCH HUNT...?
LIKE 100 YEARS BACK?
IT'S TRULY UNFORGIVABLE.
CRUNCH
TO REVIVE SUCH AN ANACHRONISTIC PRACTICE.
CRUNCH
RODRIGO'S SEARCHING FOR WITCHES AS PART OF A HUNT...?
HMM...
YOU BELIEVE I'M OVERTHINKING THIS, DEACON?
NAH, BUT YOU'RE YOUNG.
AND YOUTH BRINGS WITH IT FUSSINESS.
AT MY AGE, I'VE BEEN PLACES. SEEN AND HEARD PLENTY.
BUT, YOU KNOW, YOU RANK HIGHER THAN ME, THOMAS.
WITH YOUR EXTENSIVE STUDIES IN THEOLOGY AND PHILOSOPHY, I'M SURE YOU SEE THINGS FROM A DIFFERENT PERSPECTIVE.
NONSENSE... YOU SPEAK TOO HIGHLY OF ME, DEACON EDWIN...
NO, IT'S TRUE. THAT'S WHY I ASKED *YOU* TO STEP IN, IN MY ABSENCE.
THOMAS.
SMILE

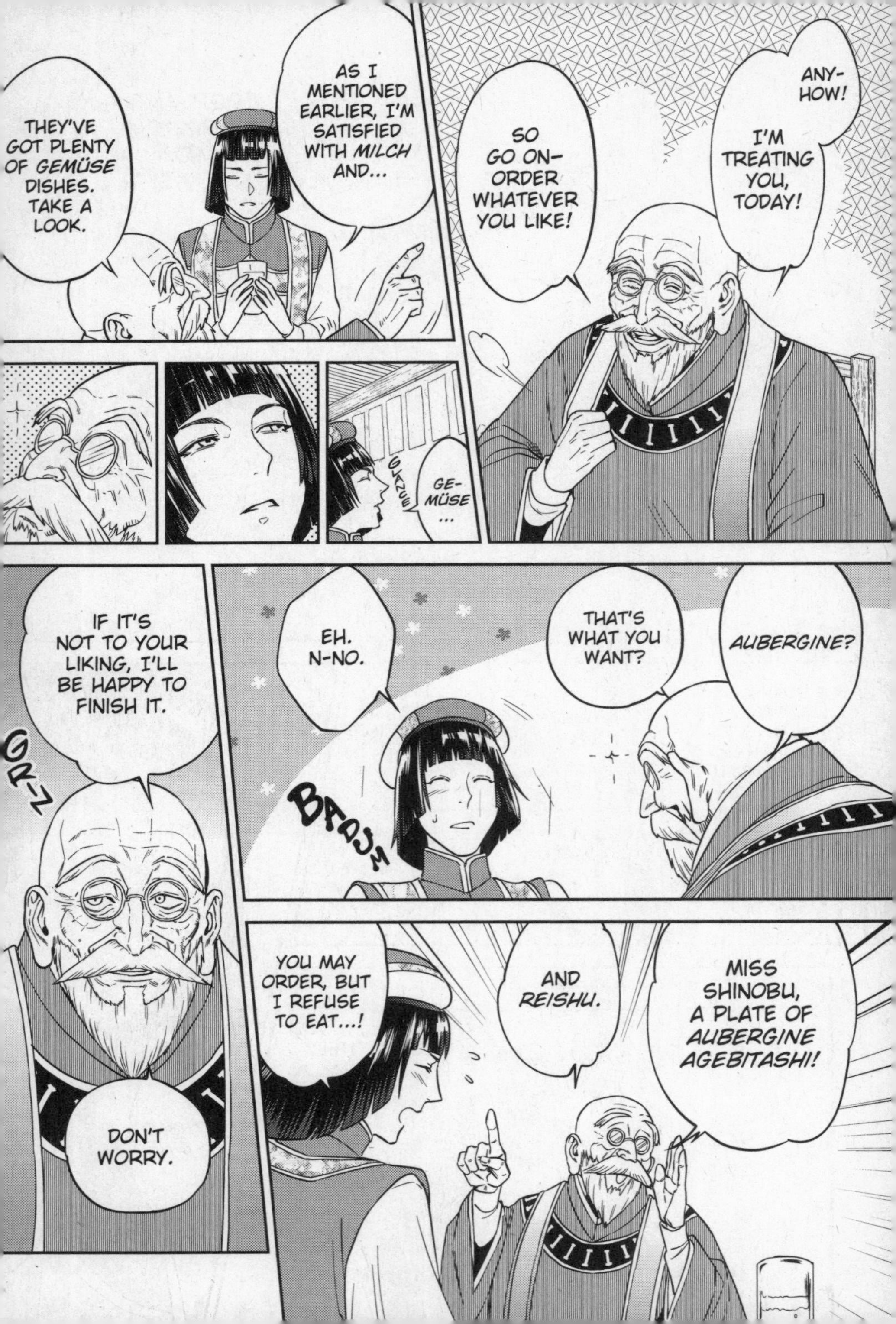
ANY-HOW!
I'M TREATING YOU, TODAY!
SO GO ON—ORDER WHATEVER YOU LIKE!
AS I MENTIONED EARLIER, I'M SATISFIED WITH *MILCH* AND...
THEY'VE GOT PLENTY OF *GEMÜSE* DISHES. TAKE A LOOK.
GLANCE
GE-MÜSE...
AUBERGINE?
THAT'S WHAT YOU WANT?
EH. N-NO.
BADUM
MISS SHINOBU, A PLATE OF *AUBERGINE AGEBITASHI!*
AND *REISHU.*
YOU MAY ORDER, BUT I REFUSE TO EAT...!
IF IT'S NOT TO YOUR LIKING, I'LL BE HAPPY TO FINISH IT.
GR-Z
DON'T WORRY.

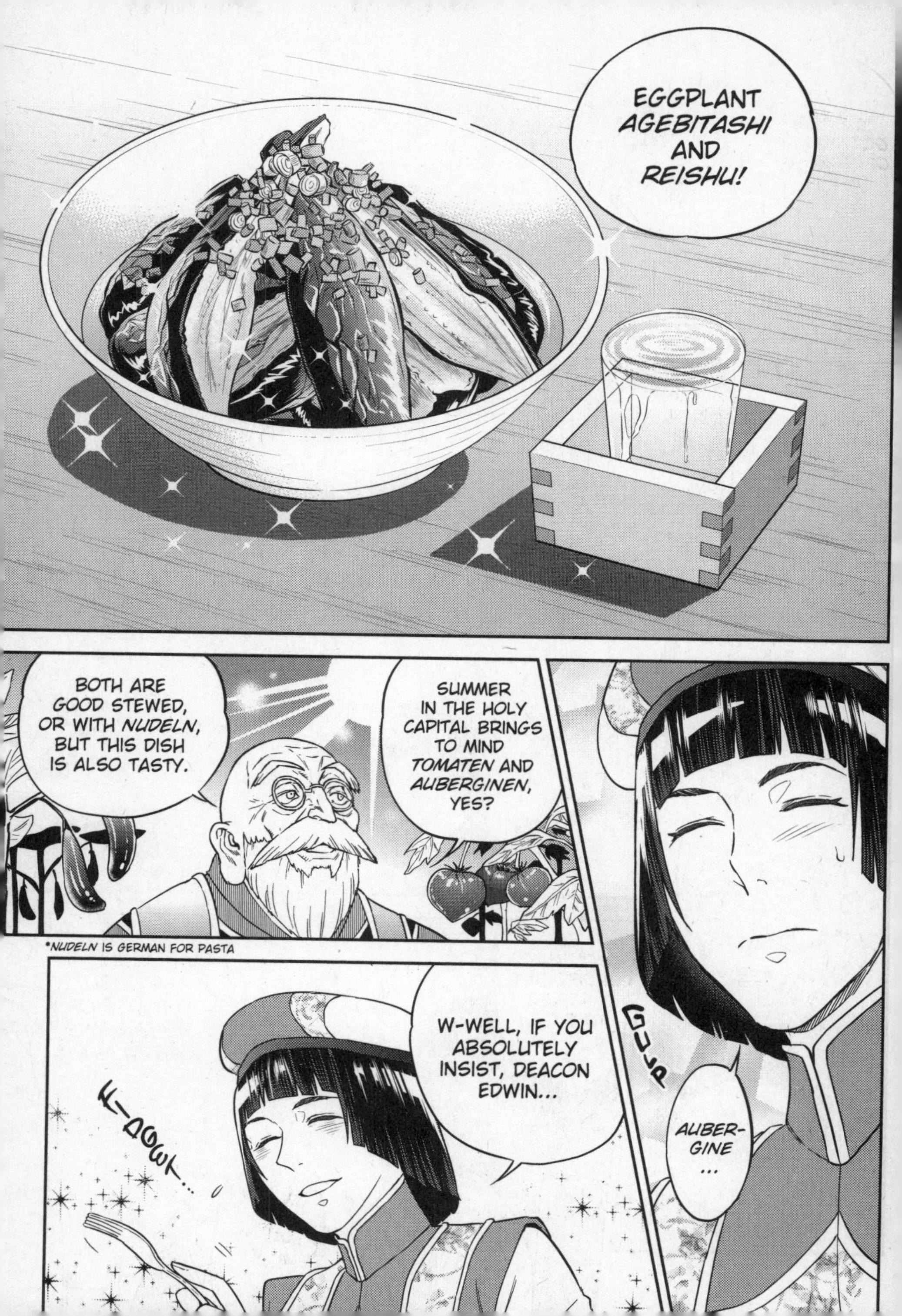
EGGPLANT *AGEBITASHI* AND *REISHU*!
GULP
AUBER-GINE ...
SUMMER IN THE HOLY CAPITAL BRINGS TO MIND *TOMATEN* AND *AUBERGINEN*, YES?
BOTH ARE GOOD STEWED, OR WITH *NUDELN*, BUT THIS DISH IS ALSO TASTY.
W-WELL, IF YOU ABSOLUTELY INSIST, DEACON EDWIN...
**NUDELN* IS GERMAN FOR PASTA*

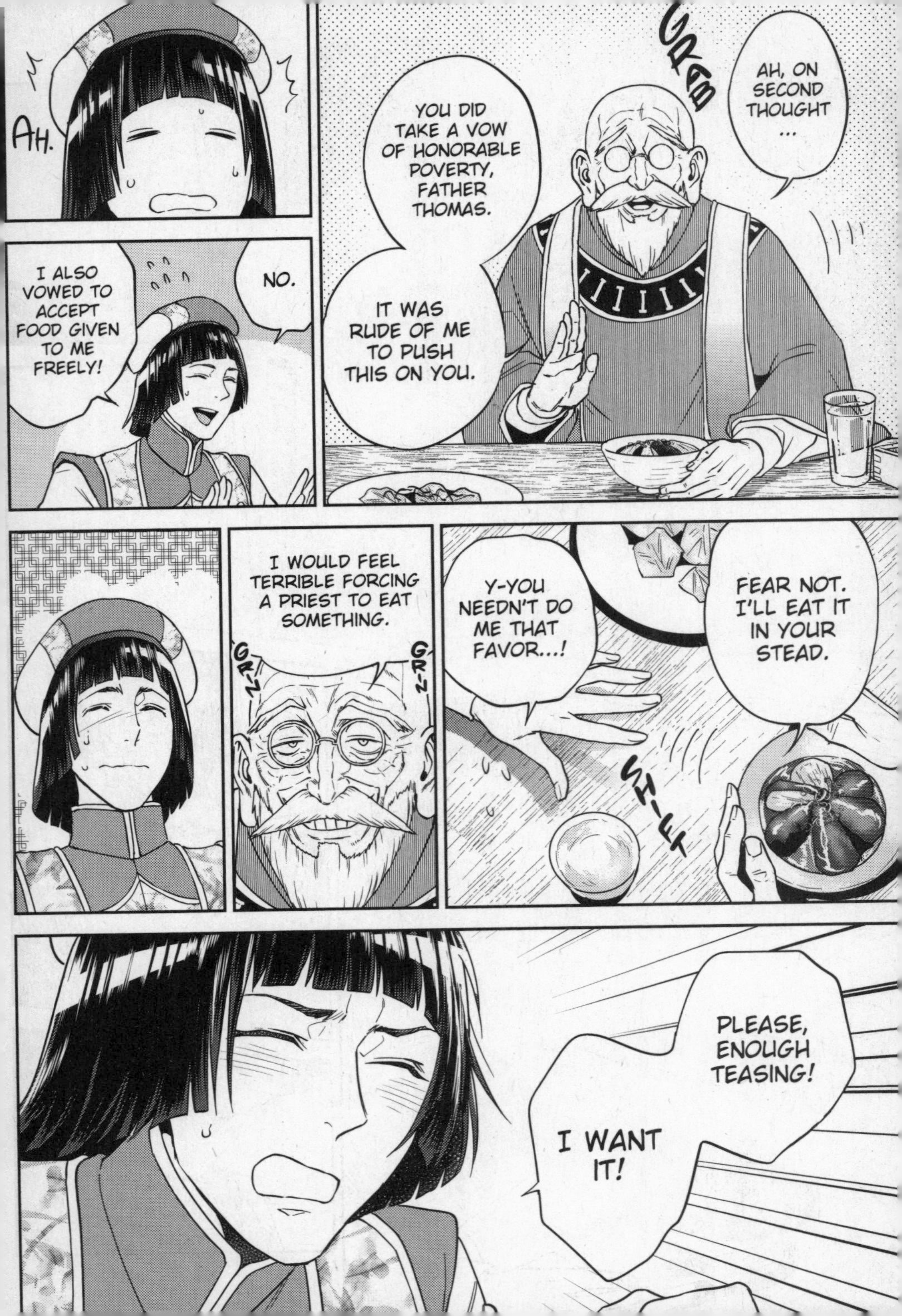
AH, ON SECOND THOUGHT ...
GRAB
YOU DID TAKE A VOW OF HONORABLE POVERTY, FATHER THOMAS.
IT WAS RUDE OF ME TO PUSH THIS ON YOU.
AH.
NO.
I ALSO VOWED TO ACCEPT FOOD GIVEN TO ME FREELY!
FEAR NOT. I'LL EAT IT IN YOUR STEAD.
Y-YOU NEEDN'T DO ME THAT FAVOR...!
SHIFT
I WOULD FEEL TERRIBLE FORCING A PRIEST TO EAT SOMETHING.
GRIN
GRIN
PLEASE, ENOUGH TEASING!
I WANT IT!

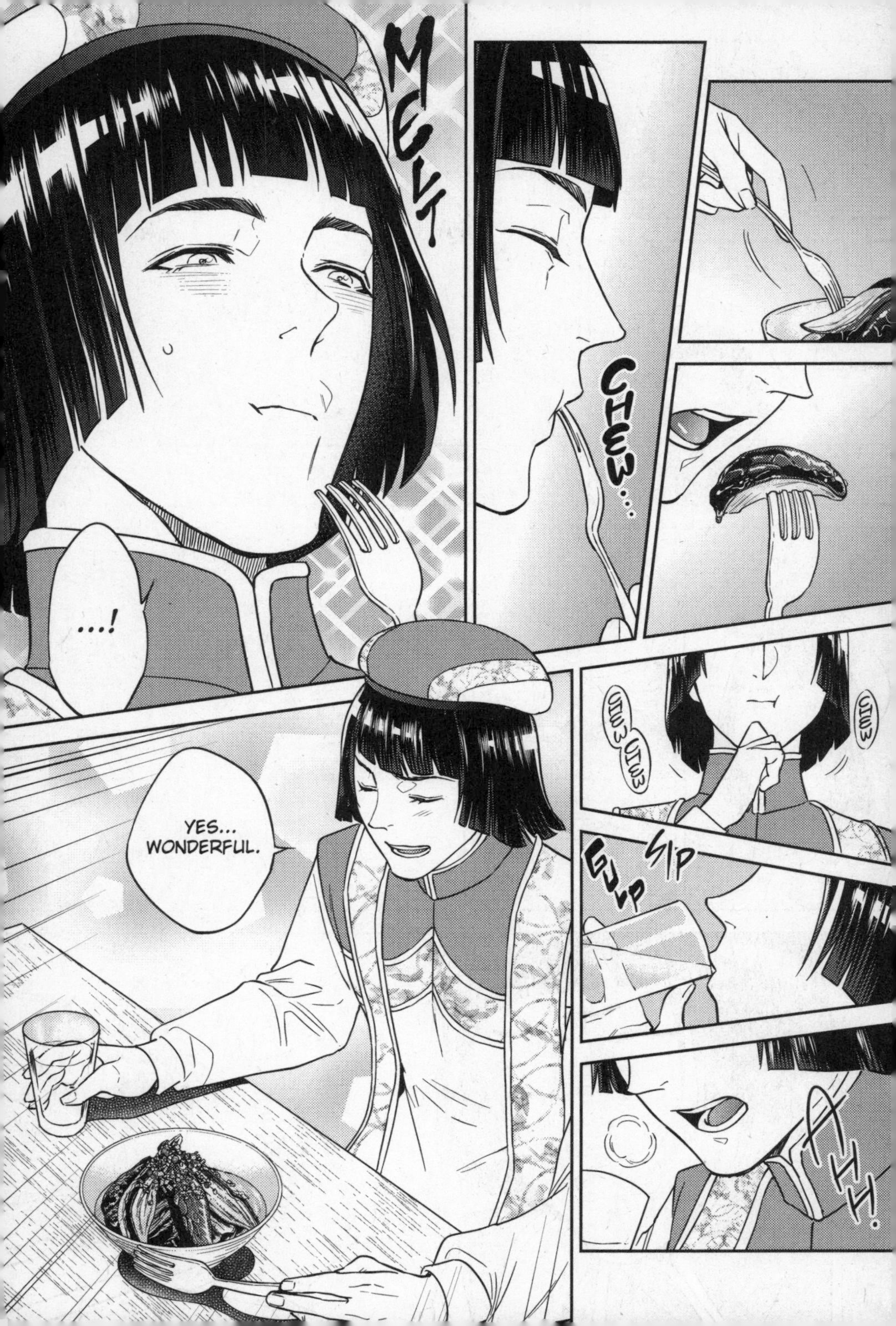
CHEW...
MELT
...!
CHEW
CHEW CHEW
SIP
GULP
AHH!
YES...
WONDERFUL.

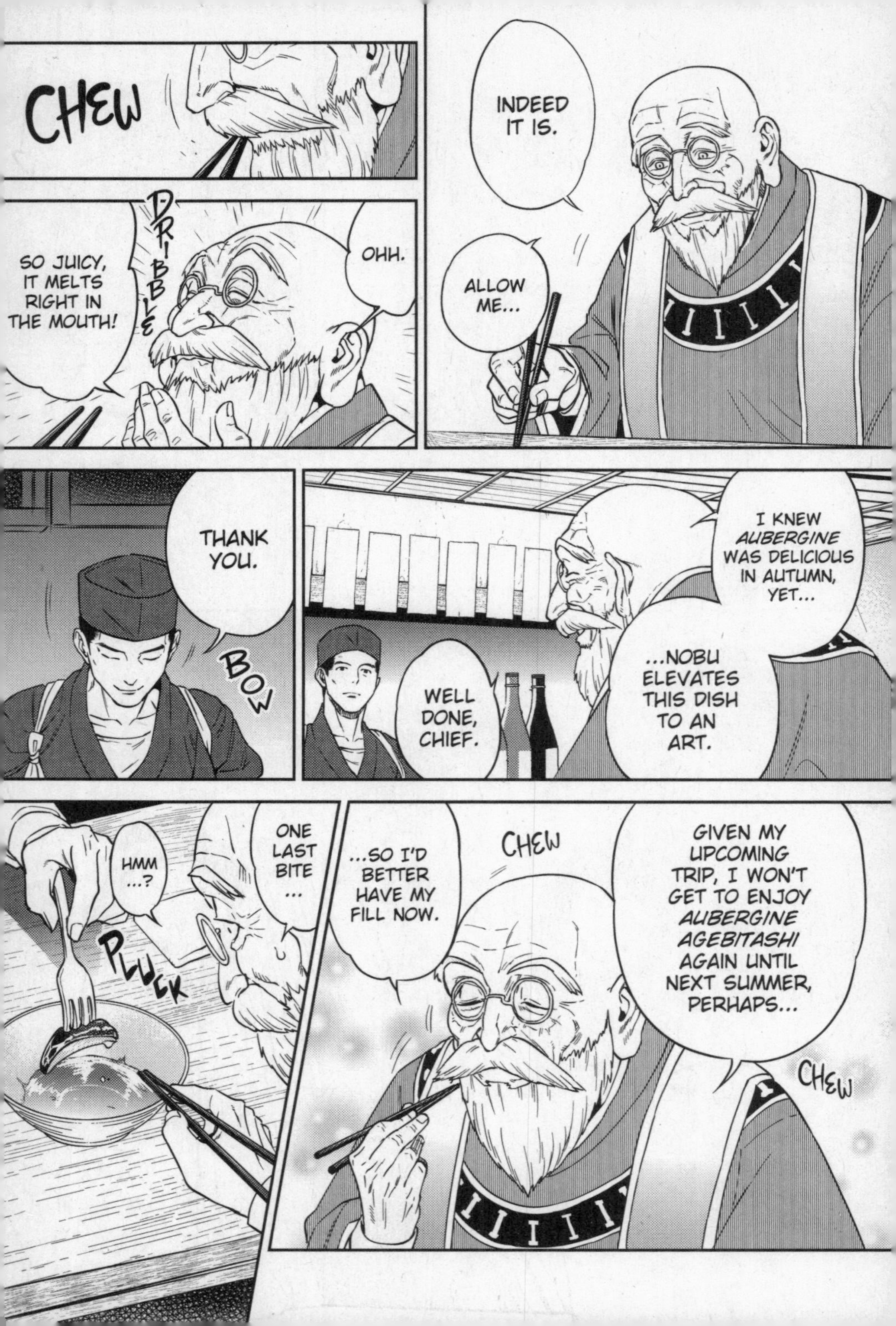
INDEED IT IS.
ALLOW ME...
CHEW
OHH.
DRIBBLE
SO JUICY, IT MELTS RIGHT IN THE MOUTH!
I KNEW *AUBERGINE* WAS DELICIOUS IN AUTUMN, YET...
...NOBU ELEVATES THIS DISH TO AN ART.
WELL DONE, CHIEF.
THANK YOU.
BOW
GIVEN MY UPCOMING TRIP, I WON'T GET TO ENJOY *AUBERGINE AGEBITASHI* AGAIN UNTIL NEXT SUMMER, PERHAPS...
CHEW
...SO I'D BETTER HAVE MY FILL NOW.
CHEW
ONE LAST BITE ...
HMM ...?
PLUCK

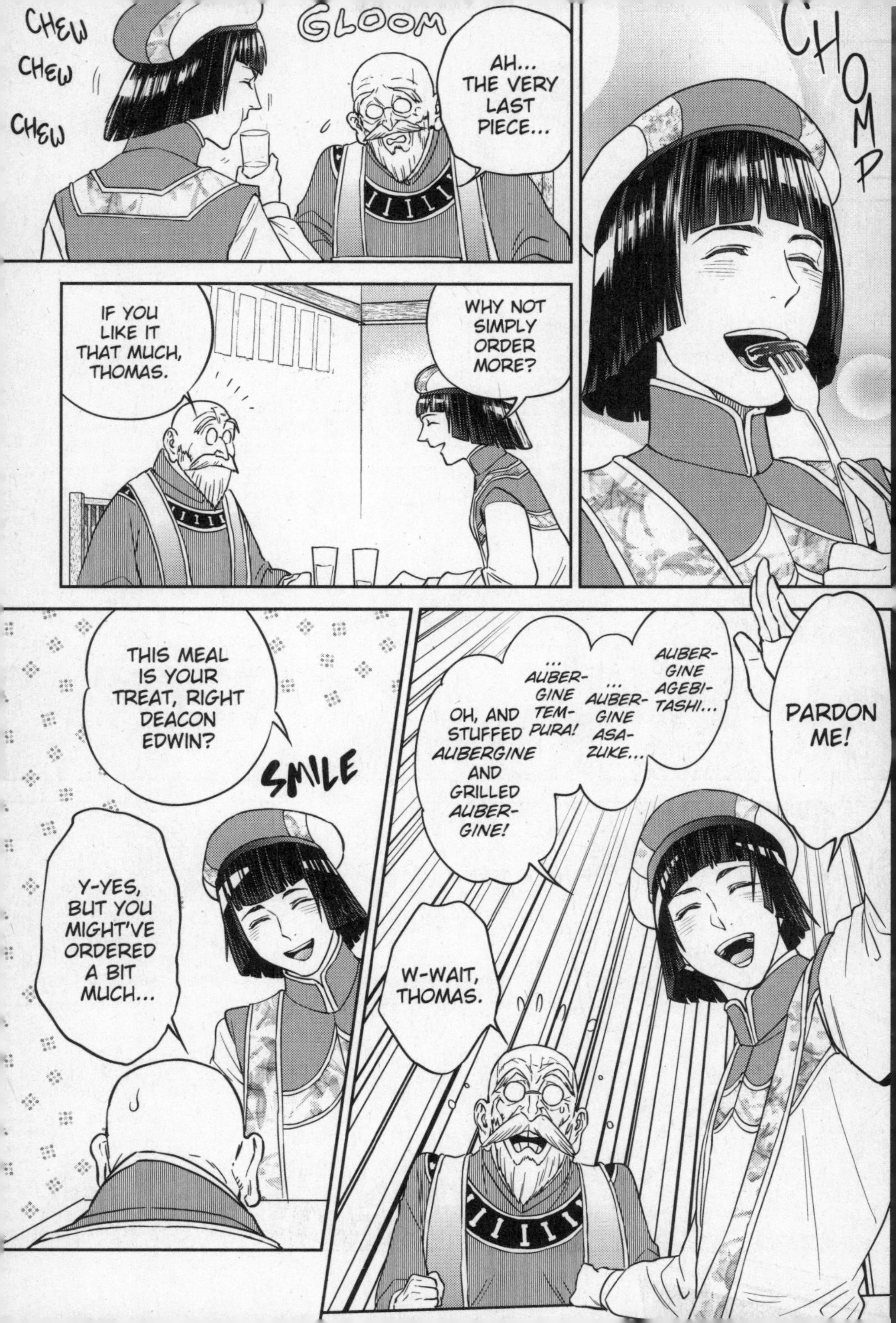
CHOMP
AH... THE VERY LAST PIECE...
GLOOM
CHEW
CHEW
CHEW
WHY NOT SIMPLY ORDER MORE?
IF YOU LIKE IT THAT MUCH, THOMAS.
PARDON ME!
AUBERGINE AGEBITASHI...
...AUBERGINE ASAZUKE...
...AUBERGINE TEMPURA!
OH, AND STUFFED AUBERGINE AND GRILLED AUBERGINE!
W-WAIT, THOMAS.
THIS MEAL IS YOUR TREAT, RIGHT DEACON EDWIN?
SMILE
Y-YES, BUT YOU MIGHT'VE ORDERED A BIT MUCH...

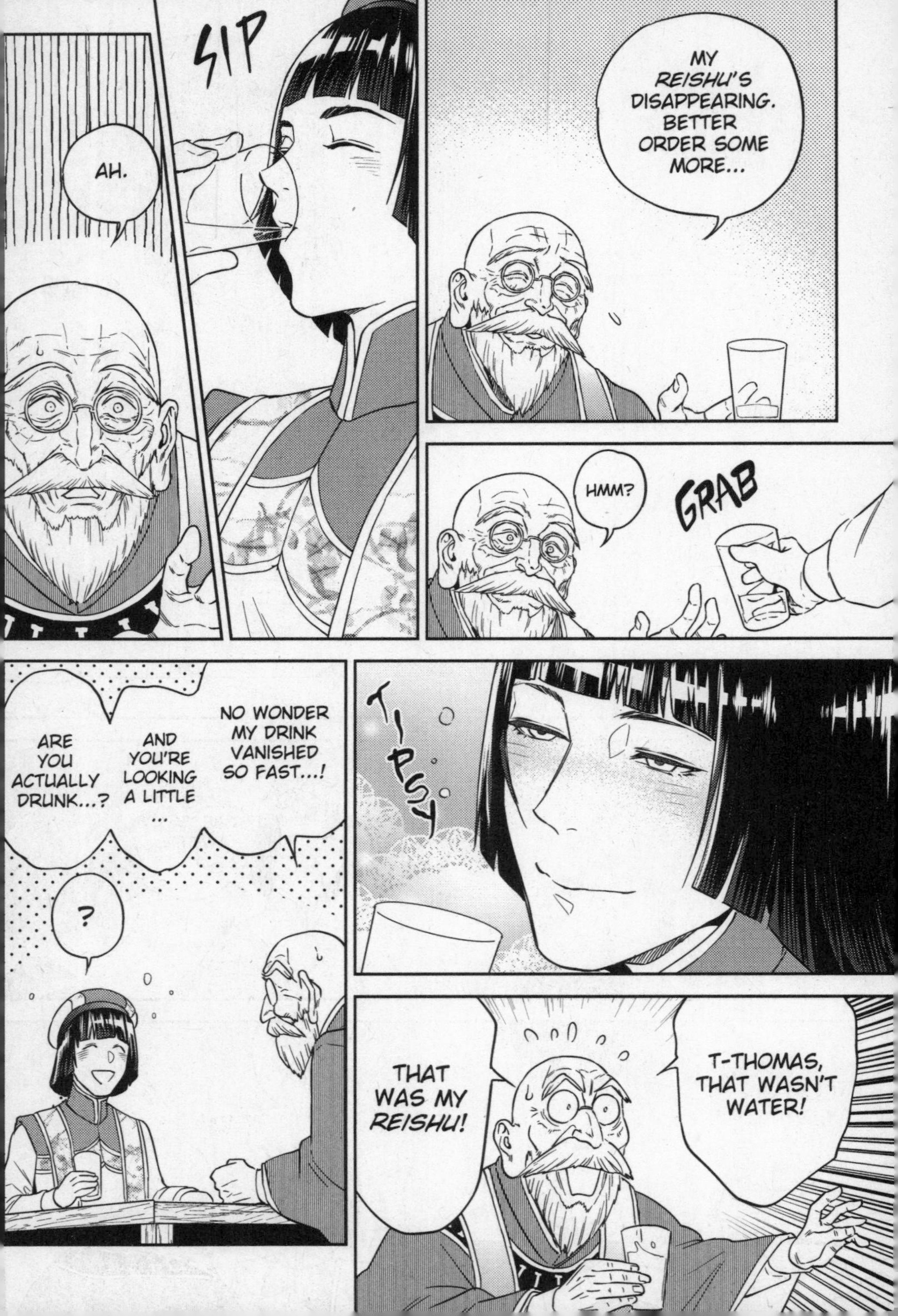
MY *REISHU*'S DISAPPEARING. BETTER ORDER SOME MORE...
HMM?
GRAB
SIP
AH.
T-I-P-S-Y
T-THOMAS, THAT WASN'T WATER!
THAT WAS MY *REISHU*!
NO WONDER MY DRINK VANISHED SO FAST...!
AND YOU'RE LOOKING A LITTLE ...
ARE YOU ACTUALLY DRUNK...?
?

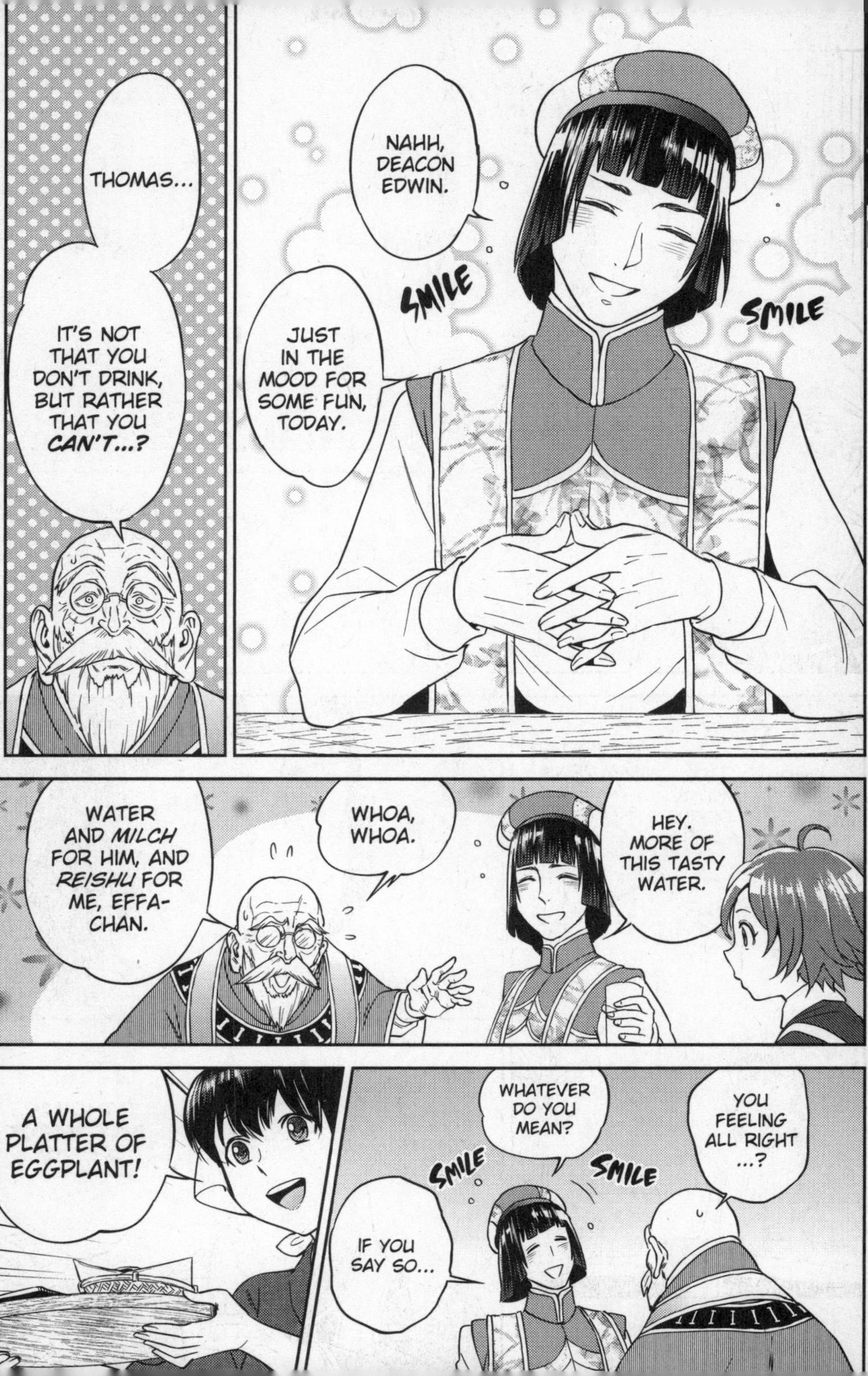
NAHH, DEACON EDWIN.
SMILE
SMILE
JUST IN THE MOOD FOR SOME FUN, TODAY.
THOMAS...
IT'S NOT THAT YOU DON'T DRINK, BUT RATHER THAT YOU *CAN'T...?*
HEY. MORE OF THIS TASTY WATER.
WHOA, WHOA.
WATER AND *MILCH* FOR HIM, AND *REISHU* FOR ME, EFFA-CHAN.
YOU FEELING ALL RIGHT ...?
WHATEVER DO YOU MEAN?
SMILE
SMILE
IF YOU SAY SO...
A WHOLE PLATTER OF EGGPLANT!

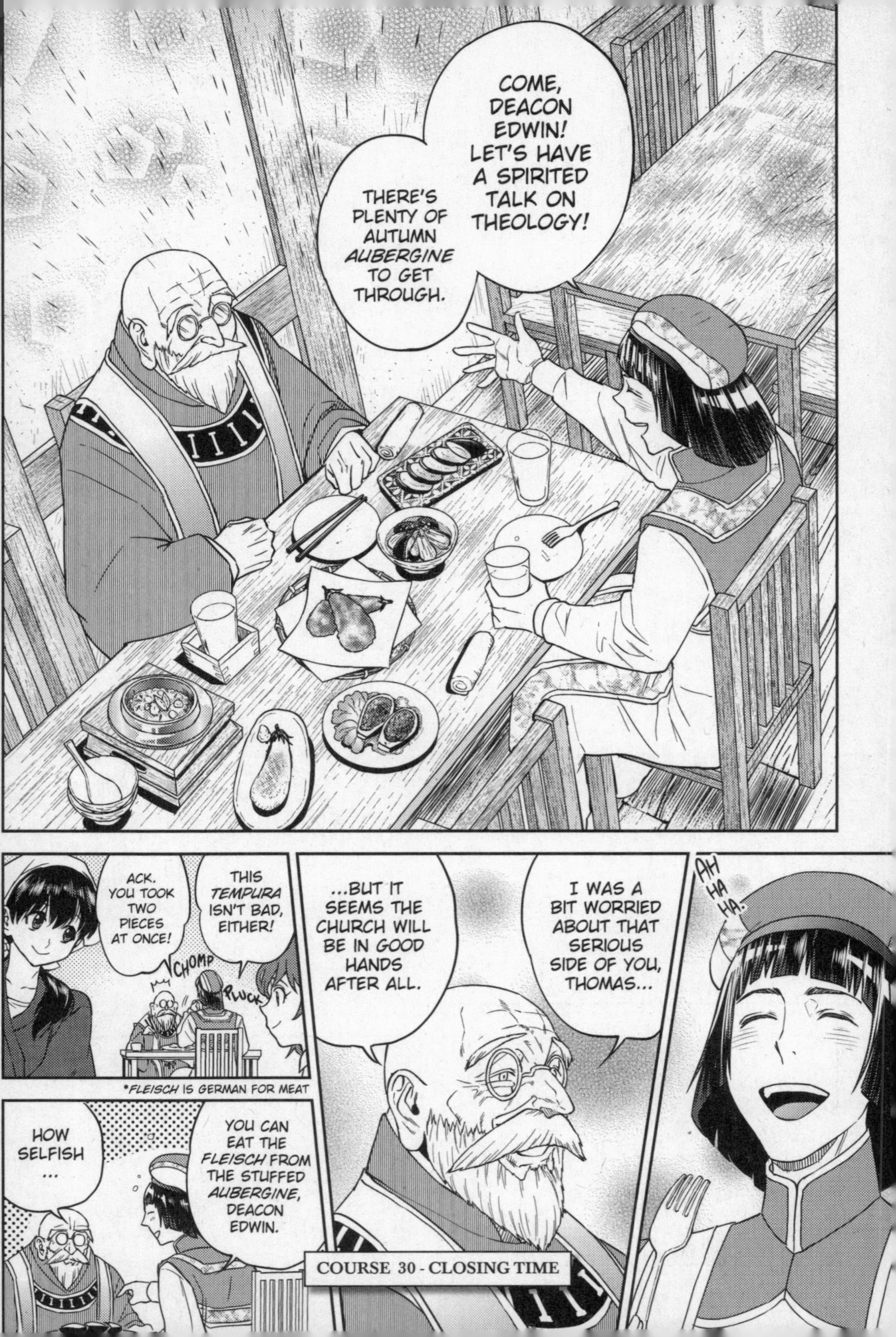
COME, DEACON EDWIN! LET'S HAVE A SPIRITED TALK ON THEOLOGY!
THERE'S PLENTY OF AUTUMN *AUBERGINE* TO GET THROUGH.
AH HA HA.
I WAS A BIT WORRIED ABOUT THAT SERIOUS SIDE OF YOU, THOMAS...
...BUT IT SEEMS THE CHURCH WILL BE IN GOOD HANDS AFTER ALL.
THIS *TEMPURA* ISN'T BAD, EITHER!
ACK. YOU TOOK TWO PIECES AT ONCE!
CHOMP
PLUCK
YOU CAN EAT THE *FLEISCH* FROM THE STUFFED *AUBERGINE*, DEACON EDWIN.
HOW SELFISH ...
COURSE 30 - CLOSING TIME

**FLEISCH* IS GERMAN FOR MEAT

Eggplant Agebitashi

OTHERWORLDLY IZAKAYA

NOBU

COURSE 31

TEMPURA FOR AN AUTUMN PALATE

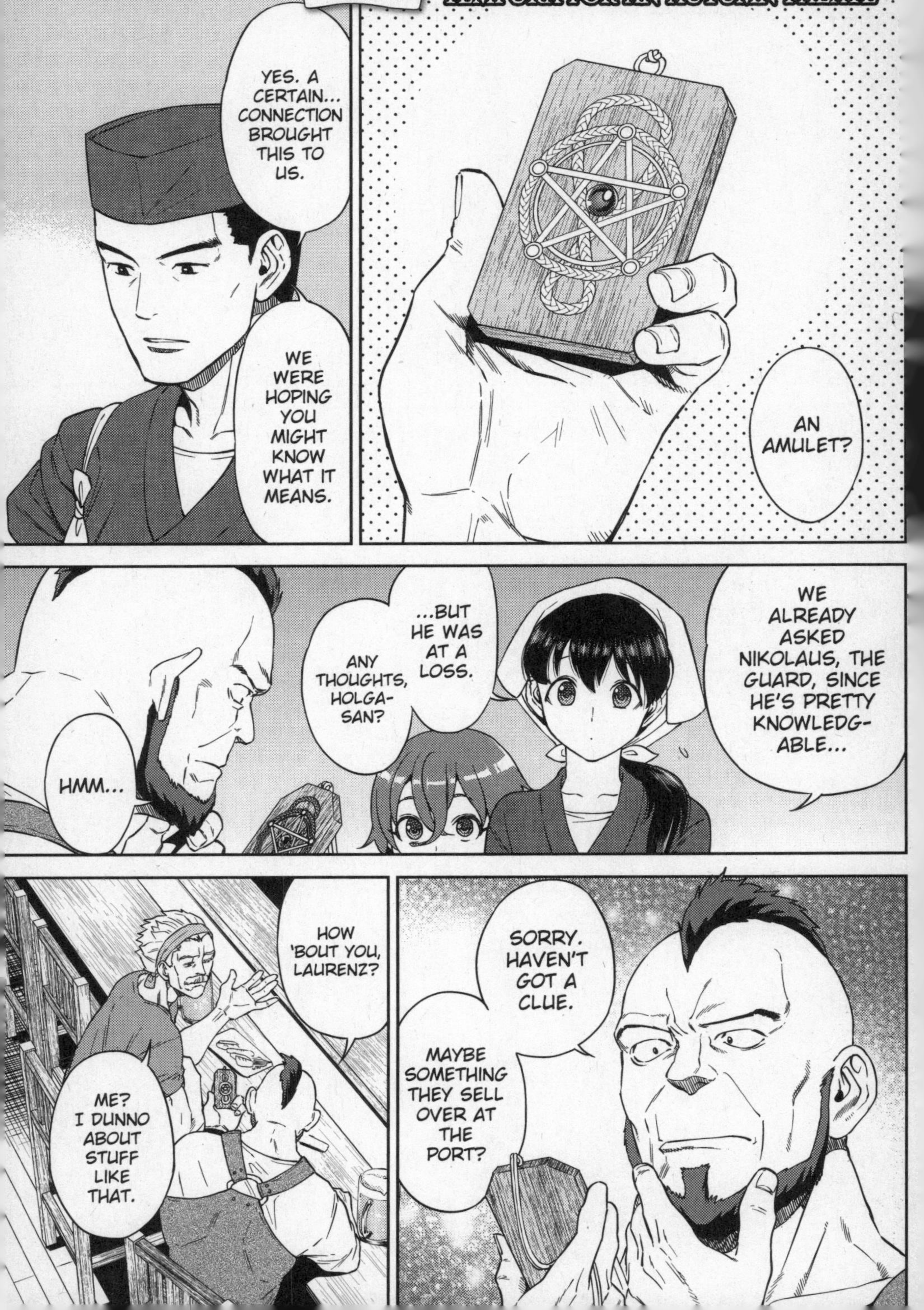
AN AMULET?
YES. A CERTAIN... CONNECTION BROUGHT THIS TO US.
WE WERE HOPING YOU MIGHT KNOW WHAT IT MEANS.
WE ALREADY ASKED NIKOLAUS, THE GUARD, SINCE HE'S PRETTY KNOWLEDG-ABLE...
...BUT HE WAS AT A LOSS.
ANY THOUGHTS, HOLGA-SAN?
HMM...
SORRY. HAVEN'T GOT A CLUE.
MAYBE SOMETHING THEY SELL OVER AT THE PORT?
HOW 'BOUT YOU, LAURENZ?
ME? I DUNNO ABOUT STUFF LIKE THAT.

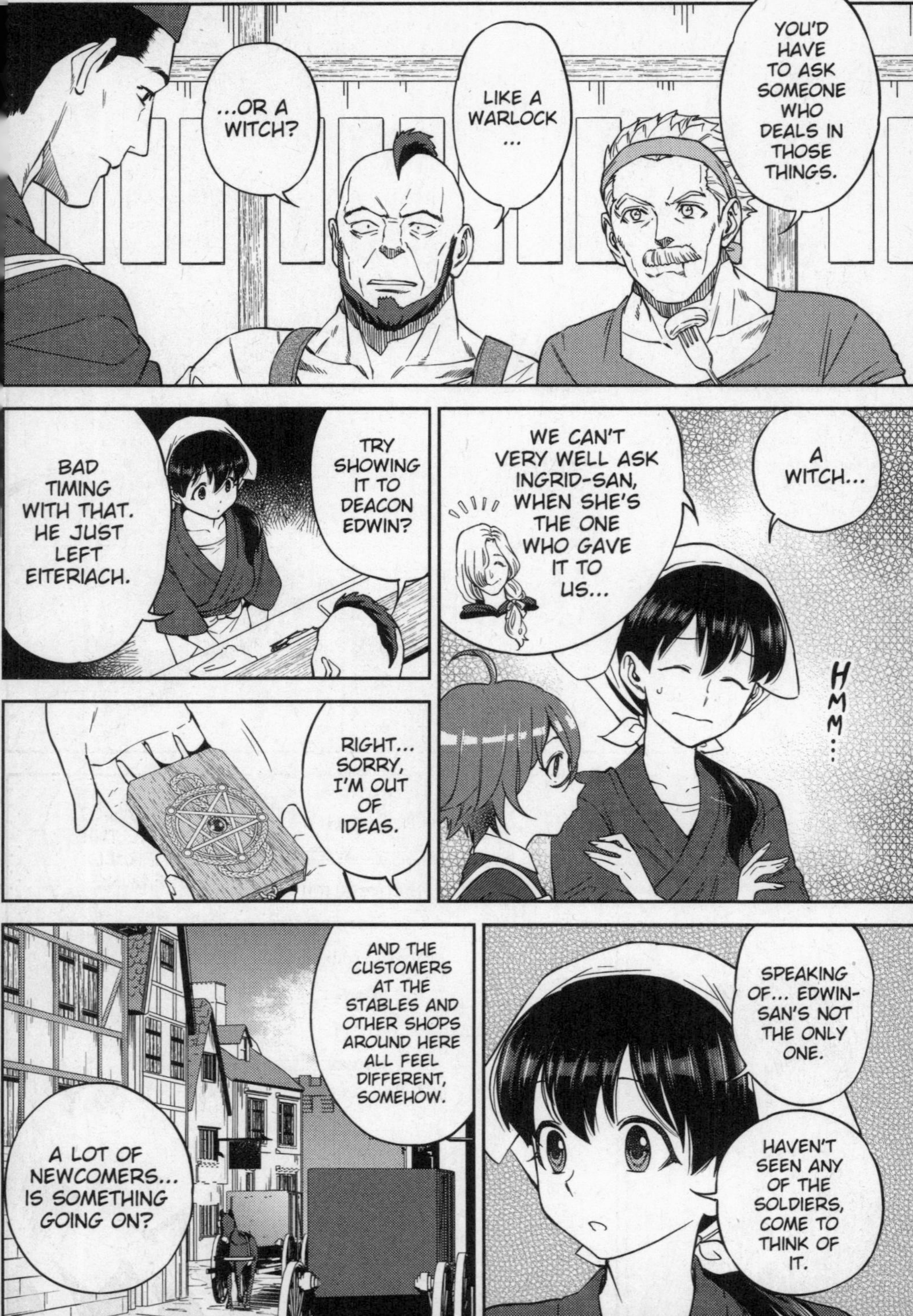
YOU'D HAVE TO ASK SOMEONE WHO DEALS IN THOSE THINGS.
LIKE A WARLOCK ...
...OR A WITCH?
A WITCH...
WE CAN'T VERY WELL ASK INGRID-SAN, WHEN SHE'S THE ONE WHO GAVE IT TO US...
HMM...
TRY SHOWING IT TO DEACON EDWIN?
BAD TIMING WITH THAT. HE JUST LEFT EITERIACH.
RIGHT... SORRY, I'M OUT OF IDEAS.
SPEAKING OF... EDWIN-SAN'S NOT THE ONLY ONE.
HAVEN'T SEEN ANY OF THE SOLDIERS, COME TO THINK OF IT.
AND THE CUSTOMERS AT THE STABLES AND OTHER SHOPS AROUND HERE ALL FEEL DIFFERENT, SOMEHOW.
A LOT OF NEWCOMERS... IS SOMETHING GOING ON?

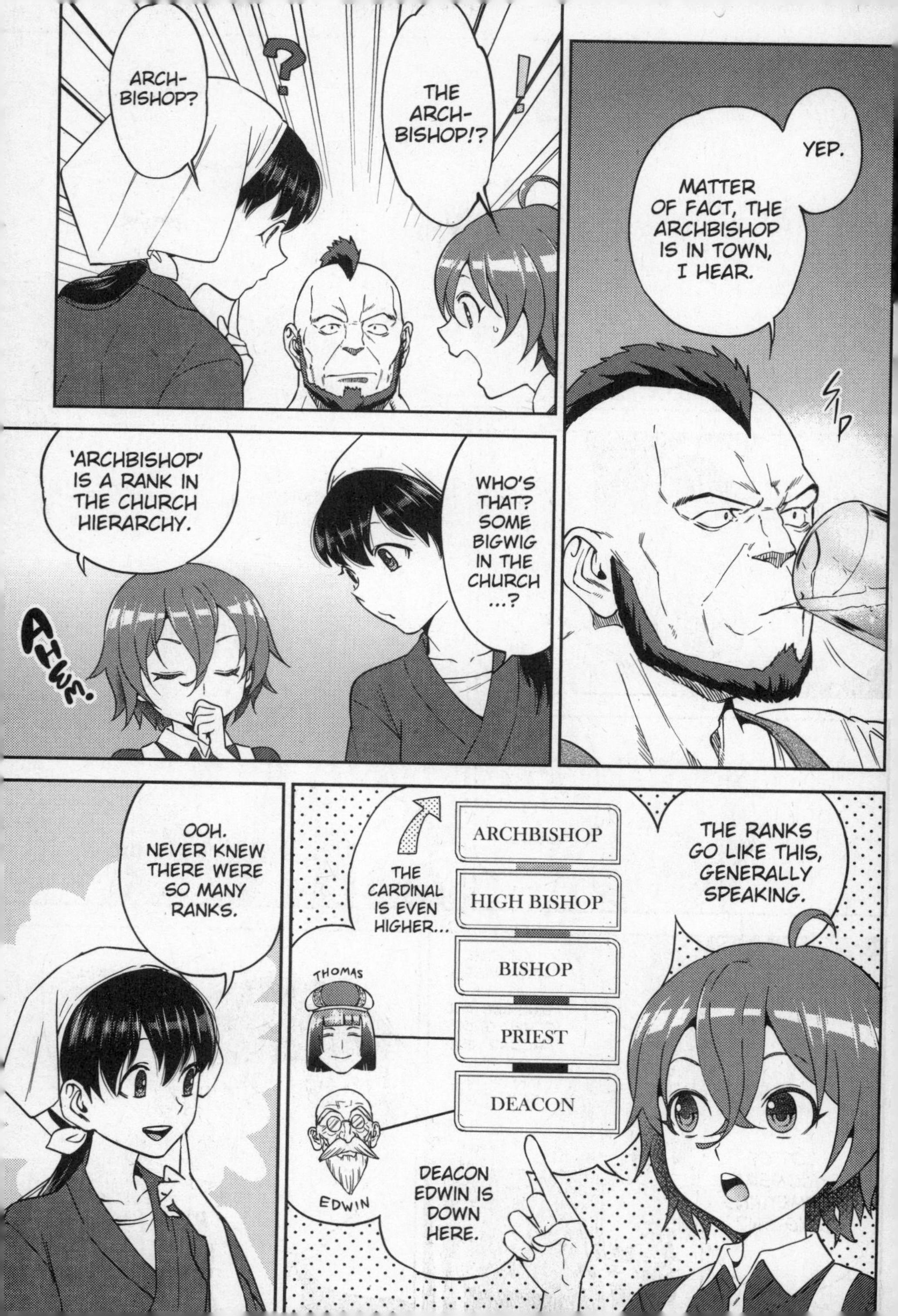
YEP.
MATTER OF FACT, THE ARCHBISHOP IS IN TOWN, I HEAR.
SIP
THE ARCH-BISHOP!?
ARCH-BISHOP?
WHO'S THAT? SOME BIGWIG IN THE CHURCH ...?
'ARCHBISHOP' IS A RANK IN THE CHURCH HIERARCHY.
AHEM!
THE RANKS GO LIKE THIS, GENERALLY SPEAKING.
ARCHBISHOP
HIGH BISHOP
BISHOP
PRIEST
DEACON
THE CARDINAL IS EVEN HIGHER...
THOMAS
EDWIN
DEACON EDWIN IS DOWN HERE.
OOH. NEVER KNEW THERE WERE SO MANY RANKS.

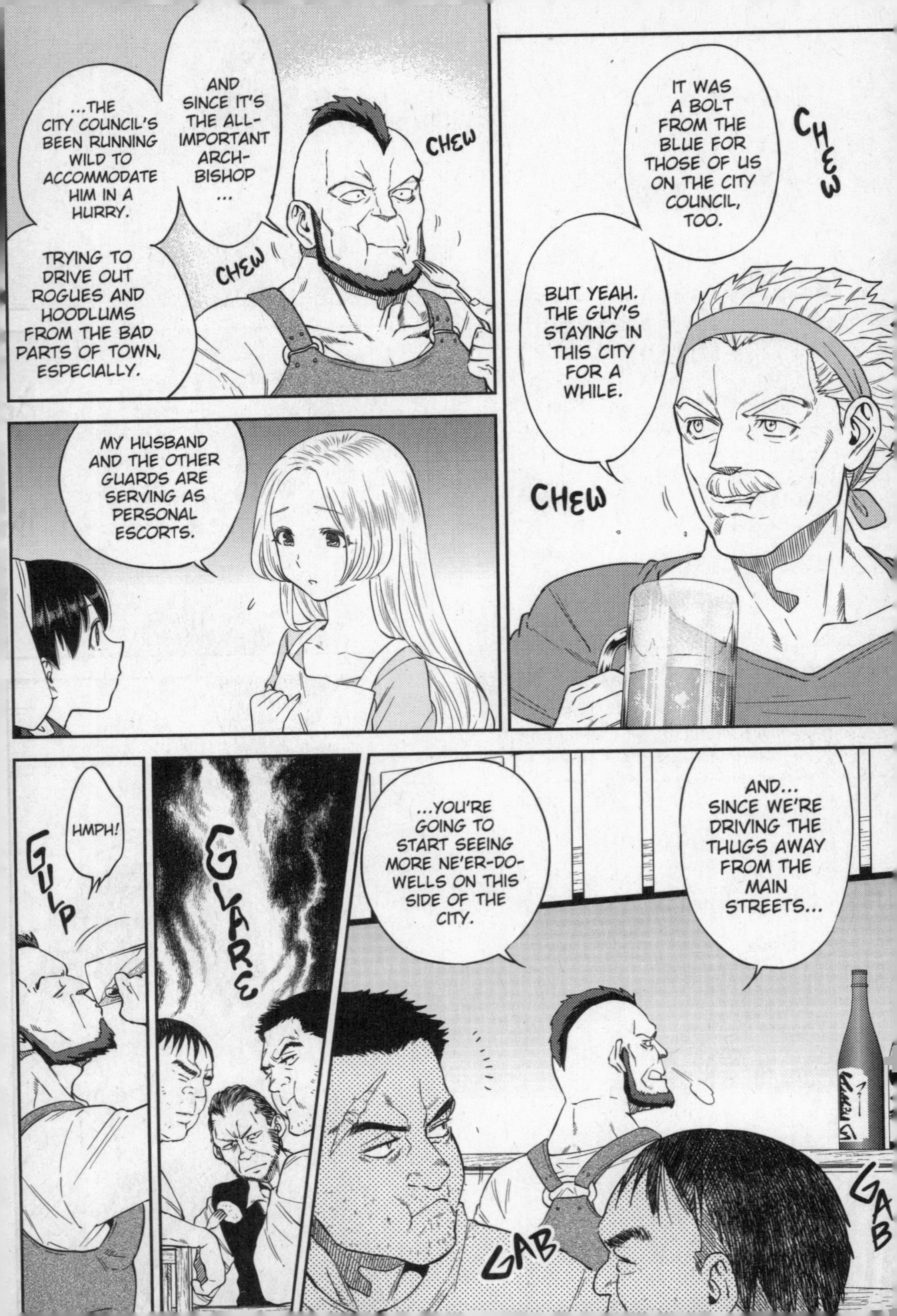
IT WAS A BOLT FROM THE BLUE FOR THOSE OF US ON THE CITY COUNCIL, TOO.
CHEW
BUT YEAH. THE GUY'S STAYING IN THIS CITY FOR A WHILE.
CHEW
AND SINCE IT'S THE ALL-IMPORTANT ARCH-BISHOP ...
CHEW
...THE CITY COUNCIL'S BEEN RUNNING WILD TO ACCOMMODATE HIM IN A HURRY.
TRYING TO DRIVE OUT ROGUES AND HOODLUMS FROM THE BAD PARTS OF TOWN, ESPECIALLY.
CHEW
MY HUSBAND AND THE OTHER GUARDS ARE SERVING AS PERSONAL ESCORTS.
AND... SINCE WE'RE DRIVING THE THUGS AWAY FROM THE MAIN STREETS...
...YOU'RE GOING TO START SEEING MORE NE'ER-DO-WELLS ON THIS SIDE OF THE CITY.
GAB
GAB
GLARE
HMPH!
GULP

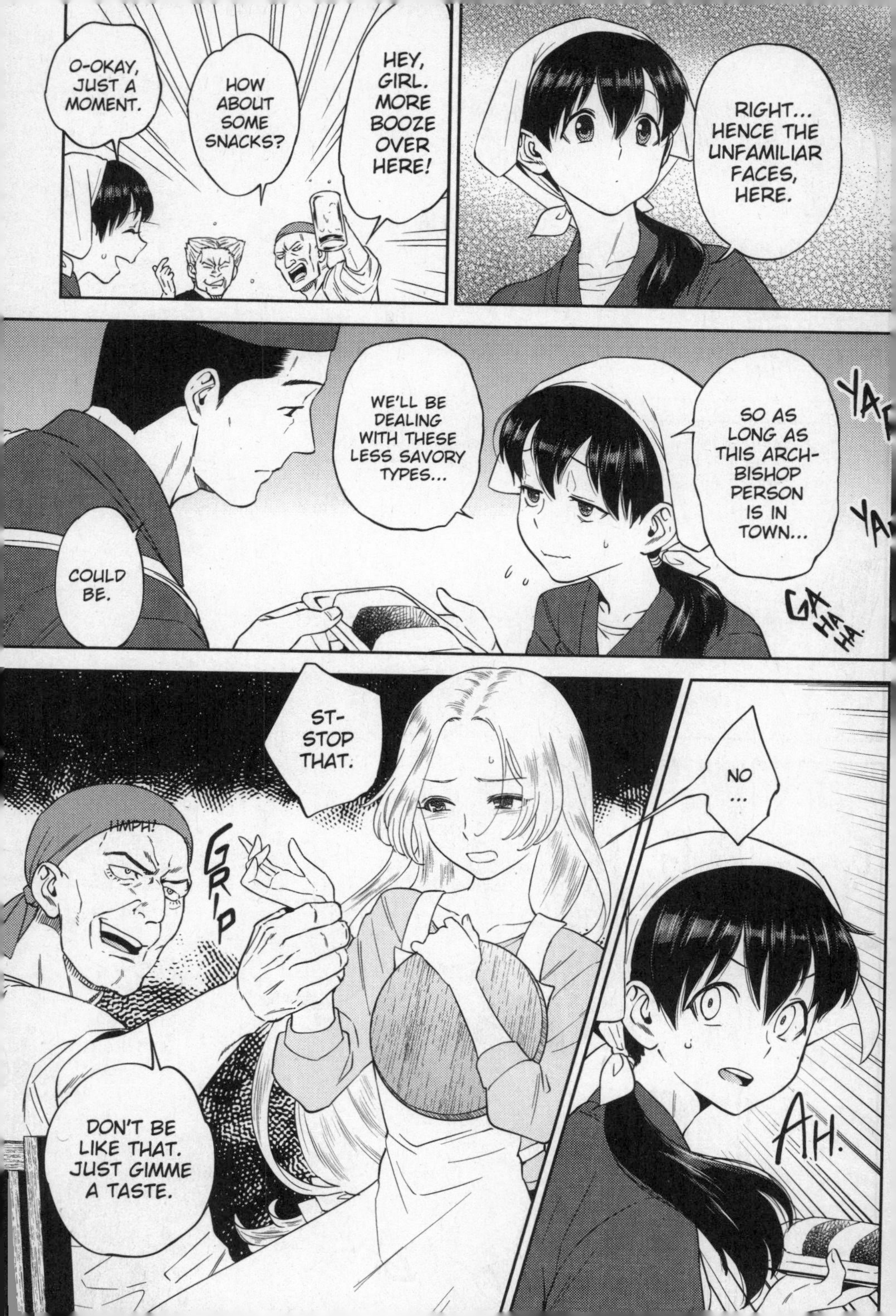
RIGHT... HENCE THE UNFAMILIAR FACES, HERE.
HEY, GIRL. MORE BOOZE OVER HERE!
HOW ABOUT SOME SNACKS?
O-OKAY, JUST A MOMENT.
YA
YA
SO AS LONG AS THIS ARCH-BISHOP PERSON IS IN TOWN...
WE'LL BE DEALING WITH THESE LESS SAVORY TYPES...
COULD BE.
GA HA HA.
NO ...
AH.
ST- STOP THAT.
HMPH!
GRIP
DON'T BE LIKE THAT. JUST GIMME A TASTE.

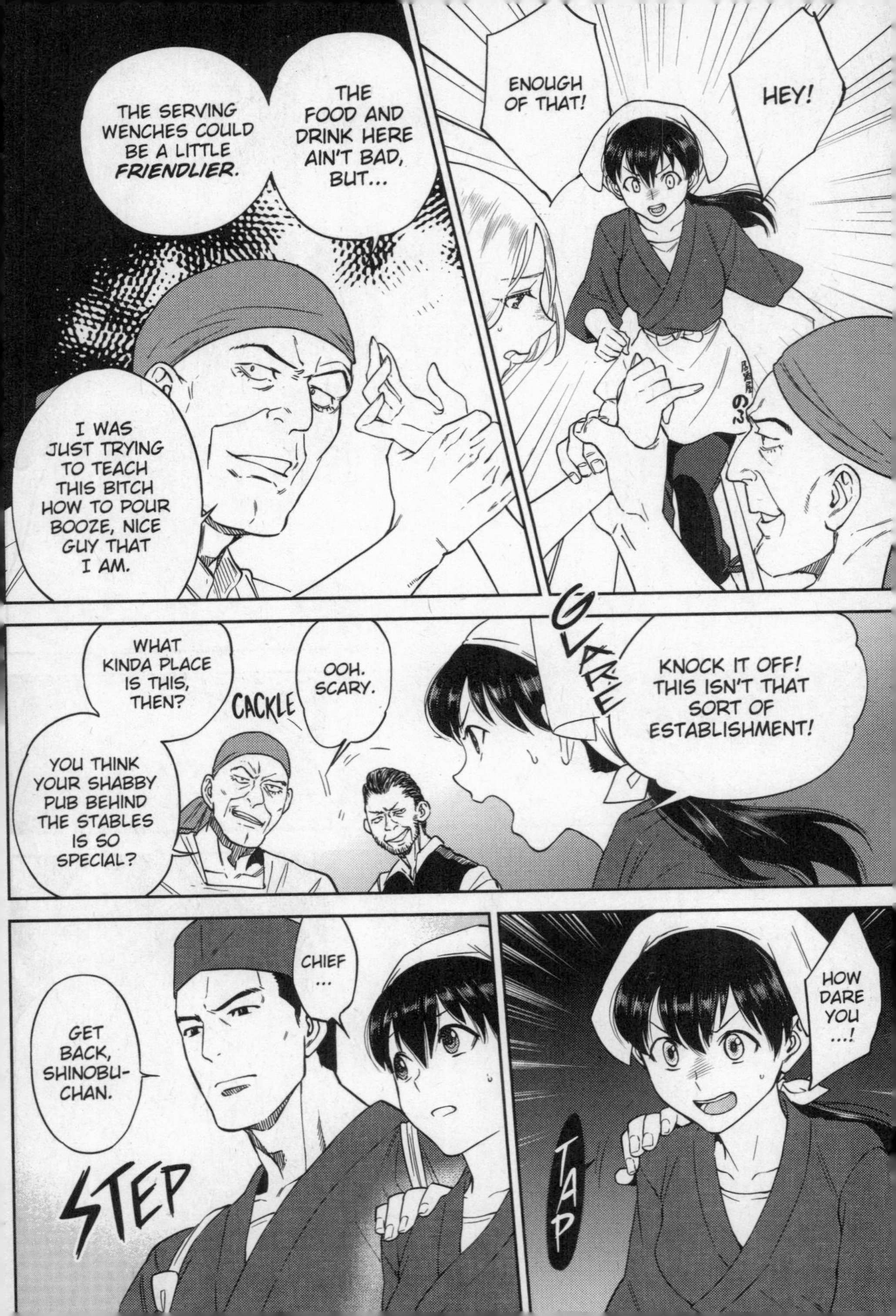
HEY!
ENOUGH OF THAT!
THE FOOD AND DRINK HERE AIN'T BAD, BUT...
THE SERVING WENCHES COULD BE A LITTLE *FRIENDLIER*.
I WAS JUST TRYING TO TEACH THIS BITCH HOW TO POUR BOOZE, NICE GUY THAT I AM.
GLARE
KNOCK IT OFF! THIS ISN'T THAT SORT OF ESTABLISHMENT!
OOH. SCARY.
WHAT KINDA PLACE IS THIS, THEN?
CACKLE
YOU THINK YOUR SHABBY PUB BEHIND THE STABLES IS SO SPECIAL?
HOW DARE YOU ...!
TAP
CHIEF ...
GET BACK, SHINOBU-CHAN.
STEP

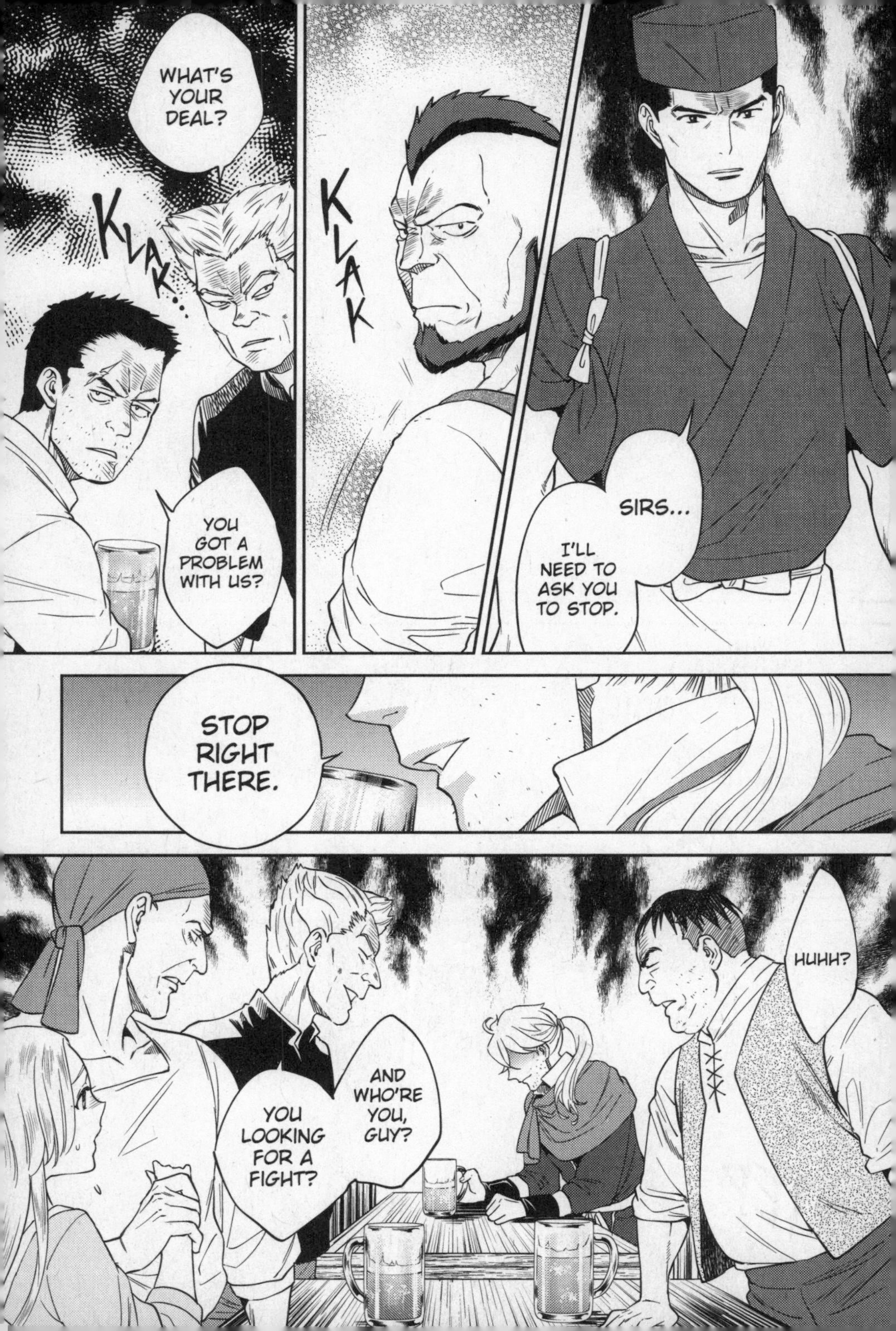
SIRS...
I'LL NEED TO ASK YOU TO STOP.
KLAK
WHAT'S YOUR DEAL?
KLAK...
YOU GOT A PROBLEM WITH US?
STOP RIGHT THERE.
HUHH?
AND WHO'RE YOU, GUY?
YOU LOOKING FOR A FIGHT?

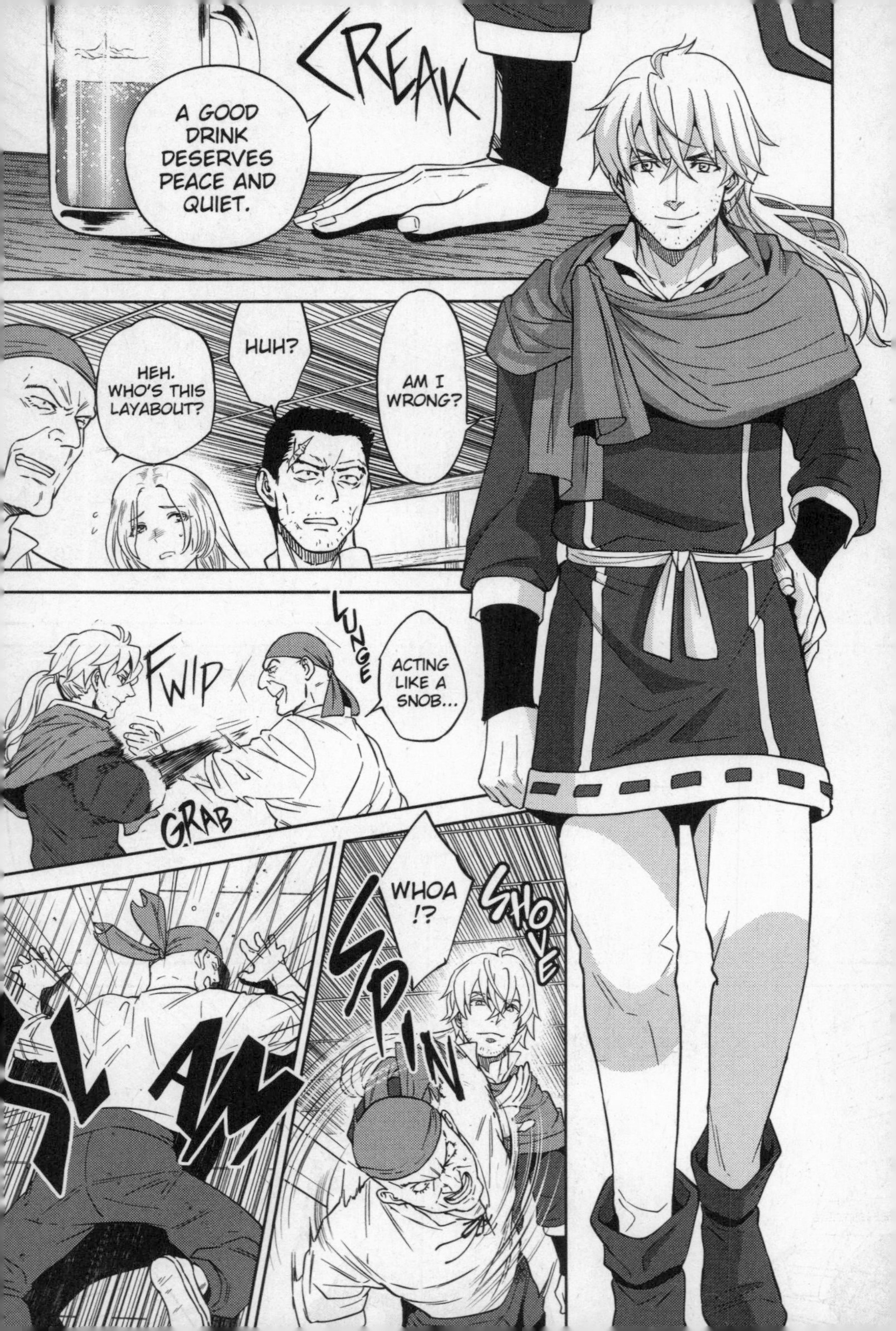
CREAK
A GOOD DRINK DESERVES PEACE AND QUIET.
AM I WRONG?
HUH?
HEH. WHO'S THIS LAYABOUT?
ACTING LIKE A SNOB...
LUNGE
FWIP
GRAB
SHOVE
WHOA !?
SPIN
SLAM

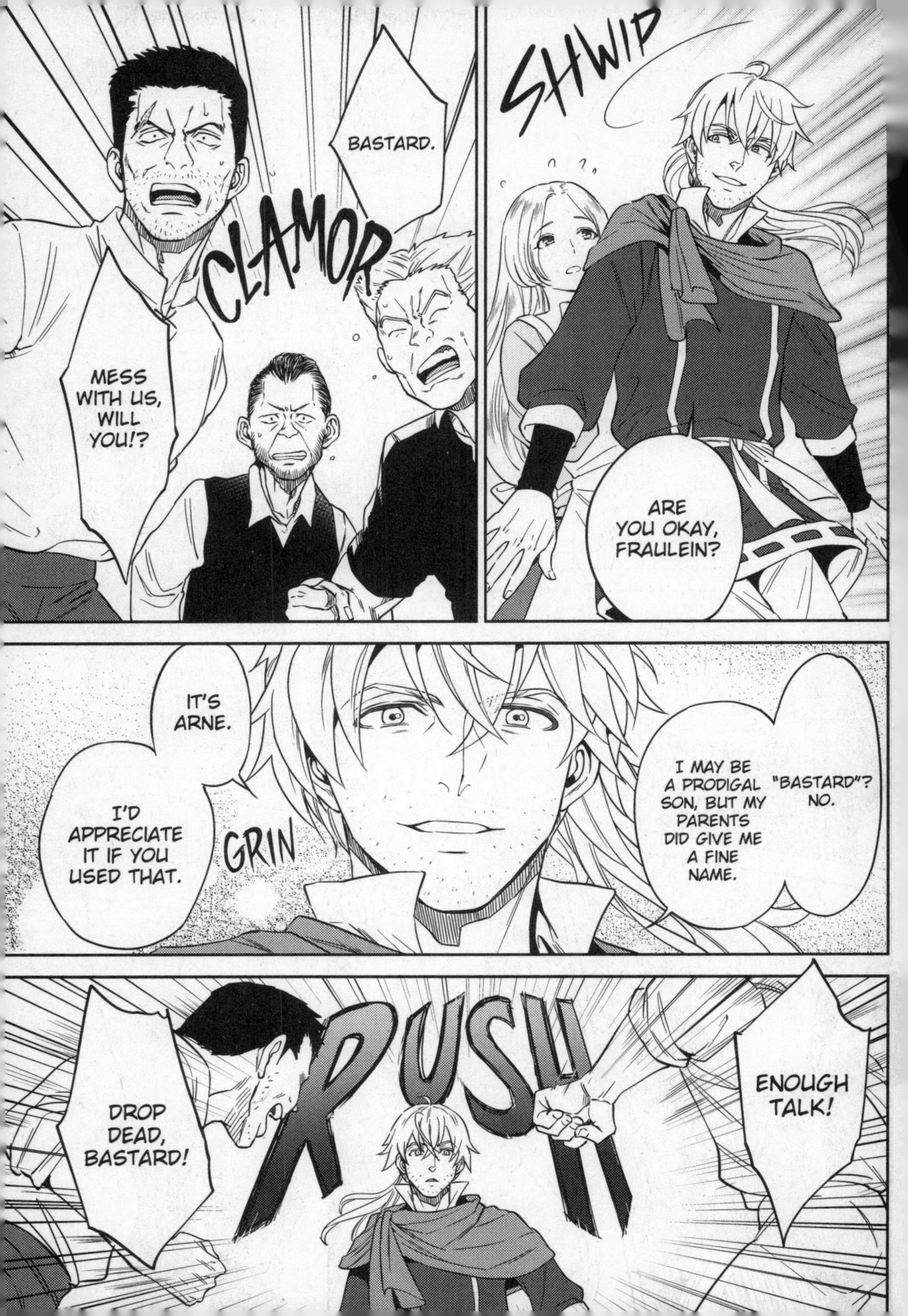
SHWIP
ARE YOU OKAY, FRAULEIN?
BASTARD.
CLAMOR
MESS WITH US, WILL YOU!?
"BASTARD"? NO.
I MAY BE A PRODIGAL SON, BUT MY PARENTS DID GIVE ME A FINE NAME.
IT'S ARNE.
GRIN
I'D APPRECIATE IT IF YOU USED THAT.
ENOUGH TALK!
PUSH
DROP DEAD, BASTARD!

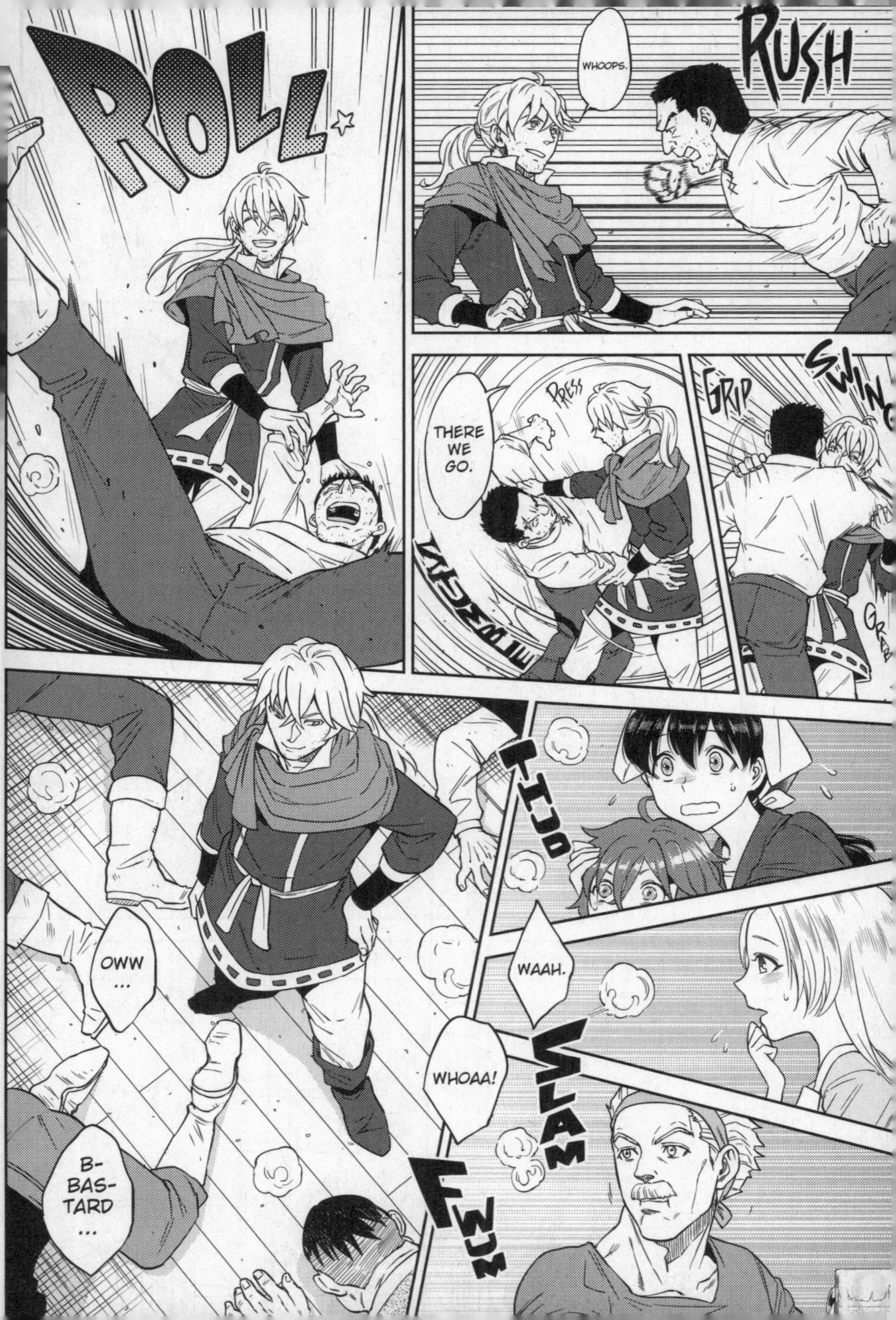

RUSH
WHOOPS.
SWING
GRIP
GRAB
PRESS
THERE WE GO.
ROLL
THUD
WAAH.
WHOAA!
SLAM
FWUM
OWW ...
B-BAS-TARD ...

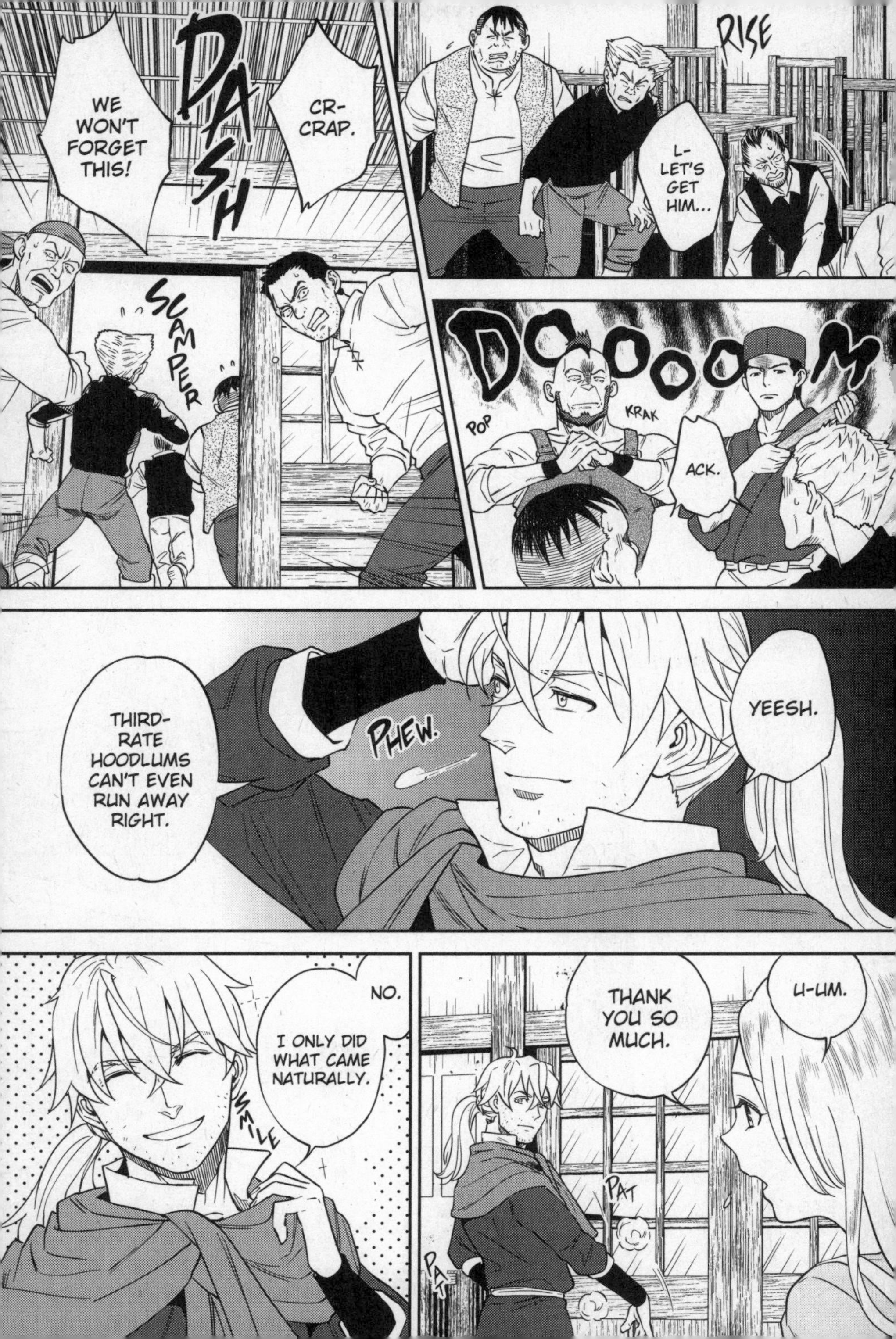
RISE
L-LET'S GET HIM...
DOOOOOM
KRAK
POP
ACK.
CR-CRAP.
WE WON'T FORGET THIS!
DASH
SCAMPER
YEESH.
PHEW.
THIRD-RATE HOODLUMS CAN'T EVEN RUN AWAY RIGHT.
U-UM.
THANK YOU SO MUCH.
PAT
PAT
NO.
I ONLY DID WHAT CAME NATURALLY.
SMILE

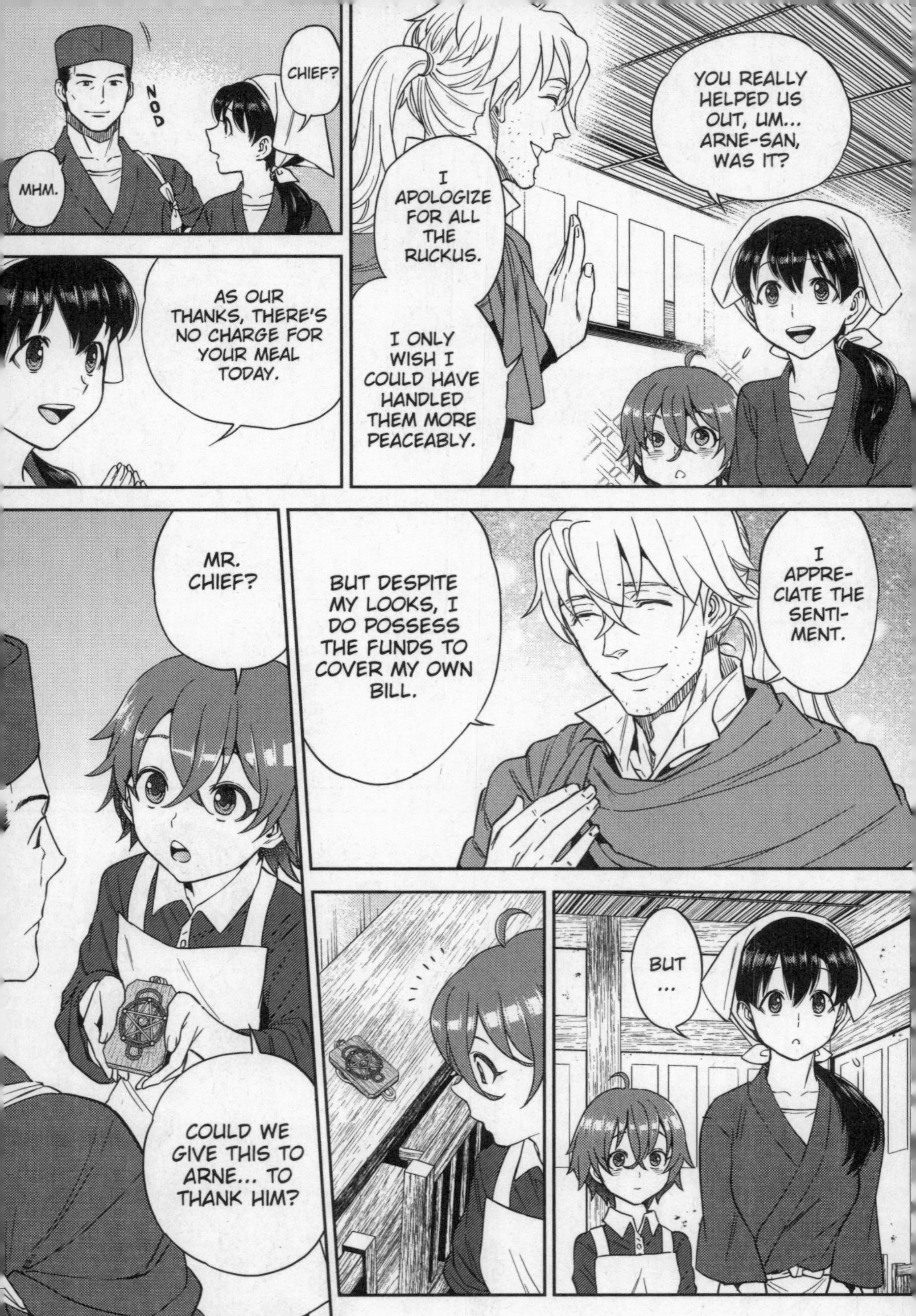
YOU REALLY HELPED US OUT, UM... ARNE-SAN, WAS IT?
I APOLOGIZE FOR ALL THE RUCKUS.
I ONLY WISH I COULD HAVE HANDLED THEM MORE PEACEABLY.
CHIEF?
NOD
MHM.
AS OUR THANKS, THERE'S NO CHARGE FOR YOUR MEAL TODAY.
I APPRECIATE THE SENTIMENT.
BUT DESPITE MY LOOKS, I DO POSSESS THE FUNDS TO COVER MY OWN BILL.
BUT ...
MR. CHIEF?
COULD WE GIVE THIS TO ARNE... TO THANK HIM?

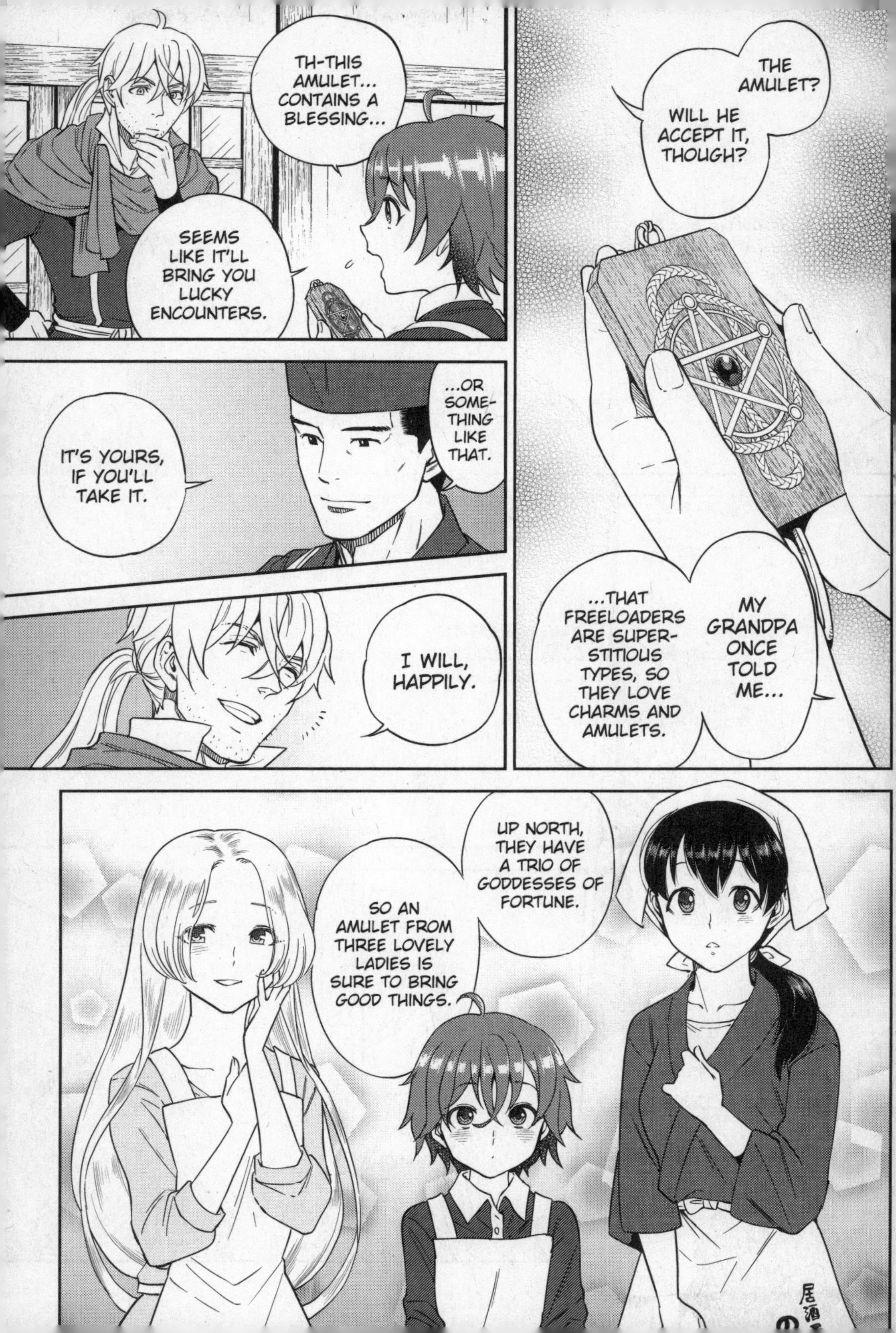
THE AMULET?
WILL HE ACCEPT IT, THOUGH?
MY GRANDPA ONCE TOLD ME...
...THAT FREELOADERS ARE SUPER-STITIOUS TYPES, SO THEY LOVE CHARMS AND AMULETS.
TH-THIS AMULET... CONTAINS A BLESSING...
SEEMS LIKE IT'LL BRING YOU LUCKY ENCOUNTERS.
...OR SOME-THING LIKE THAT.
IT'S YOURS, IF YOU'LL TAKE IT.
I WILL, HAPPILY.
UP NORTH, THEY HAVE A TRIO OF GODDESSES OF FORTUNE.
SO AN AMULET FROM THREE LOVELY LADIES IS SURE TO BRING GOOD THINGS.

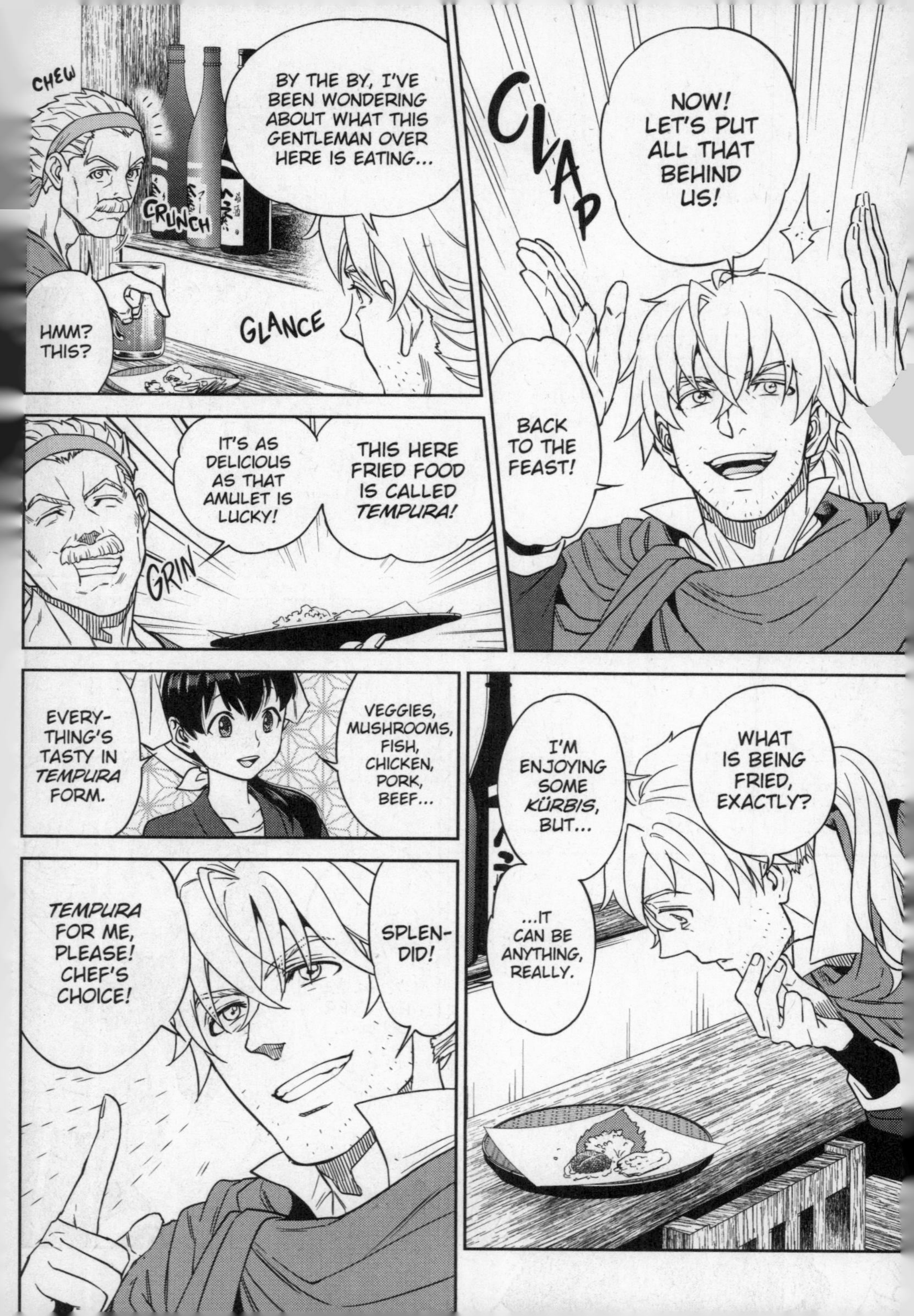
CLAP
NOW! LET'S PUT ALL THAT BEHIND US!
BACK TO THE FEAST!
BY THE BY, I'VE BEEN WONDERING ABOUT WHAT THIS GENTLEMAN OVER HERE IS EATING...
CHEW
CRUNCH
GLANCE
HMM? THIS?
THIS HERE FRIED FOOD IS CALLED *TEMPURA!*
IT'S AS DELICIOUS AS THAT AMULET IS LUCKY!
GRIN
WHAT IS BEING FRIED, EXACTLY?
I'M ENJOYING SOME *KÜRBIS,* BUT...
...IT CAN BE ANYTHING, REALLY.
VEGGIES, MUSHROOMS, FISH, CHICKEN, PORK, BEEF...
EVERY-THING'S TASTY IN *TEMPURA* FORM.
SPLEN-DID!
TEMPURA FOR ME, PLEASE! CHEF'S CHOICE!

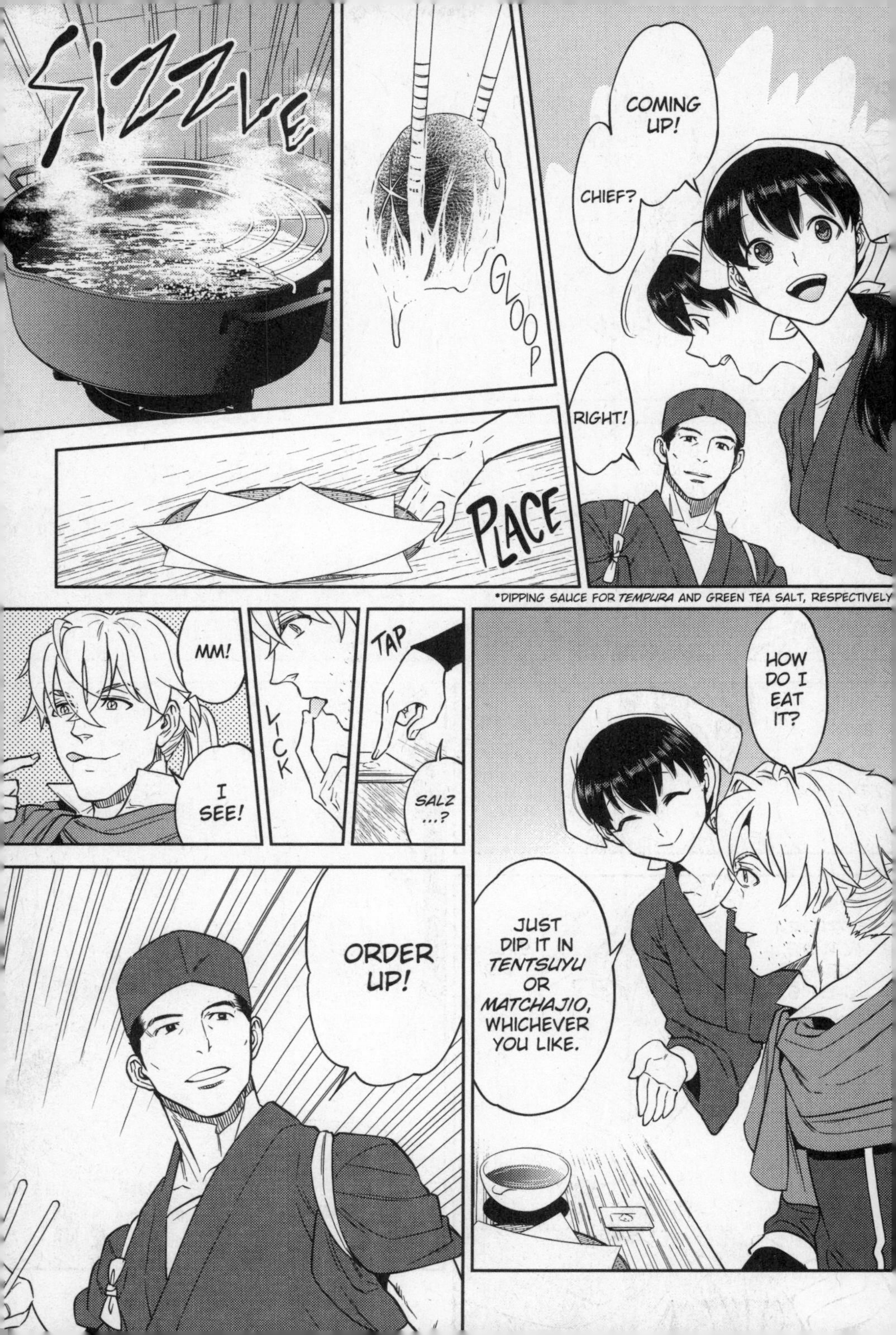
COMING UP!
CHIEF?
RIGHT!
GLOOP
SIZZLE
PLACE
HOW DO I EAT IT?
JUST DIP IT IN *TENTSUYU* OR *MATCHAJIO*, WHICHEVER YOU LIKE.
TAP
SALZ ...?
LICK
MM!
I SEE!
ORDER UP!

*DIPPING SAUCE FOR *TEMPURA* AND GREEN TEA SALT, RESPECTIVELY

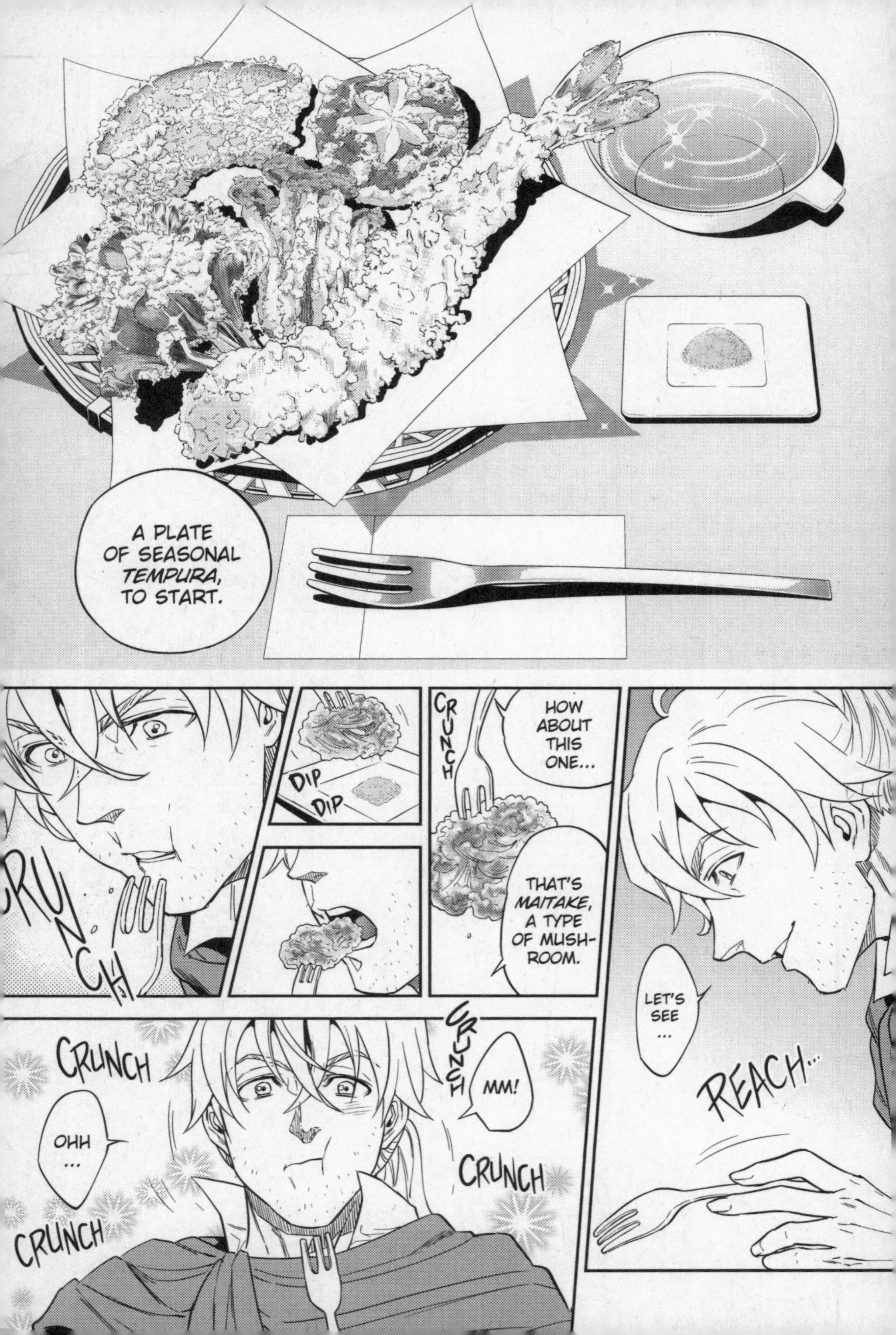

A PLATE OF SEASONAL *TEMPURA*, TO START.
LET'S SEE ...
REACH...
HOW ABOUT THIS ONE...
CRUNCH
THAT'S *MAITAKE*, A TYPE OF MUSH-ROOM.
DIP
DIP
CRUNCH
CRUNCH
MM!
CRUNCH
CRUNCH
OHH ...
CRUNCH

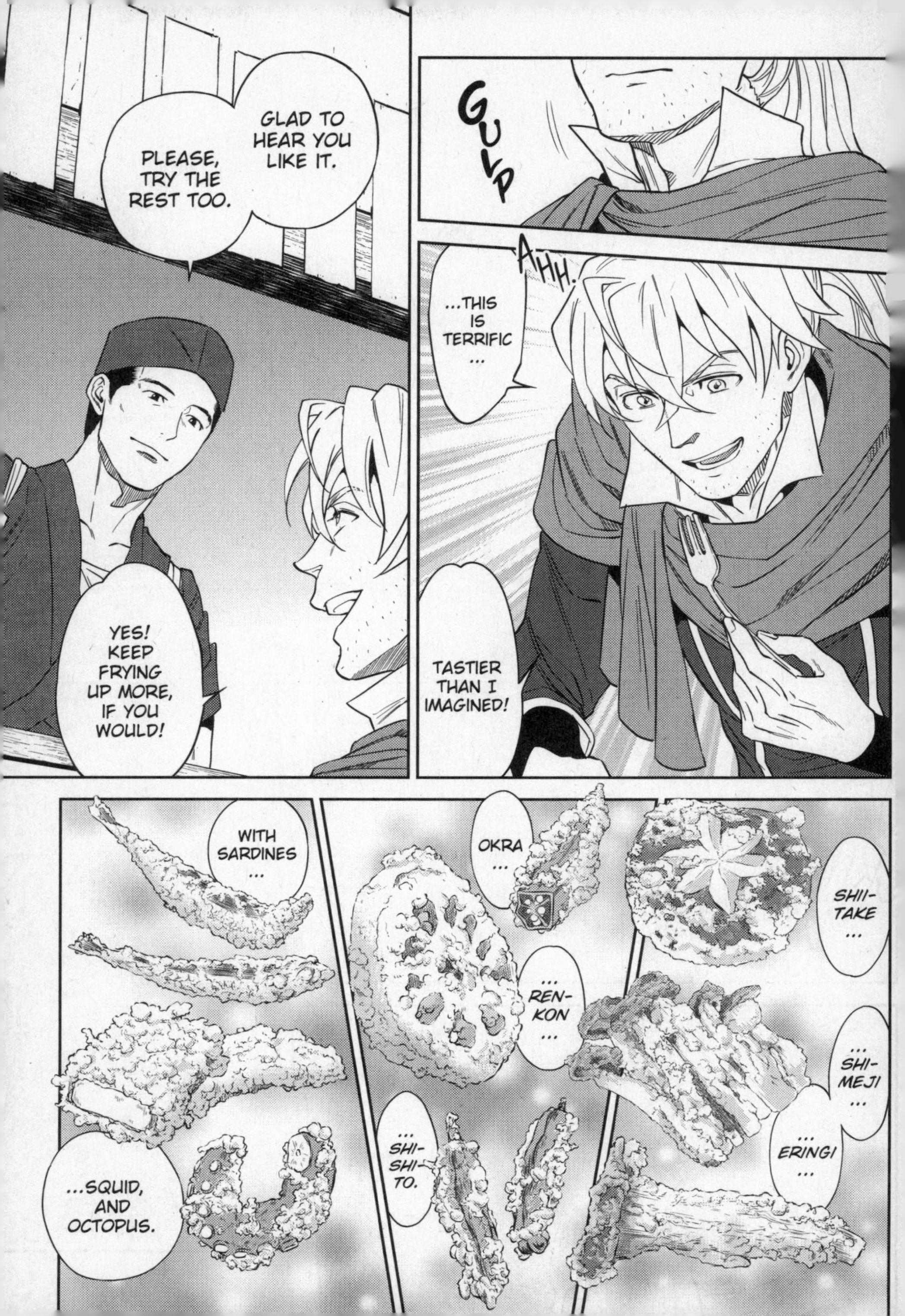
GULP
AHH.
...THIS IS TERRIFIC ...
TASTIER THAN I IMAGINED!
GLAD TO HEAR YOU LIKE IT.
PLEASE, TRY THE REST TOO.
YES! KEEP FRYING UP MORE, IF YOU WOULD!
SHII-TAKE ...
... SHI-MEJI ...
... ERINGI ...
OKRA ...
... REN-KON ...
... SHI-SHI-TO.
WITH SARDINES ...
...SQUID, AND OCTOPUS.

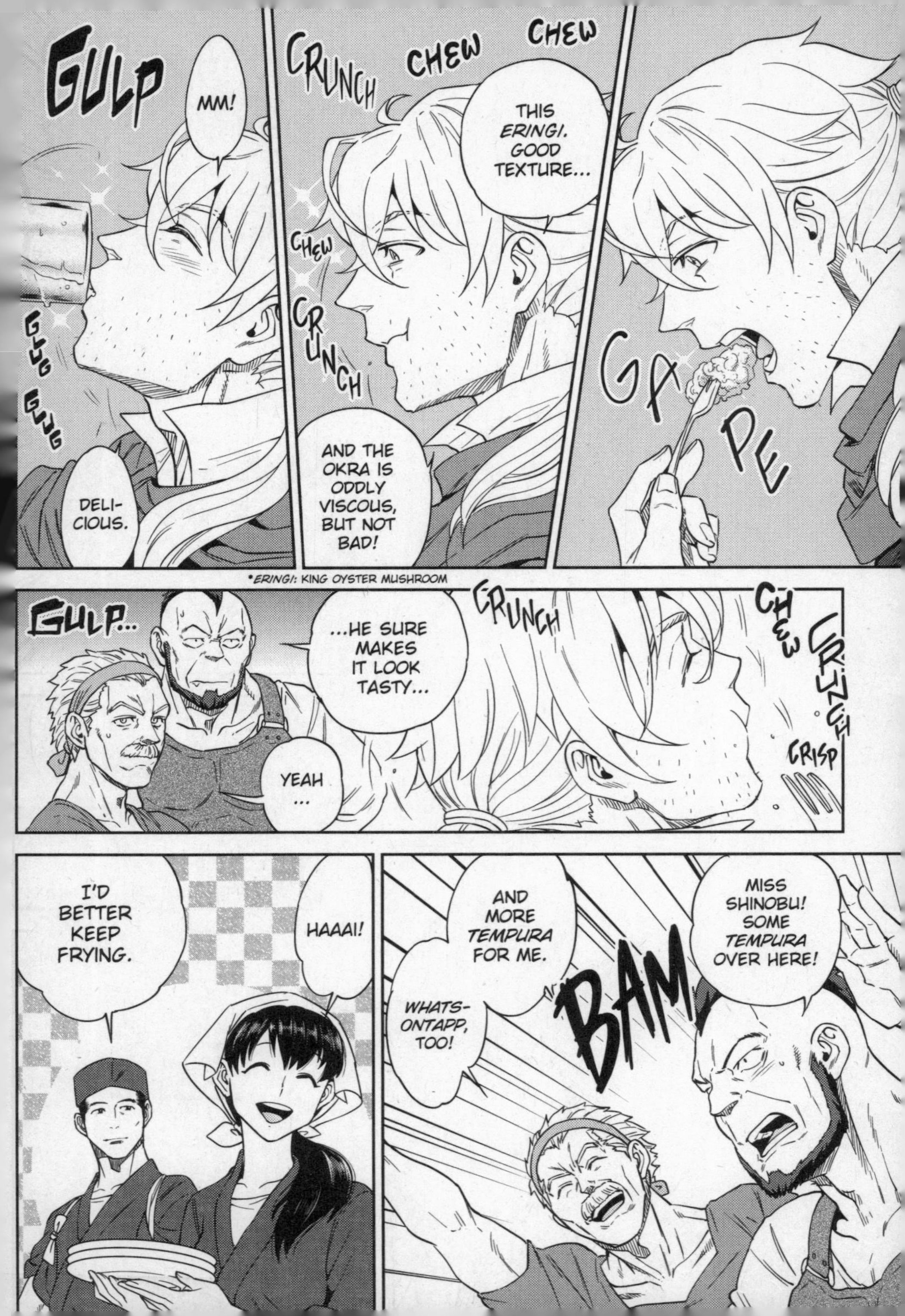
GAPE
CHEW
CRUNCH
THIS ERINGI. GOOD TEXTURE...
CHEW
CRUNCH
AND THE OKRA IS ODDLY VISCOUS, BUT NOT BAD!
GULP
MM!
GLUG GLUG
DELI-CIOUS.
*ERINGI: KING OYSTER MUSHROOM
CHEW CRUNCH
CRISP
CRUNCH
...HE SURE MAKES IT LOOK TASTY...
YEAH ...
GULP...
MISS SHINOBU! SOME TEMPURA OVER HERE!
BAM
AND MORE TEMPURA FOR ME.
WHATS-ONTAPP, TOO!
HAAAI!
I'D BETTER KEEP FRYING.

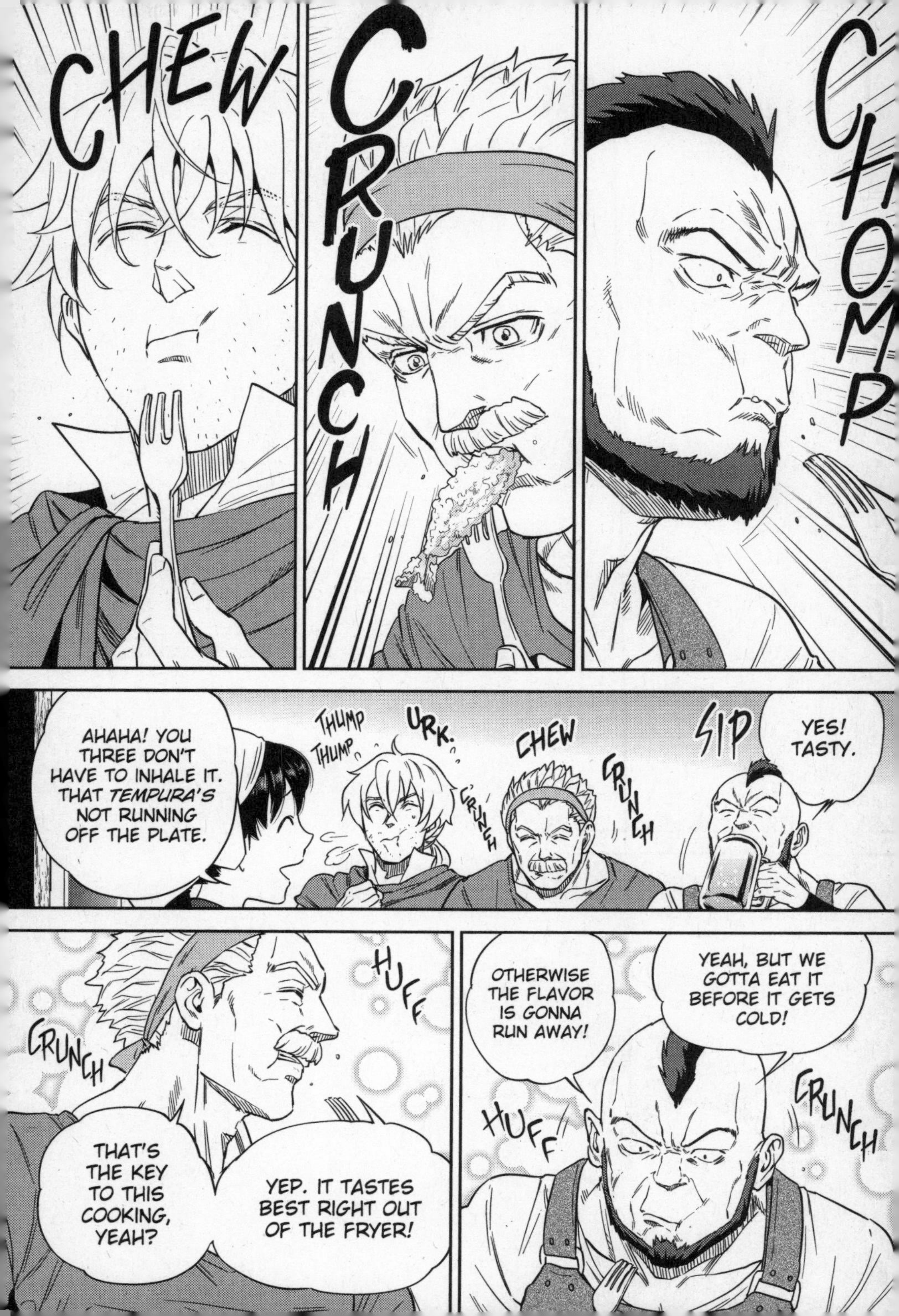
CHOMP
CRUNCH
CHEW
YES! TASTY.
SIP
CRUNCH
CHEW
CRUNCH
URK.
THUMP THUMP
AHAHA! YOU THREE DON'T HAVE TO INHALE IT. THAT *TEMPURA'S* NOT RUNNING OFF THE PLATE.
YEAH, BUT WE GOTTA EAT IT BEFORE IT GETS COLD!
OTHERWISE THE FLAVOR IS GONNA RUN AWAY!
CRUNCH
HUFF
HUFF
CRUNCH
YEP. IT TASTES BEST RIGHT OUT OF THE FRYER!
THAT'S THE KEY TO THIS COOKING, YEAH?

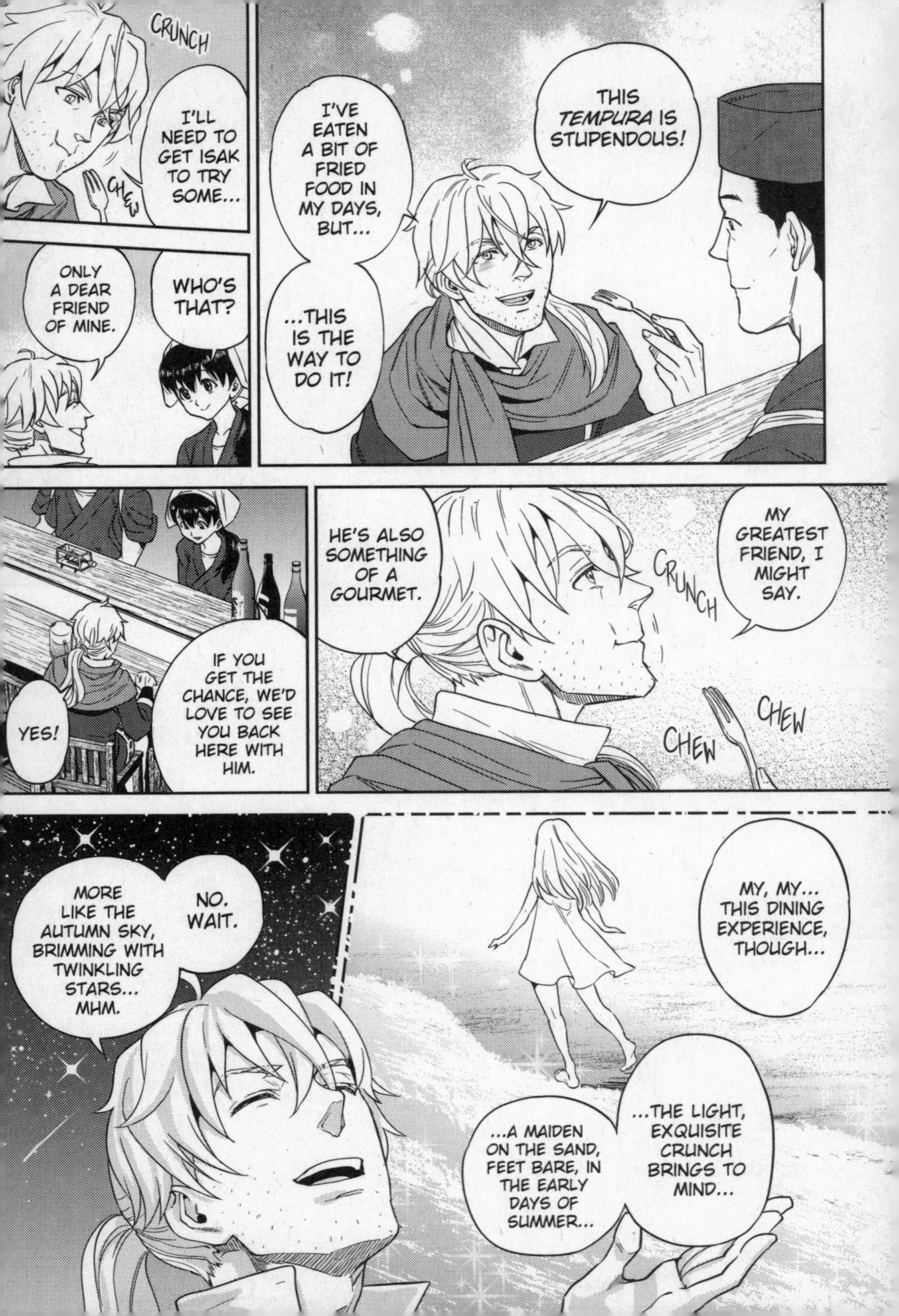
THIS *TEMPURA* IS STUPENDOUS!
I'VE EATEN A BIT OF FRIED FOOD IN MY DAYS, BUT...
...THIS IS THE WAY TO DO IT!
CRUNCH
I'LL NEED TO GET ISAK TO TRY SOME...
CHEW
WHO'S THAT?
ONLY A DEAR FRIEND OF MINE.
MY GREATEST FRIEND, I MIGHT SAY.
CRUNCH
HE'S ALSO SOMETHING OF A GOURMET.
CHEW
CHEW
IF YOU GET THE CHANCE, WE'D LOVE TO SEE YOU BACK HERE WITH HIM.
YES!
MY, MY... THIS DINING EXPERIENCE, THOUGH...
...THE LIGHT, EXQUISITE CRUNCH BRINGS TO MIND...
...A MAIDEN ON THE SAND, FEET BARE, IN THE EARLY DAYS OF SUMMER...
NO. WAIT.
MORE LIKE THE AUTUMN SKY, BRIMMING WITH TWINKLING STARS... MHM.

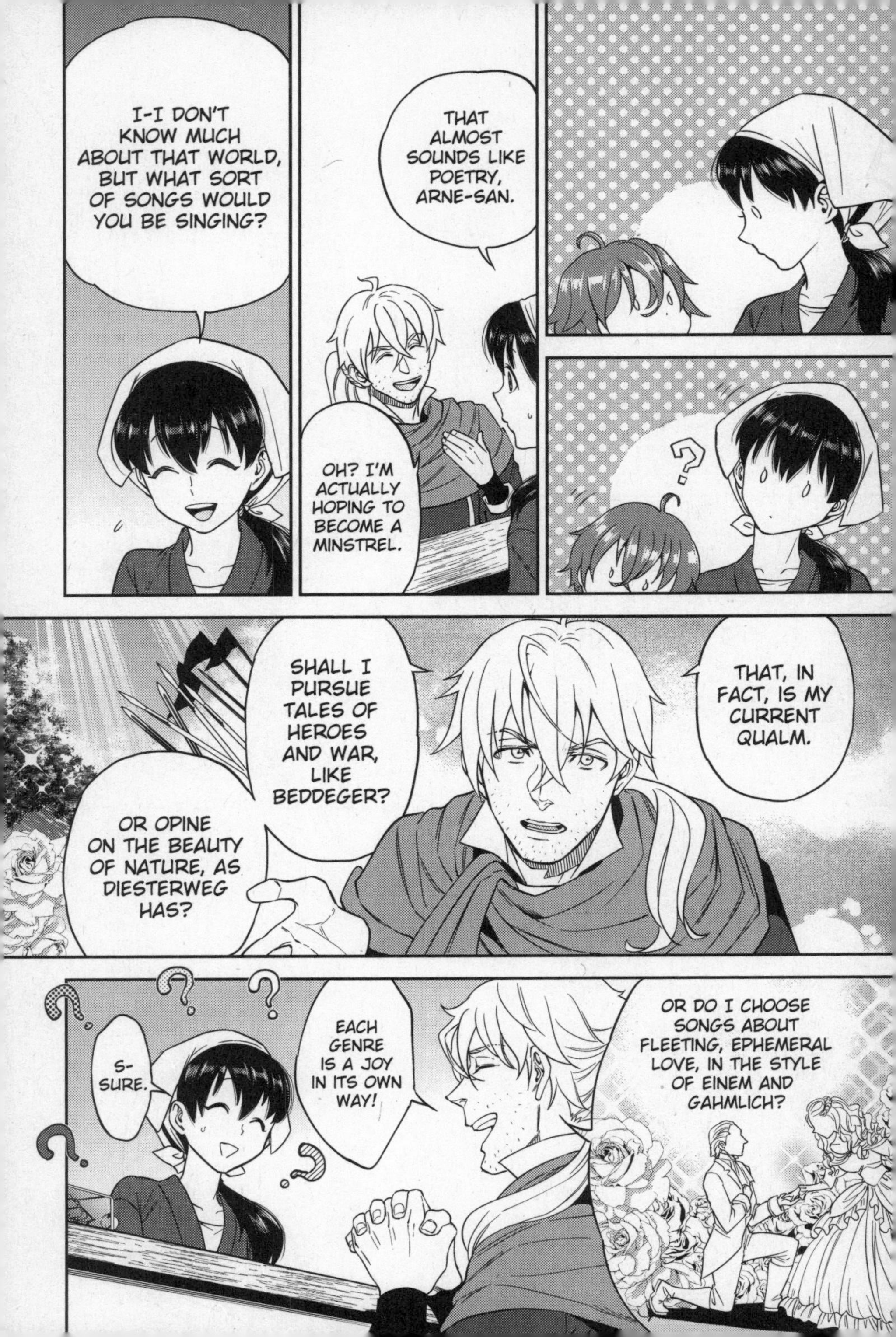
THAT ALMOST SOUNDS LIKE POETRY, ARNE-SAN.
OH? I'M ACTUALLY HOPING TO BECOME A MINSTREL.
I-I DON'T KNOW MUCH ABOUT THAT WORLD, BUT WHAT SORT OF SONGS WOULD YOU BE SINGING?
THAT, IN FACT, IS MY CURRENT QUALM.
SHALL I PURSUE TALES OF HEROES AND WAR, LIKE BEDDEGER?
OR OPINE ON THE BEAUTY OF NATURE, AS DIESTERWEG HAS?
OR DO I CHOOSE SONGS ABOUT FLEETING, EPHEMERAL LOVE, IN THE STYLE OF EINEM AND GAHMLICH?
EACH GENRE IS A JOY IN ITS OWN WAY!
S-SURE.

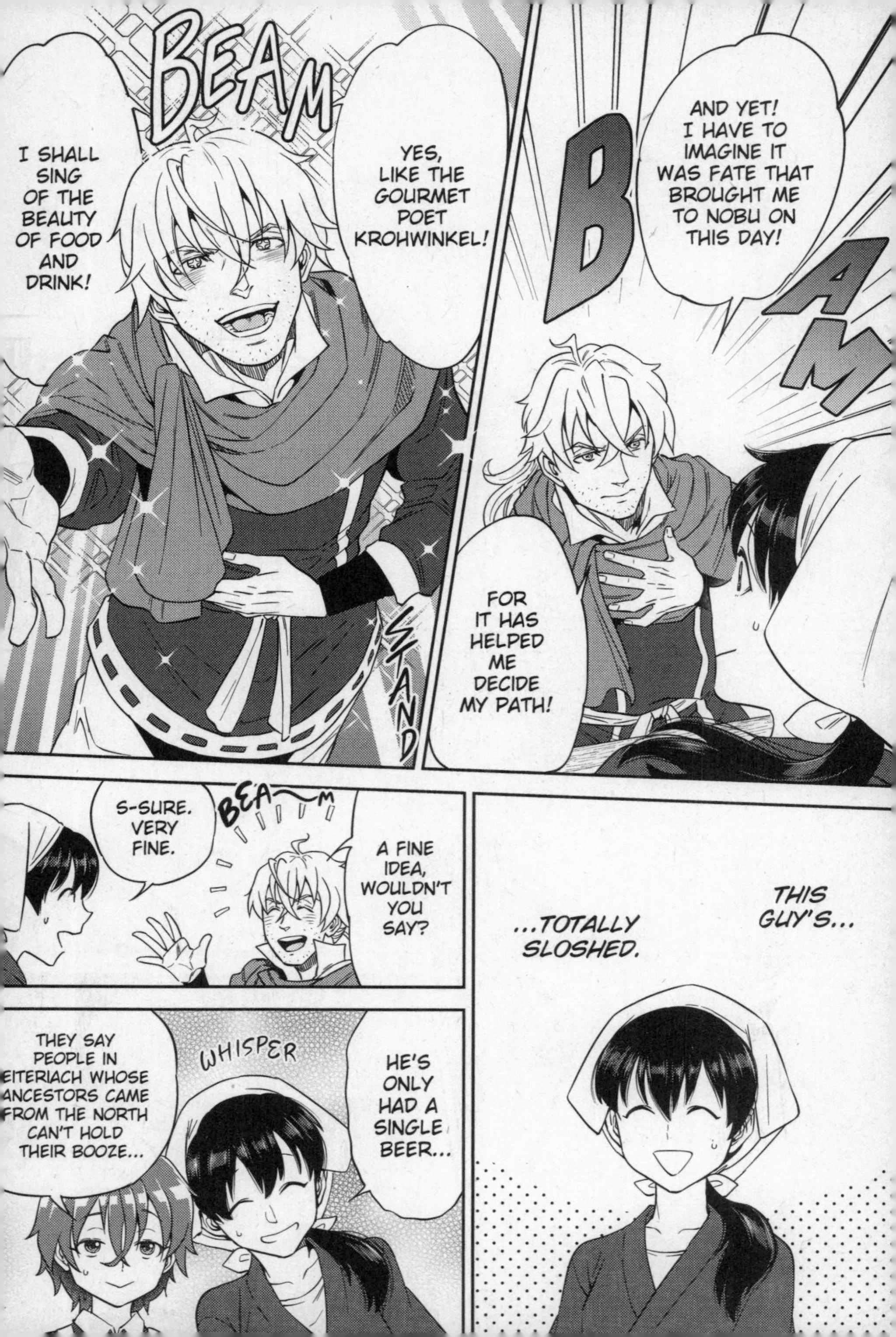

AND YET! I HAVE TO IMAGINE IT WAS FATE THAT BROUGHT ME TO NOBU ON THIS DAY!
BAM
FOR IT HAS HELPED ME DECIDE MY PATH!
YES, LIKE THE GOURMET POET KROHWINKEL!
BEAM
I SHALL SING OF THE BEAUTY OF FOOD AND DRINK!
STAND
THIS GUY'S...
...TOTALLY SLOSHED.
A FINE IDEA, WOULDN'T YOU SAY?
BEA~M
S-SURE. VERY FINE.
HE'S ONLY HAD A SINGLE BEER...
WHISPER
THEY SAY PEOPLE IN EITERIACH WHOSE ANCESTORS CAME FROM THE NORTH CAN'T HOLD THEIR BOOZE...

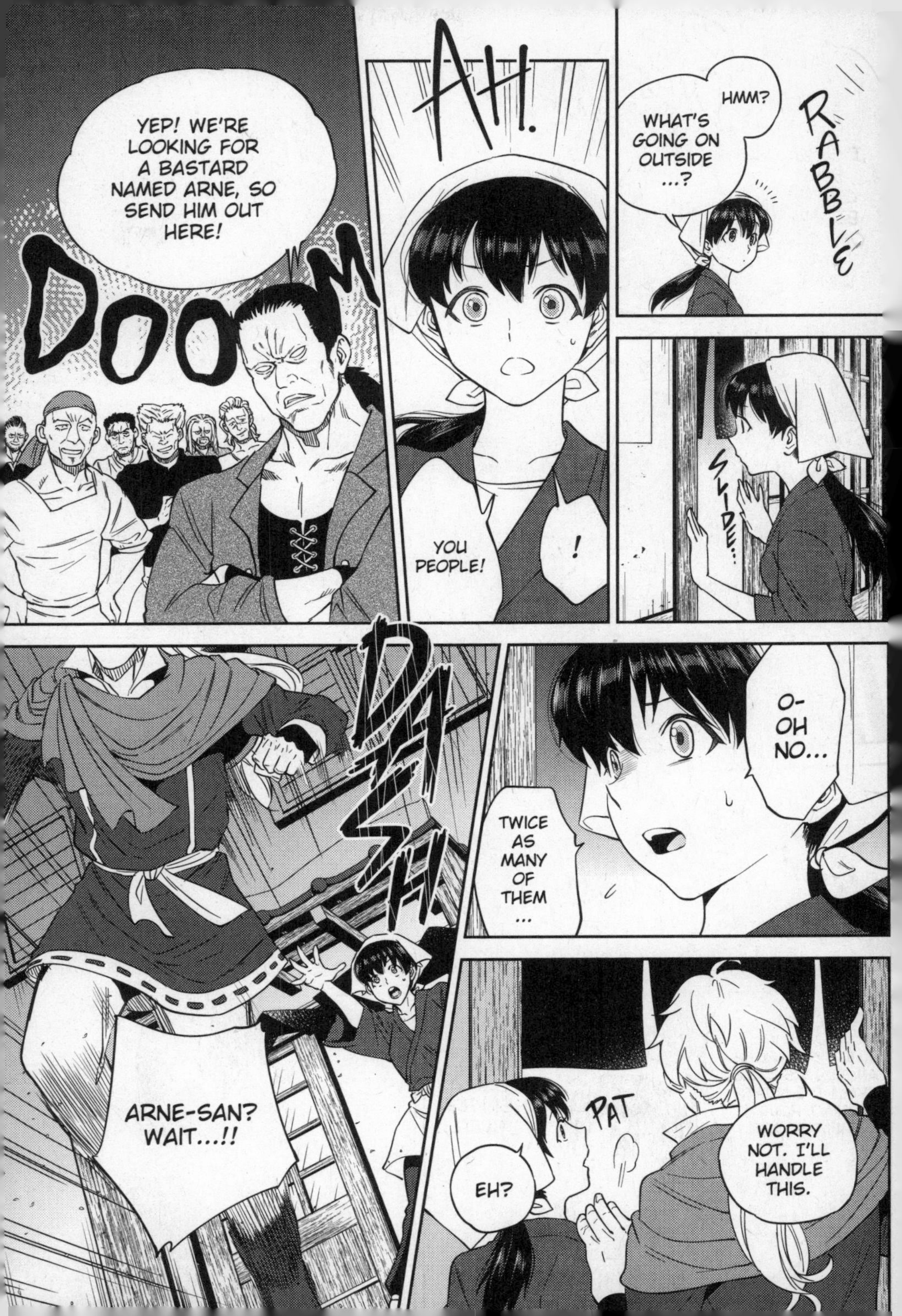
HMM?
WHAT'S GOING ON OUTSIDE ...?
RABBLE
SLIDE...
AH.
!
YOU PEOPLE!
YEP! WE'RE LOOKING FOR A BASTARD NAMED ARNE, SO SEND HIM OUT HERE!
DOOM
O-OH NO...
TWICE AS MANY OF THEM ...
WORRY NOT. I'LL HANDLE THIS.
PAT
EH?
DASH!
ARNE-SAN? WAIT...!!

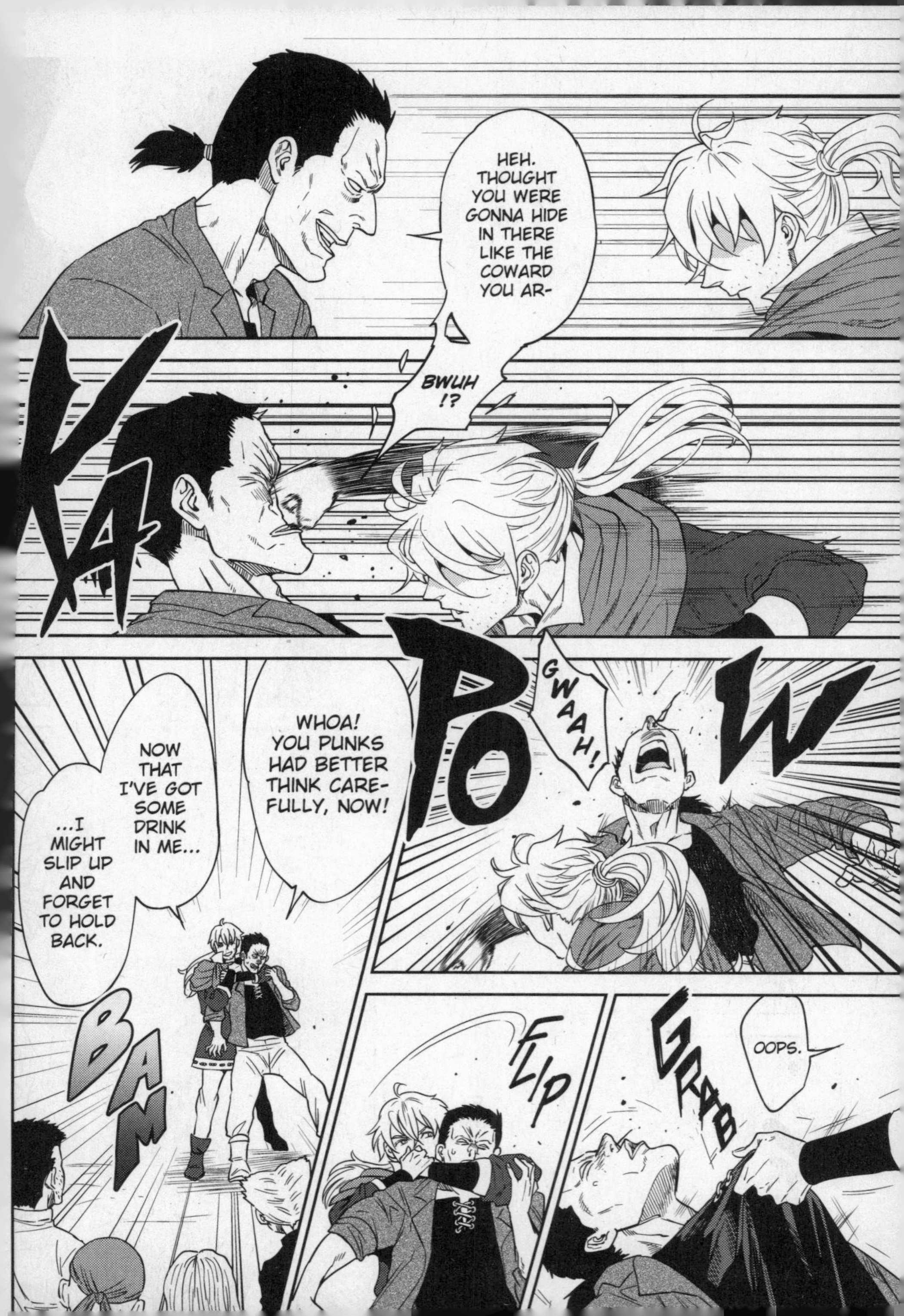
HEH. THOUGHT YOU WERE GONNA HIDE IN THERE LIKE THE COWARD YOU AR-
BWUH !?
KA
GWAAH!!
POW
OOPS.
GRAB
FLIP
WHOA! YOU PUNKS HAD BETTER THINK CARE-FULLY, NOW!
NOW THAT I'VE GOT SOME DRINK IN ME...
...I MIGHT SLIP UP AND FORGET TO HOLD BACK.
BAM

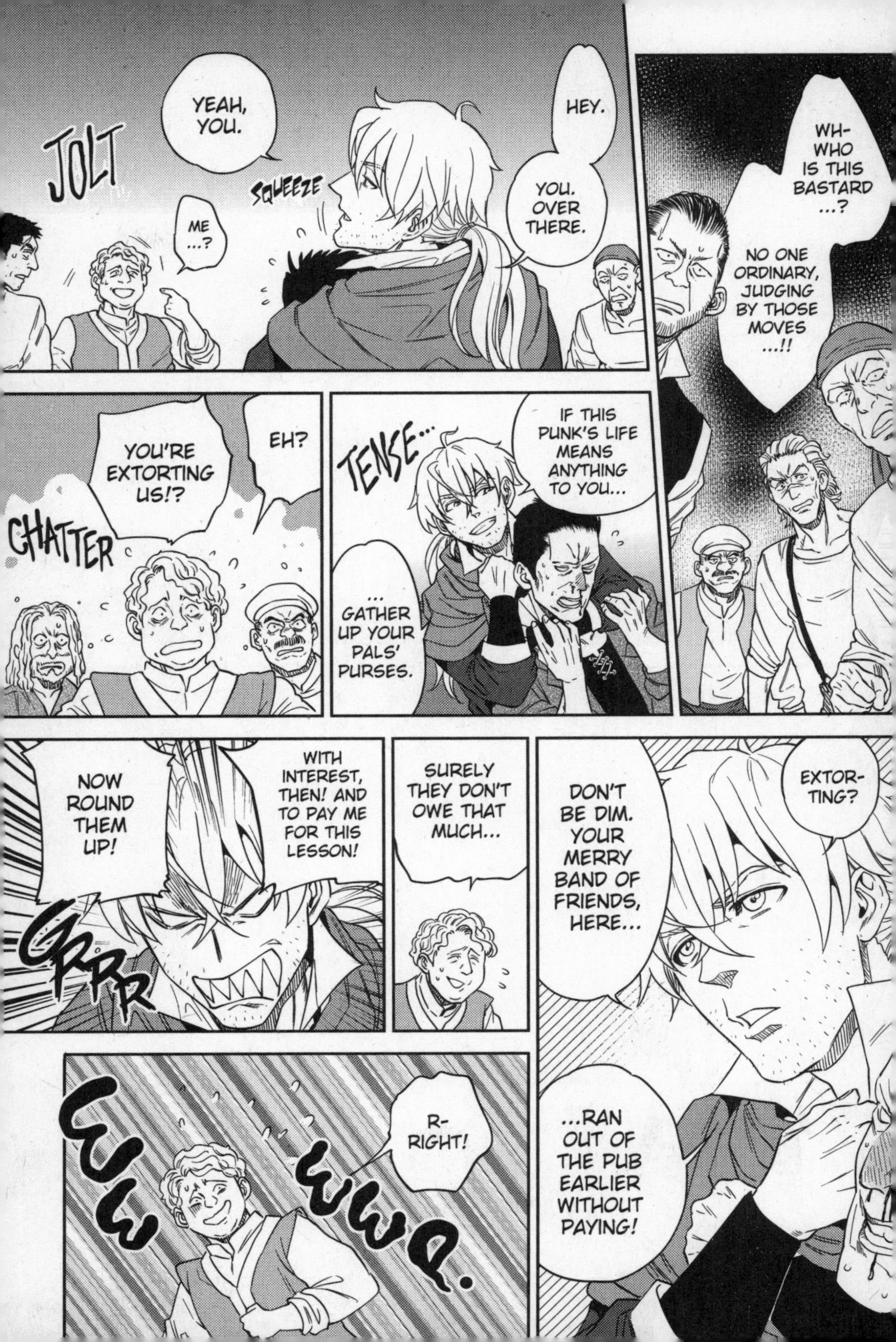
HEY.
YOU. OVER THERE.
YEAH, YOU.
SQUEEZE
JOLT
ME ...?
WH- WHO IS THIS BASTARD ...?
NO ONE ORDINARY, JUDGING BY THOSE MOVES ...!!
IF THIS PUNK'S LIFE MEANS ANYTHING TO YOU...
TENSE...
... GATHER UP YOUR PALS' PURSES.
EH?
YOU'RE EXTORTING US!?
CHATTER
EXTOR- TING?
DON'T BE DIM. YOUR MERRY BAND OF FRIENDS, HERE...
...RAN OUT OF THE PUB EARLIER WITHOUT PAYING!
SURELY THEY DON'T OWE THAT MUCH...
WITH INTEREST, THEN! AND TO PAY ME FOR THIS LESSON!
NOW ROUND THEM UP!
GRRR
R- RIGHT!
WW
WWP.

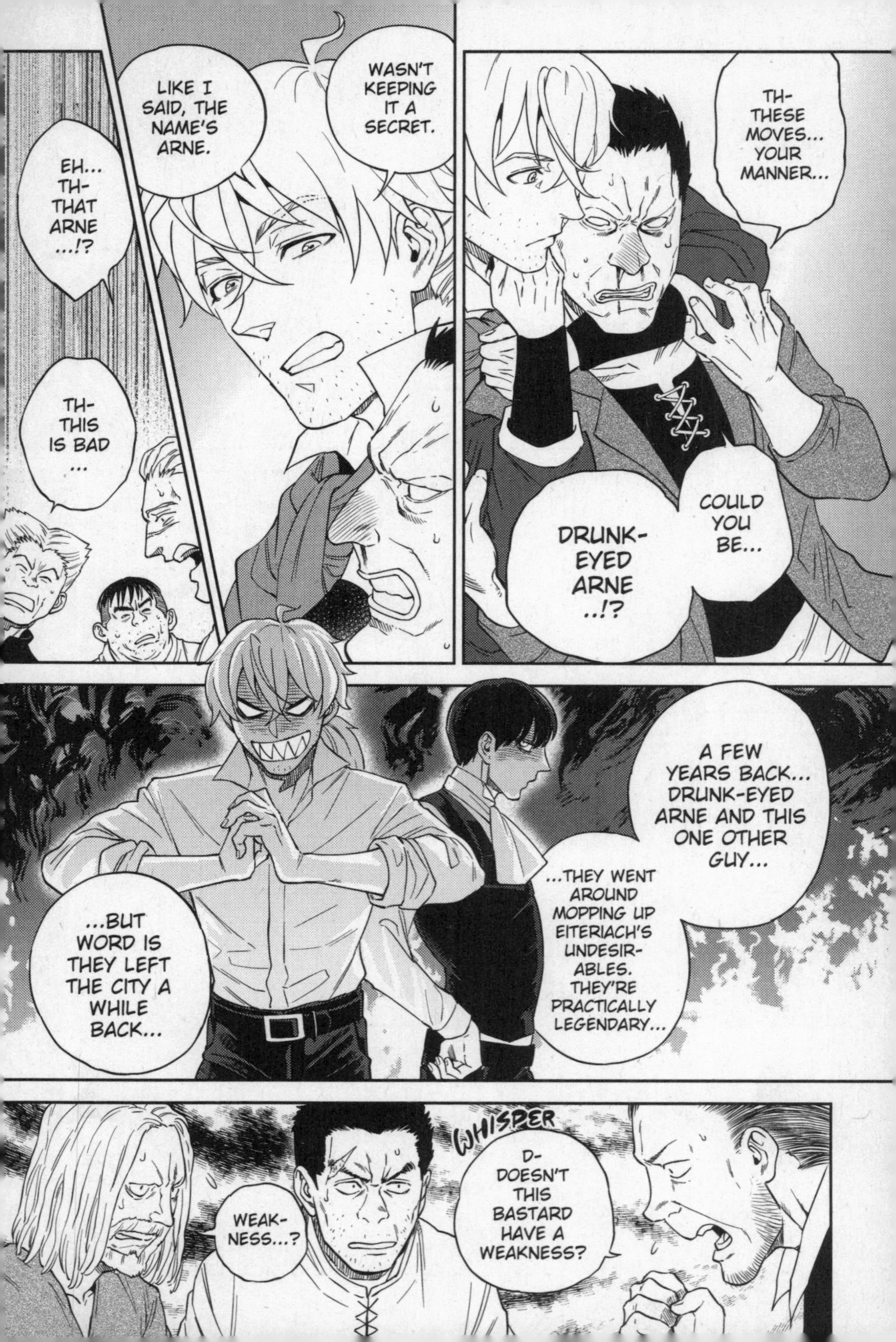
TH-THESE MOVES... YOUR MANNER...
COULD YOU BE...
DRUNK-EYED ARNE ..!?
WASN'T KEEPING IT A SECRET.
LIKE I SAID, THE NAME'S ARNE.
EH... TH-THAT ARNE ...!?
TH-THIS IS BAD ...
A FEW YEARS BACK... DRUNK-EYED ARNE AND THIS ONE OTHER GUY...
...THEY WENT AROUND MOPPING UP EITERIACH'S UNDESIR-ABLES. THEY'RE PRACTICALLY LEGENDARY...
...BUT WORD IS THEY LEFT THE CITY A WHILE BACK...
WHISPER
D-DOESN'T THIS BASTARD HAVE A WEAKNESS?
WEAK-NESS...?

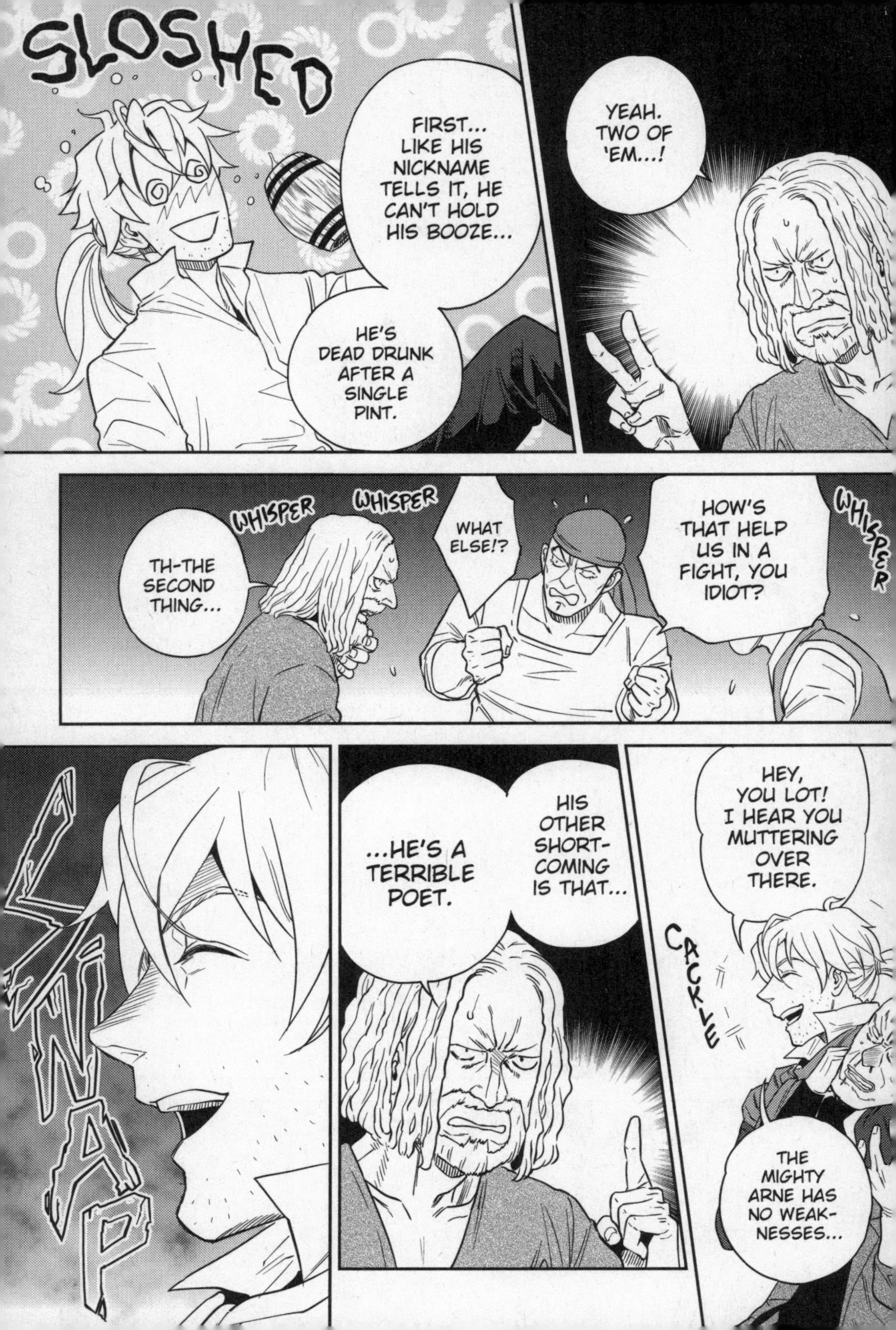
YEAH. TWO OF 'EM...!
SLOSHED
FIRST... LIKE HIS NICKNAME TELLS IT, HE CAN'T HOLD HIS BOOZE...
HE'S DEAD DRUNK AFTER A SINGLE PINT.
WHISPER
HOW'S THAT HELP US IN A FIGHT, YOU IDIOT?
WHAT ELSE!?
WHISPER
WHISPER
TH-THE SECOND THING...
HEY, YOU LOT! I HEAR YOU MUTTERING OVER THERE.
CACKLE
THE MIGHTY ARNE HAS NO WEAK-NESSES...
HIS OTHER SHORT-COMING IS THAT...
...HE'S A TERRIBLE POET.
SNAP

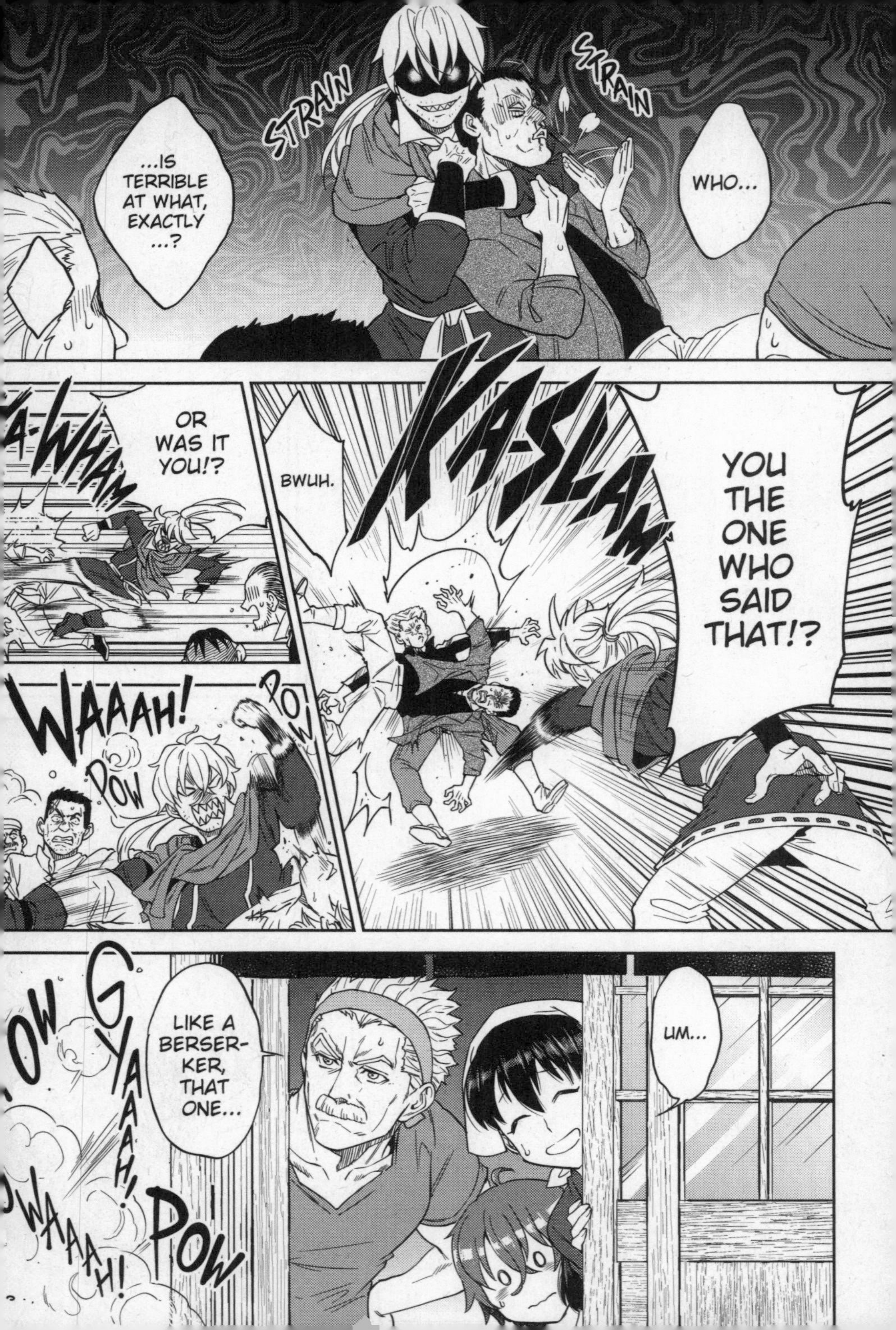

WHO...
STRAIN
STRAIN
...IS TERRIBLE AT WHAT, EXACTLY...?
YOU THE ONE WHO SAID THAT!?
KA-SLAM
BWUH.
OR WAS IT YOU!?
A-WHAM
POW
POW
WAAAH!
UM...
LIKE A BERSER-KER, THAT ONE...
GYAAAAH!
POW
OW
WAAAH!

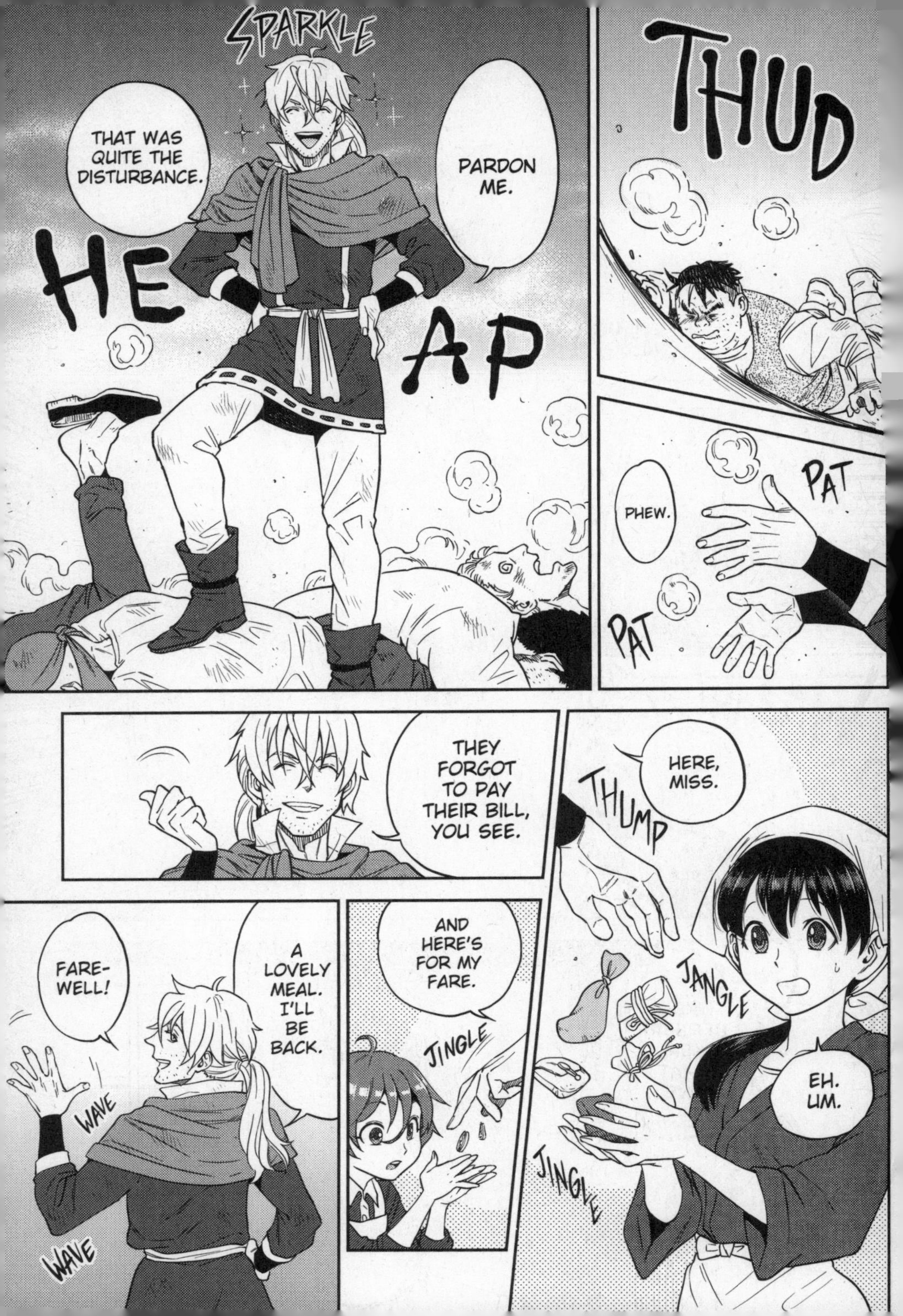
THUD
PHEW.
PAT
PAT
SPARKLE
PARDON ME.
THAT WAS QUITE THE DISTURBANCE.
HEAP
HERE, MISS.
THUMP
JANGLE
EH. UM.
JINGLE
THEY FORGOT TO PAY THEIR BILL, YOU SEE.
AND HERE'S FOR MY FARE.
JINGLE
A LOVELY MEAL. I'LL BE BACK.
FARE-WELL!
WAVE
WAVE

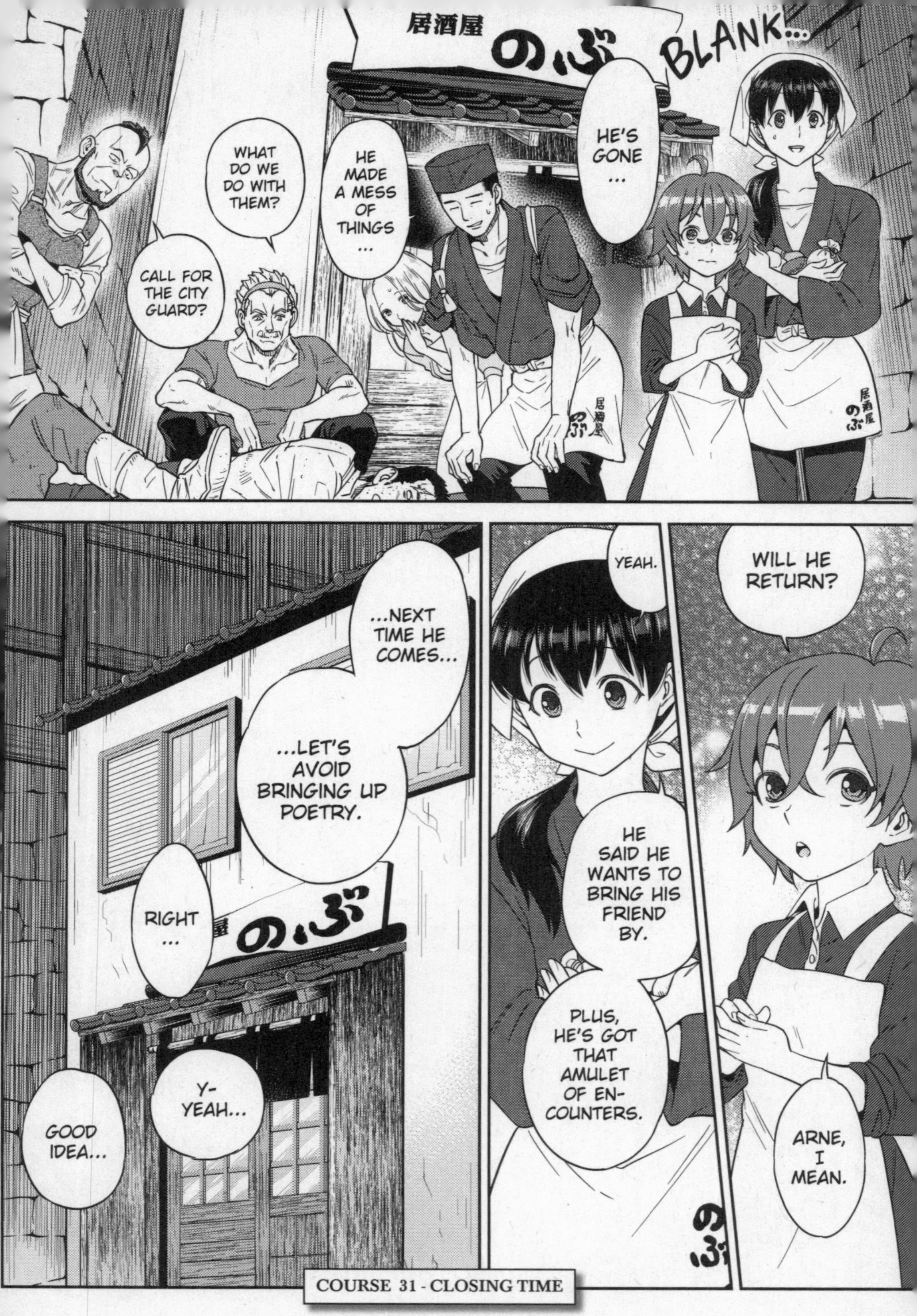
BLANK...
居酒屋
のぶ
HE'S GONE...
HE MADE A MESS OF THINGS...
WHAT DO WE DO WITH THEM?
CALL FOR THE CITY GUARD?
WILL HE RETURN?
ARNE, I MEAN.
YEAH.
HE SAID HE WANTS TO BRING HIS FRIEND BY.
PLUS, HE'S GOT THAT AMULET OF EN-COUNTERS.
...NEXT TIME HE COMES...
...LET'S AVOID BRINGING UP POETRY.
RIGHT...
Y-YEAH...
GOOD IDEA...
のぶ

COURSE 31 - CLOSING TIME

Seasonal Tempura Platter

OTHERWORLDLY IZAKAYA

NOBU

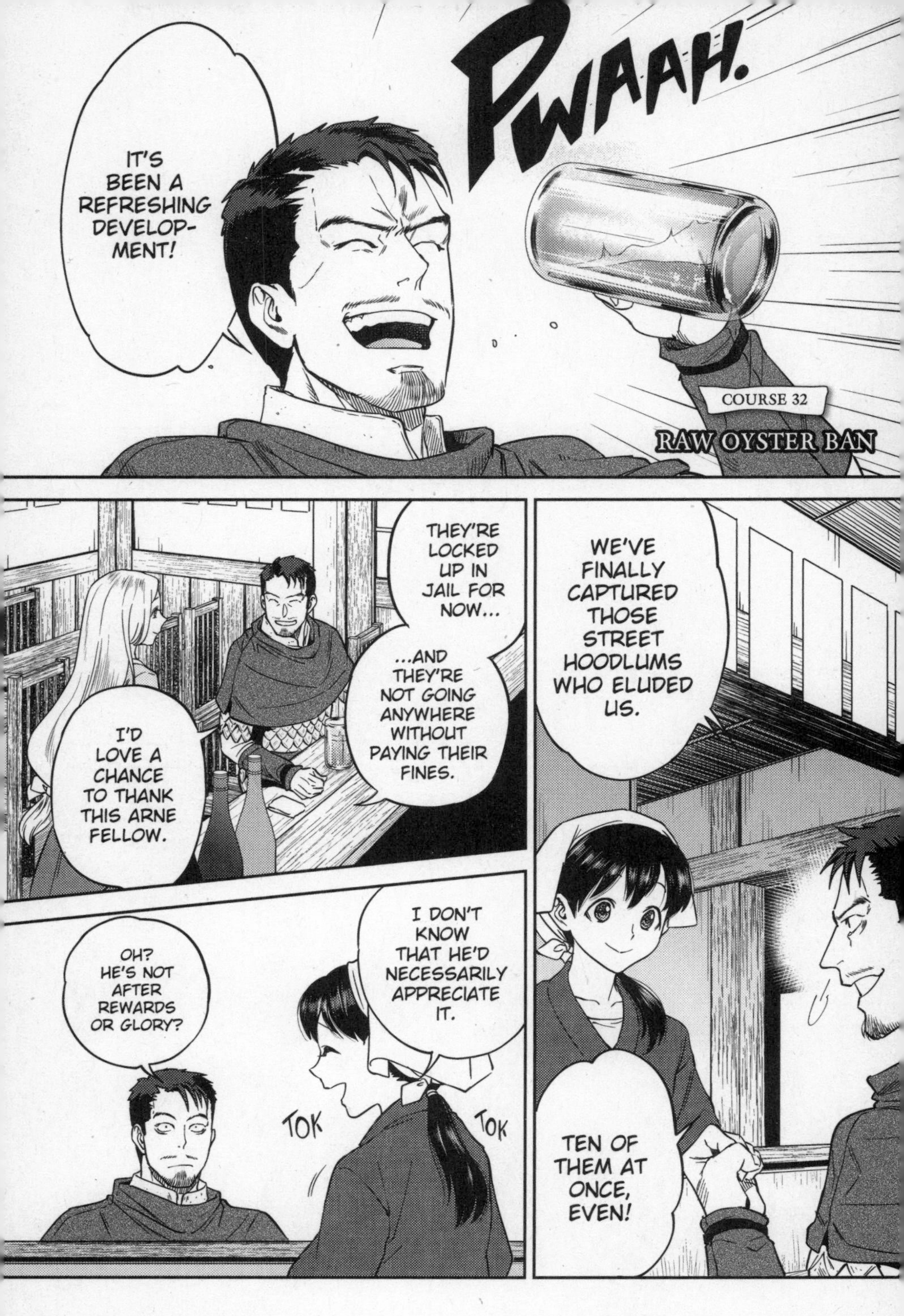
PWAAH.
IT'S BEEN A REFRESHING DEVELOPMENT!
COURSE 32
RAW OYSTER BAN
WE'VE FINALLY CAPTURED THOSE STREET HOODLUMS WHO ELUDED US.
TEN OF THEM AT ONCE, EVEN!
THEY'RE LOCKED UP IN JAIL FOR NOW...
...AND THEY'RE NOT GOING ANYWHERE WITHOUT PAYING THEIR FINES.
I'D LOVE A CHANCE TO THANK THIS ARNE FELLOW.
I DON'T KNOW THAT HE'D NECESSARILY APPRECIATE IT.
TOK
TOK
OH? HE'S NOT AFTER REWARDS OR GLORY?

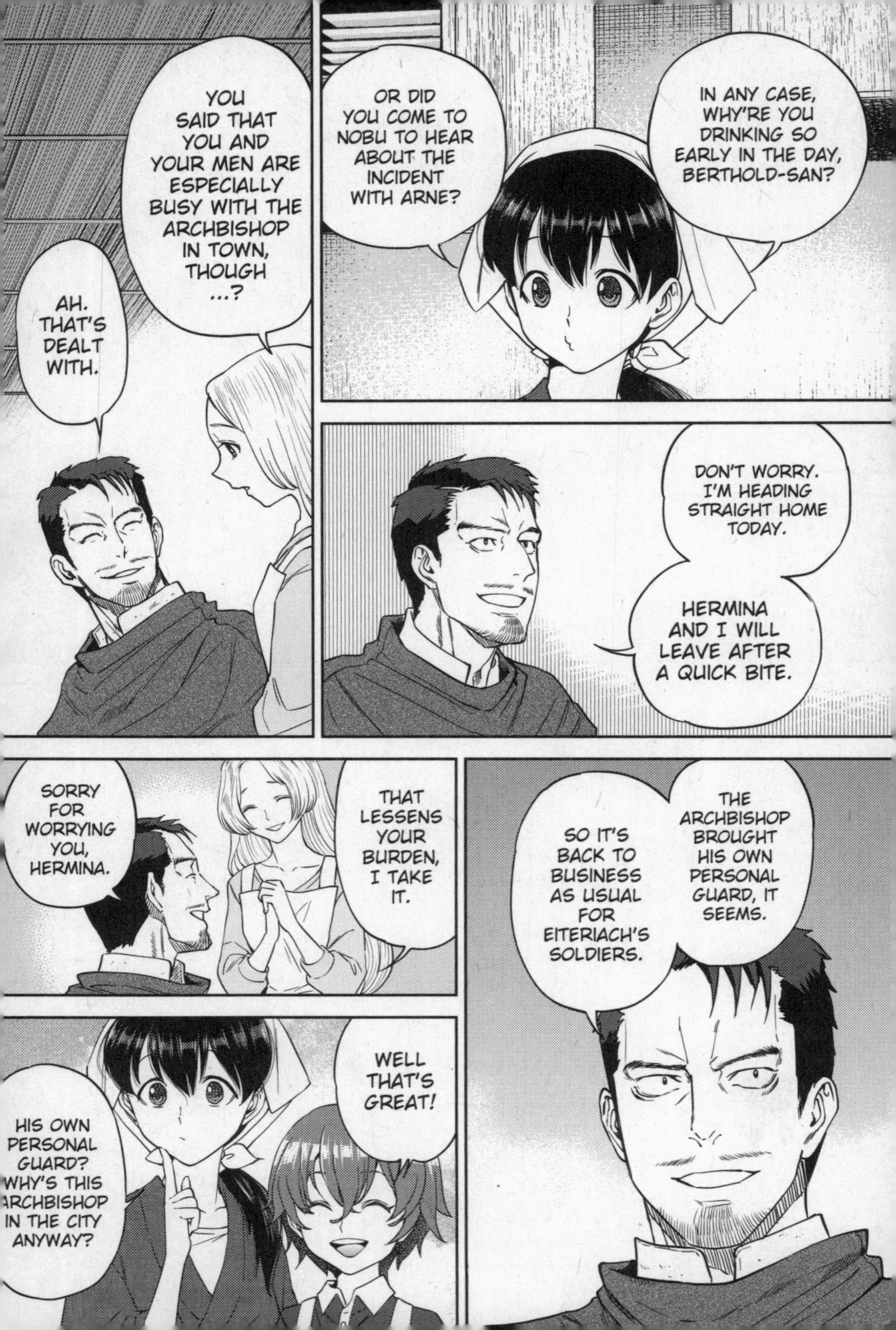
IN ANY CASE, WHY'RE YOU DRINKING SO EARLY IN THE DAY, BERTHOLD-SAN?
OR DID YOU COME TO NOBU TO HEAR ABOUT THE INCIDENT WITH ARNE?
DON'T WORRY. I'M HEADING STRAIGHT HOME TODAY.
HERMINA AND I WILL LEAVE AFTER A QUICK BITE.
YOU SAID THAT YOU AND YOUR MEN ARE ESPECIALLY BUSY WITH THE ARCHBISHOP IN TOWN, THOUGH ...?
AH. THAT'S DEALT WITH.
THE ARCHBISHOP BROUGHT HIS OWN PERSONAL GUARD, IT SEEMS.
SO IT'S BACK TO BUSINESS AS USUAL FOR EITERIACH'S SOLDIERS.
THAT LESSENS YOUR BURDEN, I TAKE IT.
SORRY FOR WORRYING YOU, HERMINA.
WELL THAT'S GREAT!
HIS OWN PERSONAL GUARD? WHY'S THIS ARCHBISHOP IN THE CITY ANYWAY?

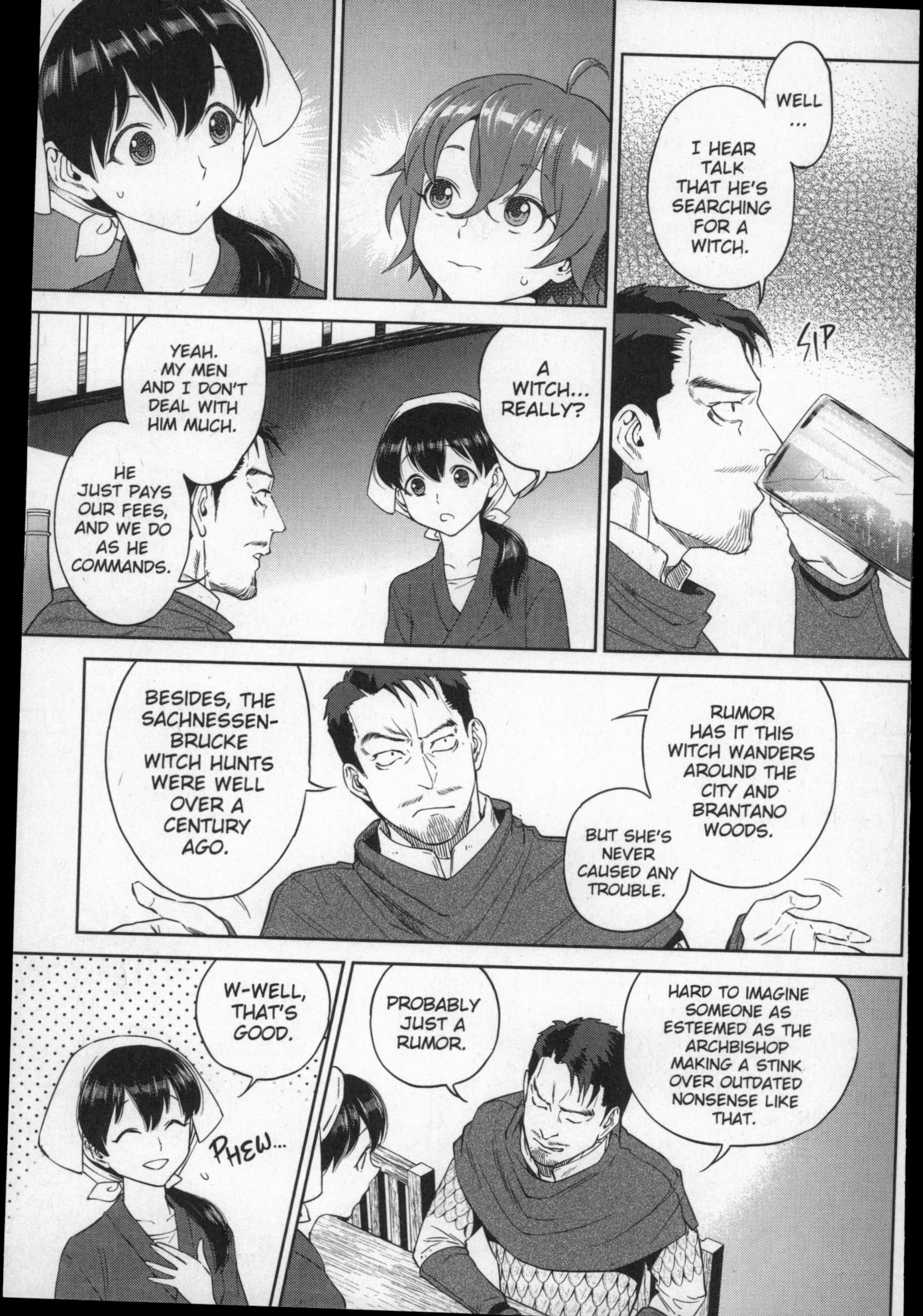
WELL ...
I HEAR TALK THAT HE'S SEARCHING FOR A WITCH.
SIP
A WITCH... REALLY?
YEAH. MY MEN AND I DON'T DEAL WITH HIM MUCH.
HE JUST PAYS OUR FEES, AND WE DO AS HE COMMANDS.
RUMOR HAS IT THIS WITCH WANDERS AROUND THE CITY AND BRANTANO WOODS.
BUT SHE'S NEVER CAUSED ANY TROUBLE.
BESIDES, THE SACHNESSEN-BRUCKE WITCH HUNTS WERE WELL OVER A CENTURY AGO.
HARD TO IMAGINE SOMEONE AS ESTEEMED AS THE ARCHBISHOP MAKING A STINK OVER OUTDATED NONSENSE LIKE THAT.
PROBABLY JUST A RUMOR.
W-WELL, THAT'S GOOD.
PHEW...

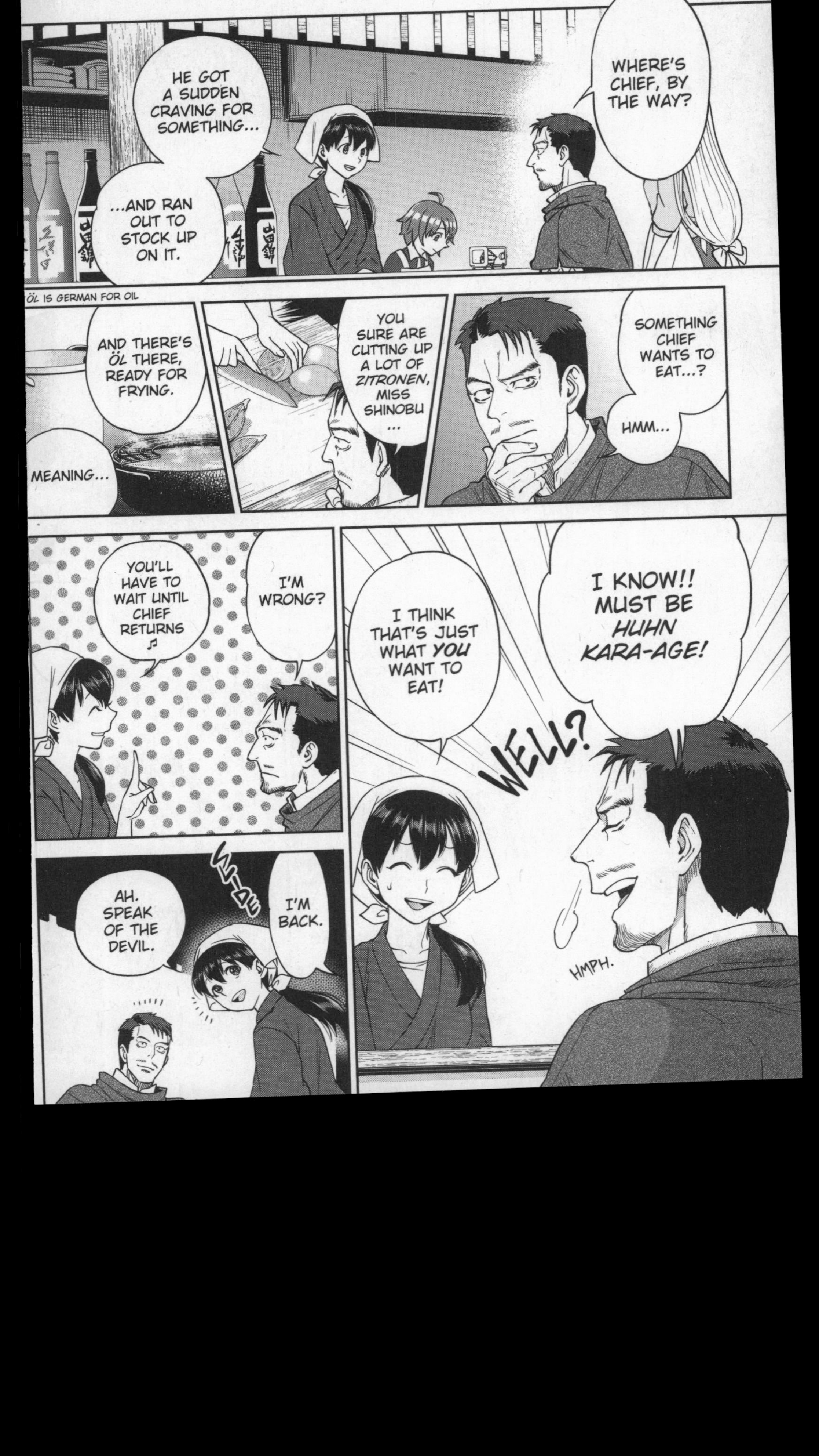
WHERE'S CHIEF, BY THE WAY?
HE GOT A SUDDEN CRAVING FOR SOMETHING...
...AND RAN OUT TO STOCK UP ON IT.
SOMETHING CHIEF WANTS TO EAT...?
HMM...
YOU SURE ARE CUTTING UP A LOT OF *ZITRONEN*, MISS SHINOBU ...
AND THERE'S ÖL THERE, READY FOR FRYING.
MEANING...
ÖL IS GERMAN FOR OIL
I KNOW!! MUST BE *HUHN KARA-AGE!*
WELL?
HMPH.
I THINK THAT'S JUST WHAT *YOU* WANT TO EAT!
I'M WRONG?
YOU'LL HAVE TO WAIT UNTIL CHIEF RETURNS ♫
SLIDE
I'M BACK.
AH. SPEAK OF THE DEVIL.

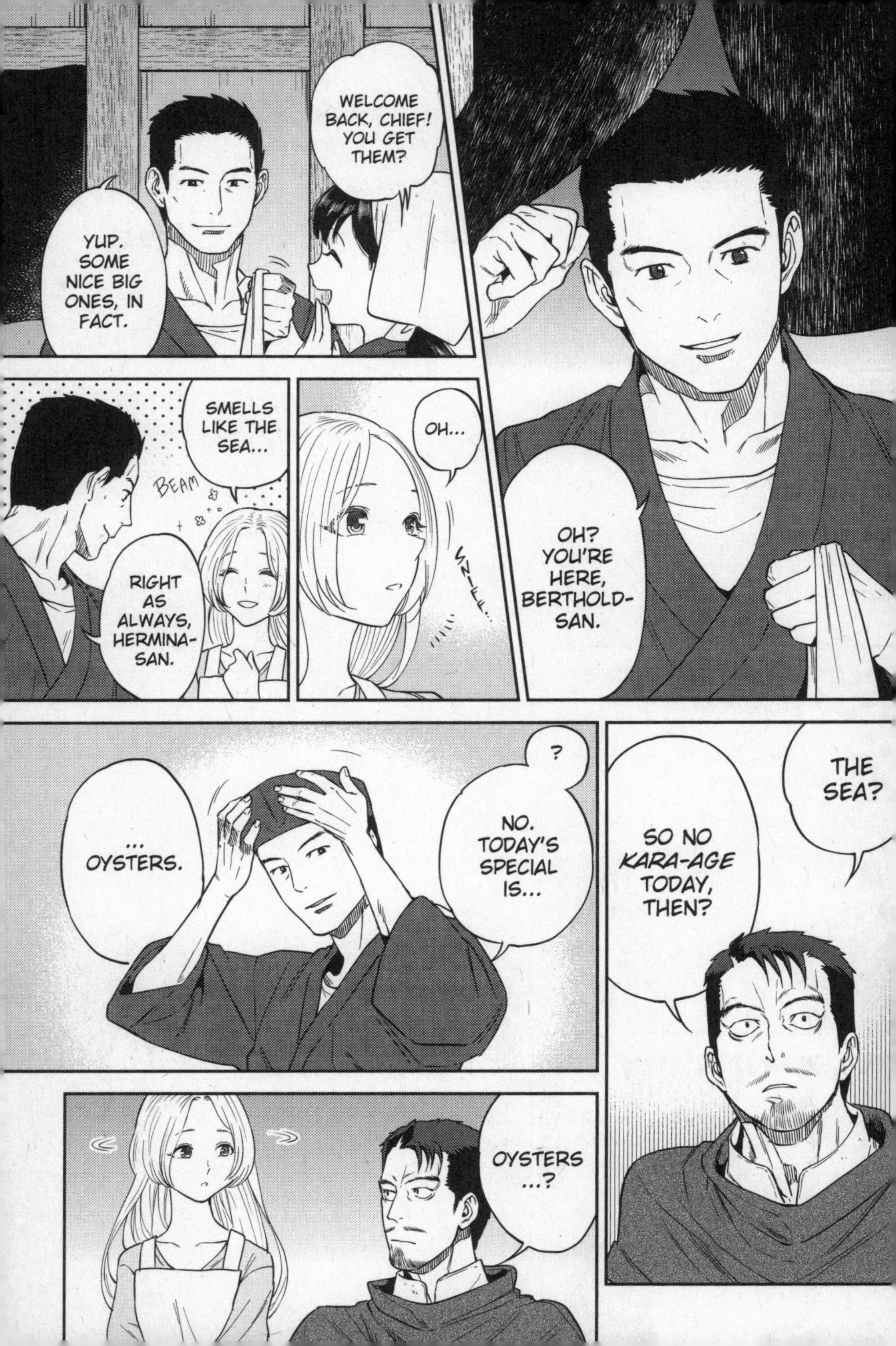

OH? YOU'RE HERE, BERTHOLD-SAN.
WELCOME BACK, CHIEF! YOU GET THEM?
YUP. SOME NICE BIG ONES, IN FACT.
OH...
SNIFF...
SMELLS LIKE THE SEA...
BEAM
RIGHT AS ALWAYS, HERMINA-SAN.
THE SEA?
SO NO *KARA-AGE* TODAY, THEN?
?
NO. TODAY'S SPECIAL IS...
... OYSTERS.
OYSTERS ...?

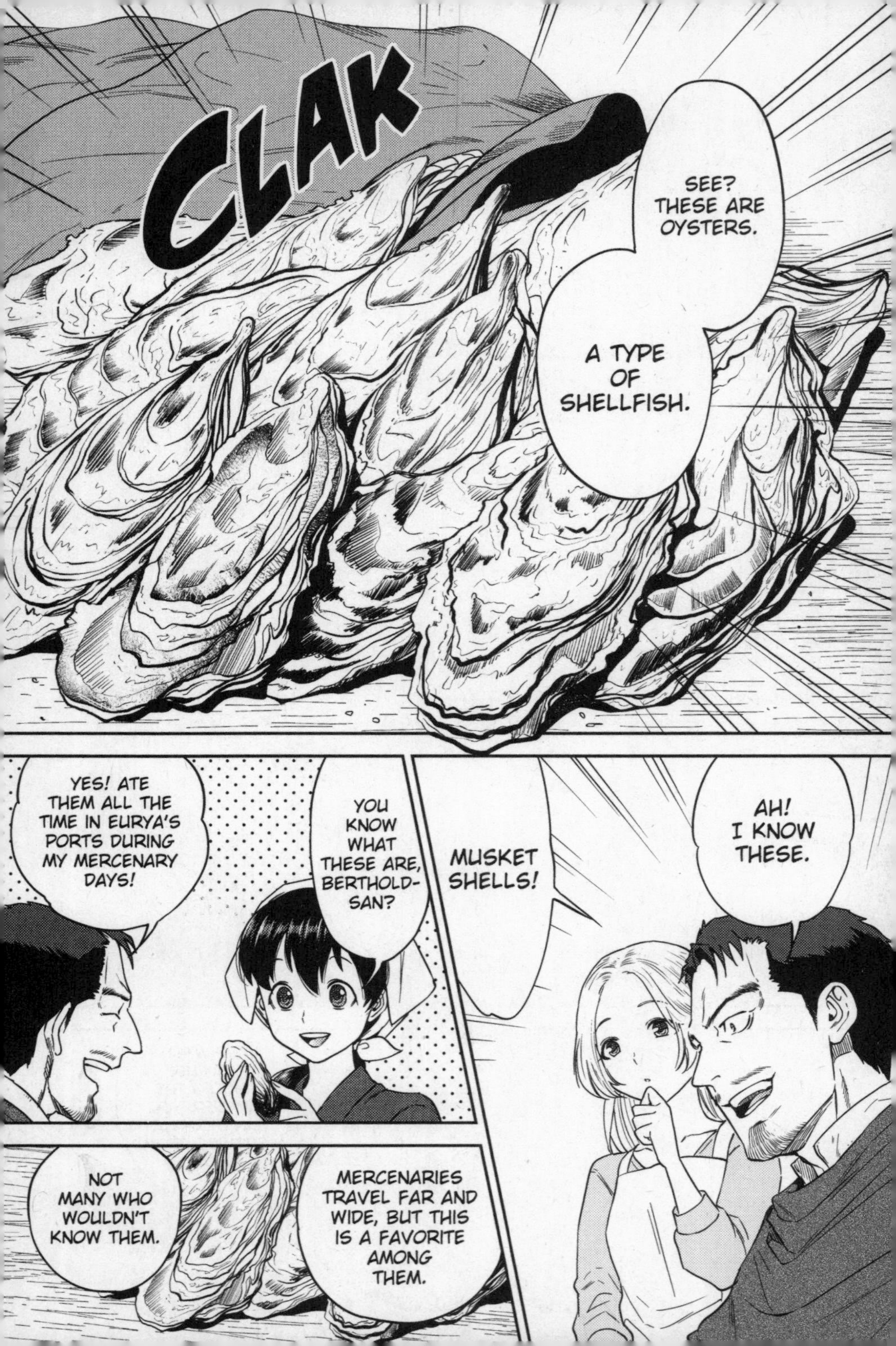
SEE? THESE ARE OYSTERS.
CLAK
A TYPE OF SHELLFISH.
AH! I KNOW THESE.
MUSKET SHELLS!
YOU KNOW WHAT THESE ARE, BERTHOLD-SAN?
YES! ATE THEM ALL THE TIME IN EURYA'S PORTS DURING MY MERCENARY DAYS!
MERCENARIES TRAVEL FAR AND WIDE, BUT THIS IS A FAVORITE AMONG THEM.
NOT MANY WHO WOULDN'T KNOW THEM.

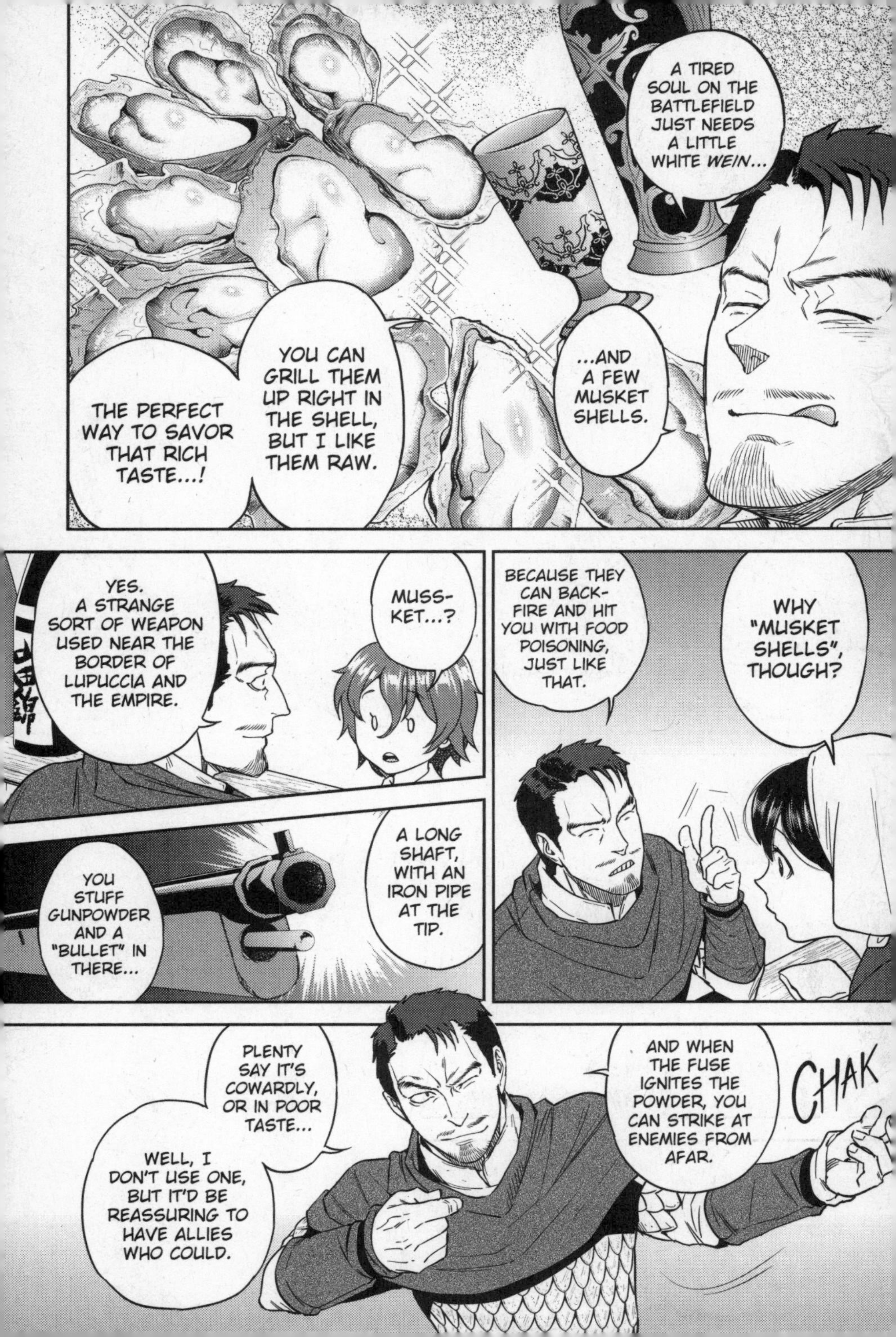
A TIRED SOUL ON THE BATTLEFIELD JUST NEEDS A LITTLE WHITE *WEIN*...
...AND A FEW MUSKET SHELLS.
YOU CAN GRILL THEM UP RIGHT IN THE SHELL, BUT I LIKE THEM RAW.
THE PERFECT WAY TO SAVOR THAT RICH TASTE...!
WHY "MUSKET SHELLS", THOUGH?
BECAUSE THEY CAN BACK-FIRE AND HIT YOU WITH FOOD POISONING, JUST LIKE THAT.
MUSS-KET...?
YES. A STRANGE SORT OF WEAPON USED NEAR THE BORDER OF LUPUCCIA AND THE EMPIRE.
A LONG SHAFT, WITH AN IRON PIPE AT THE TIP.
YOU STUFF GUNPOWDER AND A "BULLET" IN THERE...
CHAK
AND WHEN THE FUSE IGNITES THE POWDER, YOU CAN STRIKE AT ENEMIES FROM AFAR.
PLENTY SAY IT'S COWARDLY, OR IN POOR TASTE...
WELL, I DON'T USE ONE, BUT IT'D BE REASSURING TO HAVE ALLIES WHO COULD.

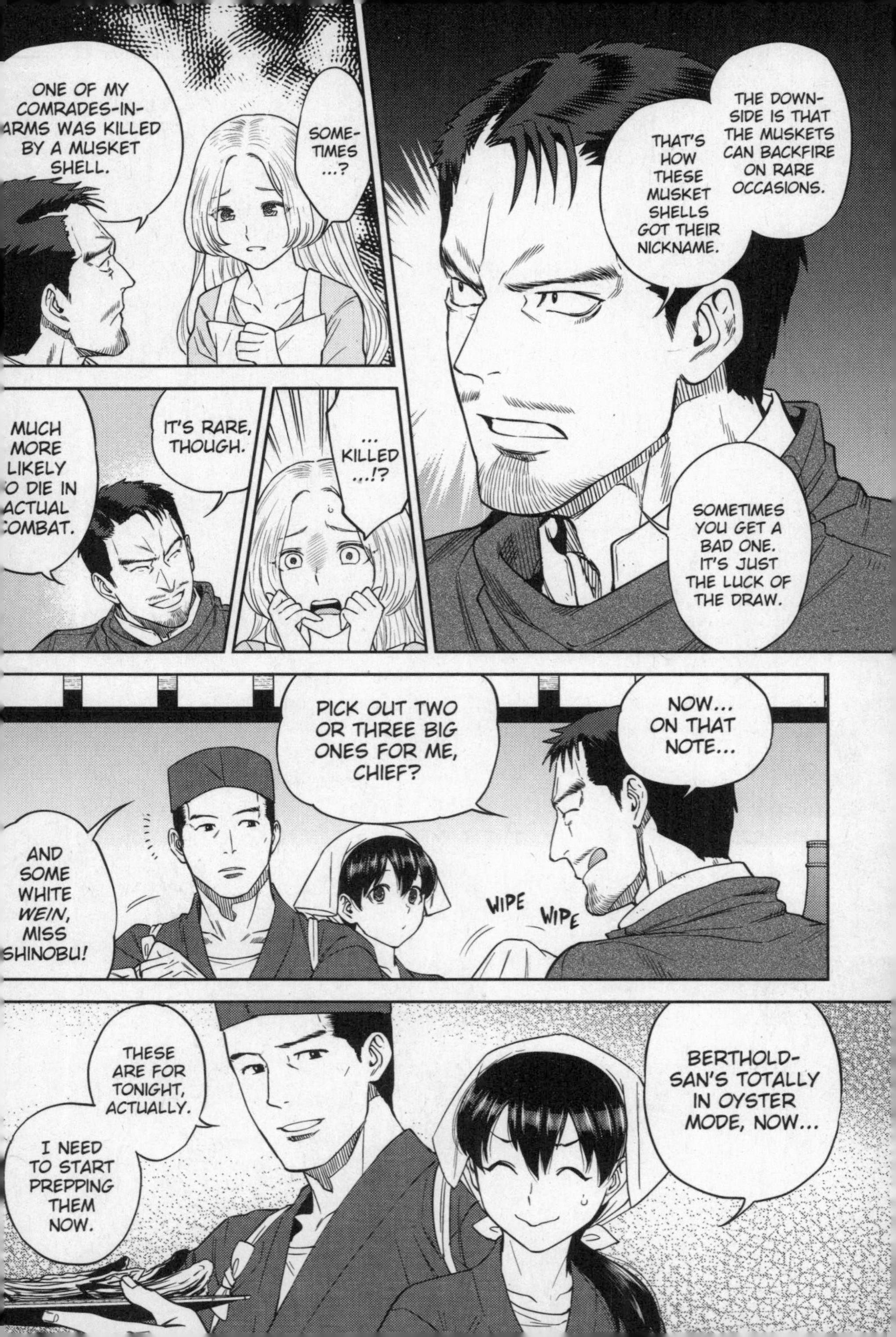
THE DOWN-SIDE IS THAT THE MUSKETS CAN BACKFIRE ON RARE OCCASIONS.
THAT'S HOW THESE MUSKET SHELLS GOT THEIR NICKNAME.
SOMETIMES YOU GET A BAD ONE. IT'S JUST THE LUCK OF THE DRAW.
SOME-TIMES ...?
ONE OF MY COMRADES-IN-ARMS WAS KILLED BY A MUSKET SHELL.
... KILLED ...!?
IT'S RARE, THOUGH.
MUCH MORE LIKELY O DIE IN ACTUAL OMBAT.
NOW... ON THAT NOTE...
PICK OUT TWO OR THREE BIG ONES FOR ME, CHIEF?
WIPE WIPE
AND SOME WHITE *WEIN*, MISS SHINOBU!
BERTHOLD-SAN'S TOTALLY IN OYSTER MODE, NOW...
THESE ARE FOR TONIGHT, ACTUALLY.
I NEED TO START PREPPING THEM NOW.

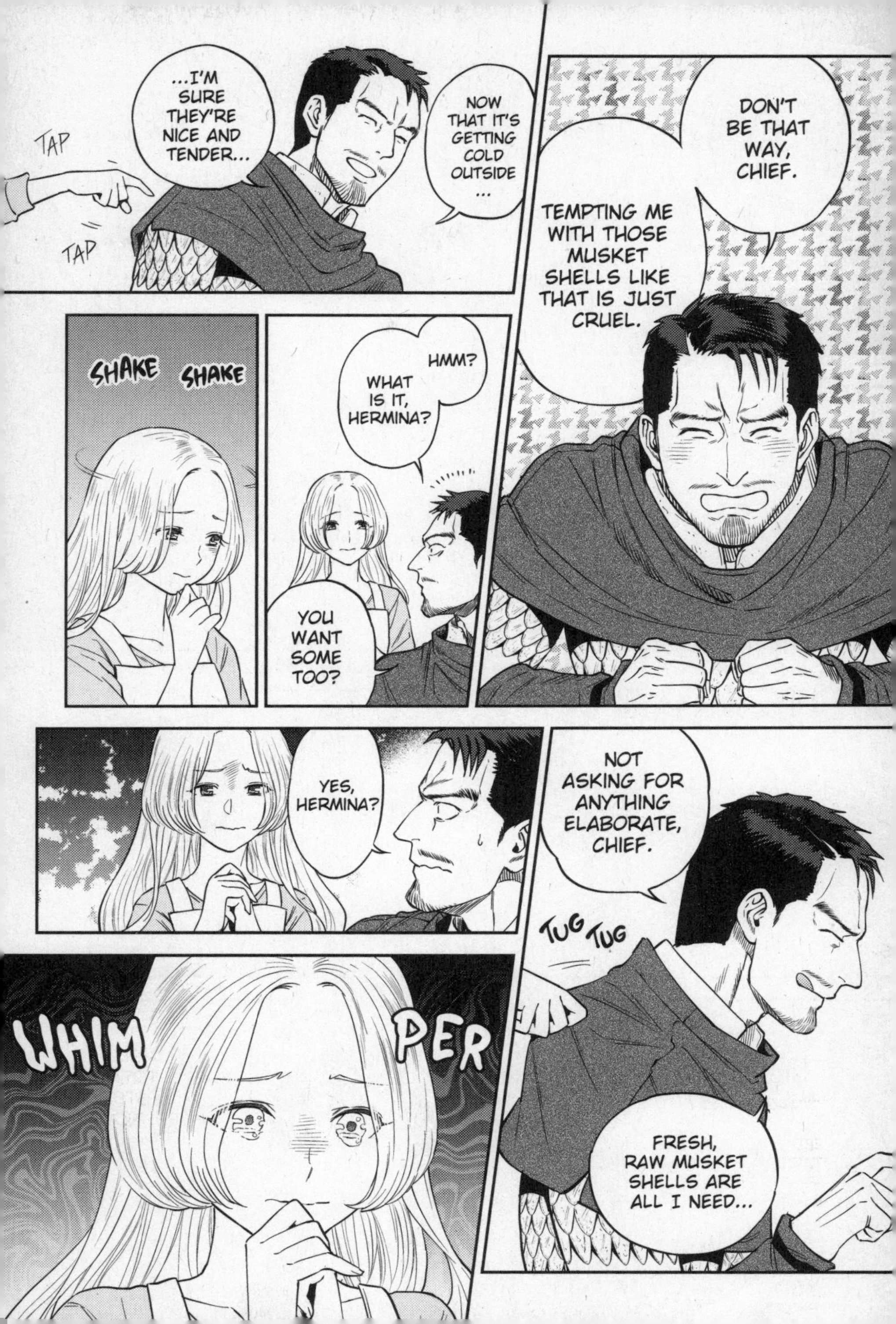
DON'T BE THAT WAY, CHIEF.
TEMPTING ME WITH THOSE MUSKET SHELLS LIKE THAT IS JUST CRUEL.
NOW THAT IT'S GETTING COLD OUTSIDE ...
...I'M SURE THEY'RE NICE AND TENDER...
TAP
TAP
HMM?
WHAT IS IT, HERMINA?
YOU WANT SOME TOO?
SHAKE SHAKE
NOT ASKING FOR ANYTHING ELABORATE, CHIEF.
TUG TUG
FRESH, RAW MUSKET SHELLS ARE ALL I NEED...
YES, HERMINA?
WHIM PER

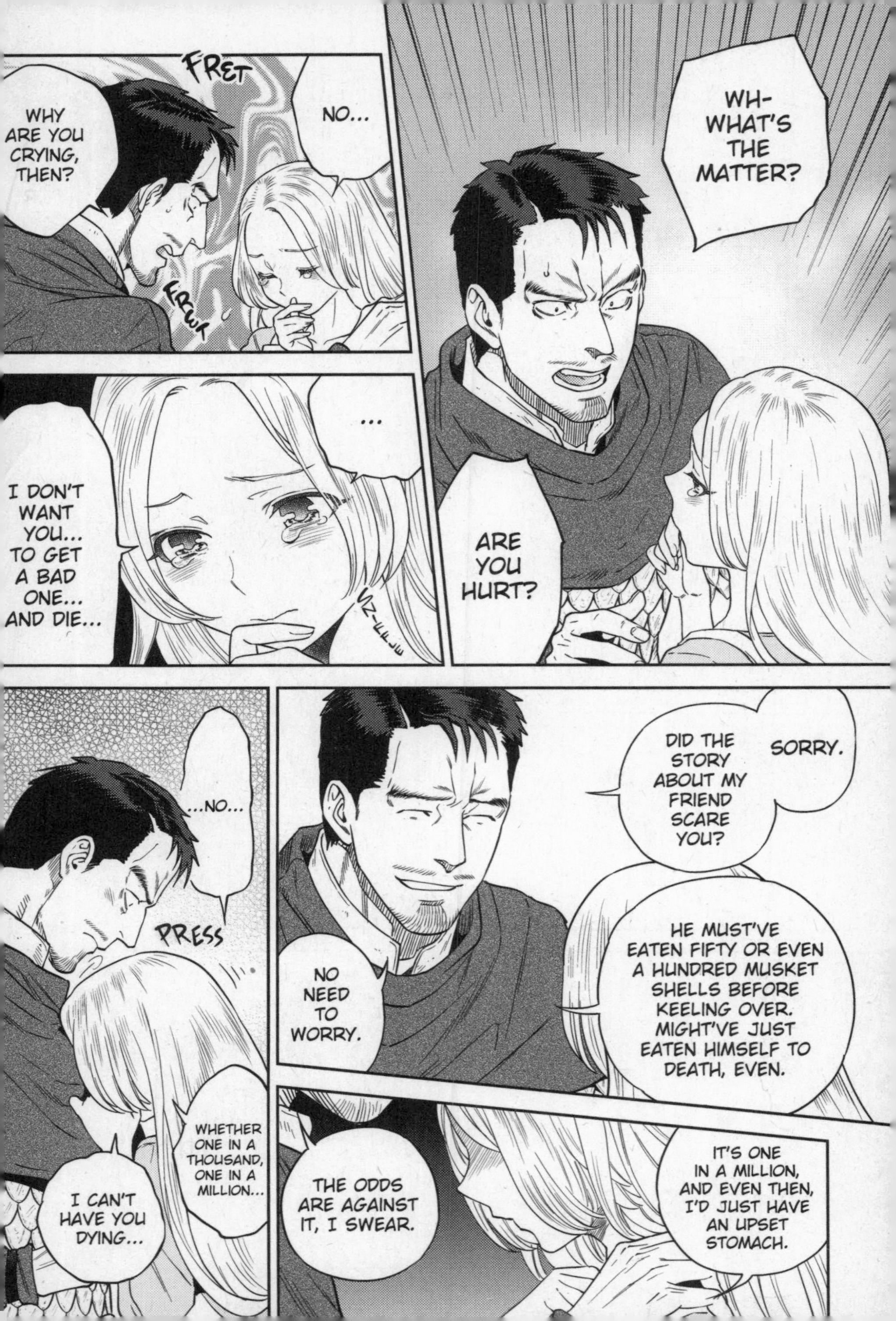
WH-
WHAT'S THE MATTER?
ARE YOU HURT?
NO...
WHY ARE YOU CRYING, THEN?
FRET
FRET
...
I DON'T WANT YOU... TO GET A BAD ONE... AND DIE...
SORRY.
DID THE STORY ABOUT MY FRIEND SCARE YOU?
HE MUST'VE EATEN FIFTY OR EVEN A HUNDRED MUSKET SHELLS BEFORE KEELING OVER. MIGHT'VE JUST EATEN HIMSELF TO DEATH, EVEN.
NO NEED TO WORRY.
IT'S ONE IN A MILLION, AND EVEN THEN, I'D JUST HAVE AN UPSET STOMACH.
THE ODDS ARE AGAINST IT, I SWEAR.
...NO...
PRESS
WHETHER ONE IN A THOUSAND, ONE IN A MILLION...
I CAN'T HAVE YOU DYING...

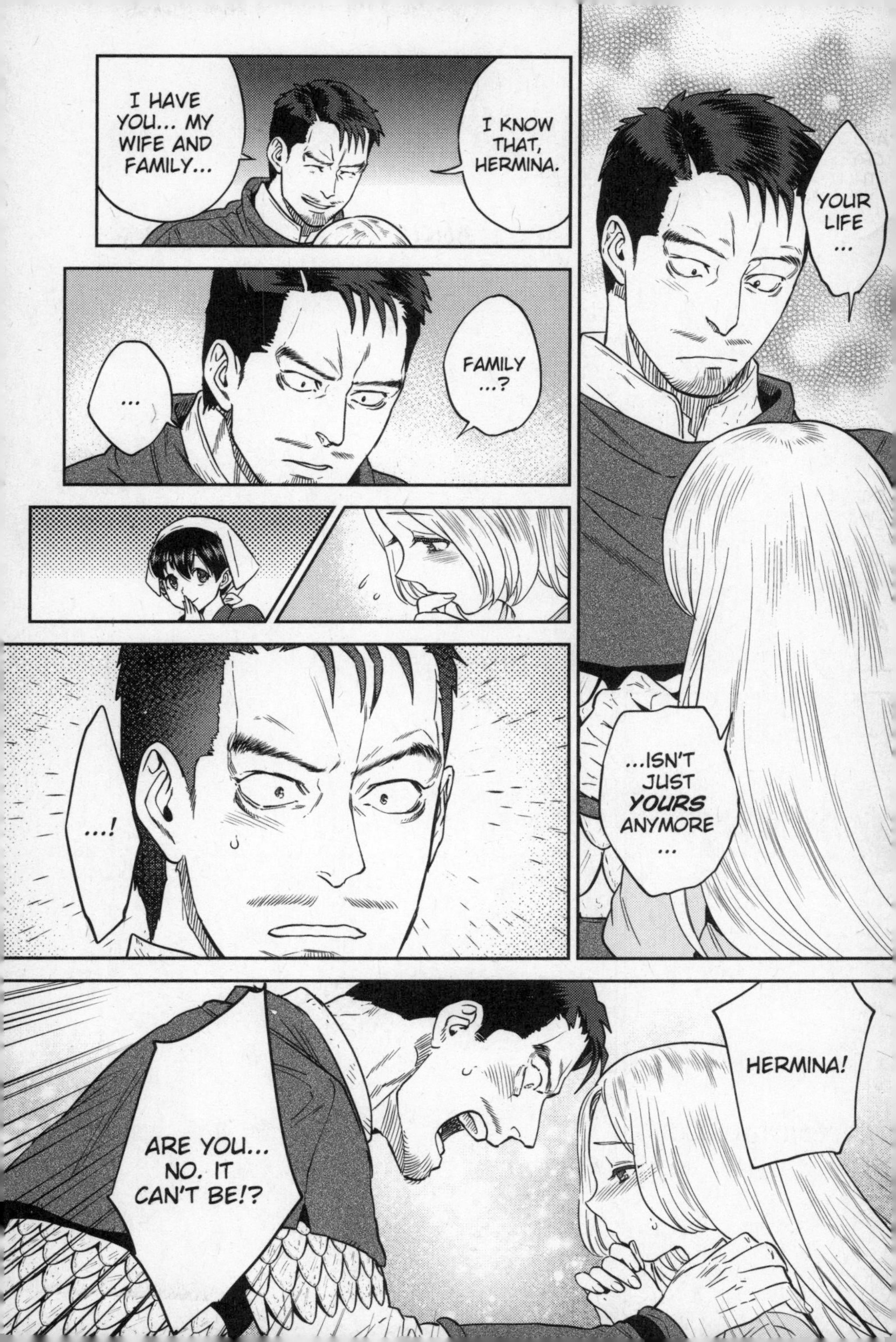
YOUR LIFE ...
...ISN'T JUST *YOURS* ANYMORE ...
I KNOW THAT, HERMINA.
I HAVE YOU... MY WIFE AND FAMILY...
FAMILY ...?
...
...!
HERMINA!
ARE YOU... NO. IT CAN'T BE!?

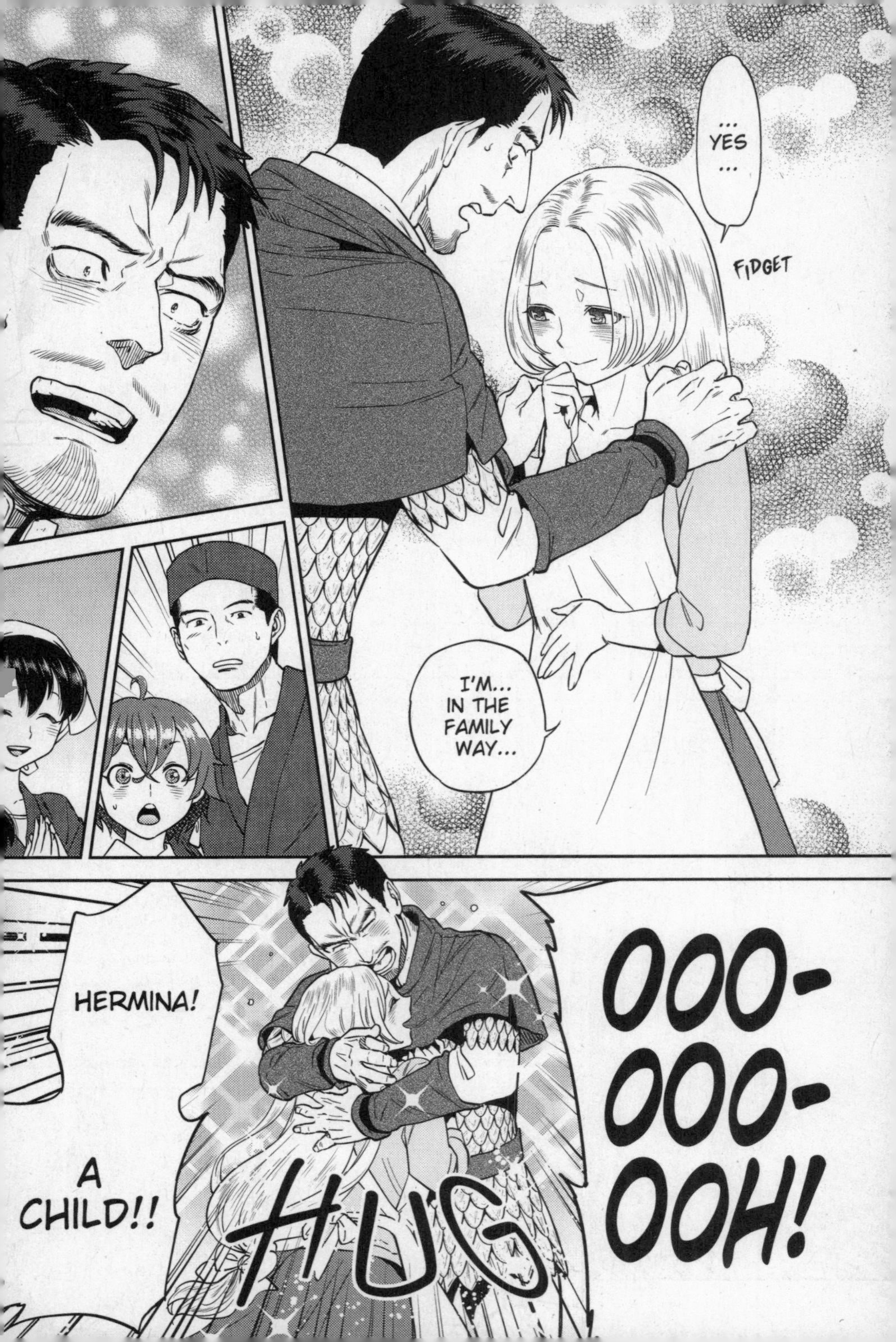
... YES ...
FIDGET
I'M... IN THE FAMILY WAY...
OOO-OOO-OOOH!
HERMINA!
A CHILD!!
HUG

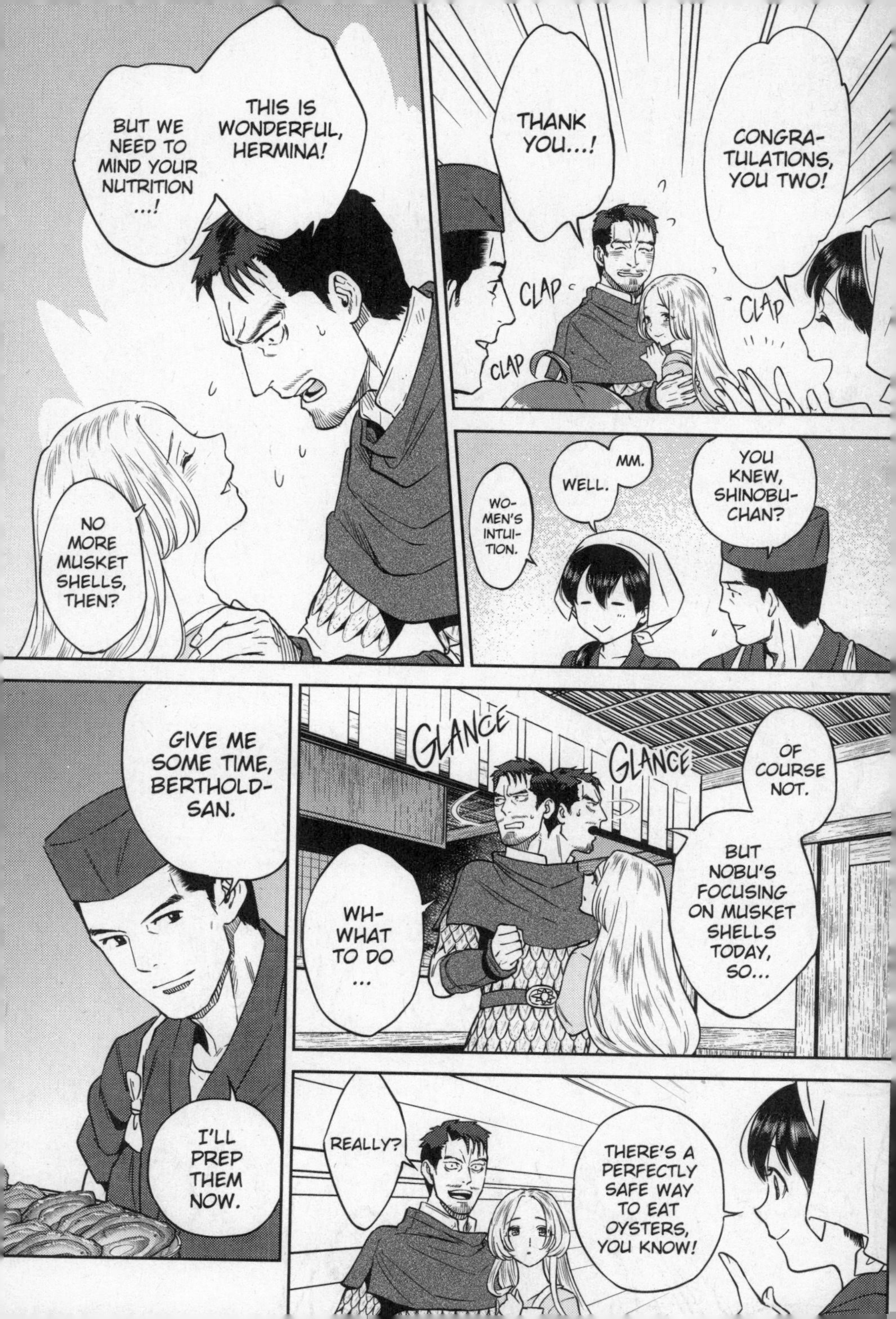

CONGRATULATIONS, YOU TWO!
THANK YOU...!
CLAP
CLAP
CLAP
YOU KNEW, SHINOBU-CHAN?
MM.
WELL.
WOMEN'S INTUITION.
THIS IS WONDERFUL, HERMINA!
BUT WE NEED TO MIND YOUR NUTRITION...!
NO MORE MUSKET SHELLS, THEN?
OF COURSE NOT.
BUT NOBU'S FOCUSING ON MUSKET SHELLS TODAY, SO...
GLANCE
GLANCE
WH-WHAT TO DO...
THERE'S A PERFECTLY SAFE WAY TO EAT OYSTERS, YOU KNOW!
REALLY?
GIVE ME SOME TIME, BERTHOLD-SAN.
I'LL PREP THEM NOW.

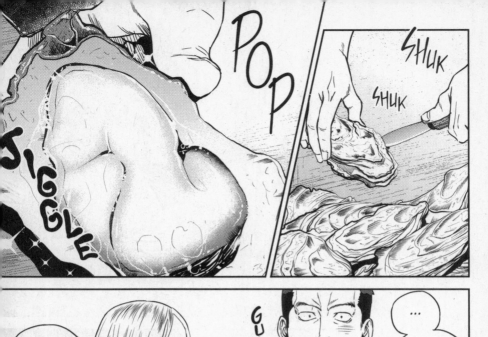

SHUK
SHUK
POP
JIGGLE
...
PLUMPER THAN I IMAGINED...
GULP...
NO HAVING THEM RAW, NOW!
WHY DON'T YOU PREP *THAT*, SHINOBU-CHAN?
SINCE I BOUGHT THE PICKLES FOR IT.
OKAY!
SHLUP
PEEL
PEEL
TOK
TOK
TOK
HMM?
IS THAT... FROM THE TIME WE HAD *HUHN NANBAN* ...?
YUP! IT'S TARTAR SAUCE!

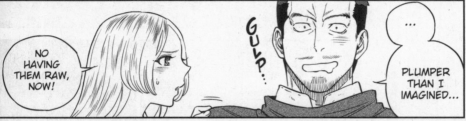

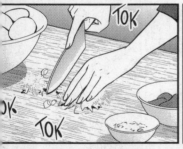

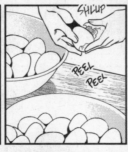

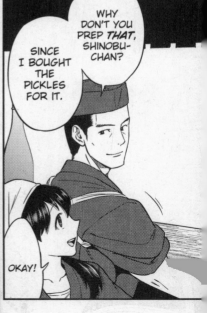

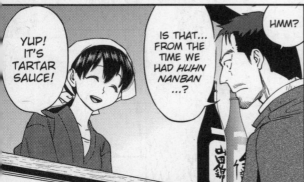

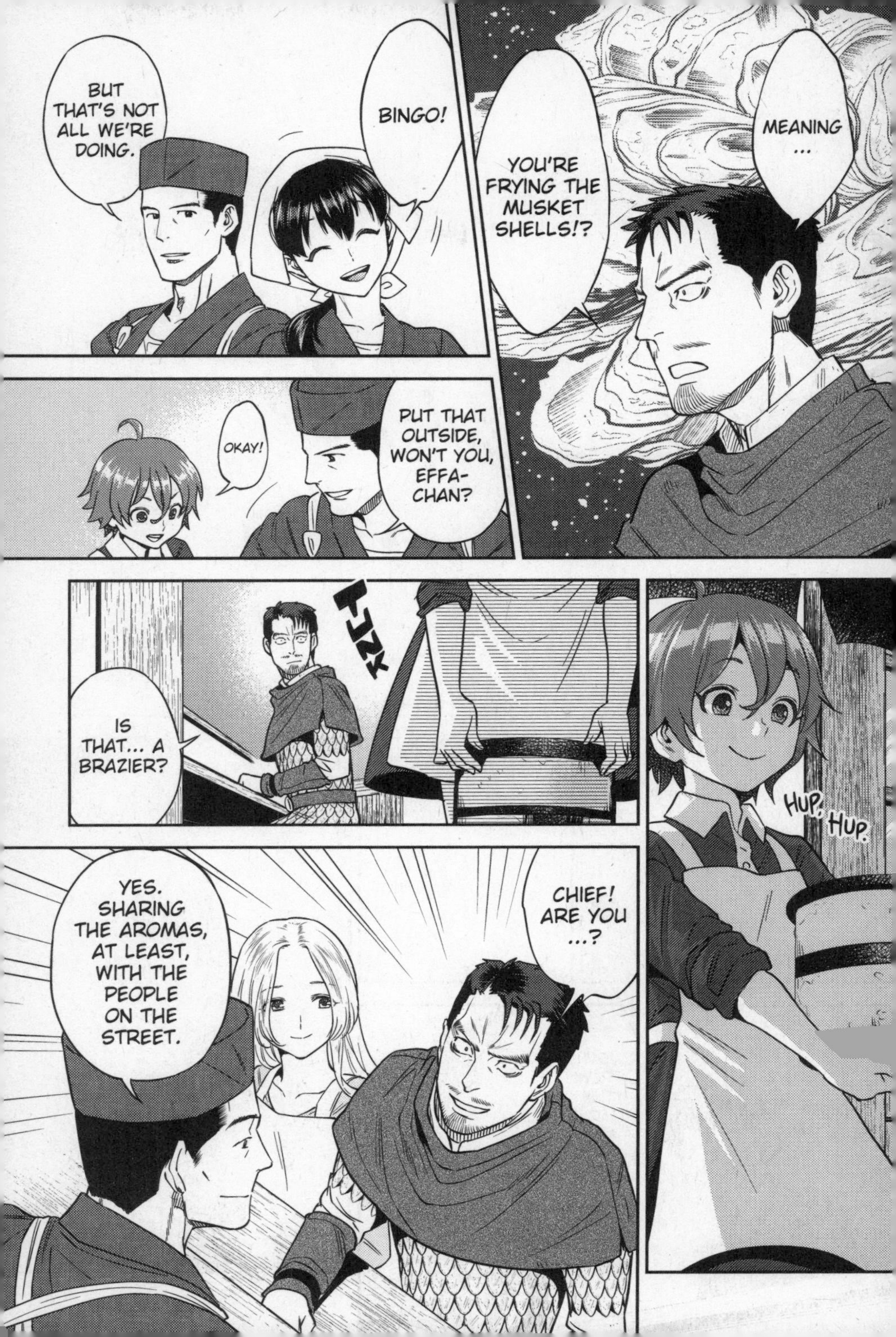

MEANING ...
YOU'RE FRYING THE MUSKET SHELLS!?
BINGO!
BUT THAT'S NOT ALL WE'RE DOING.
PUT THAT OUTSIDE, WON'T YOU, EFFA-CHAN?
OKAY!
HUP, HUP.
TUNK
IS THAT... A BRAZIER?
CHIEF! ARE YOU ...?
YES. SHARING THE AROMAS, AT LEAST, WITH THE PEOPLE ON THE STREET.

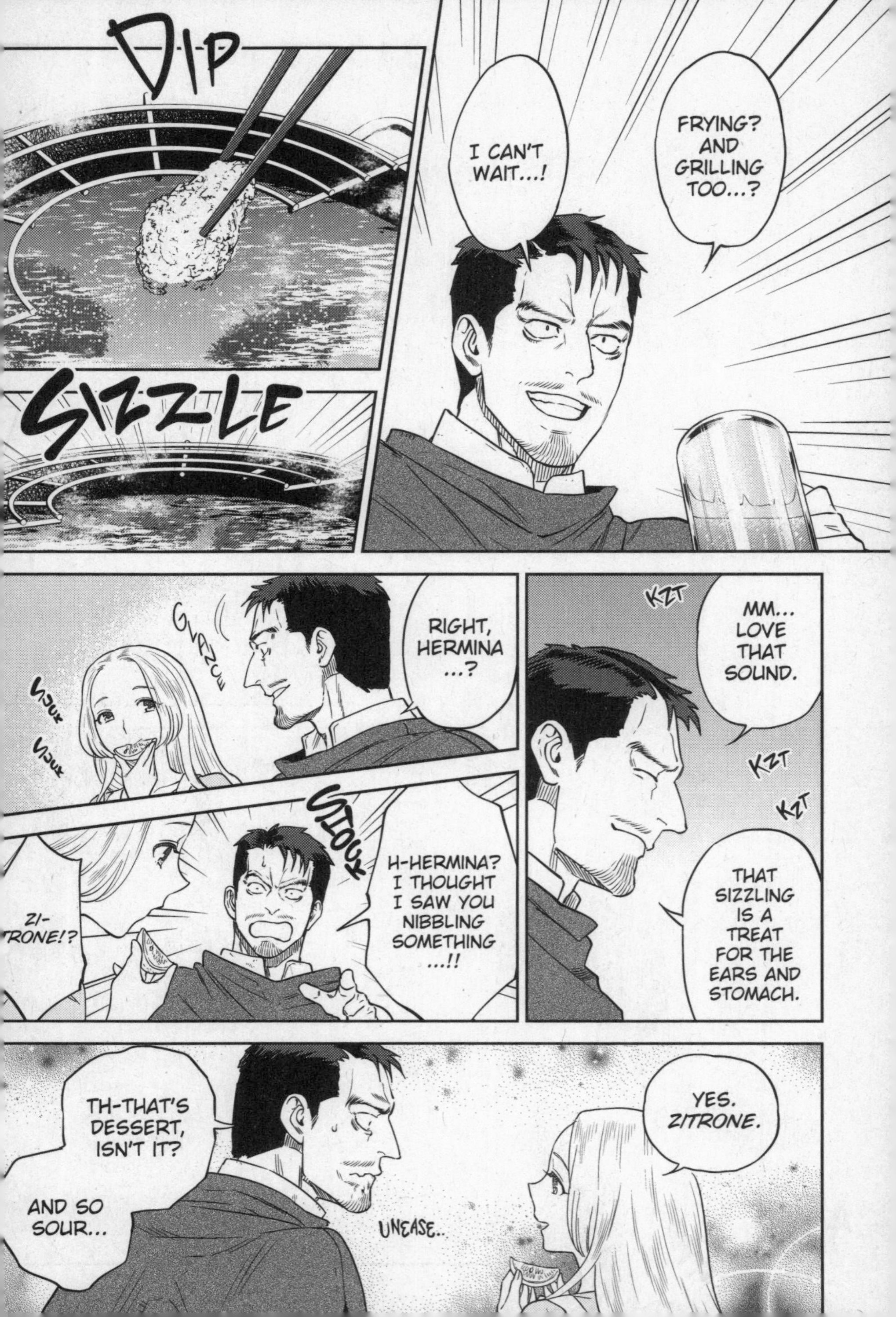
FRYING? AND GRILLING TOO...?
I CAN'T WAIT...!
DIP
SIZZLE
KZT
MM... LOVE THAT SOUND.
KZT
KZT
THAT SIZZLING IS A TREAT FOR THE EARS AND STOMACH.
RIGHT, HERMINA ...?
H-HERMINA? I THOUGHT I SAW YOU NIBBLING SOMETHING ...!!
ZI-TRONE!?
YES. ZITRONE.
TH-THAT'S DESSERT, ISN'T IT?
AND SO SOUR...
UNEASE..

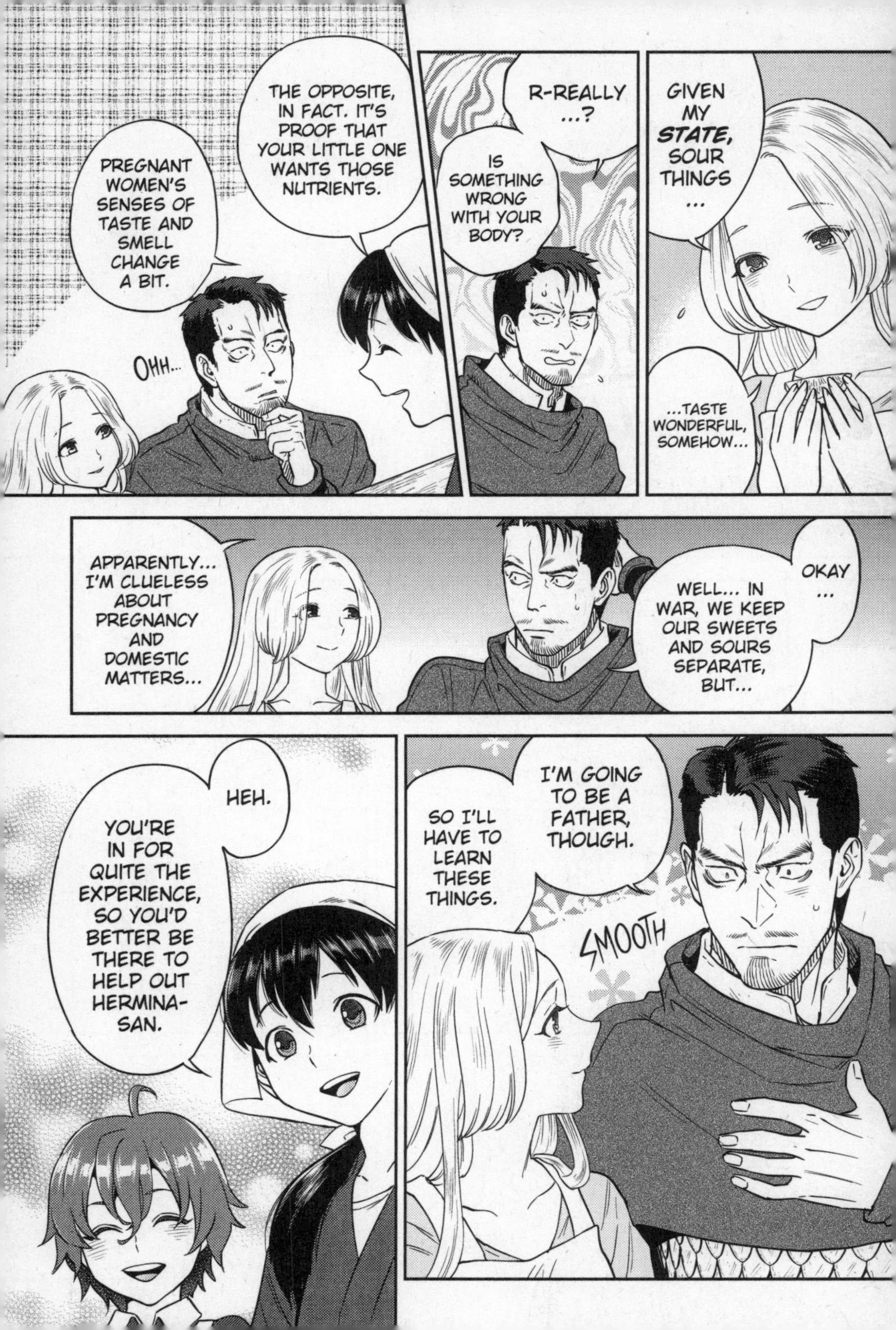
GIVEN MY STATE, SOUR THINGS ...
...TASTE WONDERFUL, SOMEHOW...
R-REALLY ...?
IS SOMETHING WRONG WITH YOUR BODY?
THE OPPOSITE, IN FACT. IT'S PROOF THAT YOUR LITTLE ONE WANTS THOSE NUTRIENTS.
PREGNANT WOMEN'S SENSES OF TASTE AND SMELL CHANGE A BIT.
OHH...
OKAY ...
WELL... IN WAR, WE KEEP OUR SWEETS AND SOURS SEPARATE, BUT...
APPARENTLY... I'M CLUELESS ABOUT PREGNANCY AND DOMESTIC MATTERS...
I'M GOING TO BE A FATHER, THOUGH.
SO I'LL HAVE TO LEARN THESE THINGS.
SMOOTH
HEH.
YOU'RE IN FOR QUITE THE EXPERIENCE, SO YOU'D BETTER BE THERE TO HELP OUT HERMINA-SAN.

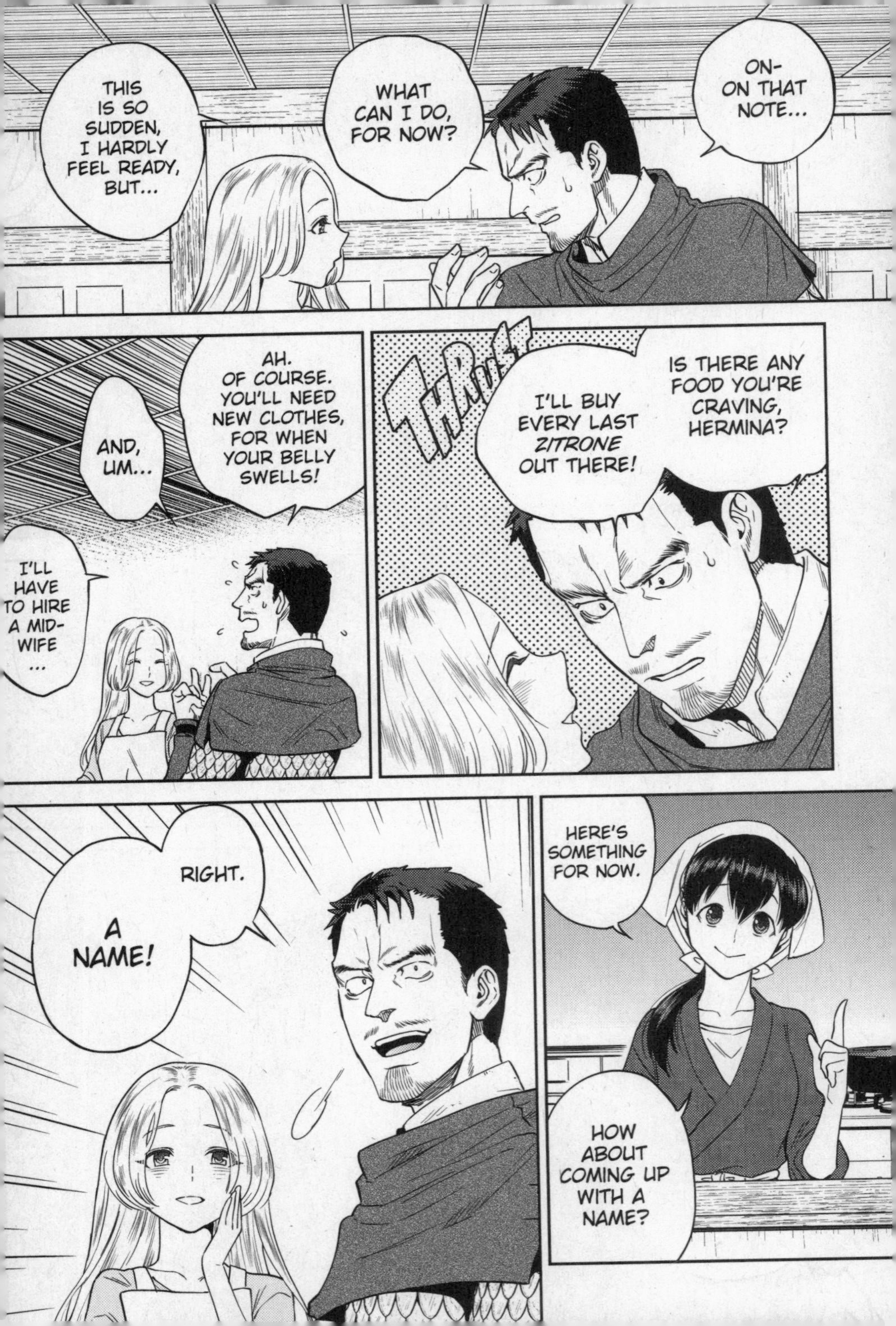
ON- ON THAT NOTE...
WHAT CAN I DO, FOR NOW?
THIS IS SO SUDDEN, I HARDLY FEEL READY, BUT...
IS THERE ANY FOOD YOU'RE CRAVING, HERMINA?
THRUST
I'LL BUY EVERY LAST *ZITRONE* OUT THERE!
AH. OF COURSE. YOU'LL NEED NEW CLOTHES, FOR WHEN YOUR BELLY SWELLS!
AND, UM...
I'LL HAVE TO HIRE A MID-WIFE ...
HERE'S SOMETHING FOR NOW.
HOW ABOUT COMING UP WITH A NAME?
RIGHT.
A NAME!

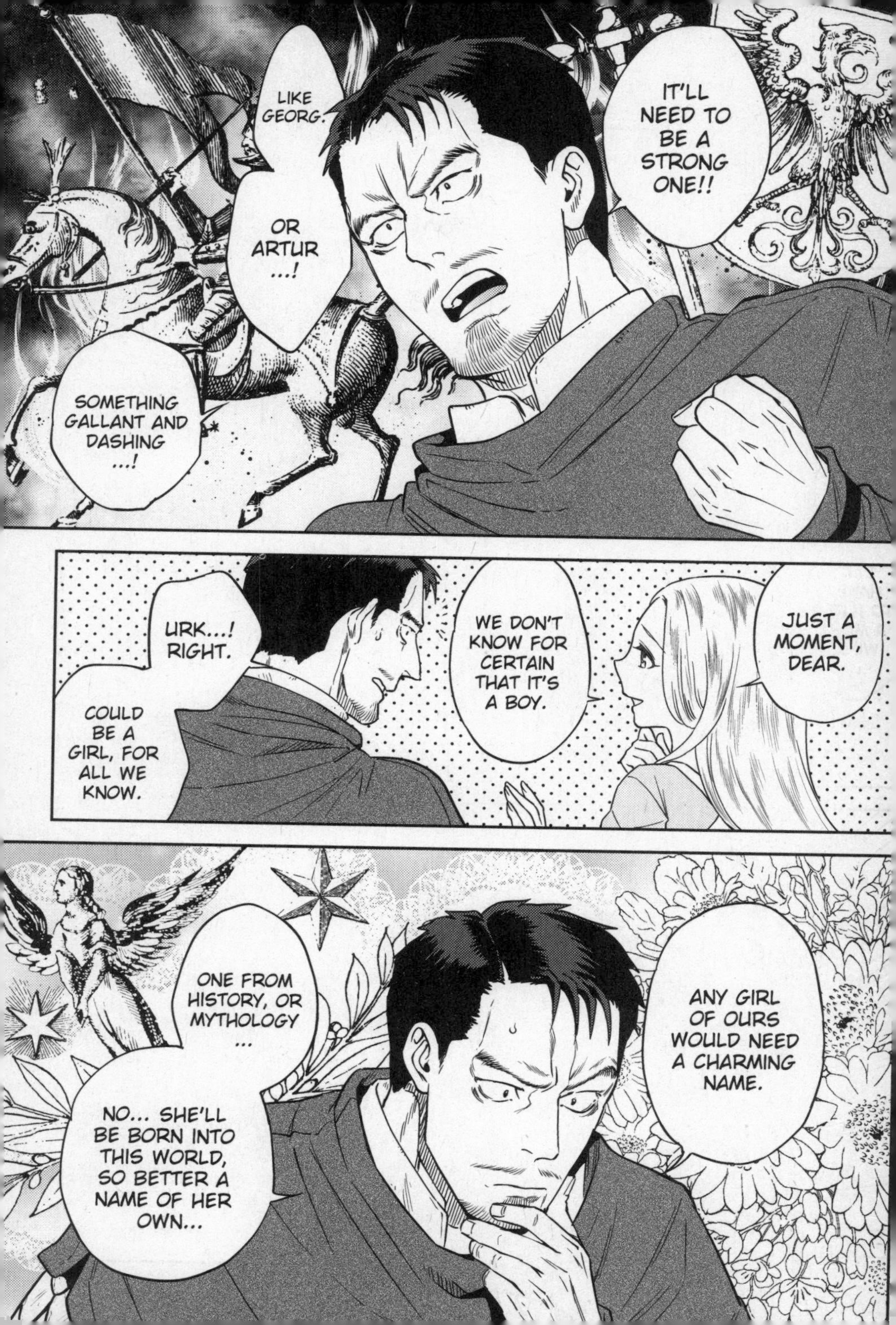
IT'LL NEED TO BE A STRONG ONE!!
LIKE GEORG.
OR ARTUR ...!
SOMETHING GALLANT AND DASHING ...!
JUST A MOMENT, DEAR.
WE DON'T KNOW FOR CERTAIN THAT IT'S A BOY.
URK...! RIGHT.
COULD BE A GIRL, FOR ALL WE KNOW.
ANY GIRL OF OURS WOULD NEED A CHARMING NAME.
ONE FROM HISTORY, OR MYTHOLOGY ...
NO... SHE'LL BE BORN INTO THIS WORLD, SO BETTER A NAME OF HER OWN...

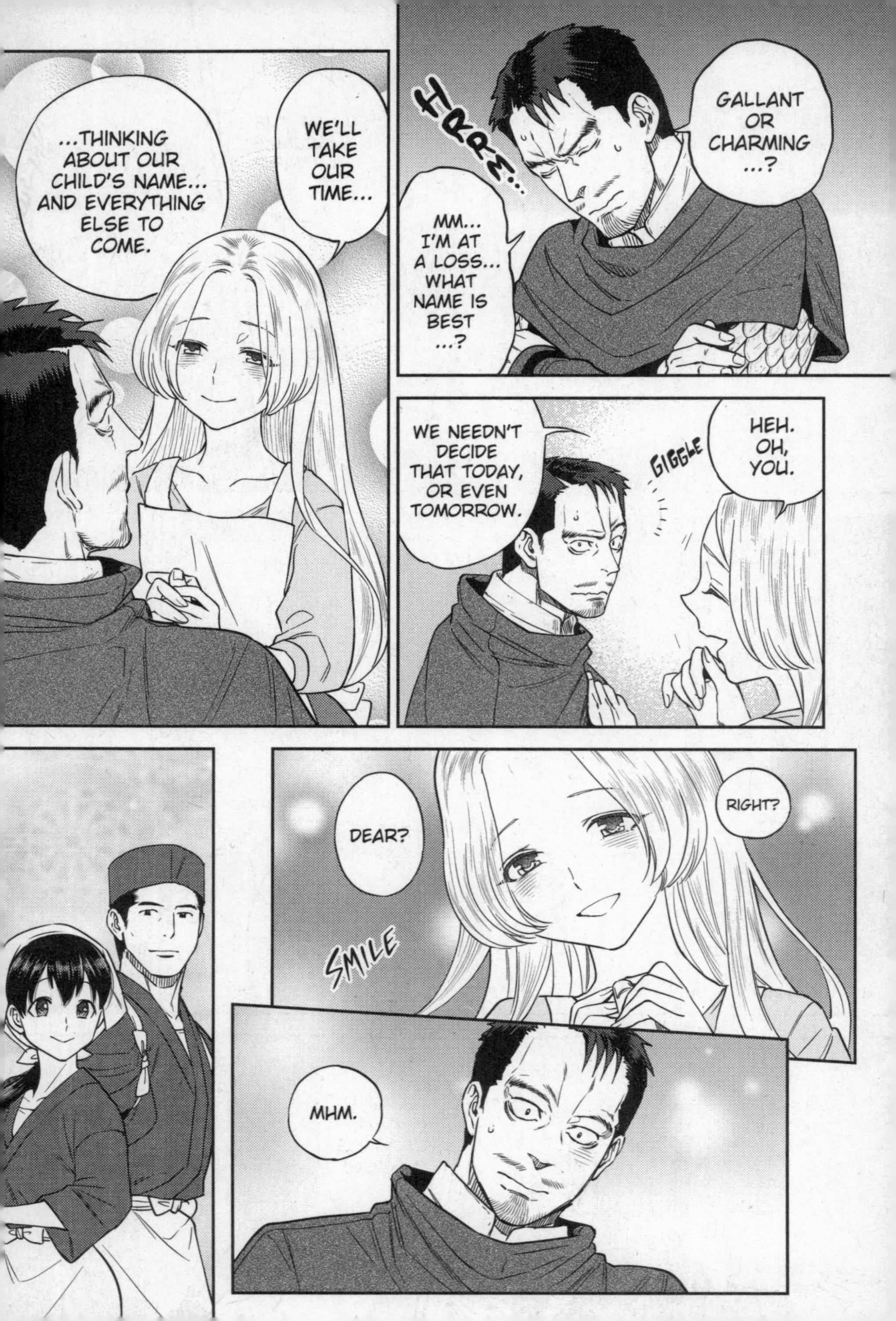
GALLANT OR CHARMING ...?
HRRE...
MM... I'M AT A LOSS... WHAT NAME IS BEST ...?
HEH. OH, YOU.
GIGGLE
WE NEEDN'T DECIDE THAT TODAY, OR EVEN TOMORROW.
WE'LL TAKE OUR TIME...
...THINKING ABOUT OUR CHILD'S NAME... AND EVERYTHING ELSE TO COME.
RIGHT?
DEAR?
SMILE
MHM.

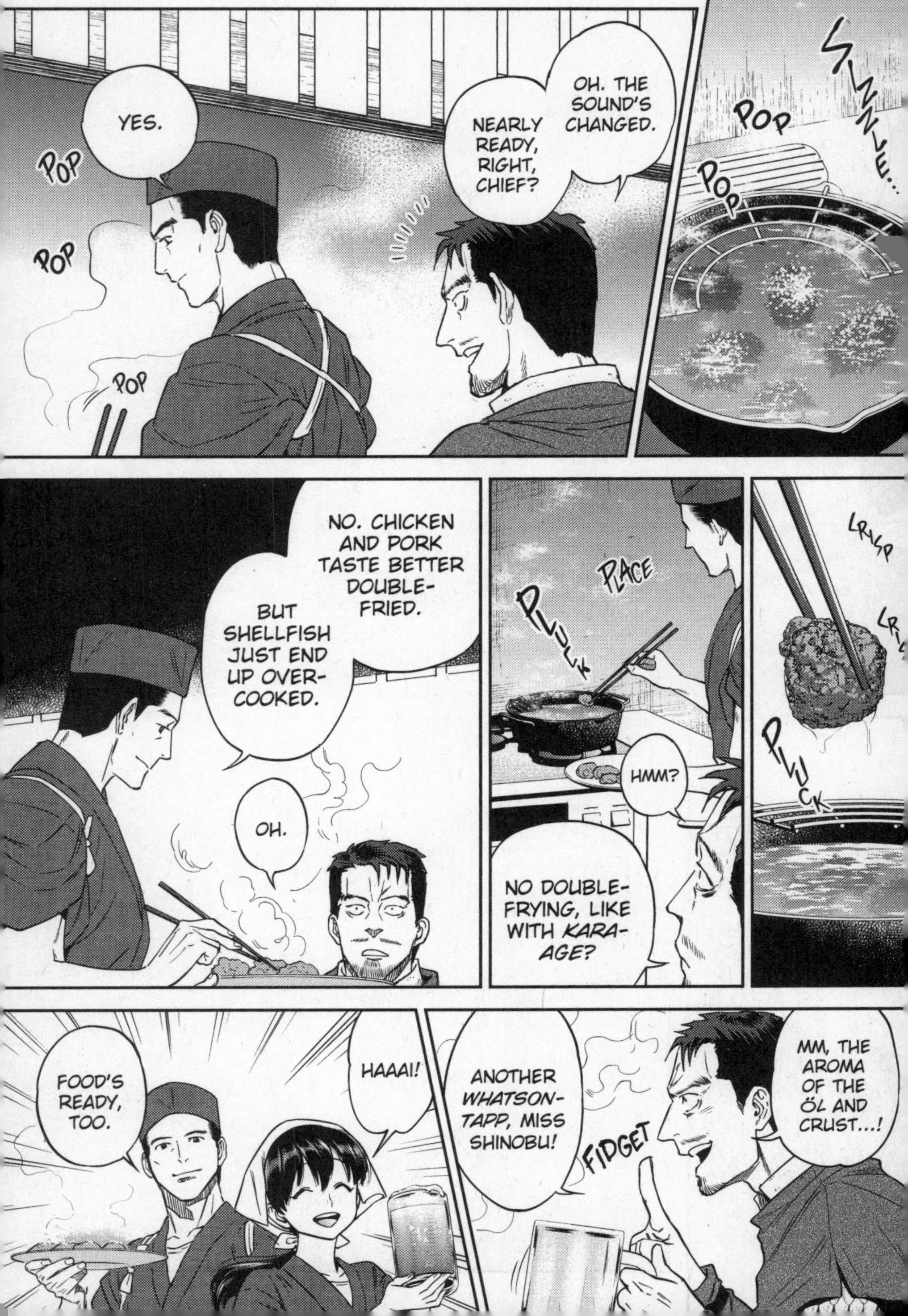
SIZZLE...
POP
POP
OH. THE SOUND'S CHANGED.
NEARLY READY, RIGHT, CHIEF?
YES.
POP
POP
POP
CRISP
PLUCK
PLACE
PLUCK
HMM?
NO DOUBLE-FRYING, LIKE WITH *KARA-AGE?*
NO. CHICKEN AND PORK TASTE BETTER DOUBLE-FRIED.
BUT SHELLFISH JUST END UP OVER-COOKED.
OH.
MM, THE AROMA OF THE ÖL AND CRUST...!
ANOTHER *WHATSON-TAPP,* MISS SHINOBU!
FIDGET
HAAAI!
FOOD'S READY, TOO.

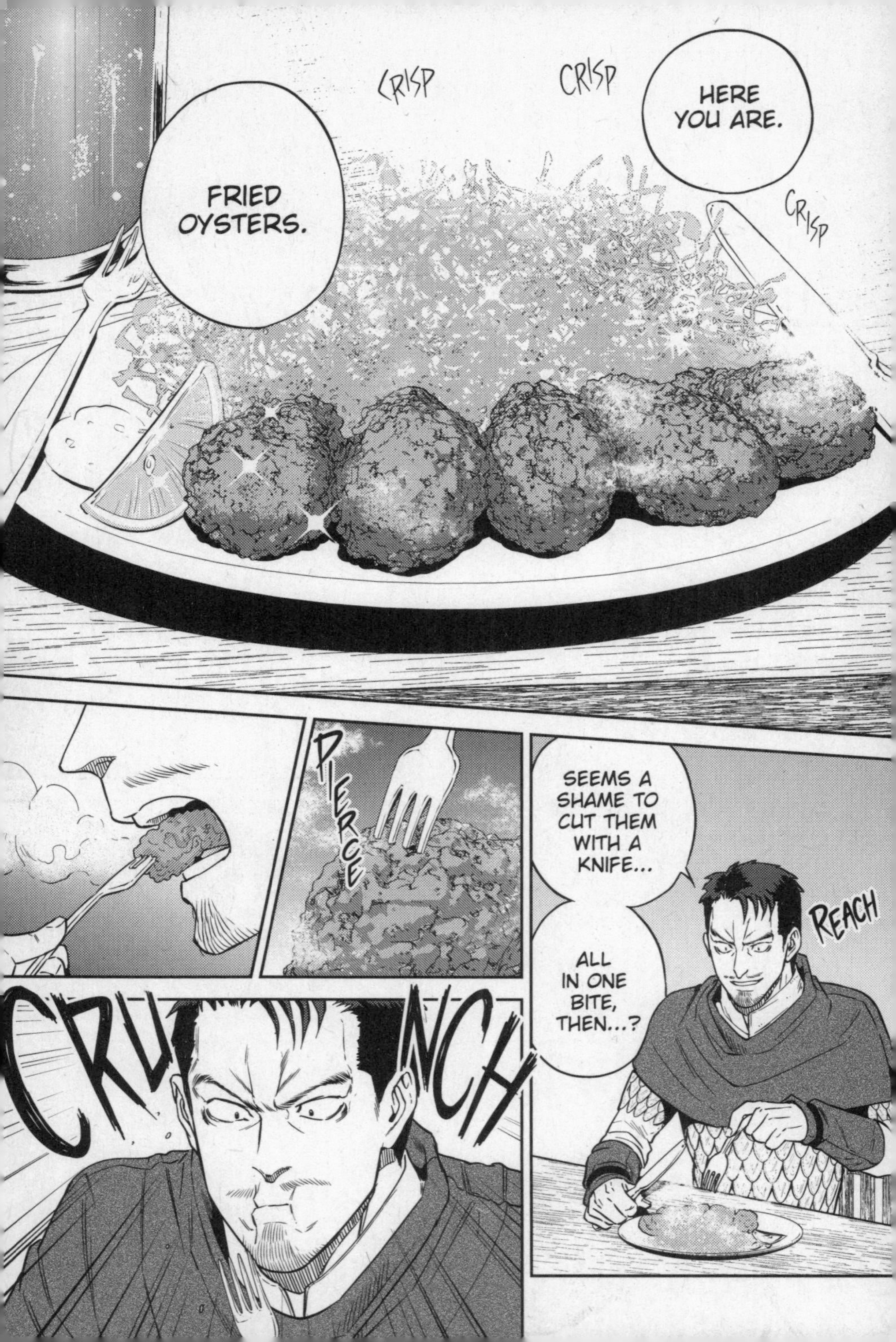
HERE YOU ARE.
CRISP
CRISP
CRISP
FRIED OYSTERS.
SEEMS A SHAME TO CUT THEM WITH A KNIFE...
REACH
ALL IN ONE BITE, THEN...?
PIERCE
CRUNCH

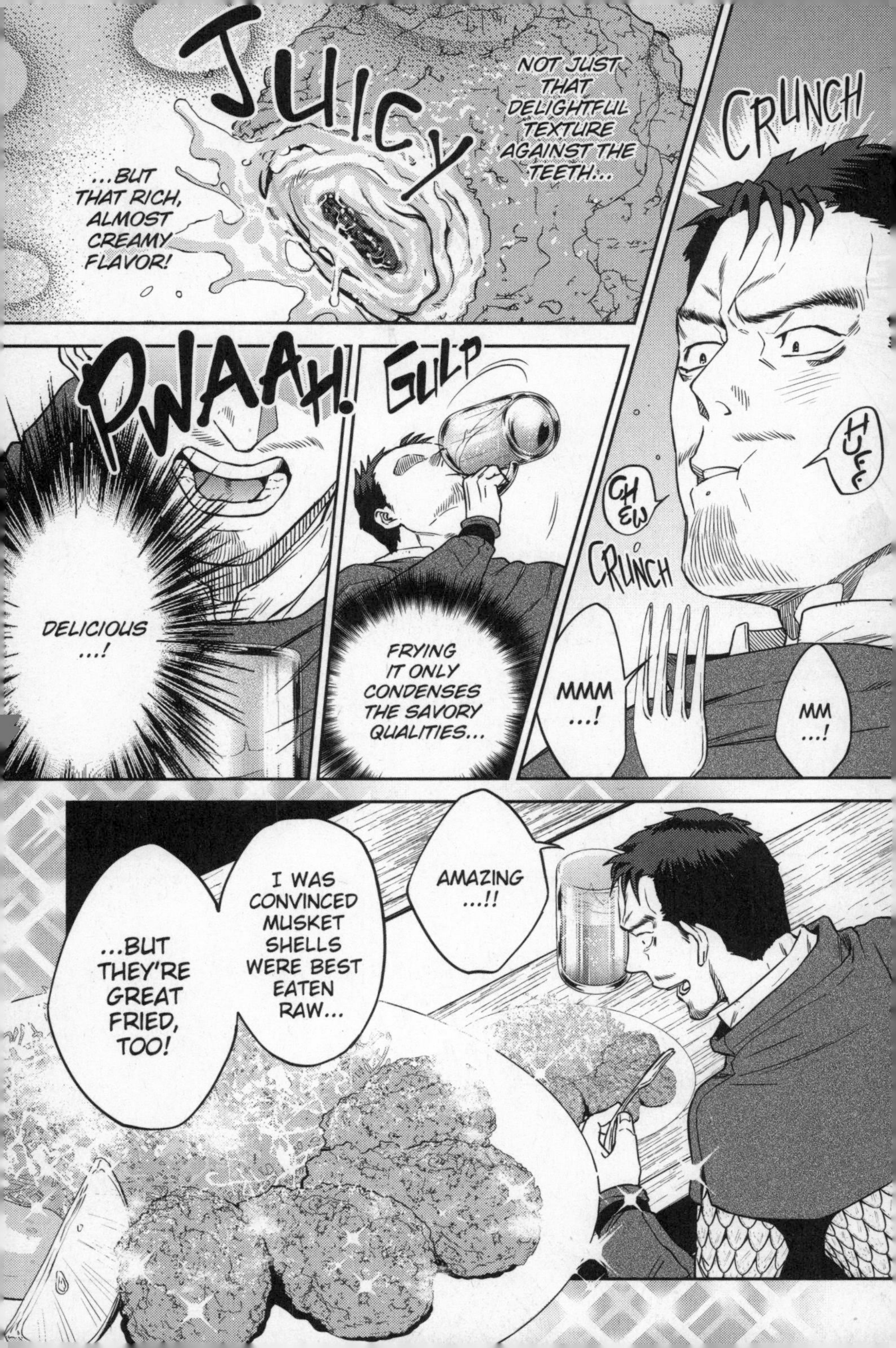
CRUNCH
HUFF
CHEW
CRUNCH
MM ...!
MMM ...!
JUICY
NOT JUST THAT DELIGHTFUL TEXTURE AGAINST THE TEETH...
...BUT THAT RICH, ALMOST CREAMY FLAVOR!
GULP
FRYING IT ONLY CONDENSES THE SAVORY QUALITIES...
PWAAH!
DELICIOUS ...!
AMAZING ...!!
I WAS CONVINCED MUSKET SHELLS WERE BEST EATEN RAW...
...BUT THEY'RE GREAT FRIED, TOO!

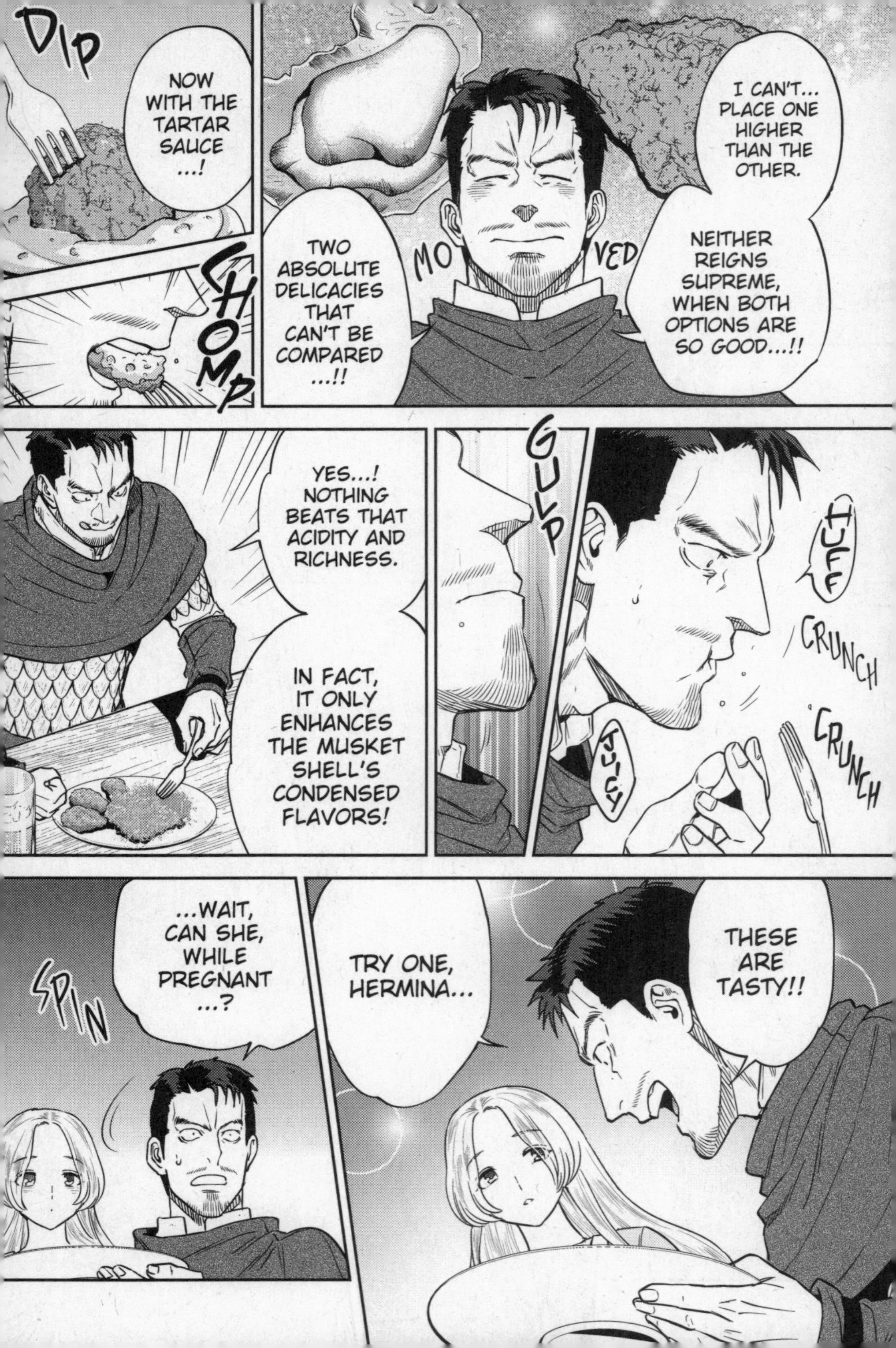
I CAN'T... PLACE ONE HIGHER THAN THE OTHER.
NEITHER REIGNS SUPREME, WHEN BOTH OPTIONS ARE SO GOOD...!!
MOVED
TWO ABSOLUTE DELICACIES THAT CAN'T BE COMPARED ...!!
DIP
NOW WITH THE TARTAR SAUCE ...!
CHOMP
GULP
HUFF
CRUNCH
CRUNCH
JUICY
YES...! NOTHING BEATS THAT ACIDITY AND RICHNESS.
IN FACT, IT ONLY ENHANCES THE MUSKET SHELL'S CONDENSED FLAVORS!
THESE ARE TASTY!!
TRY ONE, HERMINA...
...WAIT, CAN SHE, WHILE PREGNANT ...?
SPIN

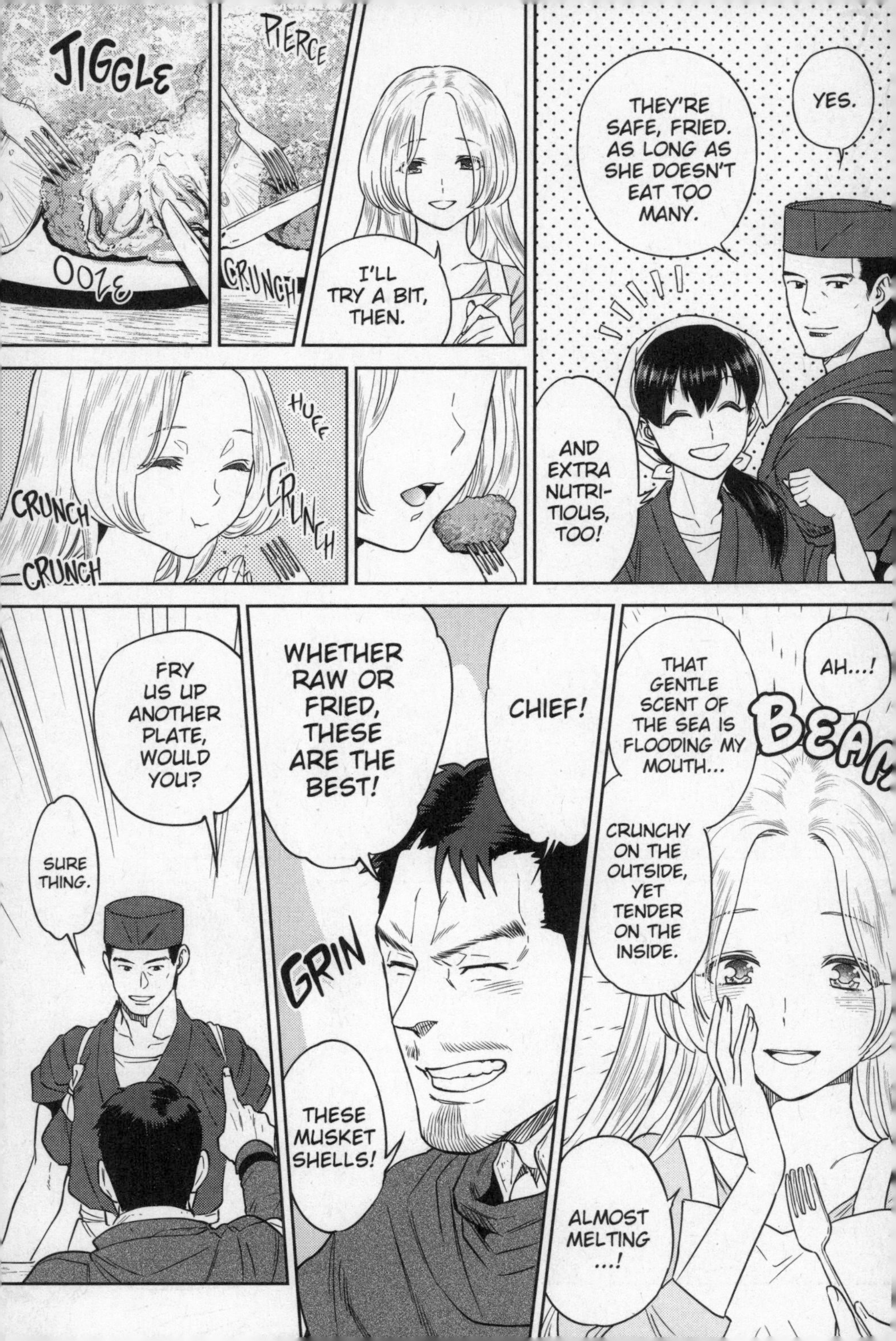
YES.
THEY'RE SAFE, FRIED. AS LONG AS SHE DOESN'T EAT TOO MANY.
AND EXTRA NUTRI-TIOUS, TOO!
I'LL TRY A BIT, THEN.
PIERCE
CRUNCH
JIGGLE
OOZE
HUFF
CRUNCH
CRUNCH
CRUNCH
AH...!
BEAM
THAT GENTLE SCENT OF THE SEA IS FLOODING MY MOUTH...
CRUNCHY ON THE OUTSIDE, YET TENDER ON THE INSIDE.
ALMOST MELTING ...!
CHIEF!
WHETHER RAW OR FRIED, THESE ARE THE BEST!
GRIN
THESE MUSKET SHELLS!
FRY US UP ANOTHER PLATE, WOULD YOU?
SURE THING.

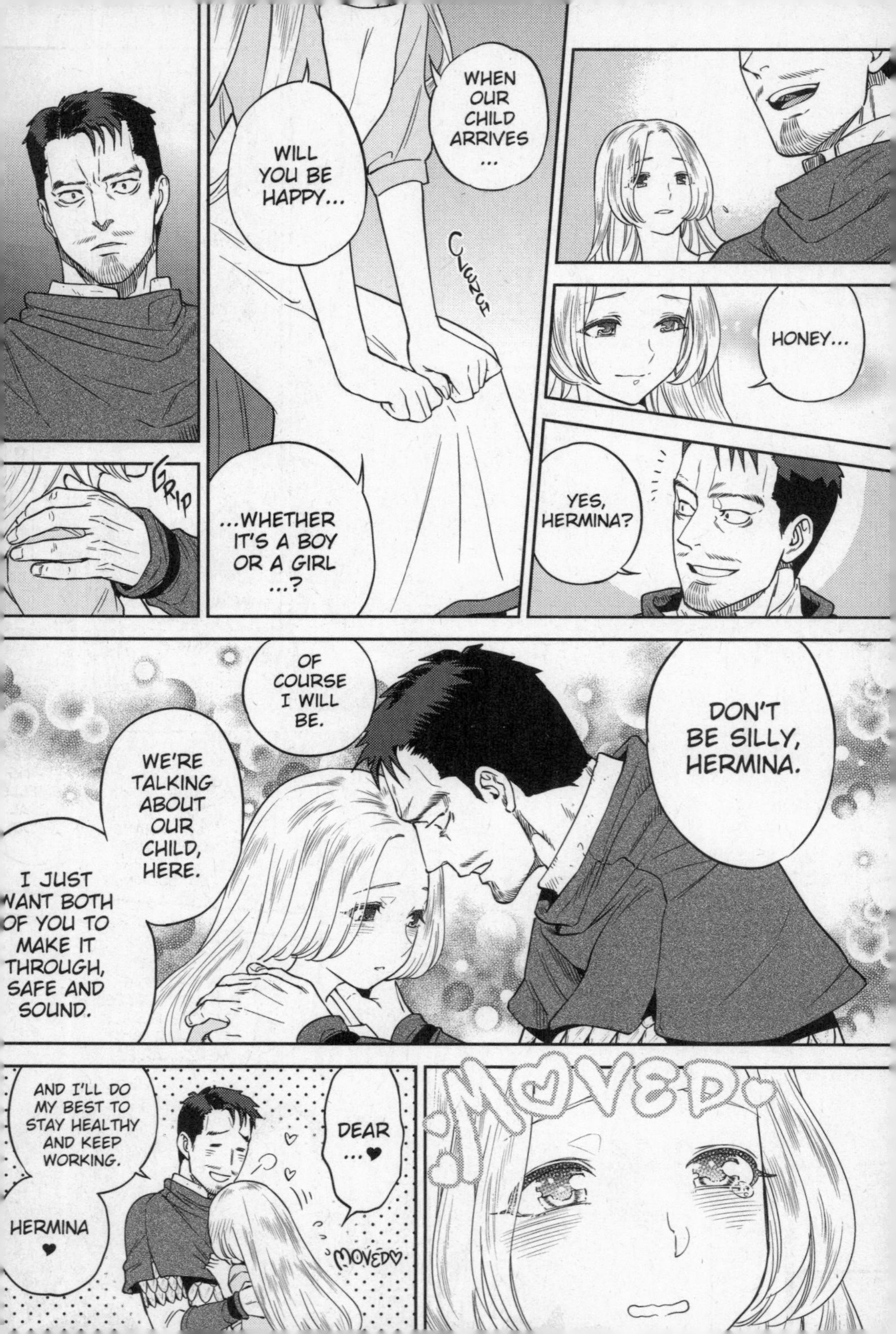

HONEY...
YES, HERMINA?
WHEN OUR CHILD ARRIVES ...
WILL YOU BE HAPPY...
CLENCH
...WHETHER IT'S A BOY OR A GIRL ...?
GRIP
DON'T BE SILLY, HERMINA.
OF COURSE I WILL BE.
WE'RE TALKING ABOUT OUR CHILD, HERE.
I JUST WANT BOTH OF YOU TO MAKE IT THROUGH, SAFE AND SOUND.
MOVED
DEAR ...♥
AND I'LL DO MY BEST TO STAY HEALTHY AND KEEP WORKING.
HERMINA ♥
MOVED

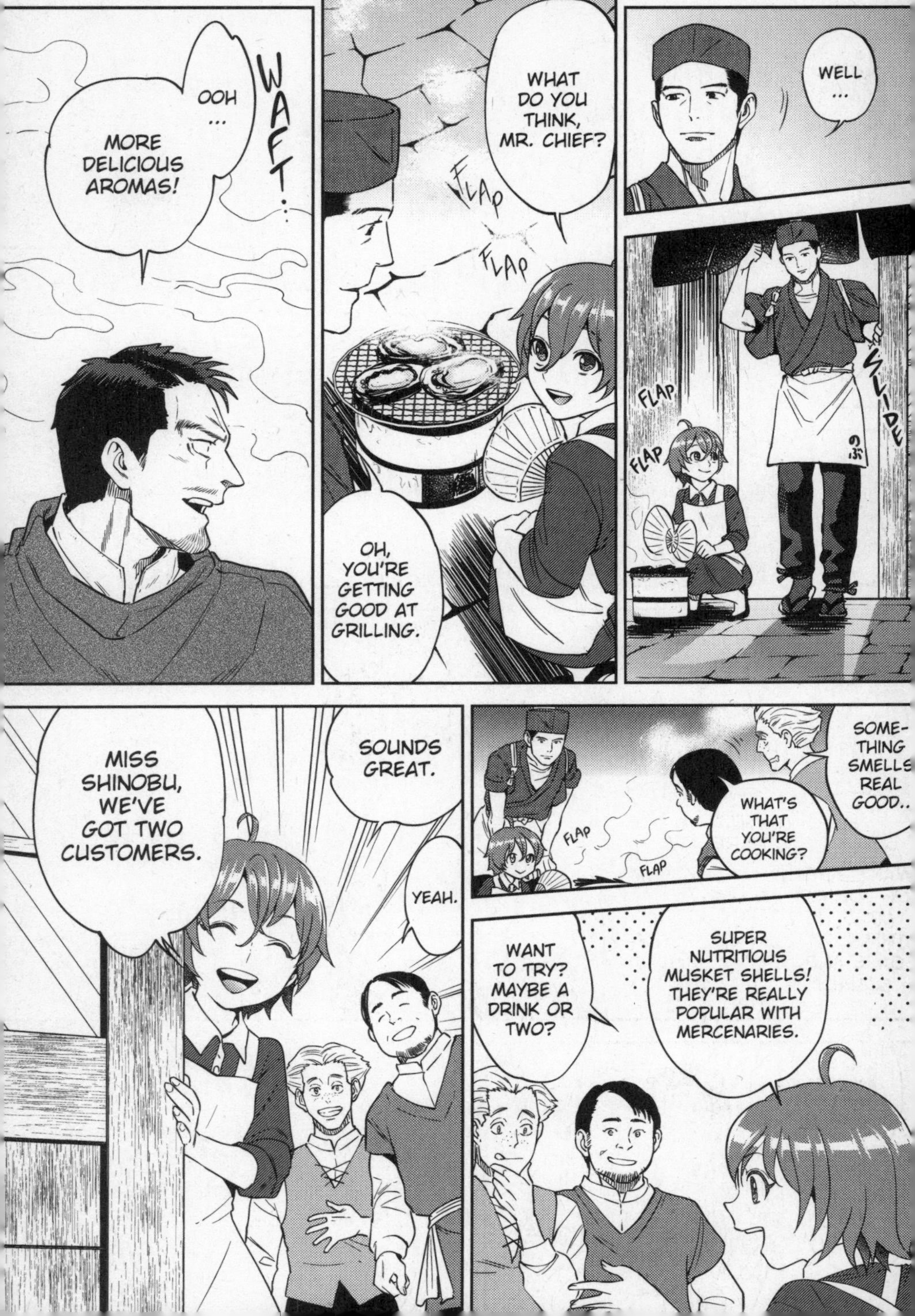
WELL ...
FLAP
FLAP
SLIDE
WHAT DO YOU THINK, MR. CHIEF?
FLAP
FLAP
OH, YOU'RE GETTING GOOD AT GRILLING.
WAFT...
OOH ...
MORE DELICIOUS AROMAS!
SOME-THING SMELLS REAL GOOD..
WHAT'S THAT YOU'RE COOKING?
FLAP
FLAP
SUPER NUTRITIOUS MUSKET SHELLS! THEY'RE REALLY POPULAR WITH MERCENARIES.
WANT TO TRY? MAYBE A DRINK OR TWO?
SOUNDS GREAT.
YEAH.
MISS SHINOBU, WE'VE GOT TWO CUSTOMERS.

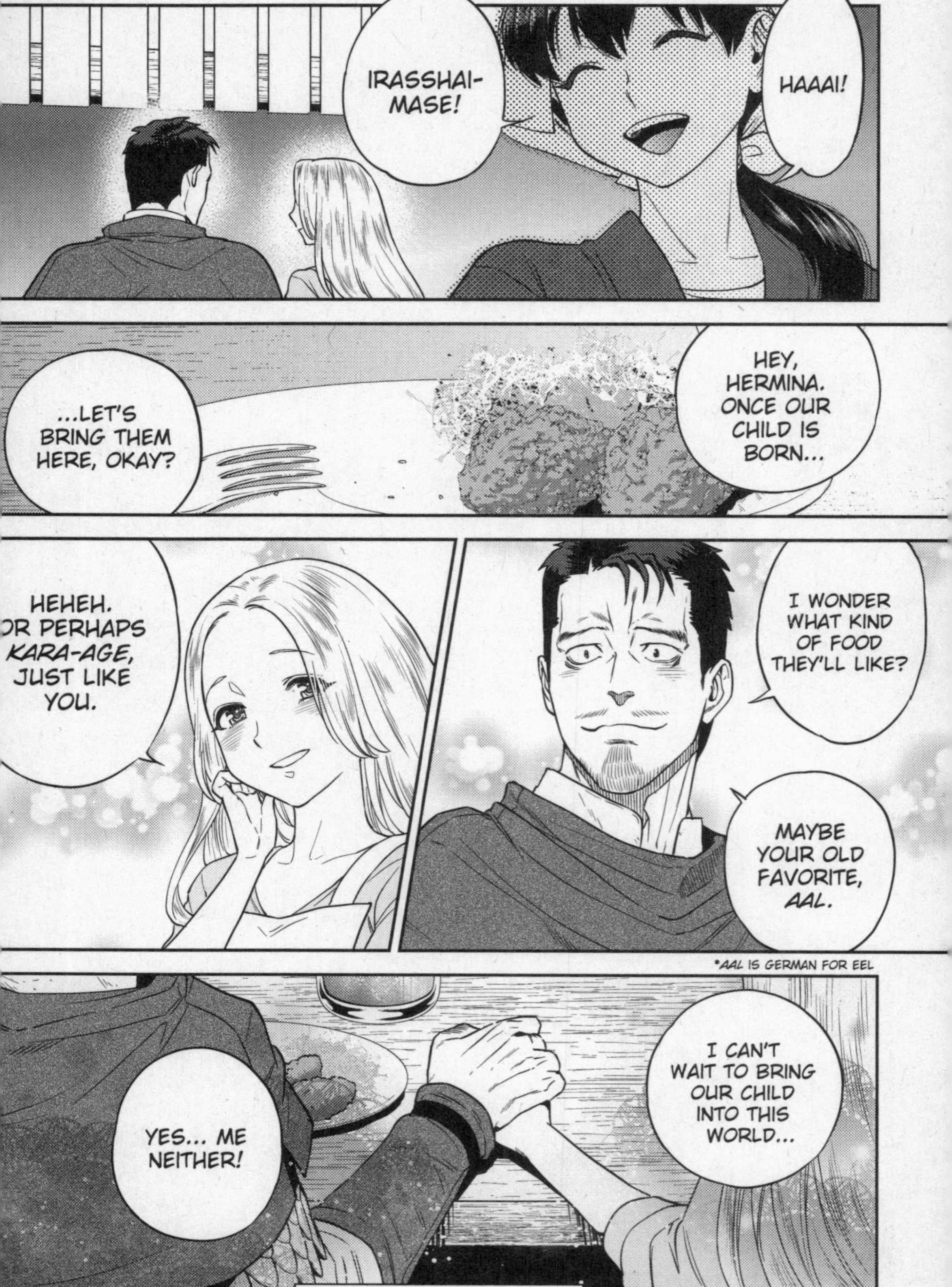
HAAAI!
IRASSHAI-MASE!
HEY, HERMINA. ONCE OUR CHILD IS BORN...
...LET'S BRING THEM HERE, OKAY?
I WONDER WHAT KIND OF FOOD THEY'LL LIKE?
MAYBE YOUR OLD FAVORITE, AAL.
HEHEH. OR PERHAPS KARA-AGE, JUST LIKE YOU.
*AAL IS GERMAN FOR EEL
I CAN'T WAIT TO BRING OUR CHILD INTO THIS WORLD...
YES... ME NEITHER!
COURSE 32 - CLOSING TIME

Fried Oysters

OTHERWORLDLY IZAKAYA
NOBU

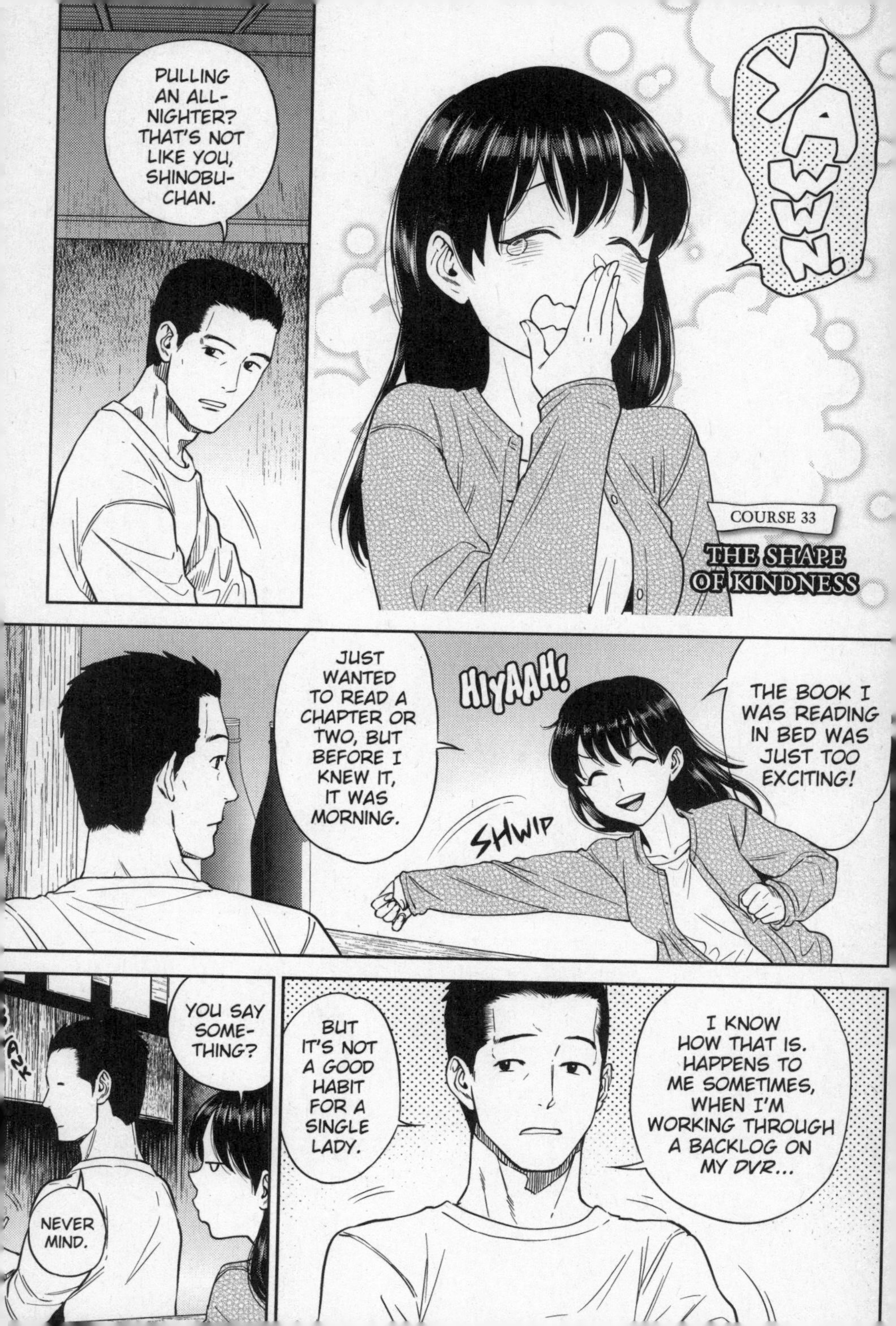

YAWN.
COURSE 33
THE SHAPE OF KINDNESS
PULLING AN ALL-NIGHTER? THAT'S NOT LIKE YOU, SHINOBU-CHAN.
THE BOOK I WAS READING IN BED WAS JUST TOO EXCITING!
HIYAAH!
JUST WANTED TO READ A CHAPTER OR TWO, BUT BEFORE I KNEW IT, IT WAS MORNING.
SHWIP
I KNOW HOW THAT IS. HAPPENS TO ME SOMETIMES, WHEN I'M WORKING THROUGH A BACKLOG ON MY DVR...
BUT IT'S NOT A GOOD HABIT FOR A SINGLE LADY.
YOU SAY SOME-THING?
NEVER MIND.

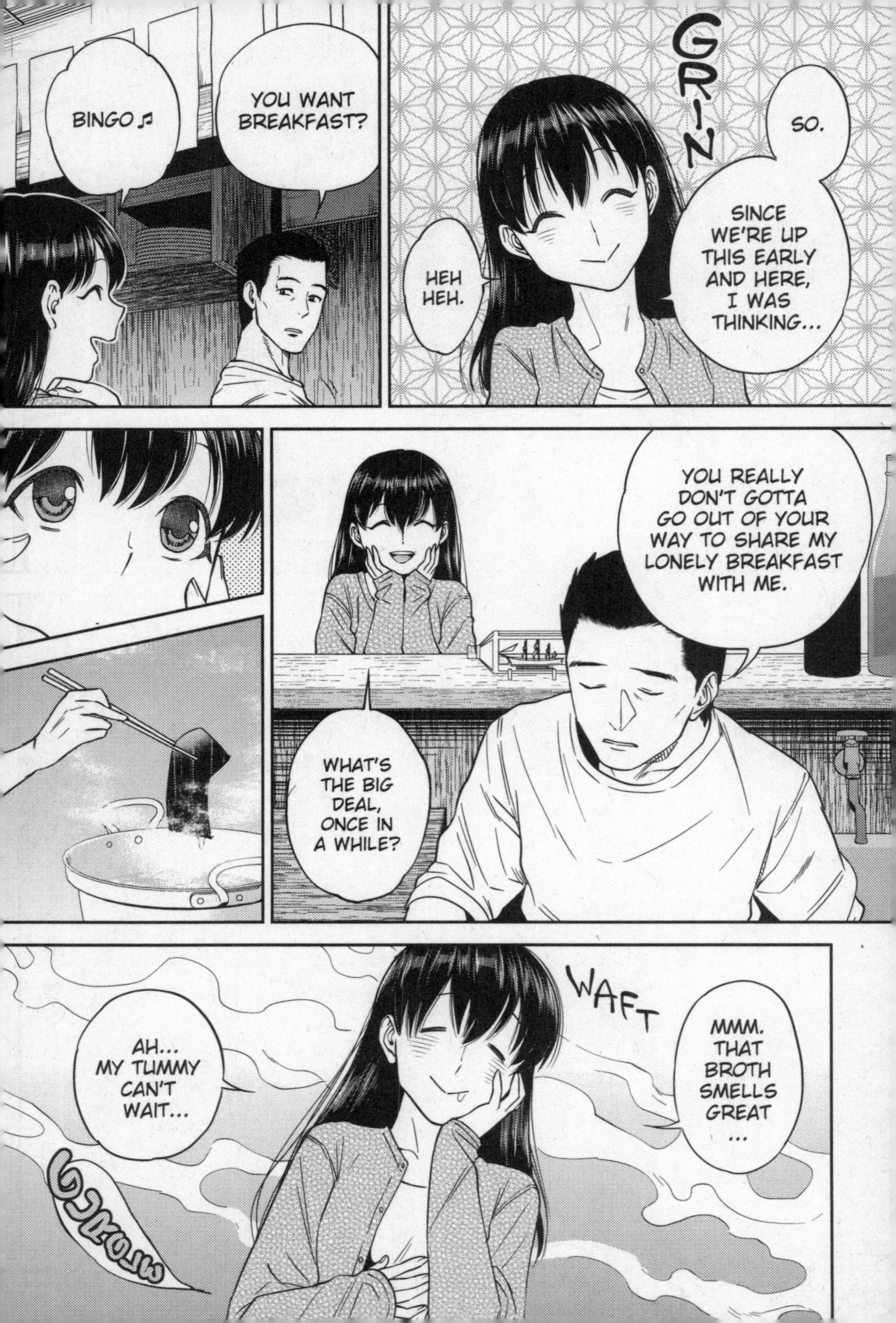
GRIN
SO.
SINCE WE'RE UP THIS EARLY AND HERE, I WAS THINKING...
HEH HEH.
YOU WANT BREAKFAST?
BINGO ♫
YOU REALLY DON'T GOTTA GO OUT OF YOUR WAY TO SHARE MY LONELY BREAKFAST WITH ME.
WHAT'S THE BIG DEAL, ONCE IN A WHILE?
WAFT
MMM. THAT BROTH SMELLS GREAT ...
AH... MY TUMMY CAN'T WAIT...

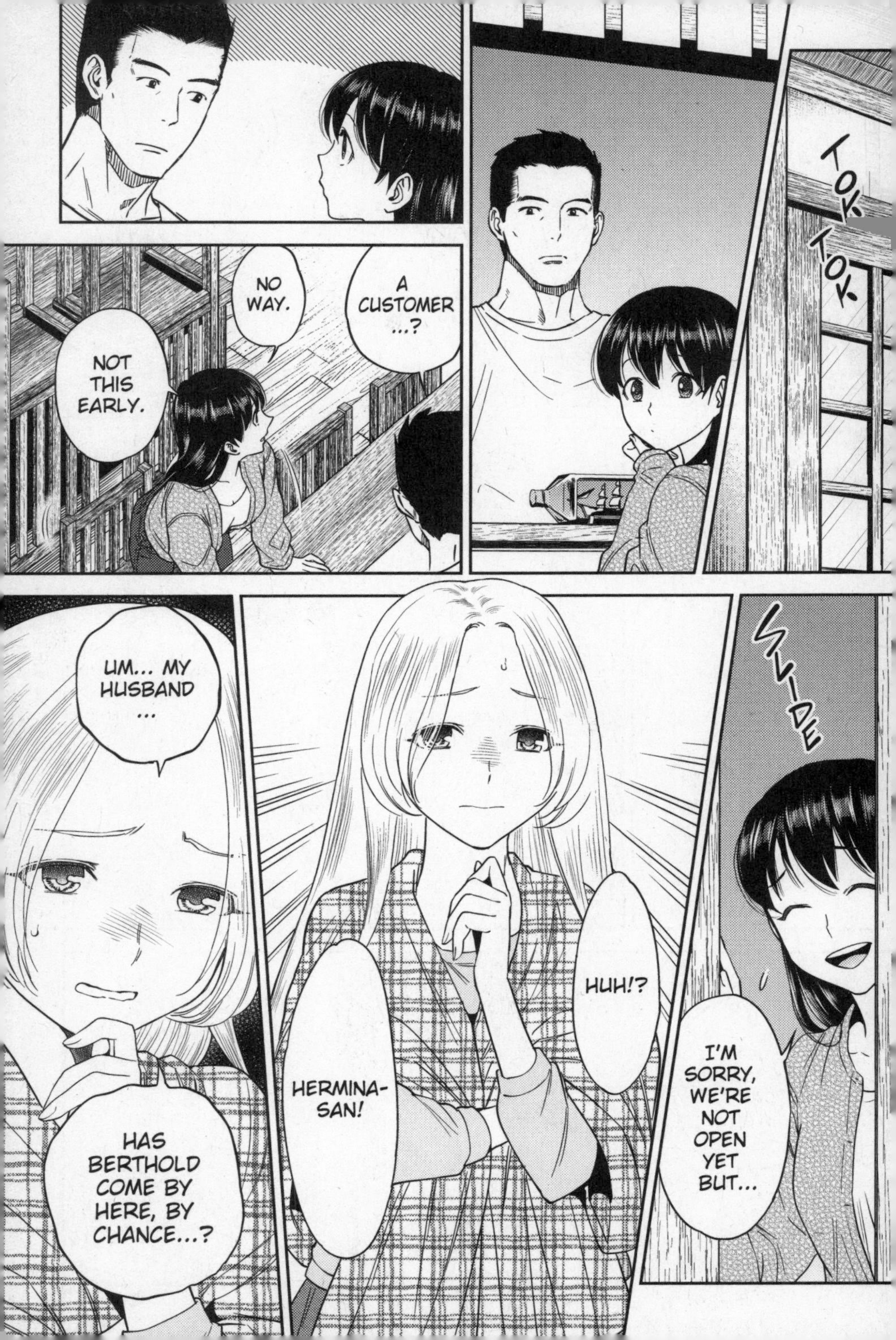
TOK TOK
A CUSTOMER ...?
NO WAY.
NOT THIS EARLY.
SLIDE
I'M SORRY, WE'RE NOT OPEN YET BUT...
HUH!?
HERMINA-SAN!
UM... MY HUSBAND ...
HAS BERTHOLD COME BY HERE, BY CHANCE...?

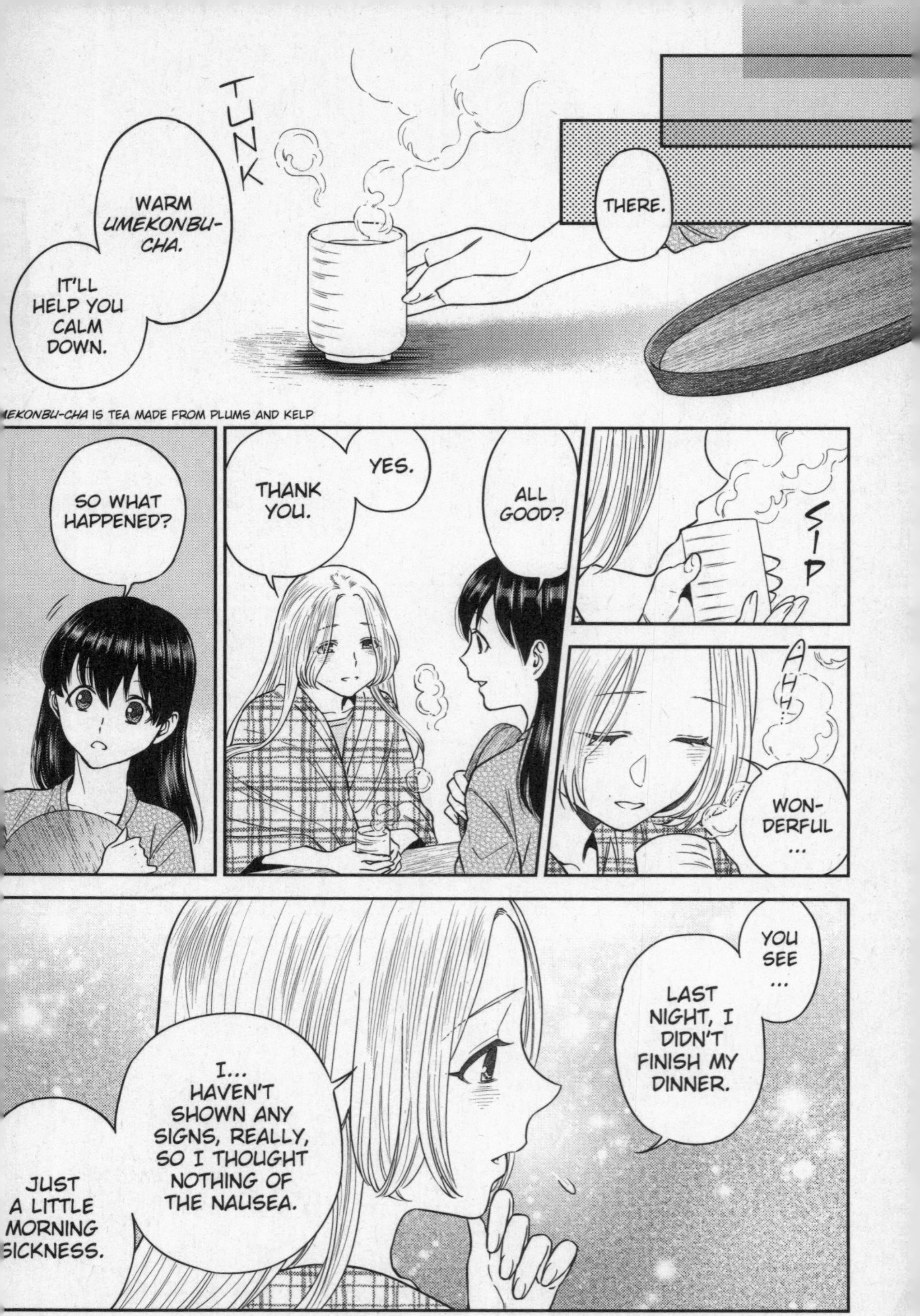
THERE.
TUNK
WARM UMEKONBU-CHA.
IT'LL HELP YOU CALM DOWN.
MEKONBU-CHA IS TEA MADE FROM PLUMS AND KELP
SIP
AHH...!
WON-DERFUL ...
ALL GOOD?
YES.
THANK YOU.
SO WHAT HAPPENED?
YOU SEE ...
LAST NIGHT, I DIDN'T FINISH MY DINNER.
I... HAVEN'T SHOWN ANY SIGNS, REALLY, SO I THOUGHT NOTHING OF THE NAUSEA.
JUST A LITTLE MORNING SICKNESS.

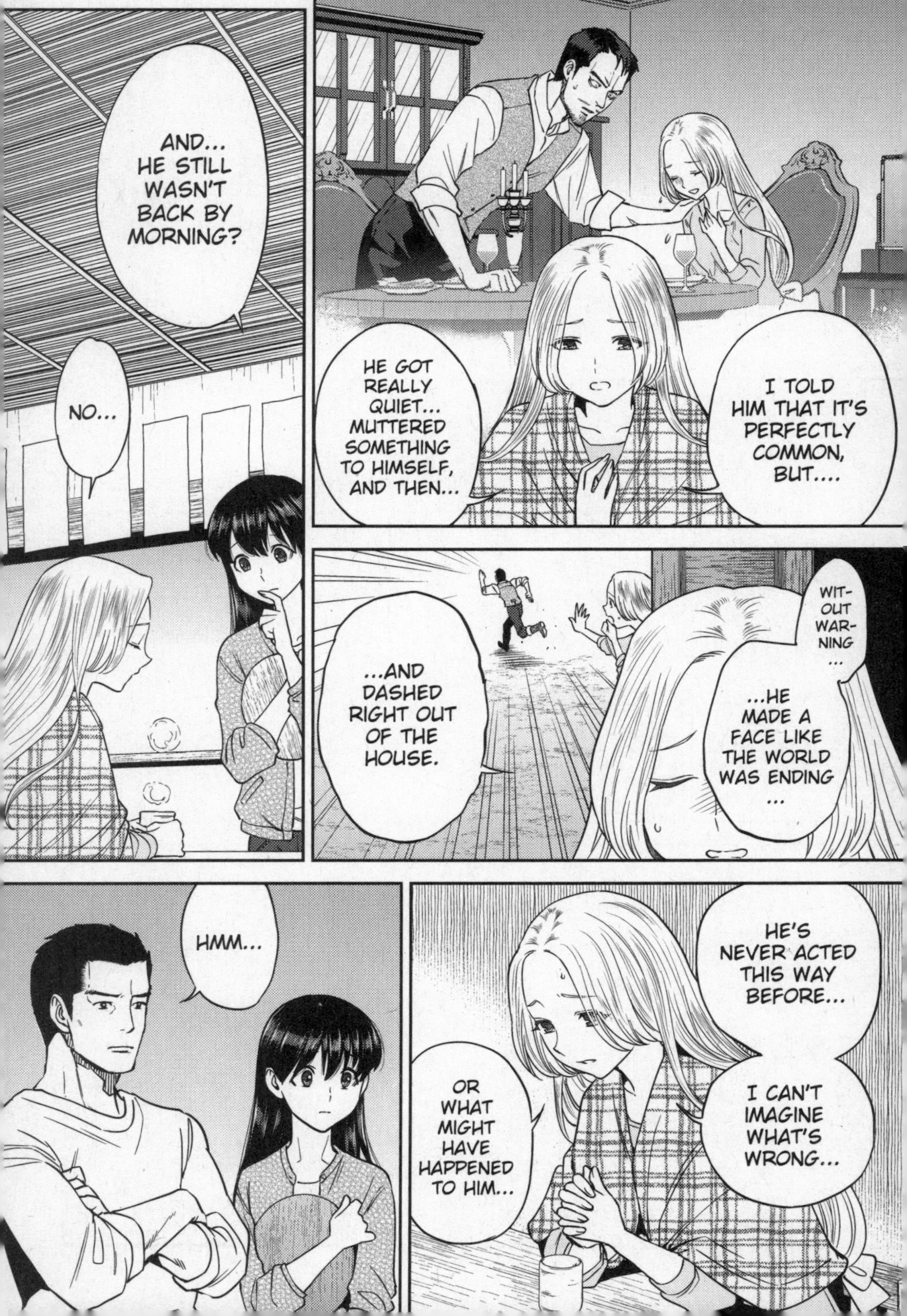
I TOLD HIM THAT IT'S PERFECTLY COMMON, BUT....
HE GOT REALLY QUIET... MUTTERED SOMETHING TO HIMSELF, AND THEN...
WIT-OUT WAR-NING ...
...HE MADE A FACE LIKE THE WORLD WAS ENDING ...
...AND DASHED RIGHT OUT OF THE HOUSE.
AND... HE STILL WASN'T BACK BY MORNING?
NO...
HE'S NEVER ACTED THIS WAY BEFORE...
I CAN'T IMAGINE WHAT'S WRONG...
OR WHAT MIGHT HAVE HAPPENED TO HIM...
HMM...

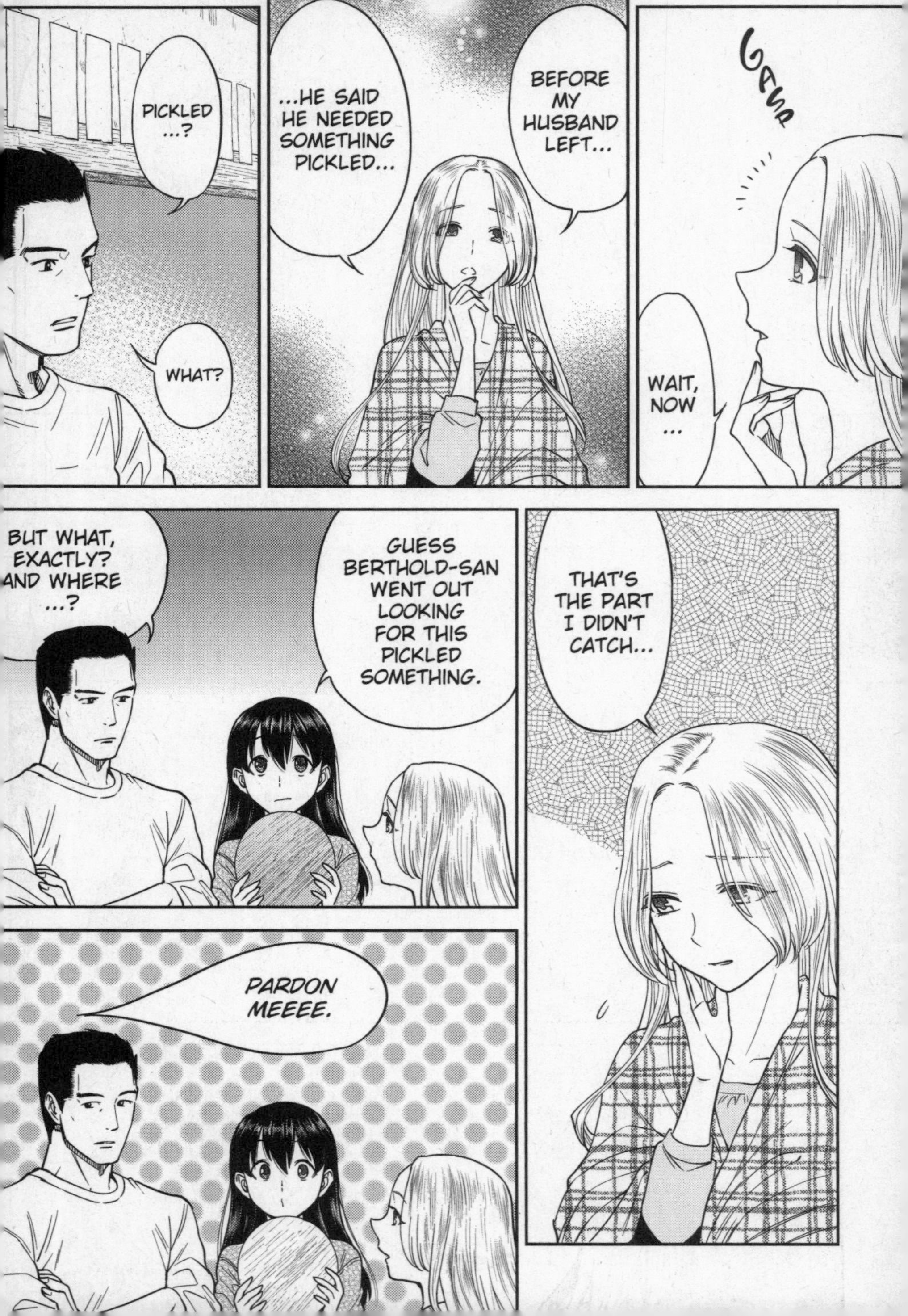
GASA
WAIT, NOW ...
BEFORE MY HUSBAND LEFT...
...HE SAID HE NEEDED SOMETHING PICKLED...
PICKLED ...?
WHAT?
THAT'S THE PART I DIDN'T CATCH...
GUESS BERTHOLD-SAN WENT OUT LOOKING FOR THIS PICKLED SOMETHING.
BUT WHAT, EXACTLY? AND WHERE ...?
PARDON MEEEE.

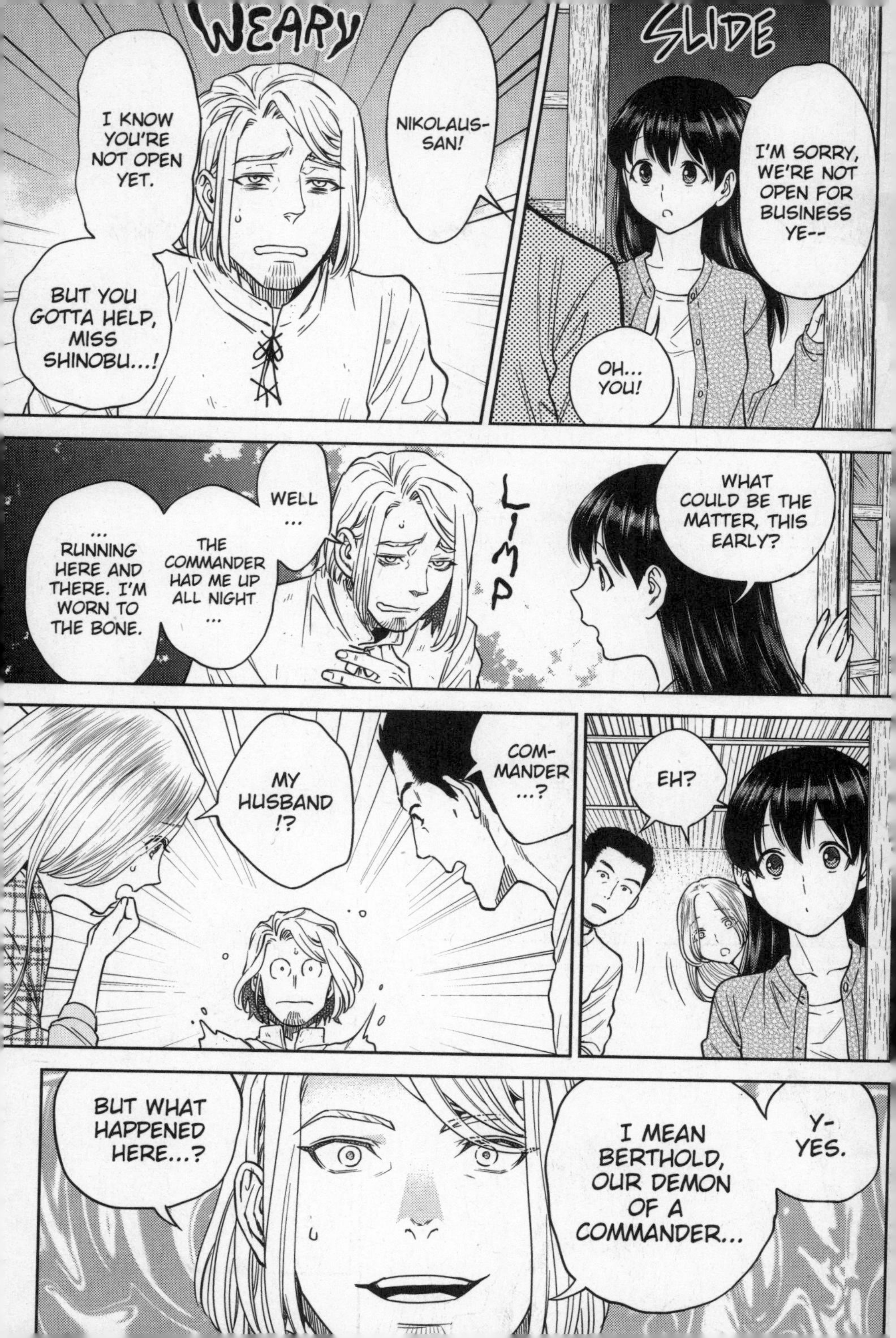
SLIDE
I'M SORRY, WE'RE NOT OPEN FOR BUSINESS YE--
OH... YOU!
WEARY
NIKOLAUS-SAN!
I KNOW YOU'RE NOT OPEN YET.
BUT YOU GOTTA HELP, MISS SHINOBU...!
WHAT COULD BE THE MATTER, THIS EARLY?
LIMP
WELL ...
THE COMMANDER HAD ME UP ALL NIGHT ...
... RUNNING HERE AND THERE. I'M WORN TO THE BONE.
EH?
COM-MANDER ...?
MY HUSBAND !?
Y-YES.
I MEAN BERTHOLD, OUR DEMON OF A COMMANDER...
BUT WHAT HAPPENED HERE...?

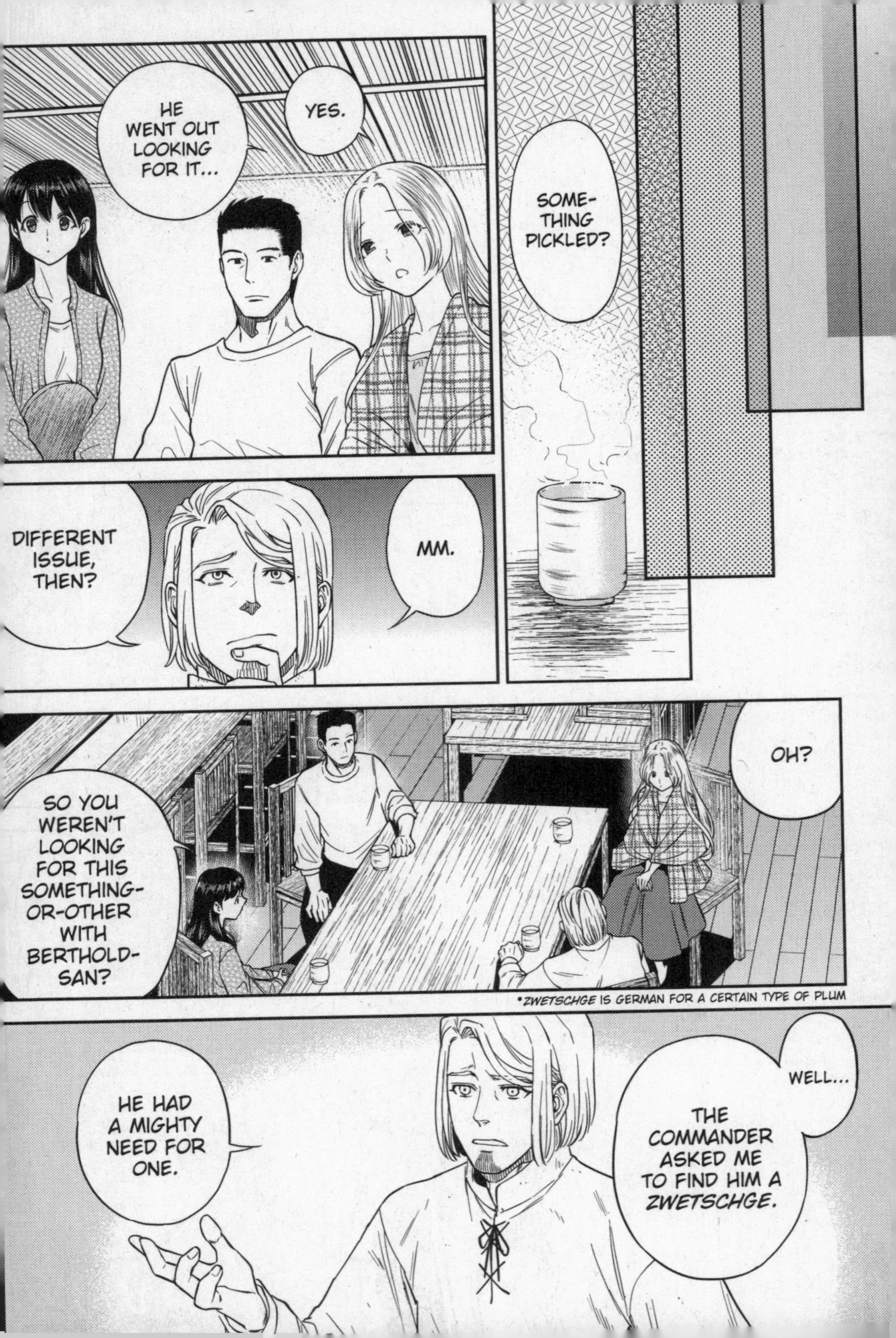
SOME-THING PICKLED?
YES.
HE WENT OUT LOOKING FOR IT...
MM.
DIFFERENT ISSUE, THEN?
OH?
SO YOU WEREN'T LOOKING FOR THIS SOMETHING-OR-OTHER WITH BERTHOLD-SAN?
WELL...
THE COMMANDER ASKED ME TO FIND HIM A *ZWETSCHGE.*
HE HAD A MIGHTY NEED FOR ONE.

**ZWETSCHGE* IS GERMAN FOR A CERTAIN TYPE OF PLUM

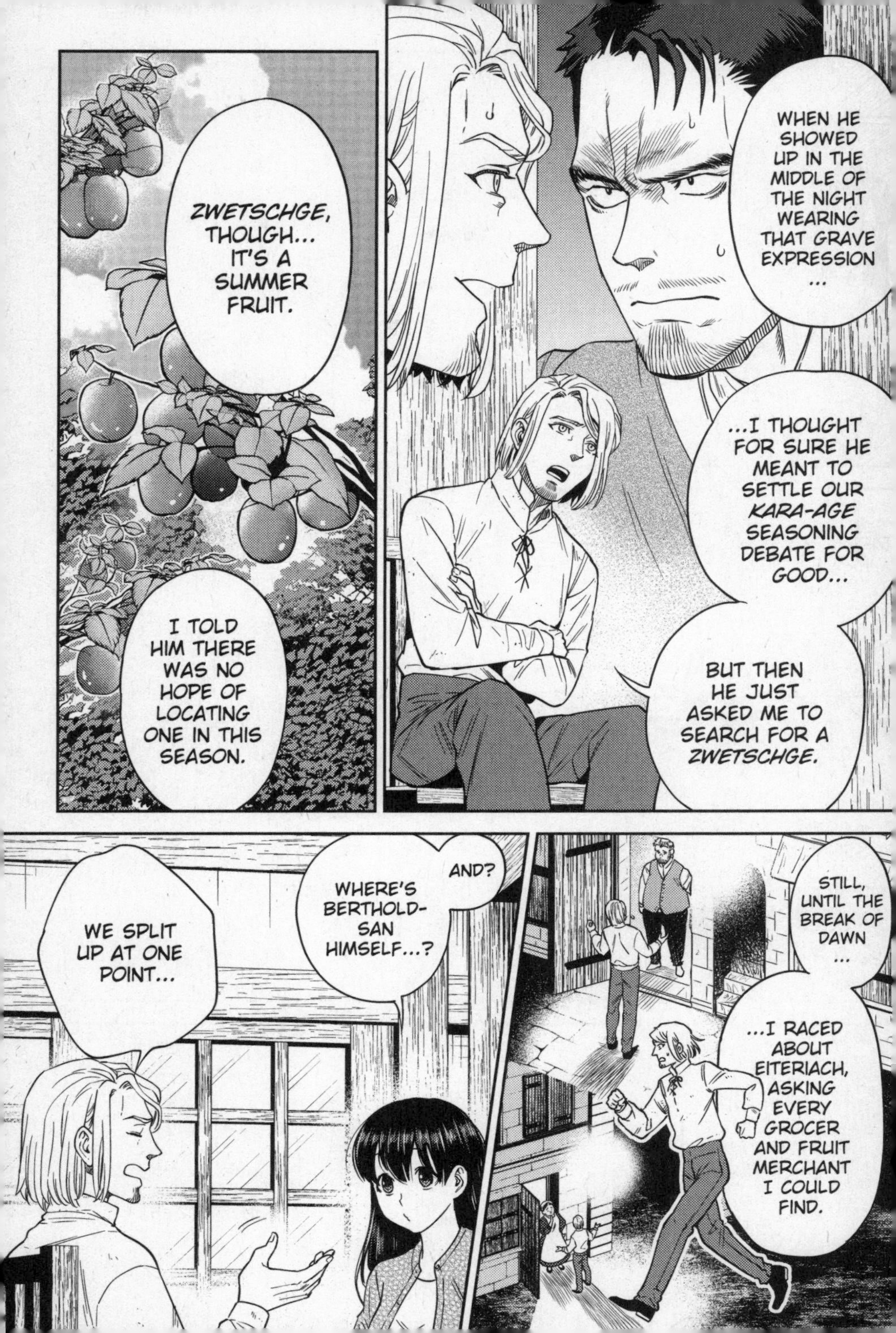
WHEN HE SHOWED UP IN THE MIDDLE OF THE NIGHT WEARING THAT GRAVE EXPRESSION ...
...I THOUGHT FOR SURE HE MEANT TO SETTLE OUR *KARA-AGE* SEASONING DEBATE FOR GOOD...
BUT THEN HE JUST ASKED ME TO SEARCH FOR A *ZWETSCHGE*.
ZWETSCHGE, THOUGH... IT'S A SUMMER FRUIT.
I TOLD HIM THERE WAS NO HOPE OF LOCATING ONE IN THIS SEASON.
STILL, UNTIL THE BREAK OF DAWN ...
...I RACED ABOUT EITERIACH, ASKING EVERY GROCER AND FRUIT MERCHANT I COULD FIND.
AND?
WHERE'S BERTHOLD-SAN HIMSELF...?
WE SPLIT UP AT ONE POINT...

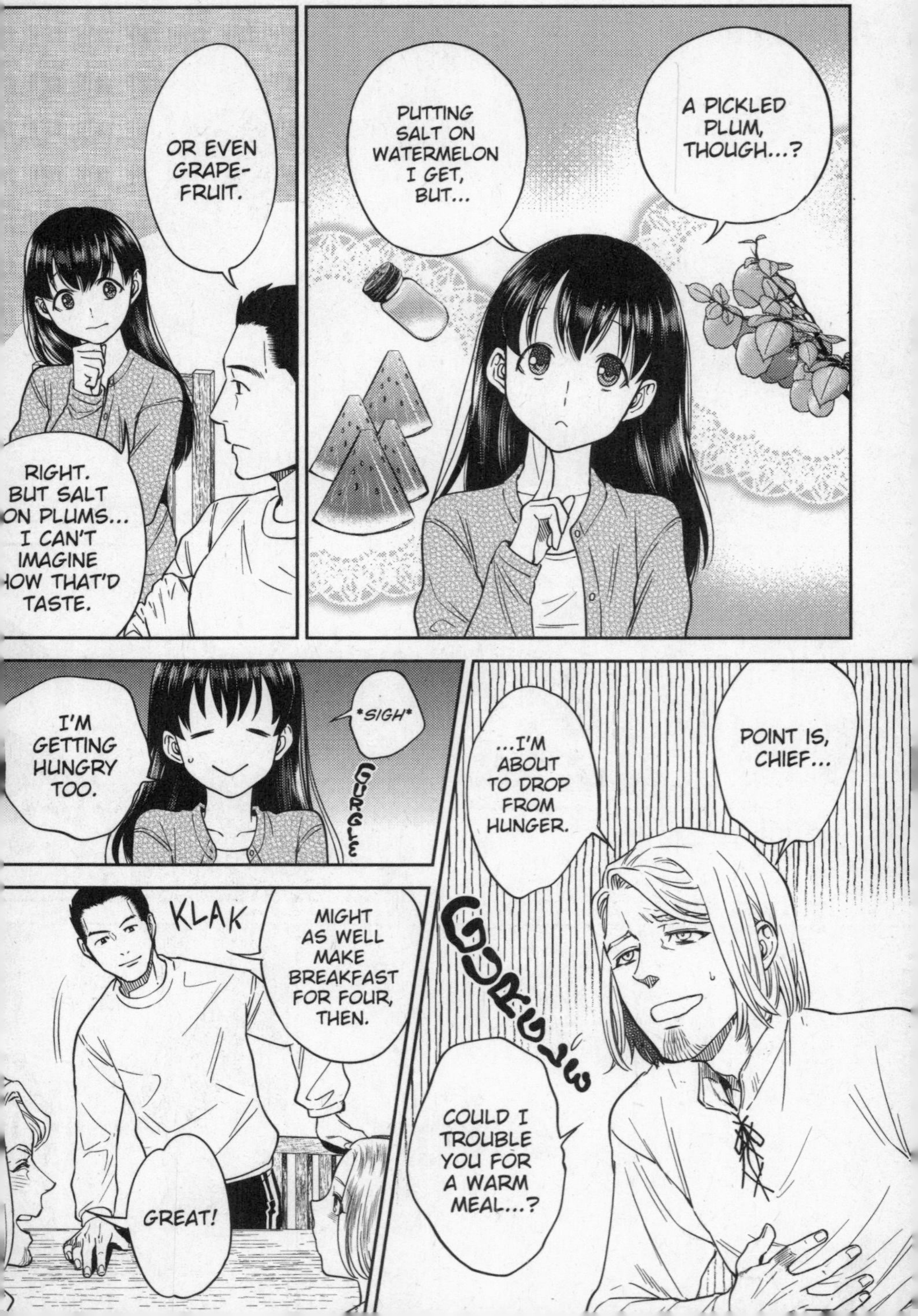
A PICKLED PLUM, THOUGH...?
PUTTING SALT ON WATERMELON I GET, BUT...
OR EVEN GRAPE-FRUIT.
RIGHT. BUT SALT ON PLUMS... I CAN'T IMAGINE HOW THAT'D TASTE.
POINT IS, CHIEF...
...I'M ABOUT TO DROP FROM HUNGER.
GURGLE
COULD I TROUBLE YOU FOR A WARM MEAL...?
SIGH
GURGLE
I'M GETTING HUNGRY TOO.
KLAK
MIGHT AS WELL MAKE BREAKFAST FOR FOUR, THEN.
GREAT!

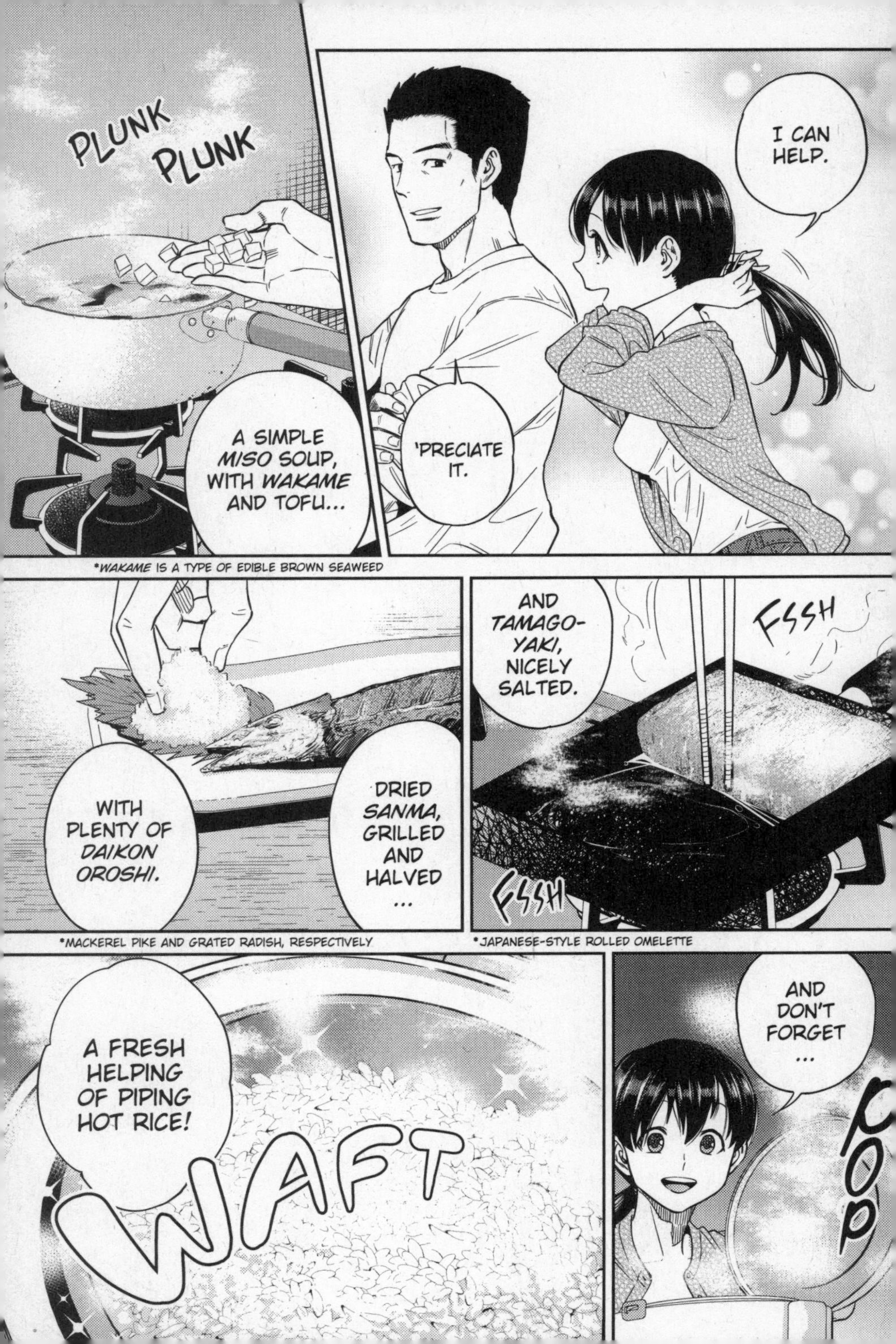
I CAN HELP.
'PRECIATE IT.
PLUNK PLUNK
A SIMPLE MISO SOUP, WITH WAKAME AND TOFU...
*WAKAME IS A TYPE OF EDIBLE BROWN SEAWEED
AND TAMAGO-YAKI, NICELY SALTED.
FSSH
FSSH
*JAPANESE-STYLE ROLLED OMELETTE
DRIED SANMA, GRILLED AND HALVED ...
WITH PLENTY OF DAIKON OROSHI.
*MACKEREL PIKE AND GRATED RADISH, RESPECTIVELY
AND DON'T FORGET ...
POP
A FRESH HELPING OF PIPING HOT RICE!
WAFT

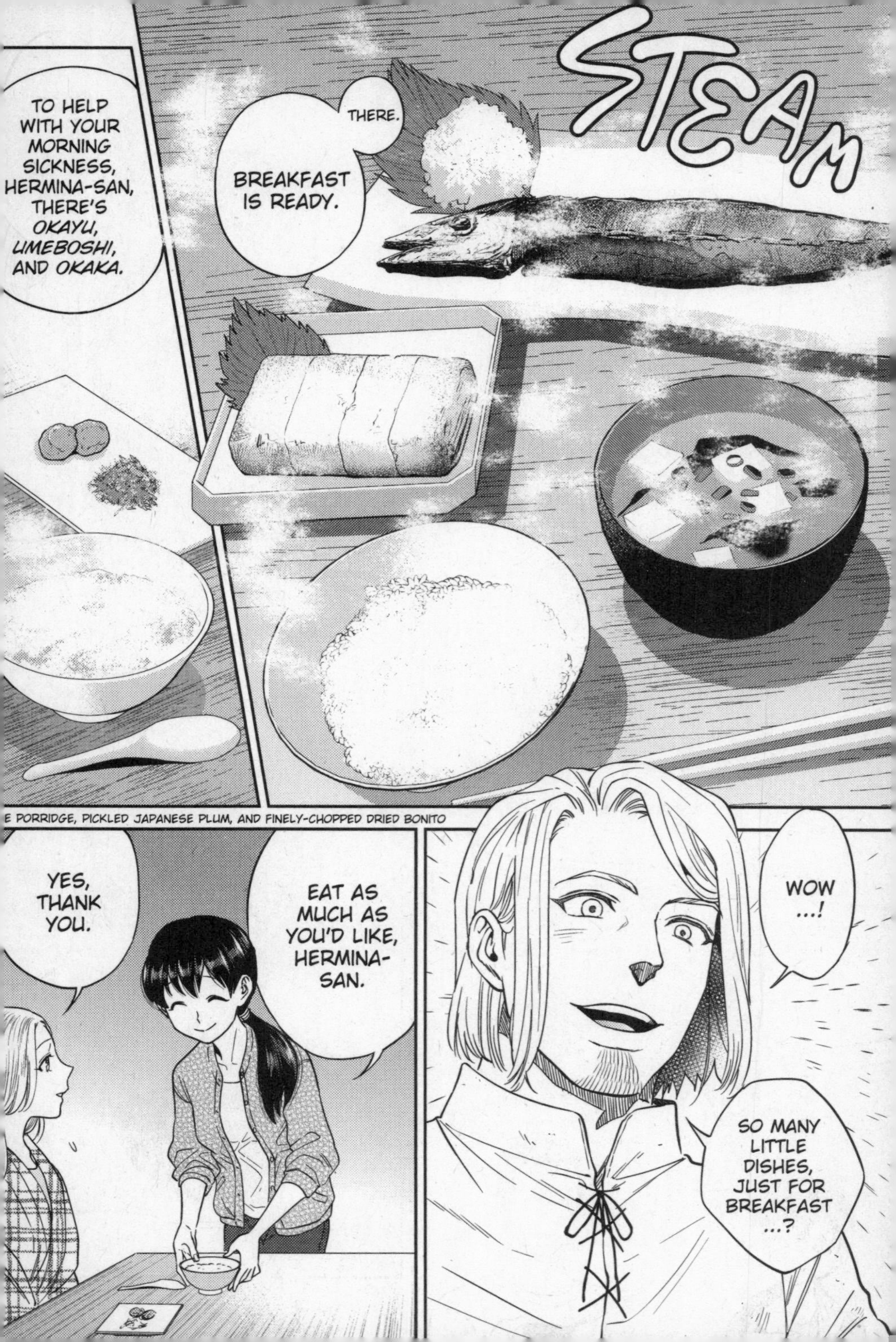
STEAM
THERE.
BREAKFAST IS READY.
TO HELP WITH YOUR MORNING SICKNESS, HERMINA-SAN, THERE'S *OKAYU*, *UMEBOSHI*, AND *OKAKA*.
E PORRIDGE, PICKLED JAPANESE PLUM, AND FINELY-CHOPPED DRIED BONITO
WOW ...!
SO MANY LITTLE DISHES, JUST FOR BREAKFAST ...?
EAT AS MUCH AS YOU'D LIKE, HERMINA-SAN.
YES, THANK YOU.

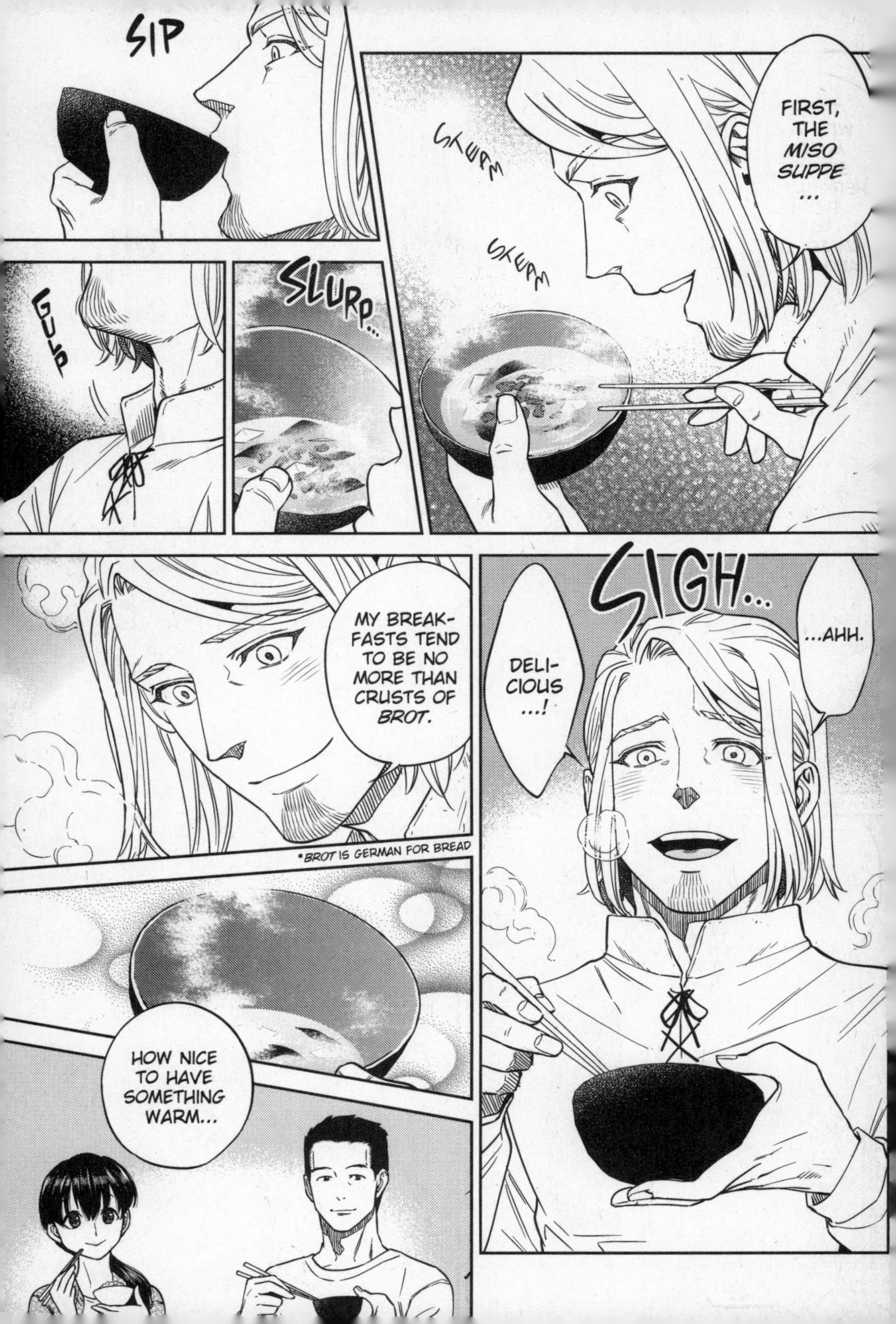
FIRST, THE *MISO SUPPE* ...
SKEWR
SKEWR
SIP
SLURP...
GULP
SIGH...
...AHH.
DELI-CIOUS ...!
MY BREAK-FASTS TEND TO BE NO MORE THAN CRUSTS OF *BROT*.
**BROT* IS GERMAN FOR BREAD
HOW NICE TO HAVE SOMETHING WARM...

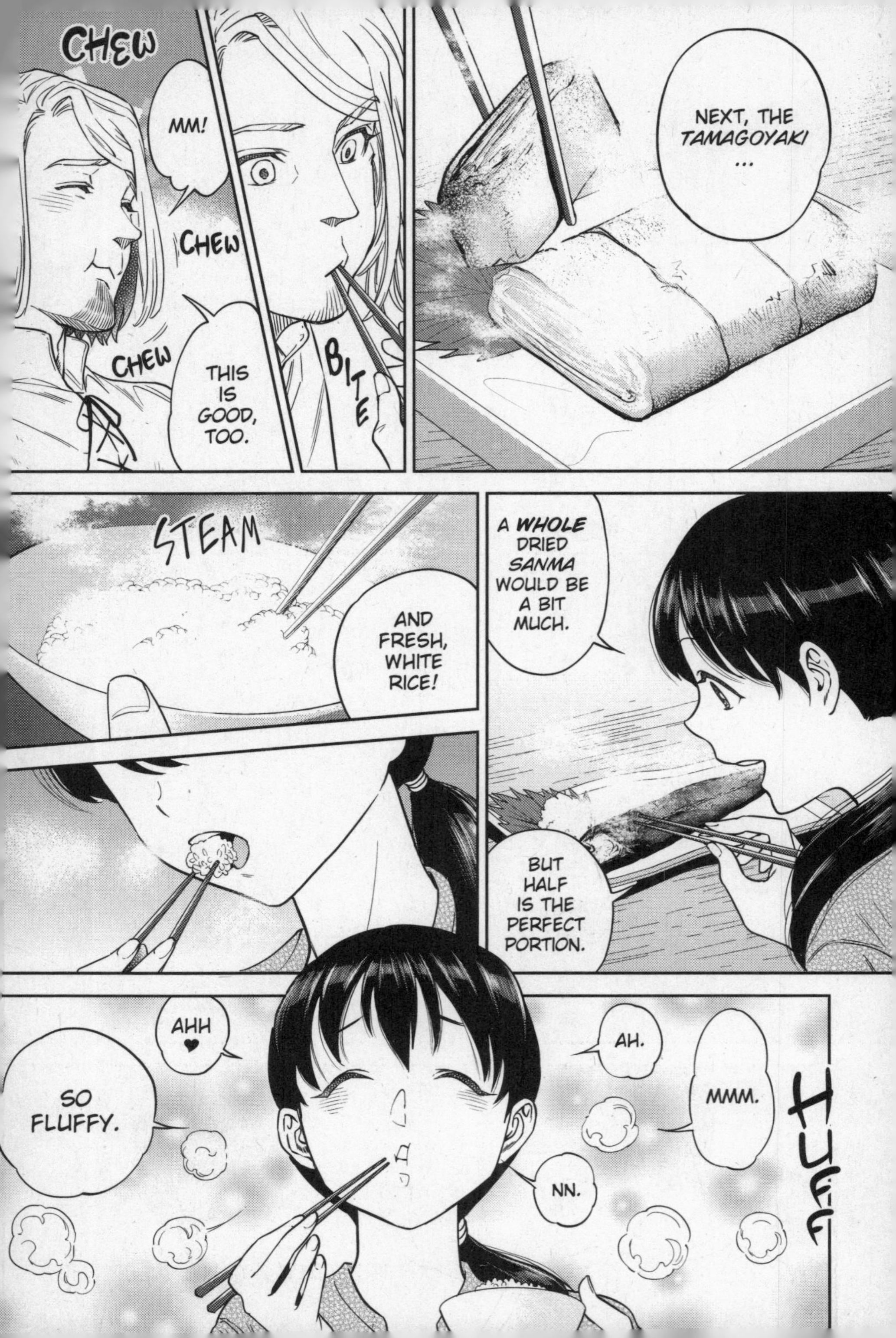
NEXT, THE *TAMAGOYAKI* ...
BITE
CHEW
MM!
CHEW
CHEW
THIS IS GOOD, TOO.
A ***WHOLE*** DRIED *SANMA* WOULD BE A BIT MUCH.
BUT HALF IS THE PERFECT PORTION.
STEAM
AND FRESH, WHITE RICE!
HUFF
MMM.
AH.
NN.
AHH ♥
SO FLUFFY.

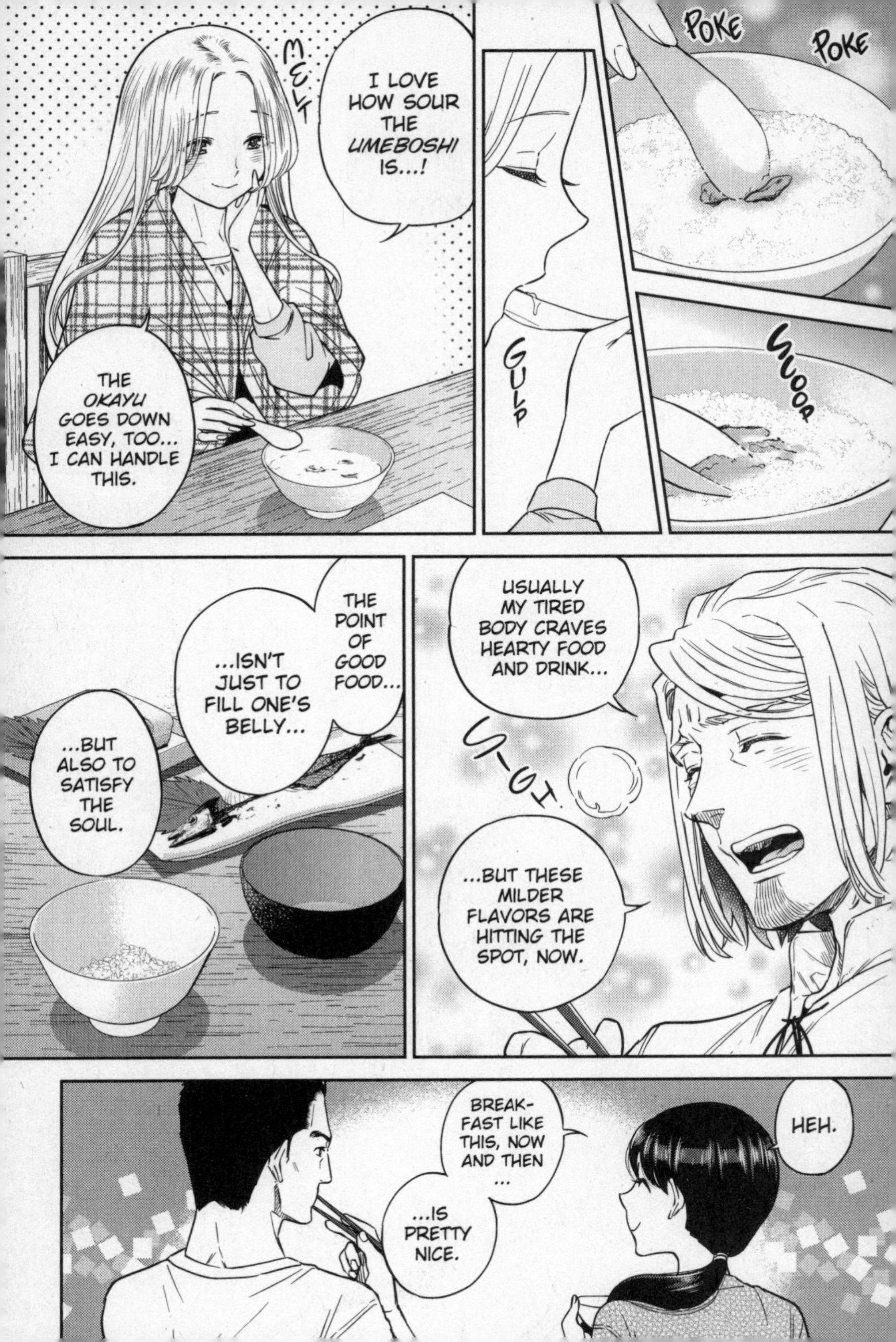
POKE
POKE
SUOOR
GULP
MELT
I LOVE HOW SOUR THE *UMEBOSHI* IS...!
THE *OKAYU* GOES DOWN EASY, TOO... I CAN HANDLE THIS.
USUALLY MY TIRED BODY CRAVES HEARTY FOOD AND DRINK...
SIGH.
...BUT THESE MILDER FLAVORS ARE HITTING THE SPOT, NOW.
THE POINT OF GOOD FOOD...
...ISN'T JUST TO FILL ONE'S BELLY...
...BUT ALSO TO SATISFY THE SOUL.
HEH.
BREAK-FAST LIKE THIS, NOW AND THEN ...
...IS PRETTY NICE.

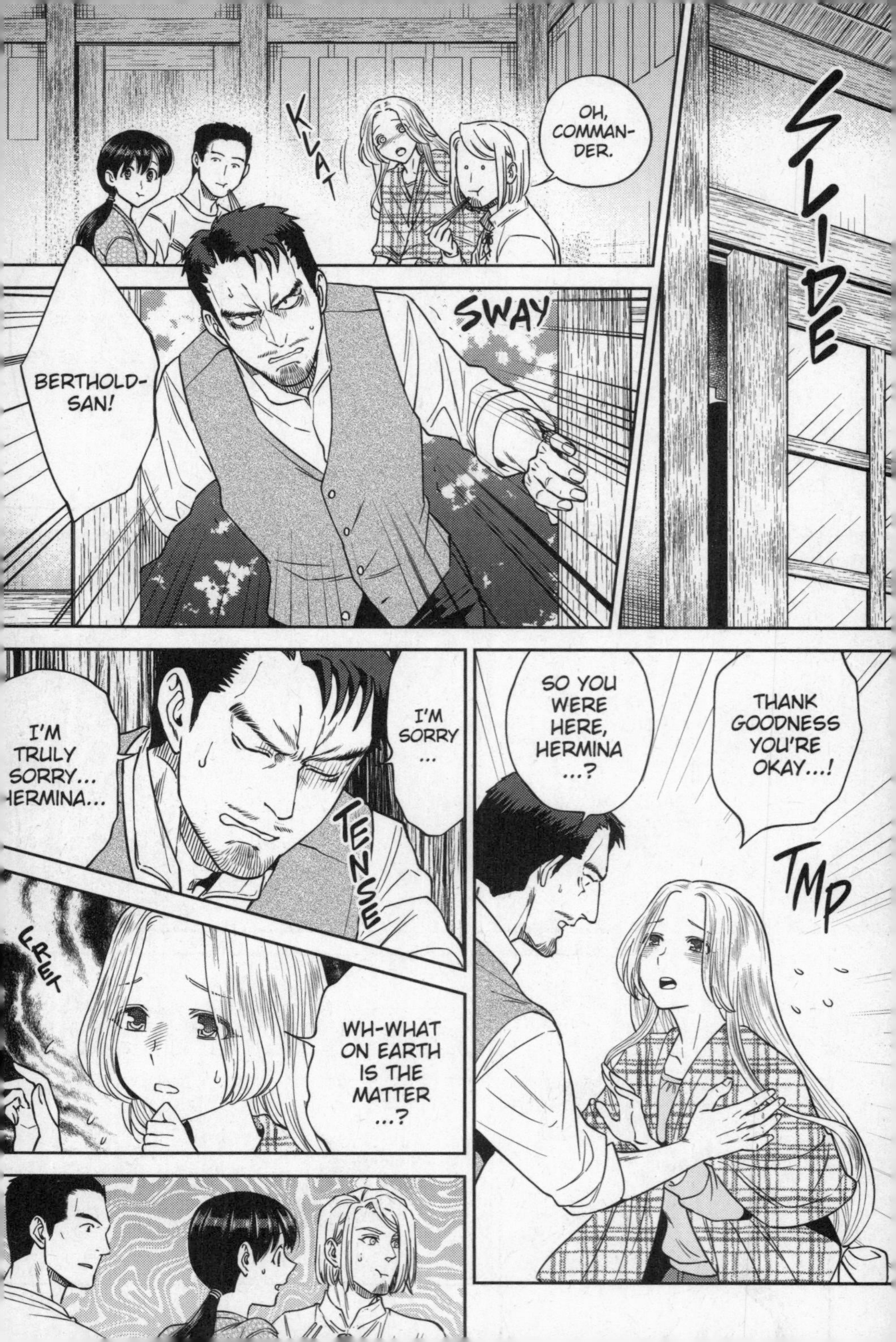
SLIDE
OH, COMMAN-DER.
KLAT
SWAY
BERTHOLD-SAN!
THANK GOODNESS YOU'RE OKAY...!
SO YOU WERE HERE, HERMINA ...?
TMP
I'M SORRY ...
TENSE
I'M TRULY SORRY... HERMINA...
WH-WHAT ON EARTH IS THE MATTER ...?
FRET

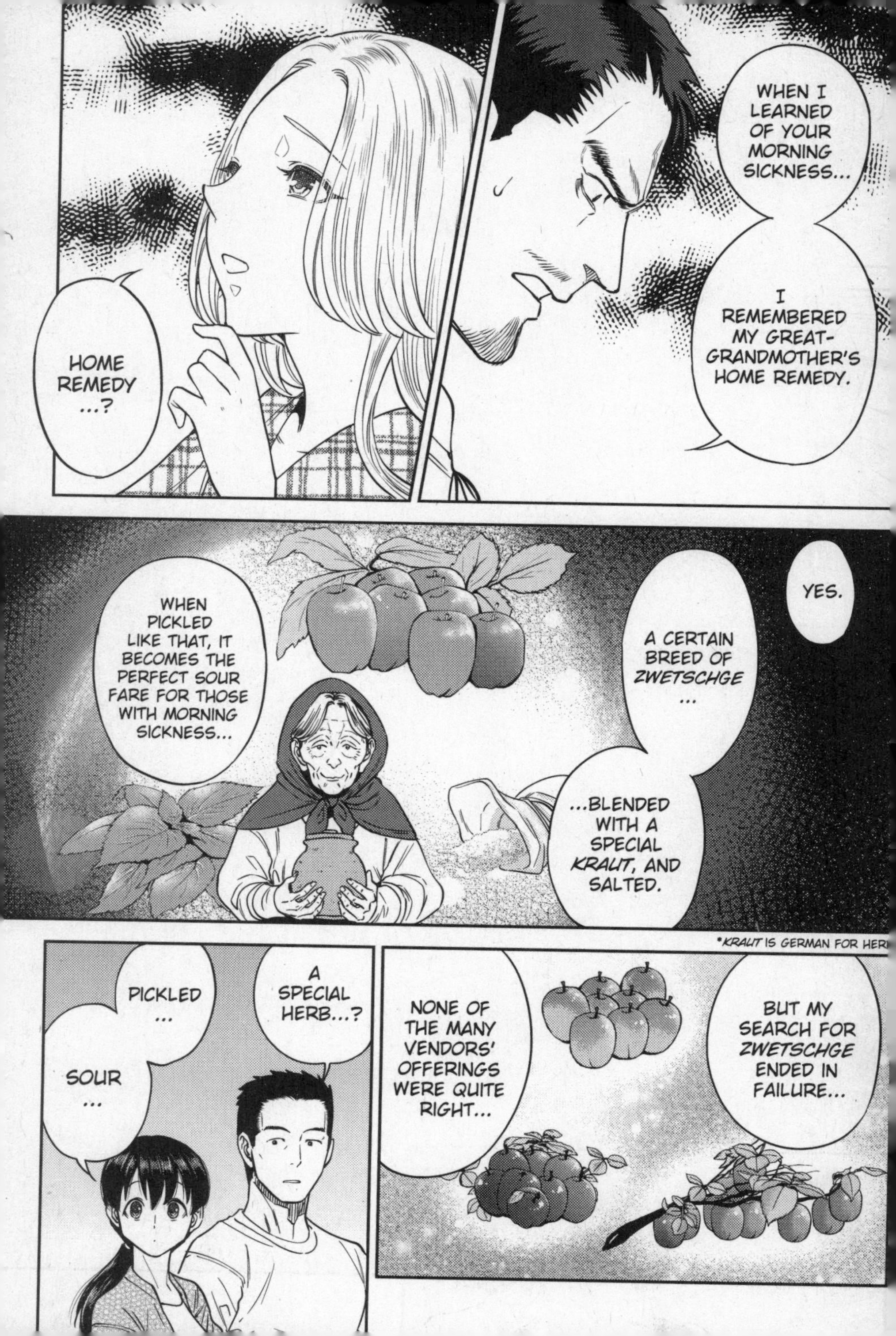
WHEN I LEARNED OF YOUR MORNING SICKNESS...
I REMEMBERED MY GREAT-GRANDMOTHER'S HOME REMEDY.
HOME REMEDY ...?
YES.
A CERTAIN BREED OF *ZWETSCHGE* ...
...BLENDED WITH A SPECIAL *KRAUT*, AND SALTED.
WHEN PICKLED LIKE THAT, IT BECOMES THE PERFECT SOUR FARE FOR THOSE WITH MORNING SICKNESS...
**KRAUT* IS GERMAN FOR HER
BUT MY SEARCH FOR *ZWETSCHGE* ENDED IN FAILURE...
NONE OF THE MANY VENDORS' OFFERINGS WERE QUITE RIGHT...
A SPECIAL HERB...?
PICKLED ...
SOUR ...

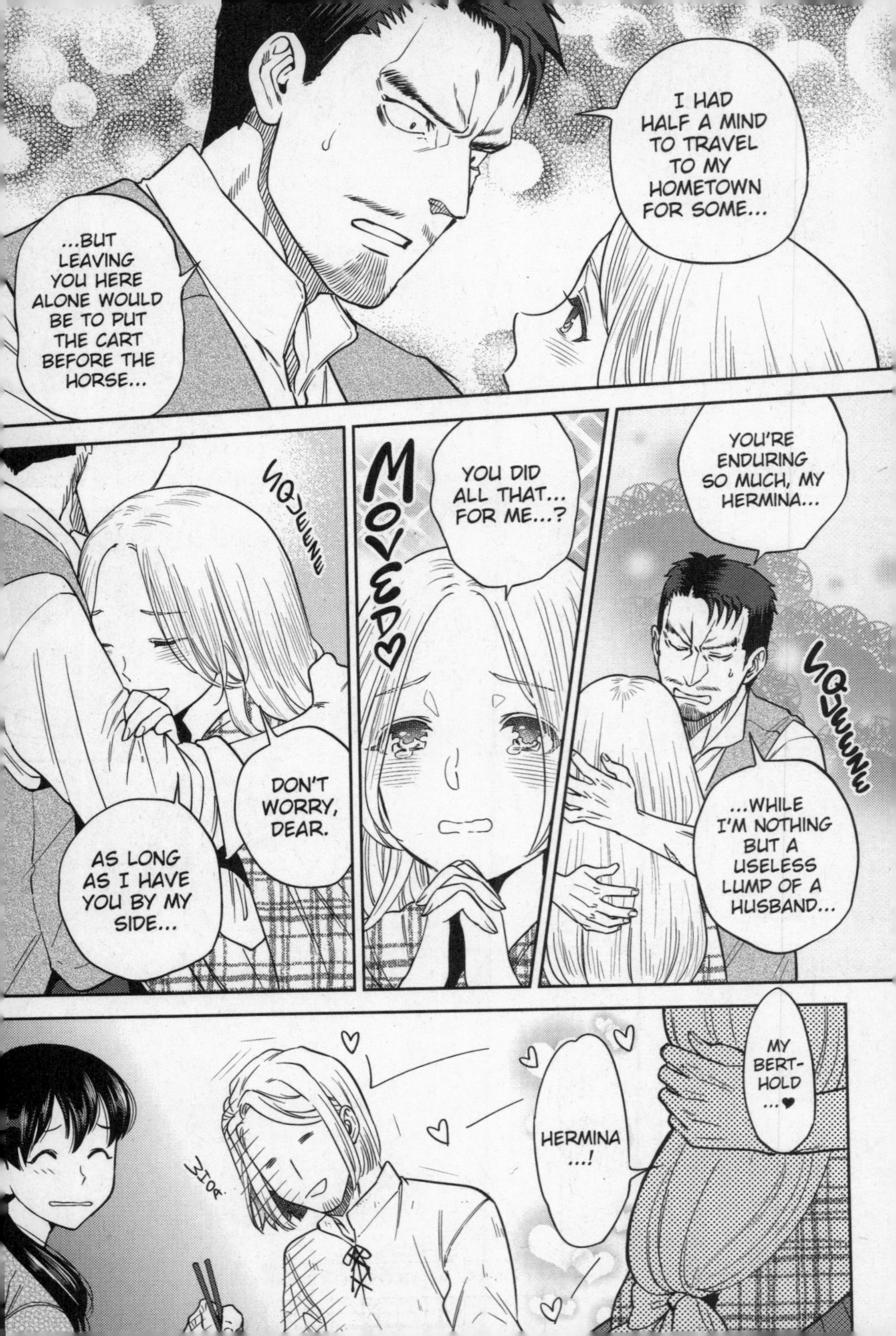
I HAD HALF A MIND TO TRAVEL TO MY HOMETOWN FOR SOME...
...BUT LEAVING YOU HERE ALONE WOULD BE TO PUT THE CART BEFORE THE HORSE...
YOU'RE ENDURING SO MUCH, MY HERMINA...
...WHILE I'M NOTHING BUT A USELESS LUMP OF A HUSBAND...
MOVED♥
YOU DID ALL THAT... FOR ME...?
DON'T WORRY, DEAR.
AS LONG AS I HAVE YOU BY MY SIDE...
MY BERT-HOLD ...♥
HERMINA ...!

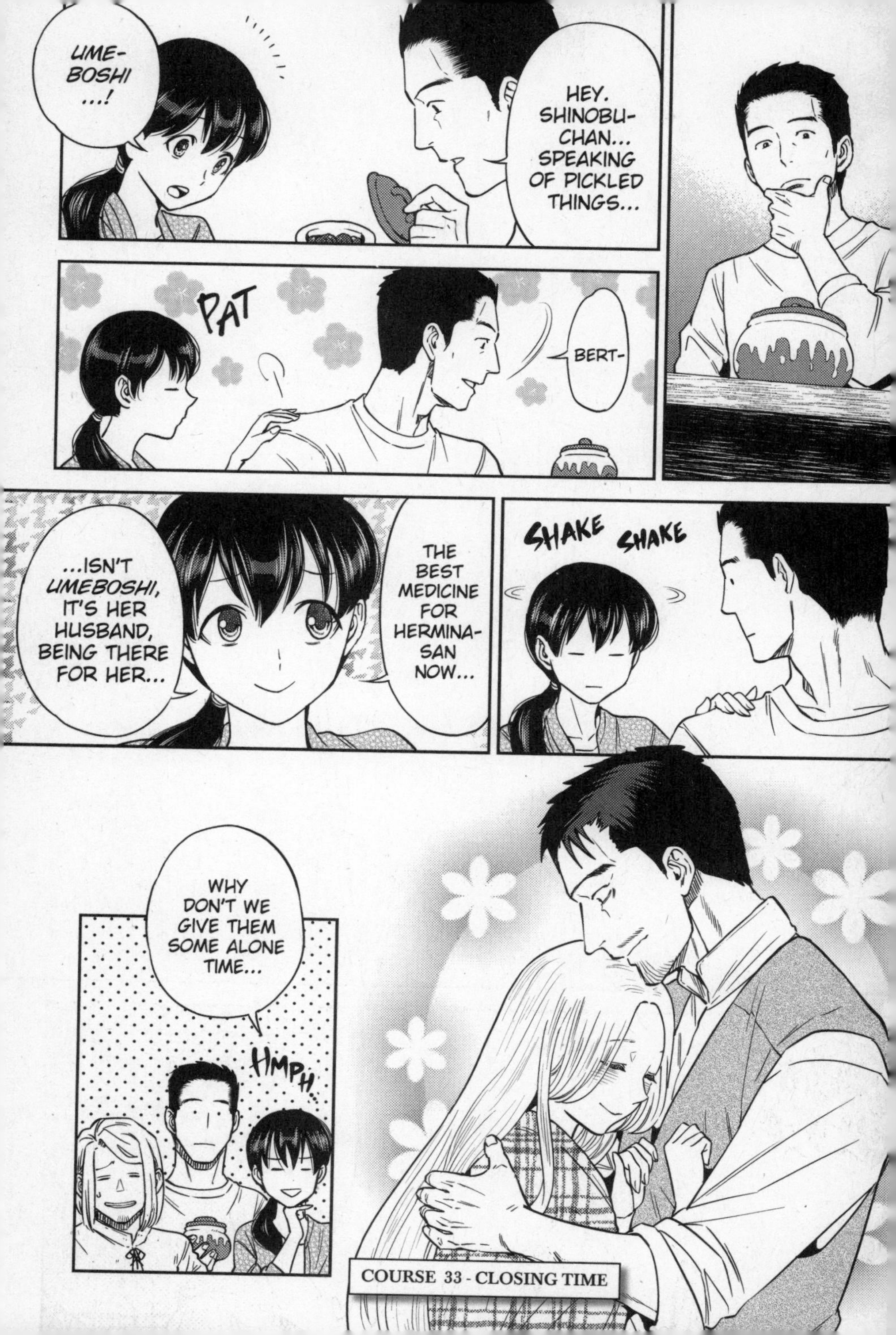
HEY. SHINOBU-CHAN... SPEAKING OF PICKLED THINGS...
UME-BOSHI ...!
BERT-
PAT
SHAKE SHAKE
THE BEST MEDICINE FOR HERMINA-SAN NOW...
...ISN'T UMEBOSHI, IT'S HER HUSBAND, BEING THERE FOR HER...
WHY DON'T WE GIVE THEM SOME ALONE TIME...
HMPH...
COURSE 33 - CLOSING TIME

Breakfast

FOOD VOCABULARY ENCOUNTERED IN THIS BOOK:

The fantasy world of "Nobu" brings together speakers of Japanese and German for a delicious cross-cultural exchange. Hans, Nikolaus, Chief, Shinobu, and the gang use a variety of foreign food vocabulary throughout, so here's a quick review of what came up in this volume!

JAPANESE

Atsukan: hot sake

Chicken Nanban: kara-age dipped in a sweet and sour sauce and topped with tartar sauce

Daikon oroshi: grated daikon (large, Japanese radish)

Edamame: soybeans, boiled and salted

Eggplant Agebitashi: lengths of eggplant first fried, then soaked in broth

Eggplant asazuke: lightly pickled eggplant

Eringi: king oyster mushroom

Kamameshi: rice stir fry cooked in an iron pot

Kara-age: one style of Japanese fried food (not limited to chicken)

Kinpira renkon: Chopped burdock root and lotus root, cooked in sugar and soy sauce

Maitake: hen-of-the-woods mushroom

Matchajio: green tea powder mixed with salt

Okaka: finely-chopped dried bonito

Okayu: thin rice porridge

Reishu: cold sake

Sanma: mackerel pike

Shiitake: a type of mushroom mostly known by its Japanese name

Shimeji: a type of mushroom rich in umami flavor

Shiokara: fermented seafood entrails

Tamagoyaki: Japanese-style rolled omelette

Tatsuta-age: meat or fish that's first marinated, then deep-fried

Tempura: Japanese deep-frying technique that uses flour and egg batter

Tentsuyu: a thin, slightly sweet, slightly salty dipping sauce for tempura dishes

Togarashi: Japanese chili pepper blend

Torinankotsu kara-age: fried chicken cartilage, specifically

Umeboshi: pickled Japanese plum

Umekonbu-cha: tea made with plums and kelp

Wakame: edible brown seaweed

GERMAN

Aubergine(n): eggplant(s)

Bohne(n): bean(s)

Brot: bread

Fisch: fish

Fleisch: meat

Gemüse: vegetables

Huhn: chicken

Knoblauch: garlic

Kohl: cabbage

Kraut: herb

Kürbis(se): pumpkin(s)

Milch: milk

Nudel(n): noodle(s), pasta

Oktopus: octopus

Salz: salt

Suppe: soup

Tintenfisch: squid

Tomate(n): tomato(es)

Wein: wine

Zitrone: lemon

Zwetschge: a subspecies of the common European plum

Nobu Characters Height Comparison (Tentative)

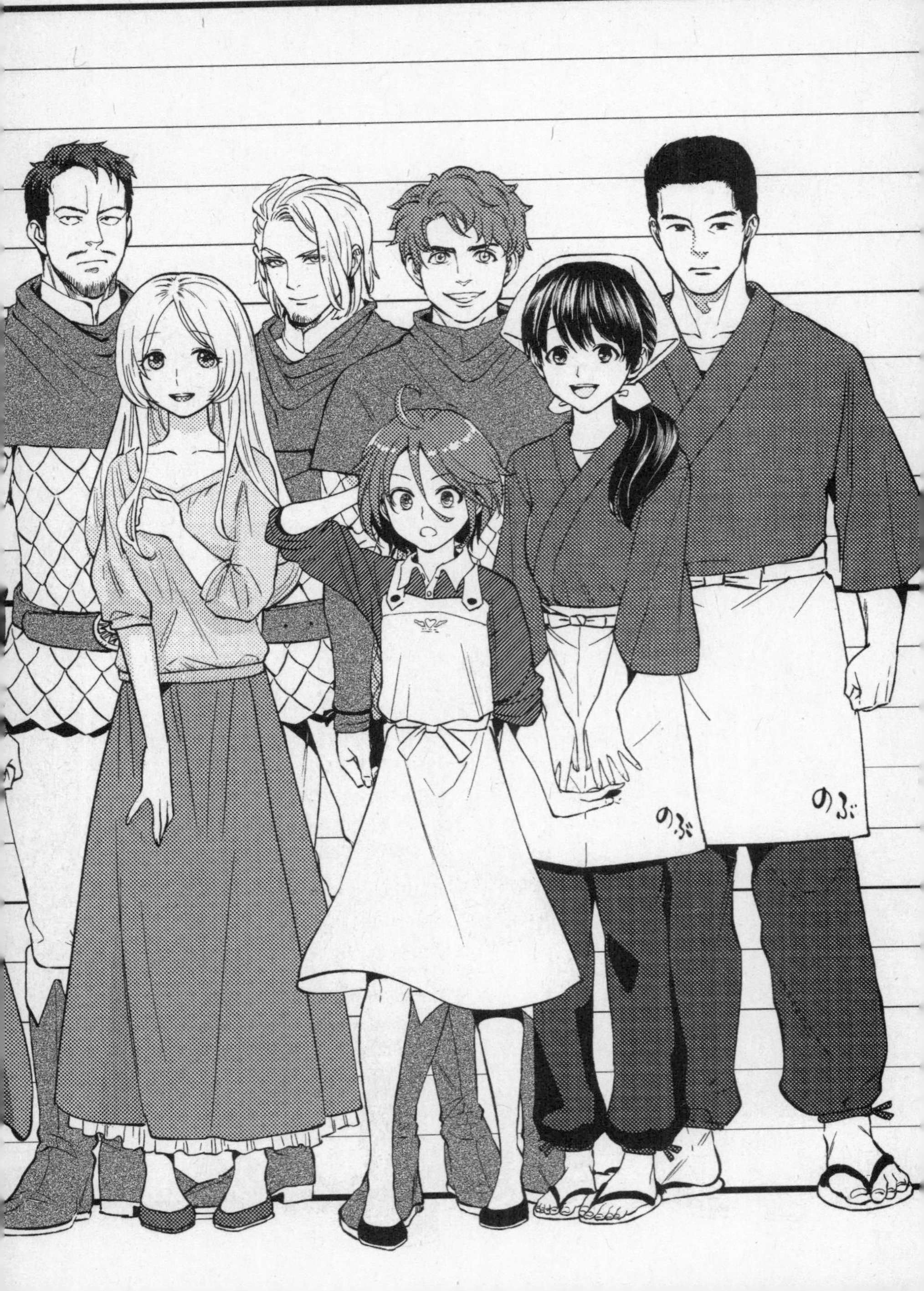
のぶ
のぶ

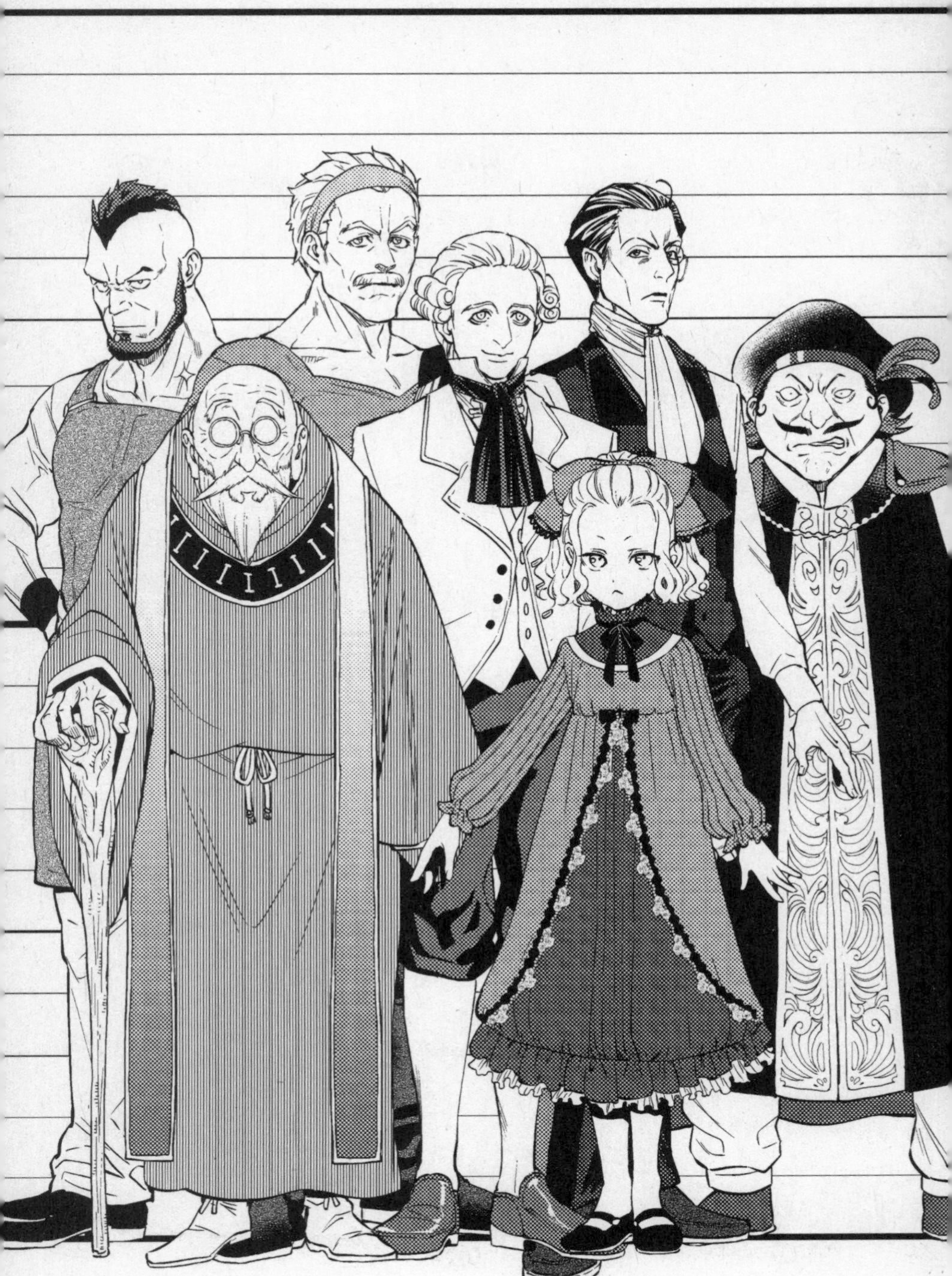

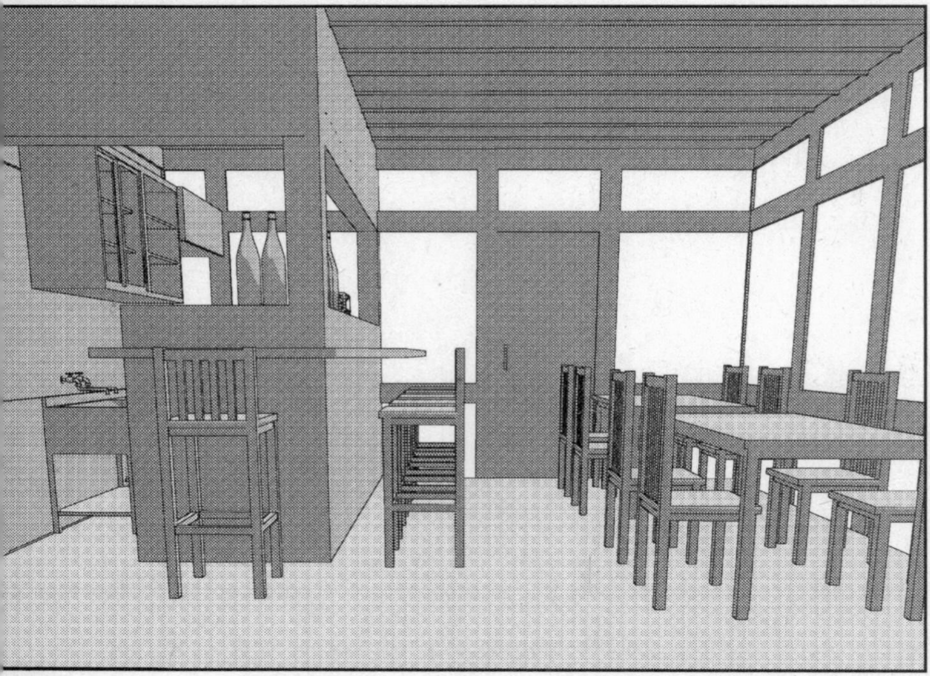

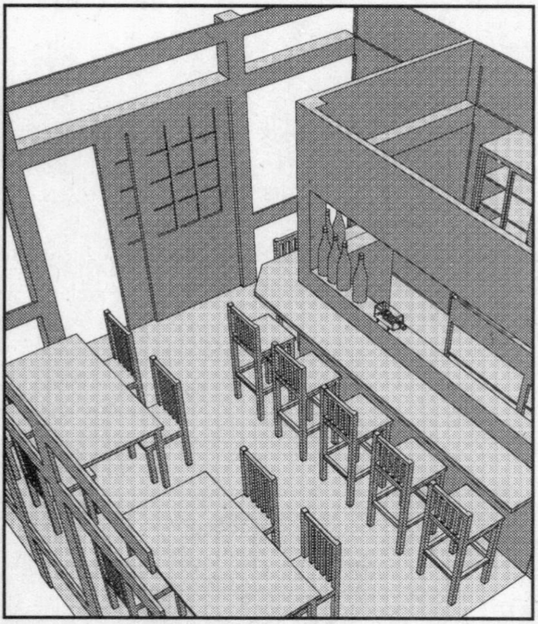

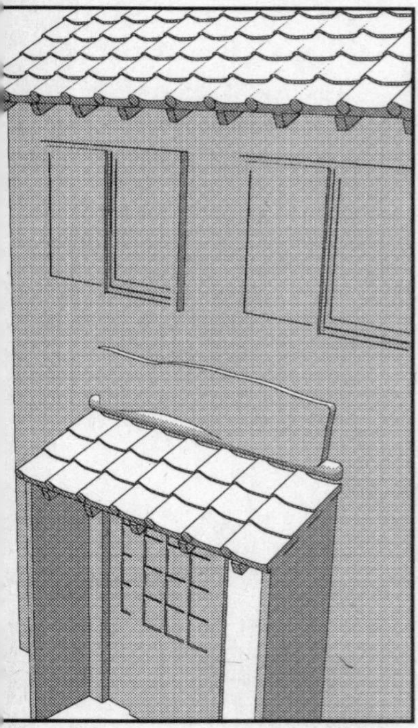

NOBU IN 3D

3D Modeling by Monkey Wrench

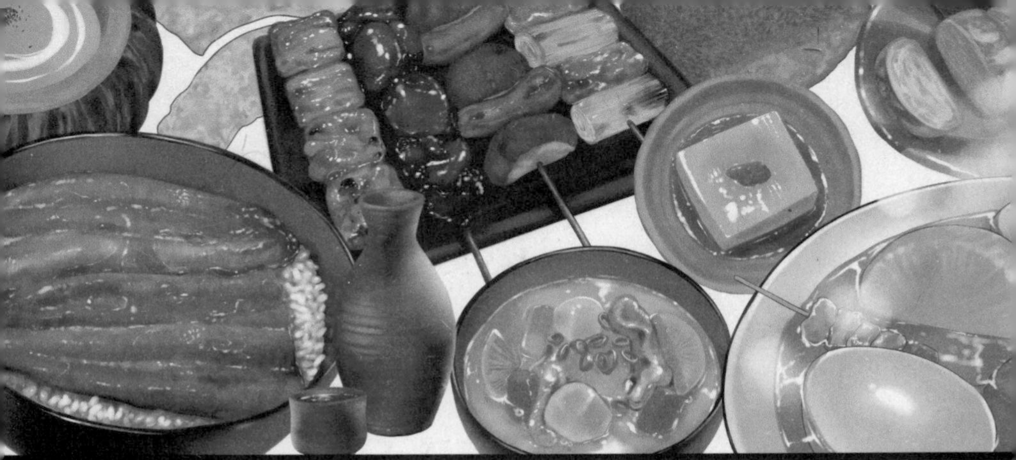

Special Thanks

To everyone who helps out!

Takashi Hashinomoto

はしのもと たかし

Monkey Wrench / Atsushi Koga

モンキーレンチ／古賀 篤

Mahuyu Konishi

小西 真冬

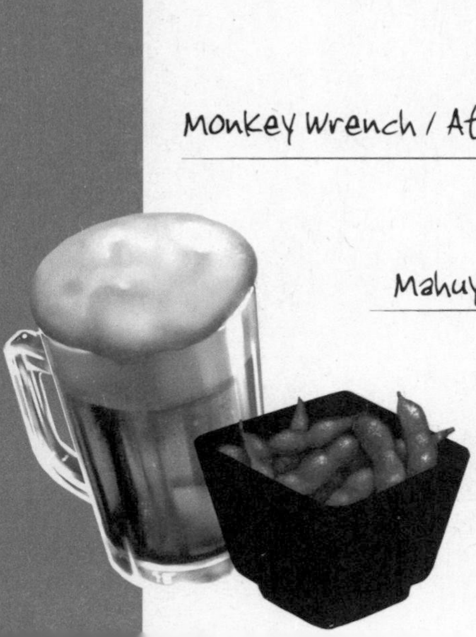

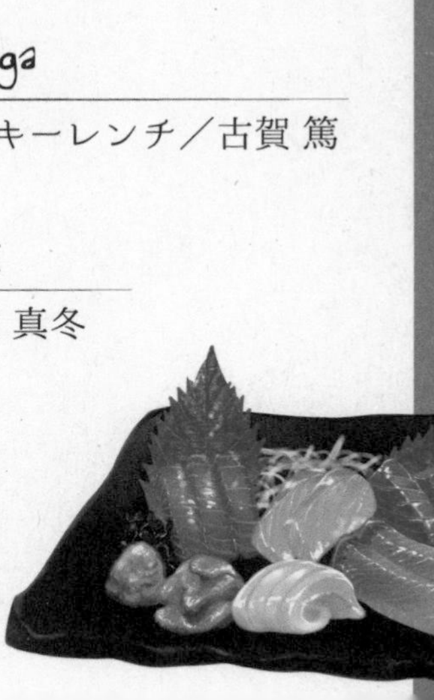

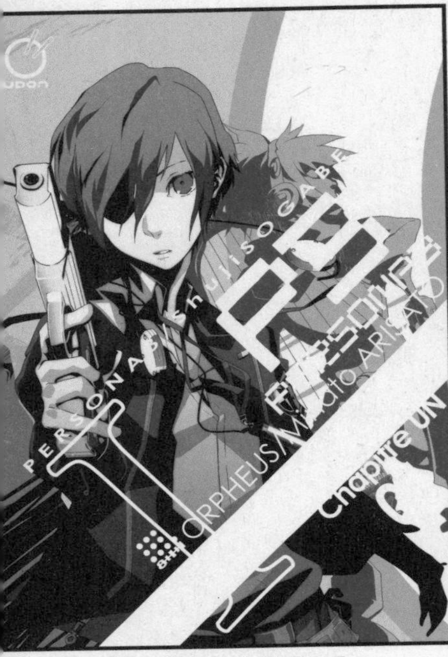
udon
Chapitre UN
ORPHEUS/Makoto ARISATO

PERSONA 3 VOL.1
ISBN-13: 978-1927925850

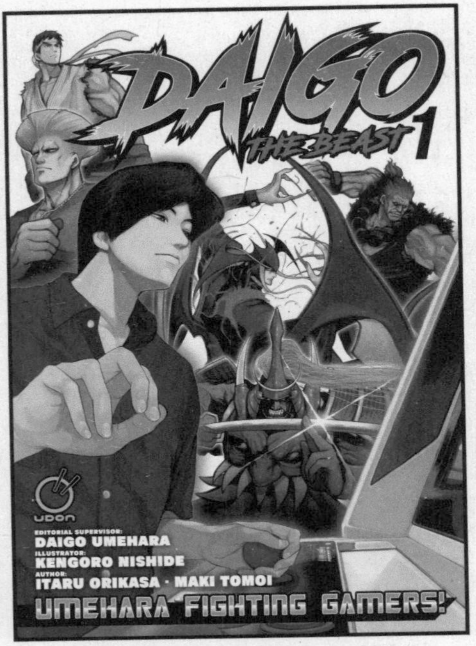
DAIGO
THE BEAST 1
udon
EDITORIAL SUPERVISOR:
DAIGO UMEHARA
ILLUSTRATOR:
KENGORO NISHIDE
AUTHOR:
ITARU ORIKASA · MAKI TOMOI
UMEHARA FIGHTING GAMERS!

DAIGO THE BEAST VOL.1
ISBN-13: 978-1772940572

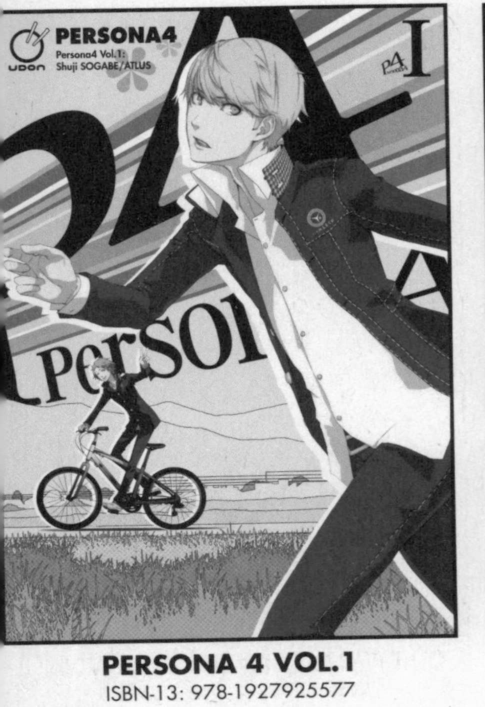
udon
PERSONA4
Persona4 Vol.1:
Shuji SOGABE/ATLUS
I
person

PERSONA 4 VOL.1
ISBN-13: 978-1927925577

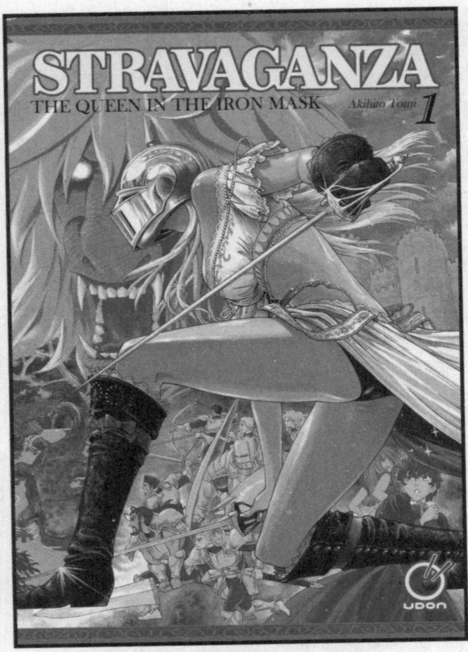
STRAVAGANZA
THE QUEEN IN THE IRON MASK
Akihito Tomi 1
udon

STRAVAGANZA VOL.1
ISBN-13: 978-1772941036

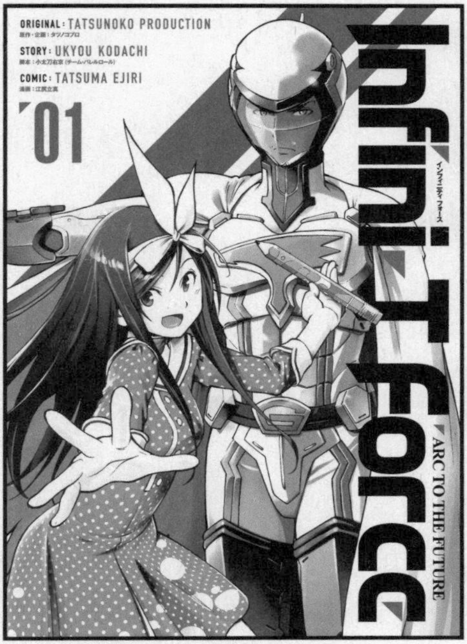
ORIGINAL: TATSUNOKO PRODUCTION
STORY: UKYOU KODACHI
COMIC: TATSUMA EJIRI
01
Infini-T Force
ARC TO THE FUTURE

INFINI-T FORCE VOL.1

ISBN-13: 978-1772940503

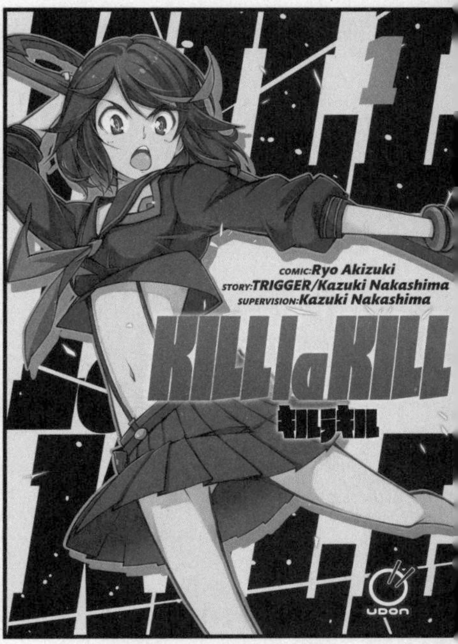
COMIC: Ryo Akizuki
STORY: TRIGGER/Kazuki Nakashima
SUPERVISION: Kazuki Nakashima
KILL la KILL
UDON

KILL LA KILL VOL.1

ISBN-13: 978-1927925492

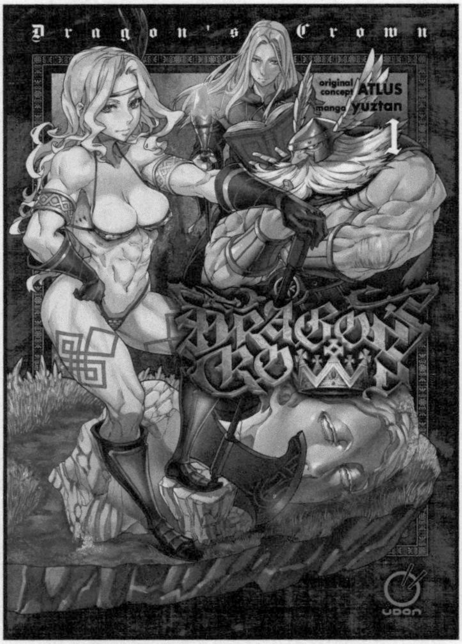
Dragon's Crown
original concept ATLUS
manga yuztan
1
UDON

DRAGON'S CROWN VOL.1

ISBN-13: 978-1772940480

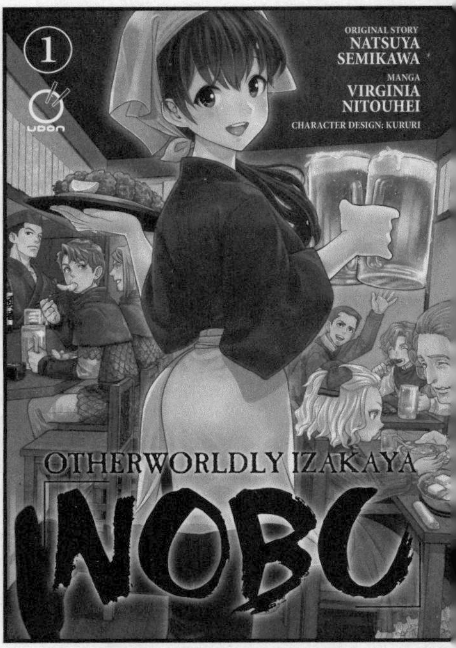
1
UDON
ORIGINAL STORY
NATSUYA SEMIKAWA
MANGA
VIRGINIA NITOUHEI
CHARACTER DESIGN: KURURI
OTHERWORLDLY IZAKAYA
NOBU

OTHERWORLDLY IZAKAYA NOBU VOL.1

ISBN-13: 978-1772940671

OTHERWORLDLY IZAKAYA
「NOBU」⑤

ENGLISH EDITION
Translation: CALEB D. COOK
Typesetting: MIYOKO HOSOYAMA
Sound Effects: EK WEAVER
Associate Editor: M. CHANDLER

UDON STAFF
Chief of Operations: ERIK KO
Director of Publishing: MATT MOYLAN
VP of Business Development: CORY CASONI
Director of Marketing: MEGAN MAIDEN
Japanese Liaisons: STEVEN CUMMINGS
ANNA KAWASHIMA

Original Story
NATSUYA SEMIKAWA

Manga
VIRGINIA NITOUHEI

Character Design
KURURI

ISEKAI IZAKAYA "NOBU" Volume 5

©Virginia-Nitouhei 2017
©Natsuya Semikawa,Kururi/TAKARAJIMASHA

First published in Japan in 2017 by KADOKAWA CORPORATION, Tokyo.
English translation rights arranged with KADOKAWA CORPORATION, Tokyo
through TUTTLE–MORI AGENCY, INC., Tokyo.

English language version published by UDON Entertainment Inc.
118 Tower Hill Road, C1, PO Box 20008
Richmond Hill, Ontario, L4K 0K0 CANADA

www.UDONentertainment.com

First Printing: November 2019
ISBN-13: 978-1-77294-108-1
ISBN-10: 1-77294-108-5

Printed in Canada